THE RELIGIOUS

INVESTIGATIONS OF

WILLIAM JAMES

THE RELIGIOUS

INVESTIGATIONS OF

WILLIAM JAMES

HENRY SAMUEL LEVINSON

THE UNIVERSITY OF NORTH CAROLINA PRESS

CHAPEL HILL

© 1981 The University of North Carolina Press

Manufactured in the United States of America

Library of Congress Cataloging in Publication Data
Levinson, Henry S
  The religious investigations of William James.

  (Studies in religion)
  Bibliography: p.
  Includes index.
  1. James, William, 1842–1910—Religion. 2. Religion—Philosophy. 3. Experience (Religion) I. Title.
II. Series: Studies in religion (Chapel Hill, N.C.)
B945.J24L437   201   80-26109
ISBN 0-8078-1468-7

CONTENTS

Preface   vii

Abbreviations   xi

PART I: *The Problem of Religion in James's America*

Chapter 1: James's Awareness of Religion   3

Chapter 2: James's Problem of Religion   25

PART II: *The Gifford Lectures, 1901–1902*

Chapter 3: James and the Science of Religions   71

Chapter 4: Religious Facts   95

Chapter 5: The Appreciation of Religion as a
Human Achievement   122

Chapter 6: Religion and a Case for the Supernatural   153

PART III: *Religion in a World of Pure Experience,
1902–1910*

Chapter 7: The Place of Religious Facts in a World
of Pure Experience   171

Chapter 8: Pragmatism and the Problem of Religious Truth   209

Chapter 9: Religious Thought in a Pluralistic Universe   240

CONTENTS

Epilogue   270

Notes   285

Bibliographical Essay   291

Index   301

PREFACE

This is a book about William James's interests in religion. It is a book of philosophical reconstruction which shows James in his own world, not ours. I have made no effort to develop a comprehensive view of James's work as psychologist, philosopher, psychical researcher, literary critic, and public orator, though James made contributions to his studies of religion in each of these roles. But I have tried to follow James's religious investigations wherever they led, even as they spilled over all sorts of proper disciplinary divisions that we make but that he did not.

I have found a great adventure in the story of the developments in James's religious inquiries. Great adventures, of course, are never very tidy. They arise in situations that are so rich with detail that any impression of them fails to register important happenings. They take surprising turns and involve subplots that, pursued in their own right, would turn into still more expansive stories. Finally, they do not really come to an end so much as haunt the listener with unanswered questions and inchoate suspicions not only about characters and events but also about himself.

I began research for this book in its middle. When I was a graduate student at Princeton working on a dissertation about James, I was rather shocked to find out that no one had written a detailed commentary or analysis of James's classic study of religion, *The Varieties of Religious Experience*, and I set out to do just that. But the more I worked on that analysis, the clearer it became that *Varieties* was the crucial segment in a series of religious investigations that spanned nearly thirty-five years and that taxed each of James's distinctive talents as a student of humanity. James's 1901–2 Gifford Lectures were rooted in Victorian debates about the role of theistic religion in culture, debates to which James had already been contributing for twenty-five years. Those lectures addressed the problem of religion that many highly cultured Victorians identified with—unable to live without religion, but unable to live with religion as it was. James wrote the lectures with special emphasis on religious movements in his own America, an elite

America centered in Boston, still self-conscious about its cultural debts to England yet openly celebrating its inheritance as a nation of Anglo-Saxons. The intellectual atmosphere in which he wrote was still highly charged by the pronouncements of Darwin and by the evolutionisms associated with his theories. The cultural milieu was also confusing; America was just finding itself in its new role as a world-class industrial, economic, and military power. Finally, James brought to his writing a personal history rooted in his own melancholy, his own search for self-esteem, his own "longing to read the facts religiously."

Part 1 places the reader in James's religious world, unfamiliar as it is to most. It first develops an overview of religion in America during James's lifetime, demonstrates the bounds of his acquaintance with those religions, and then analyzes James's "religious disease" and the "cures" that he sought to relieve it, first in personal tenacity, then in philosophy, and finally in a "science of religions."

Part 2 provides a detailed study of *The Varieties of Religious Experience*. This section locates James in relation to the emergence of the academic study of religion; demonstrates James's debts to Darwin; analyzes his understanding of religious facts and his methods for evaluating religious thought and action; and, finally, reconstructs the case for the supernatural that he mounted in his concluding lectures.

Part 3 demonstrates how James's religious interests contributed direction to his work in pragmatism and radical empiricism, and, even more importantly, how his pragmatism and radical empiricism helped resolve some of his problems concerning religion. This section considers the charges of subjectivity and capriciousness brought against James's work on religious experience and analyzes his answers to those charges. Finally, it demonstrates the emergence of a "pluralistic pantheism" in James's last works and characterizes the difference that religious thought made for James's philosophy, psychology, and cultural criticism.

The epilogue reflects on the early canonization of James's work, focusing especially on characterizations of his religious thought. While no effort is made toward developing a comprehensive picture of James-scholarship, even in its early rounds, much is given to distinguishing the James that I present in this book from early and influential renditions.

Speculation about how readers will use a book is always fraught with danger and sometimes self-fulfilling. Perhaps some readers, starved by the dearth of comprehensive analyses of *The Varieties of Religious Experience*, may turn to its middle section first. In fact, the book might be useful taken this way. But my narrative, if not James's lifework itself, will direct them to parts 1 and 3, for James's religious investigations are concatenate.

I have been studying James since I was an undergraduate at Stanford. Bill Clebsch infected me with his appreciation for James, first as my teacher and then as my most helpful colleague and demanding critic. I treasure the wealth of things that I have learned from this man, not only about James but also about teaching and writing in a university like Stanford. Clebsch read every line of this book in more than one stage of its development. He corrected more than he left standing, all to the book's credit.

Bruce Kuklick's visit to Stanford's Center for Study in the Behavioral Sciences in 1978–79 happily coincided with my leave from teaching. He responded to some of my work in its earliest drafts, urged me to retain my focus on *Varieties*, and kept me from committing various presentist fallacies.

Correspondence with John J. McDermott and H. S. Thayer helped to shape my narrative in substantive ways. So did the report made by an anonymous reader who refereed the book for The University of North Carolina Press. Among the students who have taken my seminar on James, Ned Beach must be singled out for forcing me to rethink my presentation of James's pragmatic theory of truth.

A whole battery of critics tried to lend some elegance and direction to my talkative writing style. Mike Michalson of Oberlin College, Nicholas Selby of Palo Alto, California, and, in my own department, Bill Clebsch, Van Harvey, Lee Yearley, Ted Good, and Paula Fredriksen spent long hours, out of collegiality or friendship, turning Levinsonisms into English. My editor at The University of North Carolina Press, David Perry, also rendered great service in this respect.

Thanks are due to the staff of the Houghton Library Reading Room at Harvard University, to Eugene Taylor for kindly letting me inspect some books once owned by James that are now shelved in various locations in the Harvard Libraries, to Stanford University for some financial assistance, and to the National Endowment for the Humanities for a research stipend during summer 1979. Finally, I thank Jo Guttadauro and Shirley Richardson for turning rough copy into smooth typescript and Susan Kwilecki for helping to read proof and make index.

Portions of the book appeared in my published dissertation, *Science, Metaphysics, and the Chance of Salvation* (Missoula, 1978), in *Reviews in American History* 6 (1978), and in *Publius*

9 (1979). I am grateful to the editors and publishers concerned for permission to reprint this material. Insofar as the Houghton Library of Harvard University is concerned, permission has been granted to quote from manuscripts in the William James Collection housed there.

I wrote this book at a desk in a corner of a bedroom at my home in Palo Alto, California. My wife, Cathy, and our two girls, Molly and Sarah, not only tolerated this invasion but turned it into a memorable and happy family affair. This book is dedicated to them.

ABBREVIATIONS

CER   William James, *Collected Essays and Reviews* (New York: Longmans, Green and Co., 1920).

EM   William James, "The Energies of Men," *Philosophical Review* 16 (Jan. 1907): 1–20.

EP   William James, *Essays in Philosophy* (Cambridge: Harvard University Press, 1978).

ERE   William James, *Essays in Radical Empiricism* (Cambridge: Harvard University Press, 1976).

HI   William James, *Human Immortality: Two Supposed Objections to the Doctrine* (Boston: Houghton Mifflin, 1898).

HJS   Giles Gunn, ed., *Henry James, Sr.: A Selection of His Writings* (Chicago: American Library Association, 1974).

LRHJ   William James, ed., *The Literary Remains of Henry James* (Upper Saddle River: Literature House, 1970).

LWJ   Henry James, ed., *Letters of William James*, 2 vols. (Boston: Little, Brown and Co., 1920).

MS   William James, *Memories and Studies* (New York: Longmans, Green and Co., 1911).

MT   William James, *The Meaning of Truth* (Cambridge: Harvard University Press, 1975).

PP   William James, *The Principles of Psychology*, 2 vols. (New York: Henry Holt and Co., 1890).

Prag   William James, *Pragmatism* (Cambridge: Harvard University Press, 1975).

PU   William James, *A Pluralistic Universe* (Cambridge: Harvard University Press, 1977).

SPP   William James, *Some Problems of Philosophy* (Cambridge: Harvard University Press, 1979).

SS   Henry James, Sr., *The Secret of Swedenborg* (Boston: Fields, Osgood and Co., 1869).

TC   Ralph Barton Perry, *The Thought and Character of William James*, 2 vols. (Boston: Little, Brown and Co., 1935).

TT   William James, *Talks to Teachers on Psychology and to Students on Some of Life's Ideals* (New York: W. W. Norton, 1958).

VRE   William James, *The Varieties of Religious Experience: A Study in Human Nature* (New York: Longmans, Green and Co., 1902).

WE   William James, "What is an Emotion?" in *The Emotions* by Carl Georg Lange and William James, ed. Knight Dunlap (Baltimore: Williams and Wilkins, 1922).

WJC   William James Collection, Houghton Library, Harvard University.

WTB   William James, *The Will to Believe and Other Essays* (Cambridge: Harvard University Press, 1979).

PART I

THE PROBLEM OF RELIGION

IN JAMES'S AMERICA

CHAPTER I

JAMES'S AWARENESS OF RELIGION

Religion in America During James's Lifetime

William James lived from 1842 to 1910, a period in American religious history that was dominated by the concerns of Protestant Christians. He was born during the waning, more nostalgic years of the National Period. This was a time when preachers, journalists, and public orators simultaneously sang the praises of a young republic that was realizing the pacific gospel truth and prepared the public for civil war.

In the National Period influential people in every region of the country and every contending party spoke and wrote in terms of a cluster of self-images and concepts: the image of free individuals contributing unique talents to the community; the concepts of perfection and of progress toward it; the notion that every man is equally important in the universe; the encouragement of persuasion as distinguished from coercion in religious, social, and political affairs; and a predilection for social paternalism.[1]

These were the marks of national character that James saw embedded not simply in the writings of transcendentalists like Ralph Waldo Emerson and his own father, Henry James, Sr. He also found them in the pages of E. L. Godkin's *Nation*, where he both received and transmitted his political education and sense of national vocation. They lay barely submerged in James's concern for national destiny, a topic of constant conversation among friends and family during his youth and early adulthood. They were also marks burned into Christian souls that James never met in camp meetings that he never attended, meetings which occasioned the Second Awakening during the first third of the century, at Chautauqua, Ocean Grove, Junaluska, or Bayview. They were intertwined with the gospel's message of salvation as proclaimed by Christian voluntary and missionary societies where denominational participants subordinated sectarian distinctions to the "disinterested benevolence" of Samuel Hopkins and Nathaniel Taylor.[2]

In James's youth, God's own "premises of the republic" fired the imagination of virtually every Protestant American—when every American that counted was Protestant. These people never thought of distinguishing America's vocation from the Christian quest for salvation. To be sure, there were intense controversies and divisions between sectarian groups, between groups within those sectarian groups, and between sectarian Christians and what James called "protestant Protestants," or desectarianized Christians. Old-School Presbyterians and Baptists denied the greater emphasis on the human role in redemption that New Schoolers and (in their own way) Methodists proclaimed. Unitarians affirmed "the fatherhood of God, the brotherhood of man, the leadership of Jesus, salvation by character, and the progress of man onward and upward forever."[3] This infuriated confessionalists of various sectarian stripes.

But even the conservatives who were angered by the, actually very small, Unitarian and Universalist heresies still insisted that individuals were free from earthly kings, through creed; that progress was a moral requirement, if insufficient for redemption; that perfection was the goal, though one never won so much as gracefully bestowed; and that every man had equal importance in the universe, by clarifying the religious lack and need of humankind. Sectarian and desectarianized Christians alike accused each other of breaking the sociality of persuasion that America was destined by God to realize.[4]

Fired by the demands of the Second Awakening for immediate confrontation with God and the possibility of perfect sanctification, new religious movements emerged that would attract James's curiosity and even invade his father's house. Shakers, Mormons, Millerites, Spiritualists, Swedenborgians, and transcendentalists all charted ways to attain perfect harmony with the divine, whether through communal celibacy, communal sexuality, preparedness for Christ's imminent return, reunion with the dead, openness to divine influx, or artistic inspiration.

But from the standpoint of main-line Protestant experience, the cults were embarrassing and perhaps dangerously enthusiastic examples of infidelity. Indeed, neither cults and heresies on the one hand nor right-wing confessionalists on the other increased, expanded, or triumphed during the decades immediately preceding the Civil War. During William James's first twenty years, what triumphed was the distinctive emphasis of Methodism in virtually all the denominations. Arminian views, Finneyite techniques, and a Wesleyan attitude of think-and-let-think pervaded preachers' sermons and lectures. Quite in keeping with the images of the National

4

Period, the one standard for Christian doctrine and activities was the question Will this belief or act increase the chances of salvation? This was a question James himself repeated many times, even if his understanding of salvation was different from any sectarian Christian view.

The laxity on creedal issues and the emphasis on experience that followed the triumph of Methodism was double-edged, depending on how one construed "experience." Where revivalists emphasized their postmillennialism, salvation and social responsibility went hand in hand both in the North and the South (laying the context for the later belligerence). Where they focused on experience as inward and identified conversion as *the* religious experience, salvation and social responsibility were separated. During the Civil War itself, preachers waxed thick and thin on "experience," exhorting their flocks to do battle as Christian soldiers but distinguishing the religion that every Christian got in conversion—North or South— from the politics that led to killing.[5]

For the most part, the war tended to solidify the rhetoric of the National Period, not diminish it. Especially in the North, orators of the rank of Lincoln, Horace Bushnell, and Philip Schaff spoke in measured tones that urged rededication to the destiny that the republic was created to manifest. James heard his father deliver the same message on several occasions. The war was pictured as the product of the guilt of the entire nation, the "baptism of blood" required for rebirth, purgation of evil, and return to vocation. Southern theologians like Stephen Elliott in Georgia and Richard Wilmer in Alabama pictured the war according to the doctrine of the vox populi so dominant in the National Period: God decided what course Providence would take and used the conflict to clarify the nation's divine mission.[6]

Postwar conditions undercut the nation's old sense of itself, particularly as idealized from denominational pulpits. The influx of immigrants first from Western, then Eastern, Europe; the triumph of the evolutionary sciences; and the shift from agrarian to industrial power did more to dash National Period hopes than did civil war. The immigrants were generally received as aliens and imagined as a mass, not as free individuals with gifts that the country could accept and profit from. The new sciences also asked and answered questions about groups and populations, not individuals. When these sciences were introduced on the popular level, the message displaced a prospective concern for right with a retrospective comprehension of might. In his twenties, James lamented that "Darwinism, utilitarianism, history are all eulogies of *might* as opposed to *right*" (WJC, 4478). (This was a view he would retract a decade later.)

Darwin's view, as professed by Herbert Spencer and John Fiske, undercut the notion that every man in the universe was equally important. According to Social Darwinists, importance was measured as power, and some mutations were far more powerful than others. Coercion was the reality behind the appearance of persuasion in human affairs. Certainly the invasion of the railroads into the wheatfields and ranchlands of the West and the emergence of cities to serve industry in the Northeast corroborated the theories of Social Darwinists. The captains of industry, who voiced the paternal rhetoric, looked like predators to those who were getting hurt.

These conditions not only generated "a critical period in American religion"[7] but also stimulated a spectrum of national revitalization strategies broad and intense enough to be considered "the third great awakening."[8] Dwight L. Moody's revival campaigns, mass meetings that James read about in the papers, were singled out in the 1870s by socialists as the paradigmatic mechanism for making religion the opiate of the masses. But viewed from the standpoint of the middle class he worked with and for, his message was a clear affirmation of the old consensus. It was right wing to be sure— Moody distinguished Christian education from social reform and, thus, salvation from social responsibility—but Moody's brand of revitalization was largely in consonance with the efforts of mainstream Protestant denominations. They expanded missionary efforts that had been initiated for freedmen after the war into movements to bring comfort to forsaken farmers in the West and to rescue the victims of the urban plight, as much from themselves as from industrial and city machines. But Moody's urban revivals and businessmen's prayer meetings solidified the middle classes of the North at the expense of national equilibrium. It offended southerners in every sort of church and systematically played on the themes of race and nation in ways that made new American Roman Catholics as demonic as Jews and more hateful than Buddhists on the West Coast.

Moody's efforts permeated educated classes enough for James to think of him on one occasion as representing the mood of faith in America (*EP*, 21). His revivals were sanctioned by no less a voice for liberal republicanism in the Northeast than the *Nation*, whose editors saw the enterprise as "an old-fashioned revival with modern improvements."[9] His lay ministry was a watershed for Gilded Age Protestantism, preparing the way for Andrew Carnegie's Gospel of Wealth and Josiah Strong's Imperial America.

For Moody, Carnegie, and Strong, America no longer yearned to serve as God's light for other nations; instead it proposed to take on the task of Christianizing them in its own image—and to accumulate the materials to make them powerful enough to realize this ideal. This religious fervor provided the context both for the most benevolent and thankless American missionary work abroad and for yellow journalism and subsequent imperialistic ventures in Venezuela, Cuba, Mexico, and the Philippines. President McKinley's prayers for the Christianization of Filipinos echoed the slogan of the Student Volunteer Movement for Foreign Missions, backed by Moody-inspired money: "The evangelization of the world in this generation."[10]

Crusaders like Moody were complemented as much as countered by the emerging Social Gospel movements and inner-city missions like Jerry MacAuley's Water Street Mission in New York. Many Americans during this period espoused both "imperial" evangelization *and* pacifist views: pacifism was, after all, not only a religious but a racial ideal for the white Anglo-Saxon Protestants who financed anti-imperialist leagues. Thus, James could urge missionaries to ply their persuasions on foreigners while making anti-imperialist speeches.

On intellectual fronts, the *Atlantic Monthly* (a magazine for which the young James wrote) could "report" by 1872 that Darwinism or evolution by natural selection had "quite won the day in Germany and England, and very nearly won it in America." Where Darwin's theories were seen as conflicting with biblical views of creation and the special creation of humankind, strongholds of confessionalism reacted without any sense of inevitable accommodation. Charles Hodge at Princeton Theological Seminary, a bastion of Old-School Calvinism, found Darwin's theory "absolutely incredible." Others, like the famous "infidel" Robert Ingersoll, tried to bolster their religious antipathies toward sectarian denominations by ridiculing Christianity in Darwin's name.

But religious thinkers of widely varying points of view rather quickly accepted the import of Darwin and, with his work, the significance of the new evolutionary sciences. Protestant liberals like Henry Ward Beecher in Brooklyn and Lyman Abbott in New York joined with desectarianized Protestants like Fiske in Boston and Old Schoolers like James McCosh at Princeton University in efforts to persuade congregations that "evolution is God's way of doing things." The proponents of progressive orthodoxy at Andover Theological Seminary found ways to argue that their understanding of the Gospel was most fit to survive, that the Bible recorded human experience as it was known "in our times and in our souls."

Contemporaneous with the efforts of J. W. Draper and Andrew D. White to show incompatibilities between science and religion, thinkers still deeply faithful to Calvinism continued, quite accurately, to think of themselves as scientific empiricists ready to judge impartially the hypotheses introduced by Darwin. To be sure, northern Presbyterians held heresy trials based on biblical authority just as southern Methodists censured Vanderbilt's Alexander Winchell for contradicting the Genesis account of creation in 1878. Two newly created denominations, Seventh Day Adventists (1860) and Jehovah's Witnesses (1872), reasserted Protestant reliance on the Bible and its Authorities for their claims about things in the world. But, more significantly perhaps, much of the best scientific investigation in America continued to be published in journals and magazines sponsored by Protestant colleges, seminaries, and organizations—quarterlies and annuals that James read.

Radical responses to the new climate of opinion were diverse. Some pessimistic positivists and naturalists pictured man as an "alien in an empty universe" (the phrase is William McLoughlin's), driven by forces beyond his control and attempting to cope with a simply brutal environment. But this mythologization of Darwin's work was mostly continental and hardly found echoes in the United States.

Some Unitarians, a very small if influential group of liberals, committed themselves to the total displacement of theological discourse when they founded the Free Religious Association (1867) and asserted that religion "is the effort of man to perfect himself." Felix Adler's Society for Ethical Culture (1876) worked a similar vein. But these movements together could never claim more than two thousand adherents.

Far more popular and less institutional, Helena P. Blavatsky's Theosophical Society (1875) sought to discover the fundamental truths from which the creeds of the world religions descended. Blavatsky preached a promethean brotherhood of mankind that attracted James's attention, even after Blavatsky's own spiritual exercises were uncovered as hoaxes. Based on vapid readings of Moses, Krishna, Lao-tse, Confucius, Buddha, Christ, and Darwin, among others, her message reached thousands of people in urban meetings across the country. The enthusiasm for Theosophy was echoed in the popular response to the World's Parliament of Religions held in Chicago in 1893, a conference that made Swami Vivekananda a household word in Chicago, New York, and Cambridge, Massachusetts. The parliament was hailed by Paul Carus, editor of the

Monist, a speculative journal that James read thoroughly, as the dawning of a new age of religious harmony!

But the most pervasive new movement to emerge during the period was the New Thought Alliance. Most of the groups that constituted the movement were religiously eclectic, not specifically Christian. Some, for instance, played on Eastern mystical themes that had been introduced by transcendentalists before the Civil War. Others built messages on the Vedantism and bowdlerized Buddhism that were introduced into the country at the time of the World Parliament of Religions. Those influenced by Warren Felt Evans harked back beyond Swedenborg to the hermetic tradition and Paracelsus.

But all the groups of New Thought advocated the new "therapeutic" movement founded by the patient-disciples of Phineas Parkhurst Quimby (1802–66).[11] Quimby, a mental healer that James never visited but read about curiously, was convinced that cultivating healthy attitudes could cure disease, just as wrong beliefs resulted in sickness. He combined the psychological theories of Mesmer, the theology of Swedenborg, and an inspirational presence to develop an essentially optimistic message about the capacity of the individual to save himself by letting go of his erroneous ideas and grasping for the healing truth.

Thousands of people traveled to Portland, Maine, to receive Quimby's therapy, and thousands more read the books and attended the meetings of healers who succeeded him, including Julius Dresser, his son Horatio, Henry Wood, Emmet Fox, and Ralph Waldo Trine. Those names would dot James's Gifford Lectures more than others. He thought enough of Trine to give *In Tune with the Infinite* to his son Henry for his birthday. Mental healers, forgotten now, commanded audiences and followings during their time that dwarfed other novel religious movements. They brought the problems of religion, science, and health together in ways that attracted the attention of many more conventional preachers and teachers, James among them. When, for instance, Ray Stannard Baker wrote *The Spiritual Unrest* in 1909, he found its heart in the new religious idealism which

> lays its emphasis on the power of mind over matter, the supremacy of the spirit. Its thinkers have interested themselves as never before in the marvelous phenomena of human personality, most of which were contemptuously regarded by the old materialistic sciences. The wonders of the human mind, the attribute we call consciousness, the self, the rela-

tion of mind to mind, telepathy, the strange phenomenon of
double or multiple consciousness, hypnotism, and all the related marvels, are now crowding for serious attention and
promise to open to us new worlds of human knowledge.[12]

When Baker wrote this, he invoked the "clear-sighted observer,"
Professor James, as a man of intellectual prestige to back him up.
New Thought advocates transmitted the new idealism to an enor-
mous popular audience, emphasizing the role that thinking "I do, I
know, and I will" played in the efforts of individuals to overcome
disease-breeding anxiety, or what Trine called "fearthought."

If messages like Trine's departed too radically from Calvinism to
suit the sensibilities of many American Christians, Mary Baker
Eddy's Christian Science was more assimilable. Eddy emphasized
an antithesis between the spirit and the flesh, the reality of evil as
expressed in the flesh, and the suffering and triumph of a divine
Jesus as the way of salvation from the flesh. Thus, "That which in
New Thought was the *subject* of the healing is in Christian Science
the *object* of the healing."[13] New Thinkers lay stress on the unbounded character of human possibilities, Christian Scientists on
the unbounded graciousness of Jesus Christ, Scientist. Both made
many Americans familiar with "new ranges of life succeeding on
our most despairing moments" (the phrase is William James's
[*PU*, 138]) at a time when "neurasthenia" was characterized as
"the American disease" by serious physicians concerned with
thwarting a wave of mental breakdowns, especially among the
educated in American society, a syndrome sensationalized in
George Beard's *American Nervousness* in 1882.

His Father's Christianity

James was among the most prominent of high cultural thinkers in
America concerned with the issues connecting science, health, and
religion. When he died in 1910, his book *The Varieties of Religious
Experience* (1902) had already been revised once and reprinted
eighteen times. Academics in America, Britain, Europe, and Japan
read it avidly. So did laymen in Protestant denominations as well
as their Roman Catholic and Jewish counterparts. By them, James
was hailed as a champion of religiousness whose religious thought
emerged out of an uncommon familiarity with the many and varied
modes of religious experience.

In fact, James's acquaintance with different religions was limited by region, class, inheritance, and profession. To be sure, by the time he reached maturity he could name as many religions in America and across the globe as anyone in America. He could probably give brief characterizations of major Protestant denominations and great traditions like Christianity, Buddhism, and paganism. (Many educated persons sliced the religious world into these three pieces.) But the religions he observed firsthand were primarily religions that were active around the Boston area—especially those which attracted the attention of persons who were educated, and even more especially those which attracted the sons of heretical, desectarianized Christians like James's father, who read Swedenborg and had friends in the transcendentalists' inner circle.

The Christianity that James knew most intimately was his father's: an idiosyncratic fusion of Calvinism and republicanism. Henry James, Sr., tried to articulate a Christian vision of mankind constantly laboring with God to create a universe against primordial chaos. His view was old school enough to picture God as a person and to focus on the death of personhood and the rebirth of spiritual humanity through divine grace. But it was also American enough to construe the nation's motto—e pluribus unum—as God's own. The God of Henry, Sr., was the only active or creative principle in things, but he was a worker for peace, not an absolute monarch. Salvation for him was neither a matter of beholding a sovereign monarch governing the universe nor one of serving his liege in some unearthly kingdom. Salvation was the actualization of "the principle of democracy," the assertion that "the people are rightfully sovereign, and possess the exclusive claim to the governing function" (HJS, 93). For Henry, Sr., that principle was "an actual tendency of the Divine Providence, felt all along the progress of human history, and marching now in open day to a complete and triumphant evolution" (HJS, 96).

What is more, William James's father claimed that the order that God and man would build together would effect that sociality of persuasion which he thought, especially in the wake of Christian interpretations of the Civil War, was so much a part of the Founding Fathers' vision. "The harmonic destiny of society" was to establish a time when "all coercion and restraint shall be disused in the conduct of human affairs, and when, consequently, every man will freely do unto others as he would have others do unto him" (HJS, 96–97).

The millennium, which Henry, Sr., thought inevitable, would occur when e pluribus unum—one out of many—was realized. He said in this connection that it "ought not to be forgotten . . . that the form of our polity bears on its very face, that is, in its name, an indication of the spiritual change it represents. It is not America but the UNITED STATES of *America*, 'one out of many,' as its motto reads, to which the expiring states of Europe bow, or do deepest homage, in sending over to these shores their starving populations to be nourished and clothed and otherwise nursed into citizenship, which is a condition preliminary to their being socialized," which meant, in his technical sense, Christianized or saved (*HJS*, 242).

Henry, Sr., not only expressed a variant religion of the republic but also exuded the confidence of the National Period, which his son would abandon. To be sure, he stood in counterpoint to Emerson, the period's great exemplar, first, by pitting his humanitarian socialism against the latter's individualism and, second, by insisting that individuals must be reborn as social beings before *e pluribus unum* could actually be achieved. But his democratic idealism was such that he could constantly chide the monarchies of Europe and claim that the American experiment had "thus far vindicated humanity from the charge of essential depravity" and had inaugurated "the existence of perfectly just relations between man and man." In sum, Henry, Sr., was convinced that "the American state is really become the vehicle of an enlarged human spirit. I have myself no doubt of the operation of this cause" (*HJS*, 237, 98).

From this angle his religion was more social than political. 'One out of many' articulated the relations between man and man that would eventuate when both the coercion and restraint of government were displaced by the sociality of persuasion exemplified by friends. For all his confidence, Henry, Sr., did not bow down to the idol of the Nation. He called the Nation to respond earnestly to the spirit that moved it, and should move the world. He did not worship the republic per se. Indeed, he chided the polity at appropriate times. He believed that "the State has no permanent or absolute rights over the human conscience. It was never intended for anything else than a mere *locus tenens*, a simple herald or lieutenant, to Society, while Society itself was as yet unwholly recognized, and indeed undreamt of, as the sole intellectual truth of man's Divine-natural destiny." Through commitment to the premises of the republic, Americans were not fighting "for our country only, for our own altars and firesides as men have fought hitherto, but for the altars and firesides of universal man, for the ineradicable rights of human nature itself" (*HJS*, 236, 117).

His vision of salvation was articulated in a supernatural frame of reference centered on three basic terms: Creator, Creation, and Creature. If he was attracted to Swedenborg and Fourier, he still thought that Jonathan Edwards was the most adequate philosopher. Giles Gunn has said that Henry, Sr., wanted to humanize Calvinism, not overthrow it. Perhaps it would be more in line with Henry, Sr.'s own views to say he wanted to clarify how humanized Calvinism could become. The Creature, in any case, was still utterly dependent on the Creator for being itself. The Creation was given in order to be redeemed by God and man. The Creature was fallen through his own pride and had to be delivered from evil by letting go of himself (an event that was spontaneous, thus not voluntary) and by accepting divine acceptance. Human redemption came when the moral man incarcerated by "a *law* without him" was demolished, displaced by "a life within him," making him a saint. This occurred when an influx of that divine and supernatural light broke through the harshness of self-inflating self-consciousness and moralism and caused the Golden Rule to grow natural.

But this theology which William James grew up with was different from old Calvinism in substantial ways. What Henry, Sr., had to say about "orthodox theism" lingered on in the writings of his philosopher-son. To begin with, Henry, Sr., assumed that "the Old theology" was "substantially the same in all the sects, from the old Romish down to the modern Swedenborgian." He conceived of sectarian differences, which he never explicated, as varieties of "doctrinal drapery." The old theology posited not simply God's disjunction from natural or merely carnal man but a belief that the separation was caused by a primal act of disobedience on man's part. Because this was so, according to Henry, Sr., old Calvinists believed that "creation is a failure and the destiny of the creature consequently extremely dubious if not decidedly wretched" (*HJS*, 174–75).

Human redemption occurred for these old Calvinists, according to Henry, Sr., when man was reunited with God. Reunion was achieved, first, through Christ's propitiatory sacrifice, which mitigated "the punishment rightly due to man by a God whose just demands had been betrayed," and then through divine election of single individuals who were righteous enough to be saved but not able to acquire salvation (*HJS*, 174–75).

The elder James could no longer bring himself to adore this Calvinists' God who had fallen "below the secular average of human character," phrasing that William James echoed more than once. A democrat, the father craved "a weekday Divinity, a working God, grim with dust and sweat of our most carnal appetites and passions, and bent, not for an instant upon inflating our worthless pietistic righteousness, but upon the patient, toilsome, thorough cleansing of our physical and moral existence from the odious defilement it has contracted, until we each and all present at last in body and mind the deathless effigy of his own uncreated loveliness" (SS, vi–vii).

Henry, Sr.'s desire to bring the Father down from the throne, together with his commitment to a doctrine of divine immanence, led to his focus on God's incarnation and to his inversion of the Calvinist scheme of salvation. In Calvinism, men fell collectively in consequence of the imperfection of human nature. They were elected to salvation by God when they exhibited righteous saintliness through faith. But for James, men fell individually when and because they believed they were righteous enough to receive God's salving attention. They were saved when and because they unlearned morality and self-consciousness sufficiently to identify their lives and hopes with the being and aspirations of Everyman.

He saw his rejection of old Calvinism as executed "in the sovereign interests of Christianity, very heartily worshipping the man Christ Jesus as the only God of heaven and earth" (TC, 1:15). The only role the church or organized religion had for him was to foster recognition of the snake pit of morality. Salvation occurred in society, not in ritual; in undiscriminating love for whomever, not in adoration of a Father or a Son exclusively drawn. Henry, Sr., said that the only true Christianity was a secular one—not atheological, but noninstitutional.

If his religion was a religion to which he alone expressed loyalty, it was still the religion with which his son William was most familiar. William James became intimate with it not only by reading his father's theological work and autobiographical testimony in its favor but also by living in a "daily medium" saturated with "Father's ideas." When the philosopher wrote his father four days before the latter died, he said, "All my intellectual life I derive from you; and though we have seemed at odds in the expression thereof, I'm sure there's a harmony somewhere, and that our strivings will combine" (LWJ, 1:219). His filial piety was not inflated. By then it was already clear that the philosopher's understanding of orthodox theism in America was his father's "old theology" (he never criticized it for the caricature it was), that the father's fusion of Christian and democratic themes was the son's religious "common sense," and that the father's claim that "religion begins in despair" had been corroborated by the son's own religious experience.

Orthodox Theism

Like his father, James made no attempt to understand the distinctiveness of Protestant denominations and sometimes even lumped orthodox Protestant doctrines together with Roman Catholic ones. His view of orthodox theism was actually articulated through study of fairly progressive Old School Presbyterians like McCosh, who accepted a form of the doctrine of evolution. His familiarity with sectarian Christianity was limited to an intimate acquaintance with a kind of religious *thought*: to wit, Calvinism underpinned by Scottish or Common-Sense Realism, already accommodating itself to Darwin's century.

For James, orthodox theism was "monarchial." It pictured mankind as essentially depraved, in need of punishment executed to the Lord's delight and saved from eternal damnation through divine and arbitrary election. In other words, orthodox theism was a religion of deliverance in which an optimism about the destiny of God's world was matched by a pessimism about the value of man's own work in the course of redemption.

From James's point of view, this was the theism of the colleges and seminaries in America. Intellectually, James thought, it was not all bad. To be sure, it was dogmatic and didactic and ultimately pictured divinity as a coercive power, not a persuasive one. But much could be said for the philosophical standpoint associated with this theism. In particular, college Calvinism transported the British, Christian Enlightenment from Scotland to America. This philosophical movement was geared to facilitate Calvinism's traditional marriage to science. During the period when transcendentalists were deprecating "science" as an outcome of meager "understanding," Old School Presbyterians equipped with the writings of Scotsmen like Thomas Reid, Dugald Stewart, and Thomas Brown were not only extolling science but executing its experiments. This fusion attracted both Henry James, Sr., and his philosopher-son, who read Reid, Stewart, and Brown earlier than other philosophers.

The Scottish Commonsense Realists who bolstered orthodox theism brought together four crucial elements: a commitment to a vision of mind, knowledge, and nature as fixed and related to each other in an immutable way; a commitment to restrained empiricism that restricted scientific claims to judgments based on sensory experience; a vision of inevitable scientific progress; and a view of science as doxological, not utilitarian. They were Baconians who assumed that the scientific method was a simple operation on sense-data that anyone could use with little, if any, training. They equated science with inductive method, attempted to root general laws in a meticulous survey of particulars, were greedy for "objective" facts, and distrusted hypotheses, the imagination, and, particularly, the transcendentalists' "Reason."

The Scotsmen and their American disciples allowed room for faith and Scripture by giving the scientific method a negative twist, limiting its results to a specification of nature's what, not its why. They considered induction a technique for restraining scientists from making conjectures and relying on hypotheses not demonstrably grounded on observations of a basic kind. As long as this was the normative view, science could be employed to understand and delight in a nature belonging to God.

Scottish Realism was carried from Edinburgh to Princeton by John Witherspoon in 1769, and by 1820 Scottish Realist texts had displaced Locke in most American colleges. The realist influence was so pervasive in America by 1860 that Bacon, its patron saint, was "being invoked to bless and harmonize nearly every cause in the republic. Poetry, science, philosophy, religion, psychology, medicine, law, agriculture—all found plenteous use for the quickly formulized magic of the name 'Lord Bacon.' "[14]

Old Schoolers like Charles Hodge assumed that good Christians developed the gospel message in harmony with existing assumptions about nature, mind, and knowledge. For them, the scientific revolution was anything but warfare against religion. It was a development predicated on the Protestant displacement of "Romish" coercion by persuasion and of mental dependence by intellectual freedom. For them, science simply provided tools for appreciating the wonders of God's creation as he designed, ordered, and cared for it.

To be sure, the doxological context that Old Schoolers gave science was disputed. It was confronted by many working scientists like John Tyndall and Chauncey Wright, who claimed that mechanistic and naturalistic explanations were superior to Christian doctrines of creation and Providence. But Calvinist scholars as late as McCosh contested these claims by invoking the right of any Christian scholar to review and scrutinize scientific findings and to commit to flames those that broke Baconian restraints. So long as science restricted itself to observations and right observation was viewed as the access to infallible truth, Old Schoolers could read nature as a book in which divine character was revealed. While developments in geology, organic chemistry, phrenology, polygenism, and natural history put Old Schoolers on the defensive during and after the second quarter of the nineteenth century, the

Calvinists were not forced to give up their vision of the unification of science, philosophy, and religion. Indeed, this vision, at least as a desideratum, was shared by Henry James, Sr., and his son William.

Neither of the Jameses fully shared the strategies employed by orthodox theists to monitor science. Old Schoolers executed a four-step procedure. They reminded scientists of their obligation to *facts*; underscored the humility involved in research and the derivative and provisional nature of hypotheses; demonstrated that "the Bible was the supreme existing textbook in inductive method"; and showed "how the painstaking thoroughness required in Baconian procedure undermined the claims of finality with which hasty infidel constructions were often garbed." [15]

Old Schoolers argued, in other words, that Christianity was an "experimental religion," based on "evidences" of two chief sorts: miracles and prophecies. Because miracles were seen by people and prophecies were based on things seen by people, they were on an equal par as evidence with things seen by scientists now and always. For Old Schoolers things reported as seen in the Bible were taken as facts, and facts were construed as irreproachable warrants.

Henry James, Sr., followed Swedenborg by searching for the "spiritual message" of the Bible, which meant abandoning the Old School's scriptural research program. William James, influenced by the higher criticism (he had read Strauss in French in the 1870s), echoed its American proponent, Thomas F. Curtis (1816–72), by declaring that the Bible was a "human" book, fundamentally inspired by human needs and aspirations. Both Jameses turned to other "books" to gain critical leverage on orthodox theism and to make their religious marks—Henry, Sr., to the "books" of nature and society and William to personal reflections on divine encounter.

Nonetheless, both Jameses maintained crucial attitudes originally associated with the Old-School Realists. When William wrote an editorial to the *Nation*, "The Mood of Science and the Mood of Faith," in 1874, he depicted "science" in a Baconian way. He said that physical science had earned the great authority she enjoyed because of her modest and empirical restraint. Her method of verification had "racked and riddled and cross-examined every theory and every detail of fact before letting it pass muster; and where the subject was too vague quantitatively for such control to be devised, she has avowedly held all conclusions as provisional and subject to correction." [16] James compared the rigors of Baconian science with the "moral speculations" of transcendentalists, who "insisted on defining and characterizing the entire universe in one single effort." He chided contemporary scientists who, unknowingly, perhaps, shared the transcendentalists' strategy by moving from piecemeal investigation to the creation of vast theories that, strictly speaking, were just as unverified as any of "the theosophies of the past." This was not science, but faith, where "no man's *authority* is worth a jot." Scientists like Thomas Henry Huxley and Tyndall sinned, not by articulating their grand, atheistic theories, but by asserting that they were stamped with the authority of science, while their competition was blemished with "ecclesiasticism." Faith was healthy when it was called faith, because in faith "no man is an expert beyond his neighbor." It was fanatical, however, when it borrowed authority from other enterprises by sleight of hand. According to James, Huxley and Tyndall had no more or better access to data than Beecher did when it came to the question of "the essence of life, terrestrial or other." Science was concerned with the actual, and verified its claims with evidence of things as observed. Its painstaking thoroughness undermined the "finality" of the materialisms that were promulgated by Tyndall and Huxley just as surely as it undercut the authority of papal bulls.

Religious Romanticism

James's early concern for unifying religion, science, and philosophy (a concern still voiced in his mature work) grew out of an intimate acquaintance with orthodox theism in America and withstood the deprecations of science by Romantic religionists in his own New England. His early and perduring attachment to "British Empiricism" fueled his religious investigations by making both "scientific theology" and "theistic science" desiderata (*WTB*, 104–6). His early empiricism was historically undivided from theism in America; it was an empiricism that Jonathan Edwards had felt at home with and an empiricism that Princeton Presbyterians still employed.

But unlike Old Schoolers, James played positively on tensions between religious testimony and empirical restraint. Orthodox theists tried to homogenize claims from scripture and claims from nature and ridiculed the efforts of Romantics to grant human desires, hopes, and imagination an impact on responsible thought and action. James, to the contrary, learned from Romantics like Emerson, Carlyle, Coleridge, Wordsworth, and his own father to construe the human mind like a lamp, not a mirror, and to assume the candescence of the imagination in conjunction with perception

and conception. Romantic emphasis on the human heart led to James's appreciation of the role of enthusiasm in human enterprises, including religious ones. Emerson's "antitraditional individualism" (the phrase is Sydney Ahlstrom's),[17] combined with the communitarian idealism that Emerson shared with Henry James, Sr., led to James's dual concerns for self-esteem and national (later, international) destiny. Thomas Carlyle's glorification of the heroic deed and his gospels of veracity, duty, and work influenced James's religious views enough to make him appear a moralist to critics and interpreters who found this convenient. As early as 1884, James combined Carlyle's penchant for the heroic, Emerson's understanding of the sanctity of representative individuals, and his father's insights about evil, pain, and death to construct his own Romantic vision about human destiny—but only by denying Carlyle's cynicism, Emerson's optimism, and his father's impersonalism.

Amidst all their differences, religious Romantics shared a deep respect for diversity and a great concern with harmony, for overcoming bifurcations between man and man, man and nature, and man and the divine. M. H. Abrams has caught the Romantic mood as adequately as anyone in his reflection that

> what was most distinctive in Romantic thought was the normative emphasis not on plenitude as such, but on an organized unity in which all individuation and diversity survive, in Coleridge's terms, as distinctions without division. It is well, as Coleridge put the matter, if "the understanding" operative in abstract knowledge "distinguish without dividing," and so prepare the way "for the intellectual re-union of the all in one," in "eternal reason." The norm of the highest good was thus transformed from simple unity, not to sheer diversity as such, but to the most inclusive integration,

or something Coleridge had called "multeity in unity."[18] This norm saturated the conversations that Emerson, Carlyle, and Henry, Sr., had with one another. Moreover, in conjunction with the typical Romantic ideal of "strenuous effort along the hard road of culture and civilization," the norm of "multeity in unity" defined the religious aspect of American university education as James understood it, professed it, and practiced it.

As James understood his social situation, he was part of a nation committed to maintaining human harmony through thoughtful self-government. He took democratic republican ideals as seriously as his father and committed himself to the national task of forging

equilibrium out of a plurality of human interests, which he assumed as given. The way to achieve that harmony involved education. Without education, a people would be governed by unrefined "affections for old habit, currents of self-interest, and gales of passion" (*MS*, 320). Under those conditions, the many would remain just that—plural.

The aim of higher education, James said, was to serve the republic by teaching important (wealthy, educable) people the art of persuasion, encouraging their ability to sympathize with the wants, needs, and problems of others who were different, and enabling them, above all, "to know a good man when we see him" (*MS*, 316). The social value of the college bred lay in their ability to reason, sympathize, and prefer good leaders. Those qualities would lead to a world of distinctions without divisions.

James thought that one way to accomplish this Romantic end was to ensure the liberal character of education. That was done through humanistic study broadly conceived as the study of human achievements. The humanist recapitulated the Romantics' understanding of man's upward fall by viewing the truth as something, indeed, *the* thing, to search for, not something to serve except through searching. This led to an emphasis on the investigation of problems, as distinguished from an emphasis on the transmission of answers associated with America's sectarian colleges. To be sure, university humanists sifted human creations, learning "what types of activity have stood the test of time." That was the way they acquired "standards of the excellent and durable." But this was done as much to cast doubt on currently accepted ways of thinking and acting as it was to settle opinions about past affairs.

The point of higher education for James was to forge not a certain sort of character but simply "character," or "moral tone," a functional orientation toward life that was decidedly and methodically reflective. Fully aware that very few people in America made decisions about the course of history, James assumed that he was teaching some of those people who might actually make a difference. His students would either lead or elect those who led the nation's polity, economy, and society. The task was to make those important citizens philosophical by giving them "the habit of always seeing an alternative, of not taking the usual for granted, of making conventionalities fluid again, of imagining foreign states of mind" (*LWJ*, 1:189). Philosophy meant "the possession of mental perspective." As such it was the quintessence of the militant open-mindedness of liberal education as practiced in the university, edu-

cation distinguished in James's mind from "the lifeless discussions and flabby formulas" of sectarian colleges "haunted by the consciousness of the religious orthodoxy of the country" (*EP*, 3).

It is no coincidence that the reigning problem in philosophy as practiced by professors during this "founding" period of university education in America was the problem of the one and the many. This was, or so James thought, the problem that organized philosophical investigation for each of his colleagues, and it was a direct inheritance from the Romantic norm of inclusive integration. The twin motivations for philosophical investigation, simplicity and clarity of thought, descended from the dual emphases that Romantics placed on harmony and plenitude. They would never be given their full due, according to James, "until we are fully emancipated from the traditional college regime," where philosophic problems and discussion are "*set* for us by the existence of the Church" (*EP*, 4).

Sectarianism

James was unexceptionally Romantic in his view of the philosophical quest. He thought of his office as an exercise in intellectual statesmanship. His task was to find an account of the relations that obtain among things "which will weave them into the unity of a stable system, and make of the world what one may call a genuine universe." This was the case for both moral and natural philosophers; there were no other kinds. For Romantics, a genuine universe realized the ideal of inclusive integration, and this realization involved maintaining the world's particularities but eliminating tendencies toward exclusion or domination of one particular party by another. From an ethical point of view, a genuine universe looked like a "republic," in which "we see not only that without a claim actually made by some concrete person there can be no obligation, but that there is some obligation wherever there is a claim" (*WTB*, 141, 148).

These Romantic views molded James's attitude toward religious sectarianism, or the doctrine, held by both Christian and non-Christian groups, that one religious group has *the* truth about salvation and how it is achieved or bestowed. James had no intimate acquaintance with disputes among traditional sectarian religious movements. He was aware of the revivals of Moody and Ira Sankey; he knew about the progressive orthodox movement in Andover; he could refer to Hodge and Augustus Strong as proponents of conservative confessionalism and professionalism; he could characterize the sermons of renowned liberals like Phillips Brooks in Boston and Beecher and Abbott in New York. But there is little reason to believe that he knew more about these people and movements than he found out by reading the newspapers. Their names appear now and then in his lectures on faith and reason, religion and science, positivism and romanticism, materialism and idealism. When they do, there is usually some aura of patronizing approval, if only relative to his total disapproval of life without faith.

In fact, the great exemplars of sectarianism for James were popularizers of science on the one hand and proponents of United States' "manifest destiny" on the other. James actually clashed with champions of the religion of science like William Kingdon Clifford, Huxley, Tyndall, and Henry Maudsley. In stark contrast, he never debated head-on any sectarian Christian. At the turn of the century, he vociferously chided his own country for its military escapades in Cuba, Venezuela, and the Philippines. But he simultaneously suggested that sectarian missionaries should feel free to spread their message anywhere around the world, so long as they tolerated the character of other nations and encountered others who were different in an American spirit of live-and-let-live.

James's Romantic allegiance to the norm of inclusive integration became religiously American when he began to fear that his nation was going the way of all others, lured by might, not right. He solidified his stance against sectarianism in any form when it occurred to him that America's heroes were no longer saints but labor leaders among the poor, captains of industry among the rich, and rough riders in war. Sectarian saints in America, anyhow, were traditionally persuasive; sectarian materialists and militarists were murderous. Materialism seemed rampant enough to James for him to suggest that a heraldic hog reflected American experience more accurately than an eagle. By the turn of the century, militarism—the nation's thrill to imperial battle—was dominant enough for James to lose his respect for the sacred American doctrine of the vox populi, along with his sense of humor about America's role in the world. He literally cried when Americans invaded Manila and preached that "our nation has been founded in what we may call our American religion, baptized and reared in the faith that a man requires no master to take care of him, and that common people can work out their salvation well enough together if left free to try" (MS, 43).

The New Religions

Among the new religions that appeared after 1860, James was attracted to those that he interpreted as nondogmatic, experimental, regenerative, pacifist, and spiritualist. Thus, he read New Thinkers like Ralph Waldo Trine and Julius and Horatio Dresser, but not Mary Baker Eddy, who simply added an institution to the roster of churches claiming to have found *the* way. He heartily approved the religious socialisms of Leo Tolstoy and H. G. Wells, but continued to distinguish his own religious views from those of others who spoke on behalf of religions of humanity. He was attracted to universalist tendencies of Theosophy and the cosmopolitan message of the Anti-Imperialist League, preferring intellectuals in any nation to the "partisan parties and empty quacks" in his own. On the other hand, he simply assumed that the Haymarket labor riot of 1886 had to be the work of foreigners because "Americans" did not have materialist motives, and he wrote messages to John D. Rockefeller urging charity to mental institutions in tones that paralleled Bishop Lawrence's confident Gospel of Wealth.

Reviewing the new religions he encountered, especially those that were "therapeutic," James said that "it is quite obvious that a wave of religious activity, analogous in some respects to the spread of early Christianity, Buddhism, and Mohammedanism is passing over our American world" (EM, 17). New Thought, Metaphysical Healing, and other spiritual religions were unlocking untold energies through mental discipline. The religions that employed "suggestive therapeutics," from Hatha Yoga to Christian Science, were transforming the limits of their disciples' powers, luring them into an emotional optimism that correlated human possibilities with human motives. That made the religious ferment exciting—and constructive besides.

But James, for all his attempts to receive new religions empathetically, failed to encounter old and alien ones. He treated Roman Catholics the way he treated European monarchies, and in the same breath. Roman Catholicism represented a spirit that had fallen below the secular or civilized level of humanity. During a period when the American Jewish population quadrupled, James failed to interact with Judaism at all. He followed Harvard's official, if informal, policy of taking bright Jews and making them Americans. It never occurred to him to visit the active Young Men's Buddhist Association in San Francisco when he visited there on several occasions, and the religions of Africa and Oceana were simply savage "mumbo-jumbo." It is not insignificant that the philosopher who begged his readers not to miss the joy of being other and different continually pictured "the Asian spirit" as threatening the West. Being other and different did have its limits.

CHAPTER 2

JAMES'S PROBLEM OF RELIGION

Religious Disease and Its Cures

Matthew Arnold spoke for a large class of Victorian Anglo-Saxon intellectuals when he wrote in 1875 that "at the present moment two things about the Christian religion must surely be clear to anybody with eyes in his head. One is, that men cannot do without it; the other, that they cannot do with it as it is."[1] Even if James confided to friends from his twenties on that he could not be Christian because Christ played no crucial role in the process of salvation as he understood it, Arnold's formula caught the essence of James's religious situation. By the time James was twenty-eight years old he had tried to do without religion and he had failed.

During his teens and early twenties, he had dabbled with both Epicureanism and Stoicism, common adventures for wealthy, educated, transatlantic Anglo-Saxon gentlemen at the time. He found Epicurean aestheticism too loose and ultimately comical; Stoic moralism was suffocating and tragic. His inability to devote himself to either of those classical alternatives to Christianity probably contributed to his near-suicidal depression during 1868–72, a period marked by acute acedia and its arrest by religious consolation. In a memoir quoted anonymously as part of his Gifford Lectures in 1901, he made it clear that disgust with human existence and a carking question whether life was worth living led to his despond. Personally nearly disastrous, James's acedia was far from idiosyncratic. Sloth was a common response among intellectuals to their own sense of power. As Robert Solomon has put it, in the post-Napoleonic period (and for Americans in the period immediately following the Civil War), "the Absurd was born, not of loss of religion, but of gains in humanism. The more we thought of ourselves, the less we thought of our Reality. There was no one else to blame."[2] In a period when intellectuals entertained simultaneously the notions that humanity might be divine and that the difference between the savage and the civilized rested on a series of contingencies, there were grounds for life-arresting pessimism. In such a state, James

> went one evening into a dressing-room . . . when suddenly there fell upon me without any warning, just as if it came out of the darkness, a horrible fear of my own existence. Simultaneously there arose in my mind the image of an epileptic patient whom I had seen in the asylum. . . . He sat there like a sort of Egyptian cat or Peruvian mummy, moving nothing but his black eyes and looking absolutely non-human. This image and my fear entered into a species of combination with each other. *That shape am I*, I felt, potentially. Nothing that I possess can defend me against that fate, if the hour should strike for me as it struck for him. [*VRE*, 160]

Experiences like those led to a condition that, according to James, was the opposite of nightmare. "In nightmare," he said, "we have motives to act, but no power; here we have powers, but no motives" (*WTB*, 71). The total carelessness of the catatonic, together with James's own great powers, which came and went, haunted him and left him without self-esteem. "After this," James said, "I awoke morning after morning with a horrible dread at the pit of my stomach, and with a sense of the insecurity of life that I never felt before, and that I have never felt since" (*VRE*, 160). The fear was so revelatory that "if I had not clung to scripture texts like 'The eternal God is my refuge,' etc., 'Come unto me all ye that labor and are heavy laden,' etc., 'I am the resurrection and the life,' etc., I think I should have grown really insane" (*VRE*, 161).

Neither Epicureans nor Stoics could pray, but James could not help praying. Whether or not James ever prayed again is beside the point, but it is interesting to consider that while he told James Pratt on a public questionnaire that he always felt silly praying, he privately stopped by the church in Harvard Yard on his way to work every day. In any case, he came away from his experience of morbid despair believing that neither aestheticism nor moralism could sufficiently satisfy "the religious demand" that is felt by many people as inescapable. Even if he never prayed again, he was convinced that plenty of people had to and that their religious requirements had to be accounted for by philosophers concerned with characterizing human life.

It makes no sense to pin James's depression on any one cause or set of causes. In general, he suffered from what he called "philosophical melancholy" (in essays like "Is Life Worth Living?" *WTB*, 34–56) or *Grübelsucht*, the questioning mania (in *PP*, 2:284). The new intellectual climate seemed to make all things possible, and the new materialism seemed to make them insignificant. Popular materialist tracts like Ludwig Büchner's *Kraft und Stoff* (1855), which James read thoroughly in 1862, persuaded him that existence obeyed mechanical laws inherent in "the things themselves"—laws that made both supernaturalism and idealism, or natural supernaturalism, superfluous. Büchner's deliberately shocking formula —"no force without matter; no matter without force"—haunted tough-minded students with any religious propensities during the 1860s and 1870s. James was no exception.

By comparison, Darwin's *Origin of Species* (1859) was a breath of fresh air, foisting history into the limelight, showing that if descent was actual, progress was possible, and demonstrating that fit results could be produced by chance events. But in the hands of popularizers like Huxley, Spencer, and Tyndall, Darwin's theory became a great leveler, reducing the quality of humanity to that of brutality and displacing all questions about personal and national destiny with the final solution of fatalism. James never held Darwin responsible for this pessimistic frame of mind, but it hung over his youthful intellectual crowd like a black cloud and seemed to be mirrored now and again in his own nation's emerging troubles. In an intellectual atmosphere in which self-esteem and national destiny meant just about everything, materialism challenged the very existence of a self to esteem and evolutionism, something James carefully distinguished from Darwinism, made destiny meaningless.

James delivered his lecture "Is Life Worth Living?" in 1895 before the Harvard YMCA, some twenty-five years after his own bout with psychotic melancholy. But it is an accurate narrative of James's own reflections on the period; more important, it shows that he was conscious, at least in retrospect, about how common his troubles were.

In this lecture, James attempted to show Christian students "the profounder bass-note of life." He noted that some people answer the question whether life is worth living with a temperamental optimism that makes them incapable of seriously believing that anything evil can exist. The young Rousseau was like this, as was America's own Walt Whitman. If everyone could live in such a mood, there would be no reason to ask the question. But universal optimism was a pipe dream. James said: "That life is *not* worth living the whole army of suicides declare—an army whose roll call, like the famous evening gun of the British army, follows the sun round the world and never terminates" (*WTB*, 38).

27

Even if a person never experienced an urge to commit suicide, James argued, "the plainest intellectual integrity— nay more, the simplest manliness and honor—forbid us to forget their case." The problem with life was not just abstract; it was not just that people might be governed by "kraft und stoff" or that destiny might be a sham. The problem was more tangible, accurately caught by John Ruskin when he reminded English ladies and gentlemen enraptured by the glamour of the Crystal Palace (the center of the first world's fair in 1851, and the first prefabricated public building in history, designed to demonstrate Britain's supremacy in manufacture and design) that a few feet of ground were "all that separate the merriment from the misery" (WTB, 38, 39).

While the English gentry were dining in their townhouses, untold numbers of people in London were famished and miserable, "pale from death, horrible in destitution, broken by despair" (WTB, 38). The lives of the fortunate were built on the rubble heap of the human herd. Members of that herd were not reflective enough to consider suicide. If they killed themselves, they did so helplessly. Life was not pondered by the herd, but their misery was a problem for the fortunate who were "honorable" and "manly" enough to realize that they not only shared the globe with downtrodden humans but also could do nothing to ameliorate the situation. Human misery was symptomatic of "the hard facts of nature" to Victorian intellectual ways of thinking and, hence, intractable.

James asked his audience to suppose that they were dealing with a person whose only comfort lay in knowing he could commit suicide, a person suffering from the metaphysical *tedium vitae* peculiar to reflective men. What reasons could be given for living? Ultimately, James claimed, only religious ones. Pessimism was not a moral stance; it was a religious disease, contracted when a person made religious demands "to which there comes no religious reply." He said that there were both tough- and tender-minded people but that "minds of either class may be intensely religious."[3] By "religious" he meant that they could "equally desire atonement and reconciliation, and crave acquiescence and communion with the total soul of things" (WTB, 40).

In a tough-minded person, one intellectually loyal to hard facts, like James himself, but also many of his Christian students, the disappointment of religious craving could lead to pessimism. The contradiction between the hard facts of nature and the heart's craving for divine harmony could result in a kind of inner discord. In the face of this trouble, one was left with two responses: one could cease "longing to read the facts religiously," or one could find that "supplementary facts may be discovered or believed in." These two ways of relief, James said, were really "two stages of recovery" (*WTB*, 41). Indeed, they were the stages of recovery that James had traversed himself during the preceding twenty-five years, and clarified both the sort of religion James could not live without as well as the sorts he could not live with.

James asserted that "natural religion" must inevitably lead to melancholy for intellectuals "of the nineteenth century, with our evolutionary theories and our mechanical philosophies." By natural religion he meant not only the deisms of Enlightenment philosophers but also the natural supernaturalisms of Romantics in his father's generation. Nineteenth-century intellectuals could no longer live with religions that construed nature as the adequate expression of spirit or divinity. They required as much emancipation from Romantic doxologies as their fathers had required escape from Calvinism, because they knew that "visible nature is all plasticity and indifference—a moral multiverse." Voices like Büchner's and Spencer's had made it plain to them that "if there be a divine Spirit of the universe, nature, such as we know her, cannot possibly be its *ultimate word* to man." Natural supernaturalists had been searching for divinity in the wrong book. "Either there is no spirit revealed in nature, or else it is inadequately revealed there; and (as all the higher religions have assumed) what we call visible nature, or *this* world, must be a veil and surface show whose full meaning resides in a supplementary unseen or *other* world" (*WTB*, 43).

The problem with natural supernaturalism was that the smallest unit it dealt with was "the world" or "the universe." Confronted with the actuality of human misery, students brought up under the "monistic superstition" had one plausible option. If "the world" was not good (because there was human misery) it must be evil. But, James suggested, denial of the idol of a substantially unitary world or universe was the first step of escape from philosophical melancholy. If a person owed no allegiance to "the world" then the thought of suicide was "no longer a guilty challenge or obsession." If the human misery that Ruskin spoke of was taken piecemeal and "the world" was classified as an intellectual's fiction, one could appeal to the reflective suicide "in the name of the very evils that make his heart sick there—to wait and see his part of the battle out." This, James suggested, was Carlyle's solution, the relief of melancholic pessimism through protest. Anyone with "a normally constituted heart" (that is, any genuine Victorian) was honorable enough to "take some suffering upon ourselves, to do some self-denying service

29

with our lives, in return for all those lives upon which ours are built" (*WTB*, 45, 47, 48).

According to James, people had better live without natural supernaturalism, and they could, if only through Carlylean resistance. This recommendation recapitulated his own first curative step. Upon reading Charles Bernard Renouvier's second of the "Essais" in April 1870, James found himself maintaining the latter's notion of free will—"the sustaining of a thought *because I choose* to when I might have other thoughts" (*LWJ*, 1:147). He said his first act of free will was to believe in free will and tried to discipline himself to "care little for speculation." In this mood, he asserted that

> not in maxims, not in *Anschauungen*, but in accumulated
> *acts* of thought lies salvation. *Passer Outre*. Hitherto, when I
> have felt like taking a free initiative, like daring to act origi-
> nally, without carefully waiting for contemplation of the ex-
> ternal world to determine all for me, suicide seemed the only
> manly form to put my daring into; now, I will go a step fur-
> ther with my will, not only act with it, but believe as well;
> believe in my individual reality and creative power. My belief,
> to be sure, can't be optimistic—but I will posit life (the real, the
> good) in the self-governing *resistance* of the ego to the world.
> Life shall be . . . [MS doubtful] doing and suffering and creat-
> ing. [*LWJ*, 1:148]

In other words, as he put the case generally in 1895, James "cast away all metaphysics in order to get rid of hypochondria" but was "resolved to owe nothing as yet to religion and its more positive gifts" (*WTB*, 48).

But James went on to recommend religion as a second stage of cure for philosophical melancholy. He said he meant religion "in the supernaturalist sense" or "faith in the existence of an unseen order of some kind in which the riddles of the natural order may be found explained." He argued that religion in this intellectualist sense was appropriate even if nothing positive was known of the unseen world, on the grounds that "we are free to trust at our own risks anything that is not impossible, and that can bring analogies to bear in its behalf" (*WTB*, 48, 52). "Trusting" did not carry with it any license to define in detail an unseen world or to anathematize and excommunicate those whose trust was different. This meant that no one who was "honorable" could live with any religion that exemplified the spirit of sectarianism.

The "worshippers of science" like Clifford and Huxley who tried to make life without faith respectable by insisting on "the duty of neutrality" simply lacked "scientific imagination," according to James. They failed to realize the extent to which "trusting" played a role in scientific discovery and neglected the fact that science itself responded to "an imperious inner demand on our part for ideal logical and mathematical harmonies" (*WTB*, 51). These were demands that scientists brought to data in order to wrest results from them.

Carlylean protest amounted to the courage to stake one's life on a possibility. Religious faith, according to James (echoing his brother-in-law, William Salter, spokesman for the Philadelphia Ethical Society), amounted to the belief that the possibility exists. James argued that "all the converging multitude of arguments that make in favor of idealism tend to prove . . . that the world of physics is probably not absolute" (*WTB*, 52).

He gave a curious analogy that clarified what he had in mind when he suggested that people could act as though an invisible world were real. The analogy carried through James's 1870 remark that his faith could not be optimistic. His image was startling: the physical world might lie soaking in a spiritual atmosphere in the same way that our domestic animals live in a human world that they cannot appreciate. People might be related to unseen spiritual reality the way "a poor dog whom they are vivisecting in a laboratory" is related to the intentions of the vivisector! "He lies strapped on a board and shrieking at his executioners, and to his own dark consciousness is literally in a sort of hell. He cannot see a single redeeming ray in the whole business; and yet all these diabolical seeming events are often controlled by human intentions with which, if his poor benighted mind could only be made to catch a glimpse of them, all that is heroic in him would religiously acquiesce. . . . Lying on his back on the board there he may be performing a function incalculably higher than any that prosperous canine life admits of" (*WTB*, 53).

Likewise, James suggested, the world may be "still wider" than the tragic one in which people live: "For my own part, I do not know what the sweat and blood and tragedy of this life mean, if they mean anything short of this" (*WTB*, 55). Either the unseen order explained tangible misery as adequately as James had explained vivisection to himself when he was a medical student, or life was incredible and worth living only for the sake of the protest.

James, of course, did not go on to suggest that there *was* an unseen order to provide the requisite theodicy. Instead, he took a line of thought that he had developed in light of Renouvier's "free-will" in the early 1870s. He argued that "*maybes* are the essence of the situation." He suggested that "life *feels* like a real fight—as if there were something really wild in the universe which we, with all our idealities and faithfulnesses, are needed to redeem; and first of all to redeem our own hearts from atheisms and fears" (*WTB*, 55).

People had attempted to "read" nature for signs of divinity when their trust in the Gospel itself began to fail for various reasons. James suggested that his Christian students should keep reading, but in an unlikely set of "books"—the passions of men according to men. Thus, he asked, "If needs of ours outrun the visible universe, why may not that be a sign that an invisible universe is there?" (*WTB*, 51). This question molded James's religious investigations for at least a quarter of a century, from the moment he distinguished himself as a religious investigator in 1876 until he stopped speculating about the possibility of an invisible universe and started looking for one in 1901.

Religious Tenacity, 1870–1875

In the midst of James's acute acedia, he managed to graduate from Harvard Medical School and write various reviews and notices for the *Nation*, the *North American Review*, the *Atlantic Monthly*, and the *Boston Daily Advertiser*. All of these journals were dedicated to the expression of democracy, science, and idealism, the trinity for religious republicans at the turn of the century.

Like other writings of the period, several of James's articles indicated a deep interest in "religion and medicine." They mixed concerns for the study of alleged spiritistic phenomena, medical therapies for pessimism (the religious disease), and a preoccupation with the health and well-being of the "representative American."[4]

On balance, there is no suggestion that James departed from the program of recovery from *Grübelsucht* that he had initiated in 1870 until 1875, when the death of Chauncey Wright (a mentor who became James's picture of positivism incarnate) provided an occasion for renewed *Anschauungen*. For five years, in other words, James escaped more or less successfully from hypochondria by simply willing to believe in the existence of an unseen universe which explained the riddles of manifest evil. He clung tenaciously to his belief in individual reality and creative power and posited life in the self-governing resistance of his ego to the world. Indeed, he tested his tenacity in the metaphysical club he constituted along with Charles Peirce, Oliver Wendell Holmes, Wright, and Nicholas St. John Green.

James's Carlylean method of cure was not without irony. It gave him the stability to become a professional *Grübelsuchter*, a university professor who was preoccupied with philosophical speculation by 1878 (the year he wrote two articles to appear in speculative philosophical journals).[5] In James's appreciation of Wright, written for the *Nation*, he noted that "to Wright's mode of looking at the universe, such ideas as pessimism or optimism were alike simply irrelevant. Whereas most men's interest in a thought is proportioned to its possible relation to human destiny, with him it was almost the reverse. When the mere actuality of phenomena will suffice to describe them, he held it pure excess and superstition to speak of a metaphysical whence or whither, of a substance, a meaning, or an end" (*CER*, 23).

James came to think highly of this philosophical position at times, if not in the end. Wright's labors, James wrote, were inspiring. As James saw it, philosophers' work in America to that point had been confined to "deepening enormously the philosophical *consciousness*, and revealing more and more minutely and fully the import of philosophical problems. In this preliminary task ontologists and phenomenalists, mechanists and teleologists, must join friendly hands, for each has been indispensable for the work of the other, and the only foe of either is the common foe of both—namely, the practical, conventionally thinking man, to whom . . . nothing has true seriousness but personal interests" (*CER*, 24–25).

Wright exemplified mental perspective and the sociality of persuasion to James, and neither of these characteristics abided personal tenacity—belief come hell or high water—as an adequate method of settling vexing doubts. Tenacity was adequate so long as it worked, but it succeeded only so long as a person denied his natural gregariousness by closing his ears to differences of opinion. The philosophical task was to combat the notion that personal, in the sense of egocentric, interests were ultimately authoritative in matters of human destiny.

Faith and Formal Philosophy, 1876–1881

One year, almost to the day, after James's appreciation of Wright appeared, he wrote an unsigned editorial, "The Teaching of Philosophy in Our Colleges," that represented the position of the *Nation* on the subject. G. Stanley Hall had written a letter in the same number (September 21, 1876) deploring the state of philosophy in America and urging that it be remodeled along British and German lines. Hall complained that philosophy in America was indoctrinative, not instructive, that it was taught in order to tell students what to think, not how to think. The *Nation*, speaking through James, agreed, at least that philosophy in America's sectarian colleges was "trammelled and paralyzed and made petty by the invidious presence" of orthodox religious control (*EP*, 3).

But the problem was being solved. "The sleepiest doctor-of-divinity-like repose" in America had been shaken by speculative and audacious new constructions in physical science, and eminent scientists were filling philosophical billets in university faculties. Spurred by their influence, the methods in university philosophy were becoming more investigatory. Rather than stagnate in orthodox theology, students at Harvard were reading Locke, Kant, Schopenhauer, Hartmann, Hodgson, and Spencer, and becoming intoxicated "with the liberal spirit." What doctrines these students took from their teachers was of little importance "provided they [caught] from them the living, philosophic attitude of mind, an independent personal look at all the data of life, and the eagerness to harmonize them." Without "prejudging the question whether the final results of speculation will be friendly or hostile to the formulas of Christian thought," university philosophy stood for the pursuit of truth and the resolution of human problems "as if there were no official answer occupying the field" (*EP*, 4).

The *Nation*'s sense for the great promise of university liberal education (James's editorial was written the year that Johns Hopkins was founded, an event self-consciously interpreted by many American intellectuals as the dawning of a new educational era) set the context for James's public return to the world of contemplation. He had cured himself of pessimism first by ceasing to "read the facts religiously" and then by tenaciously believing in "supplementary facts which permit the religious reading to go on." But these stages were only preliminaries to his religious investigations, which were better pursued in his role of university professor, equipped with libraries, laboratories, colleagues, and the requisite spirit.

James's first religious investigations were strictly philosophical. Between 1878 and 1881 he wrote a series of articles designed to establish his views on the motives of philosophizing, articles that argued from the structures of human behavior, especially thought, to certain conclusions about rationality. The first one, "Quelques Considérations sur la méthode subjective," appeared in Renouvier's *Critique Philosophique*.[6] A year later, "The Sentiment of Rationality" was published in *Mind*, the British journal in which Hegelians battled Scottish Common Sense. Then, in 1880, he wrote "Rationality, Activity, and Faith" for publication in the *Princeton Review*, still the center of orthodox theism from James's viewpoint.[7] Finally, in 1881, "Reflex Action and Theism" appeared in the *Unitarian Review*. James wrote each of these articles as chapters of a book, which never, however, appeared as such.

All four of these articles depended on the Darwinian view of human behavior that James had articulated in "Some Remarks on Spencer's *Definition of Mind as Correspondence*," published as a headliner in the *Journal of Speculative Philosophy*, edited by the Hegelian William Torrey Harris, in January 1878. Stalking Spencer, who claimed that the mind is "an adjustment of inner to outer relations" passively mirroring reality, on the one hand, and actively serving survival, on the other, James asserted that "the knower is not simply a mirror floating with no foothold anywhere, and passively reflecting an order that he comes upon and finds simply existing. The knower is an actor, and co-efficient of the truth on one side, whilst on the other he registers the truth which he helps to create." James further claimed that mind has a vote from birth on; that mental interests and postulates motivate behaviors that transform the world in distinctive ways; that it is impossible to completely dissociate "facts" from "values" because "facts" were evaluations; and, finally, that "the only objective criterion of reality is coerciveness, in the long run, over thought. . . . If judgments of the *should-be* are fated to grasp us in this way, they are what 'correspond' " (*EP*, 21, 22).

What Spencer forgot, according to James, was that individuals are social beings. They desire certain socially engendered qualities that may imperil their own lives and even the welfare of the community. Thus, mind does not simply serve the survival of the individual and the survival of his tribe. Individuals do not have only the means to serve ends specified by their physical environments. They often both "supply the means and the standard by which they are measured." Mind not only "serves a final purpose, but *brings* a final purpose—posits, declares it" (*EP*, 20).

Darwin provided a way for taking account of the role that such standards of appropriateness play in human life by making "spontaneous variation" and "natural selection" dual principles of evolutionary development. On Darwinian grounds, James argued that it was possible to conceive of interests as preceding "the outer relations noticed." They did not derive from physical necessity, he stated, but from "idiosyncrasies of our nervous center" or "spontaneous variations like any of those which form the ultimate *data* for

Darwin's theory." This gave him Darwinian backing for the claim that mind played an irreducible role in human life and development. To be sure, "the re-actions or outward consequences of the interests" could be expressed in nonmental terms and provided a reality principle for the selection of interests. In fact, this insight was central to the development of James's pragmatic theory of truth thirty years later. But the interest of survival, which Spencer treated as normative, was "nothing more than an objective future implication of the reaction [to some interest] as an actual fact" (*EP*, 11, 19, 18). Far from normative, according to James, Darwin understood survival as accidental to fitness, not instrumental.

From James's Darwinian point of view, thought must be analyzed using the doctrine of reflex action. That doctrine made the structural unit of the human nervous system a triad: perception, conception, and action as the components of human behavior. What is more, the doctrine assumed that "perception and thinking are only there for behavior's sake" (*WTB*, 92). This insight molded James's understanding of the motives of philosophizing and provided a context for his arguments that faith is an inevitable component of healthy thought and that theism is the most rational sort of faith.

First, James argued that philosophers aim to achieve rationality. They want to attain a mental fluency not ordinarily achieved in the fragmentary view of things that people typically have. The "philosophic interest" lies in developing a conception of "the frame of things" that will be both comprehensive and simple, an essential definition of the world that will be intellectually sufficient. Motivated by desires for "ease, peace, and rest," and a need to overcome puzzlement, philosophers try to reduce "the manifold in thought to simple form" (*EP*, 32–35). So far as their interest is theoretical or systematic, according to James, their work is governed by two aesthetic norms, unity, or simplicity, and clarity. As James described them, philosophers bring about "unity" by making associations and identifications among different sorts of things. They bring about "clarity" by distinguishing different sorts of things.

Some schools of philosophy, for example, evolutionism, seemed to crave unity or "monism" at any cost. Others sacrificed unity for clarity or "representability," for example, English empiricism. But "no system of philosophy can hope to be universally accepted among men which grossly violates either of the two great aesthetic needs of our logical nature" (*EP*, 41). Perception demanded representability; conception required unification of the facts of the world in their sensible diversity.

But according to the doctrine of reflex action, if the philosophical enterprise was healthy, philosophers' motives could not be simply theoretical or logical. They also had to be practical. Indeed, James argued, when philosophers permitted the demands of theory to govern their quest for rationality, they violated "the nature of our intelligence" and became "gnostics," or thinkers who fallaciously subordinated feeling and action to thought.

Gnosticism could be prevented, according to James, by emphasizing "the feelings of rationality in its practical aspect" (*EP*, 41). When philosophers did this, they realized that rationality had more to do with the development of abilities to deal adequately with novel situations than with the articulation of systems per se. James claimed, for instance, that empiricists happened to be right when they asserted that custom was a source of practical rational feeling. But he said that 'custom' only named and did not analyze what constitutes the feeling of practical rationality. He argued that customary conceptions feel rational *because they banish uncertainty from the future*. Novelty is the irritant that motivates people to think; expectation is the attitude that salves intelligence. From a Darwinian point of view, "it is of the utmost practical importance to an animal that he should have prevision of the qualities of the objects that surround him, and especially that he should not come to rest in presence of circumstances that might be fraught either with peril or advantage" (*WTB*, 68). Natural selection was bound to bring about the emotionally satisfying effect of expectation sooner or later.

Expectation should be (and has been) so highly prized, according to James, that a philosophical position which satisfies it will be "peacefully accepted by the mind" even if it is left logically unsystematized (*WTB*, 68). But James did not think that expectation was the sole constituent of practical rationality. For a philosophy to succeed, it must not only guarantee the future but also define what is guaranteed as congruous "*with our spontaneous powers*," one of the most significant of which is faith.

Any philosophy which either disappointed "our dearest desires," as modern German pessimism did, or contradicted "our propensities to press against objects," as modern materialism did, was bound to fail. Neither Schopenhauer nor Büchner, for instance, left the mind with anything to care for. They gave no answer to the important philosophical question What is to be done? Thus, they could not be considered serious thinkers. Serious pessimism—that is, Stoicism —stimulated "the willingness to live with energy, though energy bring pain"; serious materialism—that is, Epicureanism—permitted anesthesia or an escape from suffering "to be our rule of life" (*WTB*, 73).[8]

Here, James claimed, Christianity recognized an active impulse that differed from the energy of the Stoic and the anesthesia of the Epicurean. Faith, "the readiness to act in a cause the prosperous issue of which is not certified to us in advance," might either make life painful or facilitate an escape from suffering, but it made neither the rule of life. Faith displaced pleasure and pain as central concerns with loyalty and trust. As such, faith was an active impulse on which men commonly depended, whether they admitted it or not. The "average man" distinguished himself from the philosophers who were abnormally interested in systematicity by his "power to trust, to risk a little beyond the literal evidence." Indeed, for any normally constituted intelligence, "any mode of conceiving the universe which makes an appeal to this generous power, and makes the man seem as if he were individually helping to create the actuality of the truth whose metaphysical reality he is helping to assume," will be appealing (*WTB*, 76).

James argued that if Huxley branded faith in religious dogma "the lowest depth of immorality" and Clifford called belief that outran evidence "sin," both distorted the very nature of scientific development. To be sure, "Cette foi peut tromper, très-bien" (an intellectual faith may mislead, easily). Yet, the question was not whether faith is inevitably self-fulfilling, but whether faith is *dispensable* in a large class of experimental issues. Put negatively, the question in point was whether one is justified in rejecting a theory (like pessimism) "which many objective facts apparently confirm, solely because it does not in any way respond to our inward preferences" (*EP*, 25, 331).

Obviously, James argued, where preferences are powerless to modify or produce things, faith or "the subjective method" is totally inappropriate. But there is a class of facts that depend on personal preference, trust, or loyalty for actualization. In these cases, "faith is not only licit and pertinent, but essential and indispensable. The truths cannot become true till our faith has made them so" (*WTB*, 80). Where causes depend on personal participation for realization, loyalty is essential, even though "the effort it induces in me to make may not result in the state of things it foresees, and would fain bring to pass" (*EP*, 333). Faith did not certify the prosperity of such issues. But absence of faith abetted their elimination. Indeed, waxing Darwinian again, James suggested that such personal preferences are "the spontaneous variations upon which the intellectual struggle for existence is based. The fittest conceptions survive, and with them the names of their champions shining to all futurity" (*WTB*, 78).[9]

At this point in his argument, James reintroduced the idol he had personally abandoned a decade before. He argued that faith or the subjective method was applicable to the problems of philosophy on the grounds that these problems concerned the character of "the world." But he made this revision in his understanding: The world had no character definite enough to *require* one philosophical attitude rather than another.[10] The mistake that the adolescent *Grübelsuchter* had made was to consider the character of the world without considering his own ability to contribute to its character. Now he thought that

> in every proposition whose bearing is universal (and such are all the propositions of philosophy), the acts of the subject and their consequences throughout eternity should be included in the formula. If M represent the entire world *minus* the reaction of the thinker upon it, and if $M + x$ represent the absolutely total matter of philosophic propositions (x standing for the thinker's reaction and its results)—what would be a universal truth if the term x were of one complexion, might become egregious error if x altered its character. [*WTB*, 81]

Thus, so far as the world was concerned, beliefs about its destiny were among the phenomenal conditions "necessarily preliminary to the 'results' . . . and consequently a necessary component of the truth we seek to know" (*EP*, 335). Construing the world this way, James argued, changed the face of contemporary evolutionary philosophy. Spencer had pictured the world as M without x and had thus issued the trivial ethical standard that whatever succeeds is best. But the truly wise Darwinian, James claimed, "will . . . admit faith as an ultimate ethical factor." Any philosophy that made ethical questions "depend on the question What is going to succeed?— must needs fall back on personal belief. . . . For again and again success depends on energy of act, energy again depends on faith that we shall not fail; and that faith in turn on the faith that we are right—which faith thus verifies itself" (*WTB*, 82, 83).[11]

According to this line of thought, the world was no longer a phantom idol but a state of affairs that was constituted in part by the powers that people possessed and deployed according to their temperaments. The world's destiny depended on the rules of action that men were given or invented. Because men's active impulses were so differently fixed, a diversity of rules was inevitable. Because faithful men differed in temperament, philosophy was bound to include *Aberglaube* (a term James borrowed from Matthew Arnold), "legitimate, inexpungable, yet doomed to eternal variations and disputes" (*WTB*, 75). Loyal to the doctrine of the vox populi in 1880, James assumed that the emergence of philosophical truth ultimately depended on a fruitful conflict among theories and attitudes. It was, after all, no different in science, where "sooner or later the effects of [the scientist's] actions will undeceive him if his starting points have been falsely assumed" (*EP*, 336). Vox populi (which failed to account for the role of self-deception in both science and morals) provided a way for James to speak of "working hypotheses" and "faith" in one and the same breath.

James's own *Aberglaube* was theistic, and though he had no argument, much less proof, that divinity existed, he did argue that "*anything short of God is not rational, anything more than God is not possible*," on the grounds of the triadic structure of the human mind alone! Having rejected Büchnerian materialism "solely because it does not in any way respond to our inward preference," James argued in "Reflex Action and Theism" against moral positivists and natural supernaturalists that "a God . . . is . . . the kind of being, which, if he did exist, would form the most adequate possible object for minds framed like our own to conceive as lying at the root of the universe" (*WTB*, 93).

According to James, moral positivists were committed to the doctrine of agnosticism (a term coined by Huxley). They claimed that controversies about the character of the world were unanswerable, and thus insignificant, because the "inward nature" of the world could not be known. But, foreshadowing his pragmatic theory of meaning, James argued that so long as philosophical conceptions of the world have practical results, they are significant.

A theist could confess, along with the proponents of positivism, that "we cannot know how Being made itself or us," because theism was not an answer to the question how the world was made or why the world was made. Theism, according to James, was an answer to the question What character does the world have? (cf. *WTB*, 111). A theist had no need to discover some reality behind phenomena in order to define the inward nature of the world, or to engage in " 'Erkenntnistheorie' or philosophical ontology," because "his insight into the *what* of life leads to results so immediately and intimately rational that the *why*, the *how*, and the *whence* of it are questions that lose all urgency" (*WTB*, 107).

Indeed, James argued, positivists were correct to claim that perception must initiate thought. They were right to complain that the writings of contemporary theologians were thick on theory, thin on experience. But in their battle against theoretical excess, they lost sight of the structure of normal intelligence by placing unnatural strictures on the role of will in thoughtful human life. They proclaimed a "religion of science" intent on "suffocating all other appetites out of a nation's mind." This, James warned, would always be resisted by "our Anglo-Saxon race" because its "moral, aesthetic and practical wants form too dense a stubble to be mown by any scientific Occam's razor that has yet been formed." Anglo-Saxons would never allow positivists to characterize the world in the third person, as an "it" (*WTB*, 105, 106), for that picture totally disappointed the demands of practical rationality. The bare molecular world was an inadequate stimulus for man's practical nature. If the positivist picture were true, the world would be irrational, and it would always leave people feeling puzzled by their own wills.

Theism, to the contrary, "turns the *it* into a *thou*" (*WTB*, 106), according to James. Sectarians squabbled about the modes of revelation, the extent of Providence, the problem of evil, and, more generally, the problem of the finite and the infinite. But, James said, every theist, sectarian or not, agreed on the essential features of God: when they characterized the world as "thou," they pictured its deepest power as formally personal, individuated, and caring, fighting for righteousness as men understood it and recognizing each individual for the person he is. God was a "power not ourselves" who helped people realize their best intentions because he meant to.

James argued that the theistic conception of the world stood ready with "the most practically rational solution it is possible to conceive." Theism relieved people from the ultimate sting of tragedy by apprehending, though not comprehending, outward reality as providential. There was "not an energy of our active nature to which it does not automatically appeal, not an emotion of which it does not normally or naturally release the springs" (*WTB*, 101). The question was whether the facts of nature and the theoretical elaboration of them could always sustain theistic conclusions. James raised this issue, but did not address it. Instead, he left it in the hands of "the future history of philosophy" and turned his attention to theism's other rival, gnostic pantheism.

If positivists subordinated thought and action to perception, construed the world as an "it," and cramped intelligence by leaving active impulses without adequate stimulation, gnostics distorted the structure of human behavior by construing human knowledge as the end toward which feeling and willing are ordered. Most

Romantics were gnostics, especially those who thought they followed Hegel. They attempted to fly beyond theism by developing strategies to overcome the "ultimate duality of God and his believer, and to transform it into some sort or other of identity" (*WTB*, 106). In other words, they tried to develop a pantheism of the first person, defining "the world" as "a part of *me*." But this, for all the emotional satisfaction it might bring, was impossible.

Of course, James noted, moments of "self-surrender, of absolute practical union between one's self and the divine object of one's contemplation," surely occurred. But these religious experiences left the object "God" and the subject "I" individuated, not substantially the same. Theists in the mystical tradition found peace in emotional and practical union with their God, but they were "contented with a blank unmediated dualism." From the point of view of theorists bent on demonstrating the essential identity among sorts of things, it was an "insult to the very word 'rational' to say that the rational character of the universe and its creator means no more than that we practically feel at home in their presence, and that our powers are a match for their demands." For anyone with an insatiable speculative itch, then, dualistic theists were "the very picture of unfaithfulness to the rights and duties of our theoretic reason" (*WTB*, 106, 108).

But, James argued, from "the natural history point of view," gnosticism was an extravagant faith, resting on a misunderstanding of the role of cognition. The Darwinian knew that "the cognitive faculty, where it appears to exist at all, appears but as one element in an organic mental whole, and as a minister to higher mental powers—the powers of will" (*WTB*, 110). By arresting the course of reflex action in the "cul-de-sac" of thought, gnosticism was literally a kind of insanity. Unless theory issued in "some new practical maxim or resolve, or the denial of some old one," it was treacherously comical and bound to make the religious person suffer from that "opposite condition of nightmare," the condition James himself had felt. Gnosticism was impossible, James suggested, because no legitimate way to overcome the distinction between "me" and other powers not myself could be found. "In every being that is real," James said, "there is something external to, and sacred from the grasp of every other. God's being is sacred from ours" (*WTB*, 111).

This note ended James's first attempt to argue philosophically that people could rid themselves, in a legitimate way, of pessimism and fatalism *"by means of a very simple process of reasoning."* If James's Darwinian picture of mind was right, the philosopher's own preference could not be left out of his account of the world. If his picture of normal intelligence was right, the philosopher had better prefer theism because it satisfied the demands of practical rationality (unlike agnosticism) without playing fast and loose with the diversity of perception and the primacy of practical thought (sins committed by gnostic pantheists). In these "acts of thought" lay deliverance from debilitating melancholy and restoration to energetic theistic belief.

Human Emotion, Belief, and Will, 1882–1896

From 1882 until 1896, James maintained and elaborated the line of thought first outlined in "Reflex Action and Theism." Thus, in 1882 he wrote a piece, "On Some Hegelisms," which clarified his thought on the abnormality of gnosticism and reasserted his conviction that Hegelian attempts to overcome real diversity were a sham. To be sure, he wrote, the "many" was unified by space, time, and consciousness, but there were many consciousnesses. The world was a "sort of republican banquet . . . where all the qualities of being respect one another's personal sacredness, yet sit at the common table of space and time" (*WTB*, 201).

In 1884, James delivered his Harvard Divinity School address, "The Dilemma of Determinism," in which he argued that "the world" was ambiguous in a way that neither positivism nor monistic idealism permitted. Here, he elaborated his "$M + x$" formula of the world and reasoned that if human volitions were not indeterminate, it was impossible to account for the judgments of regret on which common morality depended. "Chance" was not the bugaboo that positivists, Hegelians, and orthodox theists alike tried to picture it. Calling a human action a matter of chance simply asserted that "there is something in it really of its own, something that is not the unconditional property of the whole. If the whole wants this property, the whole must wait till it can get it." Varying his analogy slightly from his article on Hegelisms, he insisted that "the universe may actually be a sort of joint-stock society . . . in which the sharers have both limited liabilities and limited powers" (*WTB*, 120–21).

Then, in 1885, James wrote "Necessary Truths and the Effects of Experience." Published as the last chapter of *The Principles of Psychology* in 1890 (2:617–88), this essay elaborated his Darwinian account of mind and pushed the formula 'mind proposes, environment disposes' to its limits. Indeed, if most of the pieces

James wrote from 1882 until 1890 were devoted to the work of the *Principles*, they directly concerned advances in his religious investigations at three points: the theory of emotions, the psychology of belief, and the problem of self-consciousness.

In 1884, James developed the physiological account of human emotion that was later to be known as the "James-Lange Theory of the Emotions." Read apart from "Spencer's Definition" and "Reflex Action and Theism," James's "What is an Emotion?" was subsequently sanctified as the seminal work in American behavioral psychology.[12] James argued in it that emotions are feelings of bodily changes, not pieces of mental stuff. But however the work was used or abused by others, it emerged out of the doctrine of reflex action that James had articulated against Spencer in order to make room for mental spontaneity.

James had personally felt the absence of emotion in his severe melancholy roughly fifteen years before. The same "French correspondent" who reported the experience of that sick soul who turned out to be James asked the reader of *The Varieties of Religious Experience* to

> conceive yourself, if possible, suddenly stripped of all the emotion with which your world now inspires you, and try to imagine it as it exists, purely by itself, without your favorable or unfavorable, hopeful or apprehensive comment. It will be almost impossible for you to realize such a condition of negativity and deadness. No one portion of the universe would then have importance beyond another; and the whole collection of its things and series of its events would be without significance, character, expression, or perspective. Whatever of value, interest or meaning our respective worlds may appear endued with are thus pure gifts of the spectator's mind. The passion of love is the most familiar and extreme example of this fact. If it comes, it comes; if it does not come, no process of reasoning can force it. . . . So with fear, with indignation, jealousy, ambition, worship. If they are there, life changes. And whether they shall be there or not depends almost always upon non-logical, often on organic conditions. And as the excited interest which these passions put into the world is our gift to the world, just so are the passions themselves *gifts*,—gifts to us, from sources sometimes low and sometimes high; but almost always non-logical and beyond our control. [*VRE*, 150–51]

In the sort of psychological neuralgia James called "anhedonia," there was no emotion. Life was "corpse-like," clinically inert.

Conversely, James claimed that "a purely disembodied human emotion is a non-entity." On grounds of introspection, James claimed that "whatever moods, affections, and passions I have, are in very truth constituted by, and made up of, those bodily changes we ordinarily call their expression or consequence; and . . . that if I were to become corporeally anesthetic, I should be excluded from the life of the affections, harsh and tender alike, and drag out an existence of merely cognitive or intellectual form" (WE, 18).

James thought he had lived such a life of "merely cognitive or intellectual form" in the years around 1870. The task that he set for himself was to account for the difference between that apathetic existence and his life thereafter, which was often charged with breathtaking energy. His own clinical observations left him convinced that the change did not result from any process of reasoning. It resulted from something nonlogical. There was no subjective method one could employ to establish emotionality. Without emotionality, without motives, faith was irrelevant. The subjective method depended on some excited interest, which in turn depended on passions given to people from sources beyond their control. Thus, for instance, James felt consoled when he found himself praying. Only in response to that consolation did he commit himself to certain habits of mind suggested by Renouvier.

In light of this experience, James reasoned that emotional states were not immediately induced by perception per se, because it was possible to *see* things without emotion. Common sense was wrong. It said "we lose our fortune, are sorry, and weep; we meet a bear, are frightened and run." The more accurate statement was that "we feel sorry because we cry, angry because we strike, afraid because we tremble. . . . Without the bodily states following on the perception, the latter would be purely cognitive in form, pale, colourless, destitute of emotional warmth." Bodily states made the difference between apathetic and pathetic life. Without them, "we might . . . see the bear, and judge it best to run, receive the insult and deem it right to strike, but we could not actually *feel* afraid or angry" (WE, 13).

According to James's doctrine, whistling to keep up courage was no figure of speech. If apathy coincided with anesthesia, emotion should accompany arousal. Certain moral corollaries ensued. For instance, if a person refused to express a passion, it died. In general, "if we wish to conquer undesirable emotional tendencies in ourselves we must assiduously, and in the first instance, cold-bloodedly, go through the *outward motions* of those contrary dispositions we prefer to cultivate. The reward of persistency will infallibly come, in the fading out of the sullenness or depression, and in the advent of real cheerfulness and kindliness in their stead" (WE, 22). This advice came from the former pathological *Grübel-suchter* who committed himself to caring for "the *form* of my action" and to recollecting that "only when habits of order are formed can we advance to really interesting fields of action" (*LWJ*, 1:148). James himself had turned to cultivating "outward motions" in order to cooperate with the "unseen" powers that had restored his own emotionality.

As a theoretical advance, James's work on emotions was important because it gave substance to the claim made by Darwin in *The Expression of the Emotions in Man and Animal* (1872) that specifiable internal processes are tied together with specifiable visible manifestations associated with things like anger and fear. But in the doing, James made the bold claim that the language of "expression" was itself faulty. This language motivated research on the mental stuff inside the mind that might be the thing expressed. This made the theory of emotions inevitably speculative by construing the mind as a Cartesian theater instead of a process. James suggested that the location of emotion was the body, not the mind, and that 'emotion' categorized certain bodily states of affairs, some clinically observable, some surgically so. Contrary to mind-stuff theorists, he tried to demonstrate that "no new principles have to be invoked . . . beyond the ordinary reflex circuit" (WE, 28) to account for passion. But this left unanswered the question of how an apathetic patient was restored to emotionality, a question that remained unanswered until James developed his allegiance to Frederic Myers's doctrine of the subconscious.

In any case, James's theory of emotions clarified what he thought was going on when someone suffered from religious disease, and then again when someone was on the way toward cure. It also laid the basis for his psychology of belief.[13] In *The Principles of Psychology*, James argued that "belief" meant "the sense of reality" and was a kind of feeling "more allied to the emotions than anything else" (PP, 2:283). Belief was the feeling that a person had when theoretic agitation ceased, a feeling that, if often unverbalized, always presented itself in bodily ways.

On the grounds established by his theory of emotions, James argued that doubt and inquiry, not disbelief, were the true opposites of belief. The *locus classicus* of pathological belief was the sort of drunkenness in which "a deepening of the sense of reality . . . is gained"; that of pathological doubt was the questioning mania, "the inability to rest in any conception and the need of having it confirmed and explained" (*PP*, 2:284). Beyond both belief and doubt lay that state of anhedonia, of simple, formal perception where "everything is hollow, unreal, dead" (*PP*, 2:285), both within and without.

Belief, according to James, was not simply thought. Following Franz Brentano, he held that belief presupposed thought. Belief was not a "proposition"; it was "the psychic attitude in which our mind stands towards the proposition taken as a whole" (*PP*, 2:287), the attitude of conviction. With Alexander Bain, James held that belief was the basic and primitive attitude toward things or thoughts: "The primitive impulse is to affirm immediately the reality of all that is conceived" (*PP*, 2:319). Hence, James insisted, "As a rule, we believe as much as we can. We would believe everything if only we could" (*PP*, 2:299). Both children and savages were credulous. If a newborn were presented with an illusion of a candle, that illusion would be "its all, its absolute." There would be no alternative to suggest its status as illusory. If the observing psychologist claimed the candle was unreal, he would mean that there was a world known to him which is real, a world in which the candle did not belong. But, James argued, it was fallacious to confuse the psychologist's illusion with the newborn's reality.

According to James, initial credulity is undercut only when thoughts contradict one another. If someone dreams of a winged horse, the beast is real so long as it maintains its dream-role. But, "if with this horse I make an inroad into the *world otherwise known,* and say for example, 'That is my old mare Maggie, having grown a pair of wings where she stands in her stall,' the whole case is altered; for now the horse and the place are identified with a horse and place otherwise known, and *what* is known of the latter objects is incompatible with what is perceived with the former" (*PP*, 2:289).

These considerations led James to the general claim that "*the whole distinction of real and unreal, the whole psychology of belief, disbelief, and doubt, is thus grounded on two mental facts— first, that we are liable to think differently of the same; and second, that when we have done so, we can choose which way of thinking to adhere to and which to disregard*" (*PP*, 2:290).

But James argued that there were many ways of thinking, many worlds that persons identified themselves with, so that "no general offhand answer can be given as to which objects mankind shall choose as its realities. The fight is still under way" (*PP*, 2:316). If the "complete philosopher" was motivated by a desire to assign each one of these worlds a status and relate one to the other, common people typically lived unreflectively in one world after the other, without bothering to conceive their relations. These worlds included the world of things, with their primary and secondary qualities; the world of science, or of things with their secondary qualities excluded and the laws of their motion added; the world of formal truths; the world of "idols of the tribe," illusions or prejudices common to the race; the various supernatural worlds, including those of faith and fable; the various worlds of individual opinion; and an indefinite number of worlds of sheer madness.

If most people relied on things of sense as their practical reality, this was not inevitably so, according to James. The things of theology provided a principle of reality for some; those of science, for others. But even in these special cases, James suggested, "these things are usually real with a less real reality than that of the things of sense." The things of sense were normally the things that people thought they were *required* to deal with, so they were "either our realities or the tests of our realities. Conceived objects must show sensible effects or else be disbelieved" (*PP*, 2:294, 301).

But in any case, a person's paramount reality was the world with which he identified. In other words, "as thinkers with emotional reaction, we give what seems to us a still higher degree of reality to whatever things we select and emphasize and turn to WITH A WILL." These things, and all the things connected with them, are "'our living realities." The "ego . . . is the hook from which the rest dangles, the absolute support." Indeed, the tendency to believe whatever incited an action was so strong that "the greatest proof that a man is *sui compos* is his ability to suspend belief in presence of an emotionally exciting idea. To give this power is the highest result of education" (*PP*, 2:297, 308).

On these grounds, the difference between 'belief' and 'will' was analytic. They were both psychic attitudes toward thoughts or things. But in the case of will the object was a goal that depended on personal activity for realization, whereas "objects of belief are those which do not change according as we think regarding them." Whether the mind was believing or willing, however, it did the same thing: it looked at an object and consented to its existence, espoused it, and claimed reality on its behalf. Both belief and will were "a certain relation between objects and the Self, . . . two names for one and the same psychological phenomenon" (*PP*, 2:320, 321).

As James understood the self, this analysis of belief and will implied that rivalry and conflict between the different worlds of belief were bound to be mirrored in rivalry and conflict between different selves, and vice versa. When a person chose a way of thinking, he simultaneously chose a practically real world and "one of many possible selves or characters" (PP, 1:310). Just as and when men arranged their various worlds in some order, so they developed a hierarchy of their various selves according to some scale of worth.

To be sure, according to James, "a man's Self is the sum total of all that he can call his, not only his body and his psychic powers, but his clothes and his house, his wife and his children, his ancestors and friends, his reputation and works, his lands and horses, and yacht and bank-account" (PP, 1:291). But a man ordered these things according to a feeling of self-esteem that was inevitably social in character. James had written as early as 1878 that the most important things in a person's environment were other people. In Principles he suggested that the emotion that beckons a person on "is indubitably the pursuit of an ideal social self, or a self that is at least worthy of approving recognition by the highest possible judging companion, if such companion there be." (PP, 1:315). The self that was incited to act by the presence of such a judge was "the true, the intimate, the ultimate, the permanent Me which I seek" (PP, 1:291, 315, 316). "Enlightened" scientists who spent time thinking up reasons for and against praying missed the psychological point. They forgot to mention that the reason why people do pray

> is simply that we cannot help praying. . . . The impulse to pray is a necessary consequence of the fact that whilst the innermost of the empirical selves of a man is a Self of the social sort, yet it can find its only adequate Socius in an ideal world.
>
> For most of us, a world with no such inner refuge when the outer social self failed and dropped from us would be an abyss of horror. I say 'for most of us,' because it is probable that individuals differ a good deal in the degree in which they are haunted by this sense of an ideal spectator. It is a much more essential part of the consciousness of some men than of others. Those who have the most of it are possibly the most religious men. But . . . only a non-gregarious animal could be completely without it. [PP, 1:316]

If only a nongregarious animal could be completely without it, then among humankind, only the insane might qualify.

49

James was certain enough of this position to underscore it a year after the publication of *Principles*, when he wrote "The Moral Philosopher and the Moral Life."[14] There he argued, as he had earlier, that it was possible to be morally strenuous without believing in a god, but impossible without believing in some sort of intimate, ultimate, permanent me. Belief in a god simply upped the ante. When a person believed that a god was "one of the claimants" to whom he owed obligations, "the infinite perspective open[ed] out." In the presence of divinity, as opposed to "finite demanders," a person displayed more intense energy and endurance and faced tragedy joyously. For these reasons, James argued, "the strenuous type of character will on the battlefield of human history always outwear the easy-going type, and religion will drive irreligion to the wall" (*WTB*, 160, 161).

James's work on the human emotions, belief, and the self solidified his initial philosophical positions on faith and theism. From his "natural history point of view" a person required emotionality, not from time to time but all the time, not in some pursuits but in all pursuits. Without it, that person failed to take care of himself, in environments that demanded "nervous anticipations" on his part. Because "every living thing is but a bundle of predispositions to react in particular ways upon the contact of particular features of the environment" (WE, 12), the abilities to believe, inquire, and will were fundamentally propitious. Radical skepticism and agnosticism, on the other hand—and taken as practical attitudes—were debilitating. Because the self was inevitably social, a person was required to commit himself to goals as "one of us." Moreover, when a god was "one of us," that person endured tragedy in order to realize his sharable desires all the more joyously.

But James was left with a problem. As he stated it in *Principles*: "If belief consists in an emotional reaction of the entire man on an object, how *can* we believe at will? We cannot control our emotions" (*PP*, 2:321). If "emotions" were analyzable, without remainder, as physiological change and a person had no control over physiological changes, he could not emote at will. Hence, he could not will to believe. Starting his religious investigations from reflections on the personal and social problem of pessimism, the religious disease, James responded to the problem in two ways that were, prima facie, contradictory.

On the one hand, James argued that a *process of reasoning* could be employed to overcome pessimism. On the other, he argued that the displacement of melancholy by emotionality was the outcome of a *nonlogical process*, something out of personal control. Working within the context of rational psychology, the psychology of self-consciousness, James suggested this solution: there was no way to believe at will "abruptly," but "*gradually* our will can lead us to the same results by a very simple method: *we need only in cold blood* ACT *as if the thing in question were real, and keep acting as if it were real, and it will infallibly end by growing into such a connection with our life that it will become real*. It will become so knit with habit and emotion that our interests in it will be those which characterize belief" (*PP*, 2:321).

If a person could will, and some could not, he could will to believe this way. But this view suggested another problem. James freely admitted that it was just as easy to will to believe that some women were witches or that Jews were demons as it was to act in cold blood as though one's self were free to make differences, so long as these "objects of will" hung together with the other parts of one's world satisfactorily enough. How, then, could someone judge when it was legitimate or responsible to will to believe?

The Doctrine of the Will to Believe, 1896

James took up the problem of the right to try to believe in "The Will to Believe," delivered before various Ivy League philosophy clubs in 1896. Students at Brown had read "Is Life Worth Living?" and were eager to discuss its issues with the author (*WTB*, 311). James made the visit and was satisfied enough with the proceedings to return with a theory meant to answer objections that students had expressed about his "subjective method."

At Brown and elsewhere, James said that the opposite attitude from pessimism was belief in "the religious hypothesis." Religious faith was faith in something that will happen. A world with religious significance was a world that was salvable (however the agents of salvation were specified), a world in which right would triumph over might. James said that his intent was to defend "our right to adopt a believing attitude in religious matters, in spite of the fact that our merely logical intellect may not have been coerced" (*WTB*, 311, 13).

As he had in his earlier essay on "the subjective method," James argued from the procedure of scientific investigation. But here, instead of arguing that it was legitimate to *reject* theories that had some "objective" backing if they failed to satisfy "our inward preferences," he argued that a person could responsibly *accept* conceptions not proven true, so long as they met certain psychological and logical conditions.

After establishing the intent of his essay, James executed his argument in ten sections. First, he argued that certain conditions obtain whenever a person is in the process of deciding which of two competing beliefs to hold. Whenever a person decides between competing beliefs, each belief is a" live hypothesis"; each belief appeals "as a real possibility to him to whom it is proposed" (*WTB*, 14). The reality or "liveness" of any such belief is relative, measured by a person's willingness to act as if it were true. Beliefs are live for someone when they guide his conduct. If one or another belief could not guide a person's conduct, then the decision between them would be dead for him: it would be no decision at all.

What is more, James argued, decisions are "forced" if the options comprise a "complete logical disjunction." Decisions cannot be forced unless they are live, because both options in a forced decision must be possible choices. What distinguishes forced live decisions from other live ones is that there is "no possibility of not choosing" one of the two options presented. James suggested, the imperative "either accept this truth or go without it" presents a forced option (*WTB*, 15). All other sorts of decision, James argued, are avoidable.

According to James, decisions about what to believe were either "momentous" or "trivial." They were "momentous" the more they generated some sort of difference that could be experienced; they were "trival," the less they did so. Momentous decisions were obviously live ones, but they need not be forced. The same held for trivial decisions. "Genuine decisions," James argued, are live, forced, and momentous.

But, in his second section, James argued that it was not enough to point out that personal decisions about competing beliefs are either live or dead, forced or avoidable, momentous or trivial. Other conditions held whenever a person made these decisions. Most important, decisions were never presuppositionless. They were inevitably made with reference to a body of beliefs that a person maintained. Whereas no belief was sacrosanct, many were compelling enough to inhibit attempts not to believe them. A person was irresponsible if he believed himself well and energetic when he was "roaring" with rheumatism and bedridden, just as he was unwarranted in claiming that two dollars really amounted to one hundred. A person might say these things, James suggested, but he was "impotent to believe them." He asserted that Hume was right in claiming that there were "matters of fact" and "relations between ideas" on which persons depended; though he departed somewhat from Hume by claiming that these "ideas" were "there or not there for us if we see them so." In any case, the brunt of James's point was that persons held certain beliefs about certain things "which cannot be put there by any action of our own" (*WTB*, 15–16).

Indeed, James argued, these "matters of fact" and "relations between ideas" compose the *live* beliefs without which live decisions could not be made. They constitute the "pre-existing tendency to believe" necessary for live decisions to occur. From this point of view, talk about willing to believe seemed silly in some cases, vile in others. A person was silly to try to believe something that contradicted what he took as evidence. And if he construed attendance to evidence as a duty, "wishful thinking" or trying to believe "what you know ain't true" was vile. Clifford exemplified this sense of duty when he proclaimed that "it is wrong always, everywhere, and for everyone, to believe anything upon insufficient evidence" (*WTB*, 18).[15]

But, James argued in his third section, "pure" reason was not the only alternative to wishful thinking. "Our willing nature"—such things as fear, hope, prejudice, passion, partisanship, class, and milieu—always plays a role in decisions between competing beliefs. Normally, "we find ourselves believing, we hardly know how or why," and "all for no reasons worthy of the name" (*WTB*, 18). A "mixed-up state of affairs" conditioned a person's total view. In particular, a decision to try to believe something instead of a competing belief might be made, in part, simply because the attempt seemed like the most valuable thing to do.

James's fourth section underscored the inescapability of interest in many cognitive decisions. As a matter of fact, interest provided the context for conviction. Indeed, in a certain sort of instance, *if* a person was to decide between competing beliefs, he *had to* permit his "passional" nature to govern his decisions. The thesis that James wished to defend was this: "Our passional nature not only lawfully may, but must, decide an option between propositions whenever it is a genuine option that cannot by its nature be decided on intellectual grounds; for to say, under such circumstances, 'Do not decide but leave the question open,' is itself a passional decision,— just like deciding yes or no,—and is attended with the same risk of losing the truth" (*WTB*, 20).

To be sure, James argued in his fifth section, "absolutists" could never construe James's thesis as acceptable, because they claimed some unquestionable intellectual standard on which one must base all decisions involving belief. But "empiricists" could. Empiricists measured the value of beliefs by their consequences for their conduct as investigators. They admitted the axiological character of their behavior *as* investigators.

In his sixth section, James argued that the constraint that absolutists labored under was that "no concrete test of what is really true has ever been agreed upon." Empiricists, to the contrary, were in accord with the assumptions of investigation and with historical fact, by maintaining that each and every opinion was "reinterpretable or corrigible" (*WTB*, 22). While absolutists contrived foundations to warrant their opinions, empiricists warranted hypotheses according to "the total drift of thinking" and cared little about the "origins" of belief. (As a historical judgment about the empiricist tradition, James's view was idiosyncratic.) On empiricist grounds, sheer desire could propose and sustain belief. The consequences of those beliefs should dispose of them one way or another.

In his seventh section, James suggested that empiricists could be divided into two groups, according to their definitions of scientific duty. Some empiricists committed themselves to searching for the truth; others meant, above all, to avoid error. Thinkers like Clifford took the latter course. But, James argued, either definition was an expression of "our passional life" (*WTB*, 25). Neither "duty" rested on any absolute cognitive foundation.

This led to James's eighth point: the commands to avoid error and to grasp for truth were undeniably influenced by emotional attitudes. But someone might argue that once one command or the other was established, no other passional step needed to be taken *in investigation*. James admitted that "in scientific questions, this is almost always the case; and even in human affairs in general, the need of acting is seldom so urgent that a false belief to act on is better than no belief at all" (*WTB*, 26). Scientists could normally bide their time, especially in their role as spectators of nature. But when scientists identified themselves as agents attempting to control their surroundings sufficiently to satisfy their own interests, they could not always wait upon the long run of experience to initiate action. Sometimes situations presented problems urgent enough to demand experiment, an enterprise that inevitably carried the risk of false belief with it.

Indeed, James argued that the keenest and most useful investigator was the one "whose eager interest in one side of the question is balanced by an equally keen nervousness lest he be deceived. Science has organized this nervousness into a regular *technique*, her so-called method of verification" (*WTB*, 26–27). The "religious hypothesis" per se did not preclude this nervousness, even as it depended on the "eager interest" of the person attempting to prove it true. The dichotomy between detachment and commitment that some drew to distinguish the scientific from the religious was false.

James argued in his ninth section that moral questions were among those "whose solution cannot wait for sensible proof." This claim was more than incautious; it was sloppy. James issued with one hand what he had retracted moments before: plenty of moral issues were better decided on grounds of sensible proof. Only some moral questions required rather immediate action. In some cases, a moral agent, like an investigator, provided, *by his own conduct*, some of the evidence that would confirm or deny the opinion he was trying to believe. The same was true with some beliefs concerning the intentions of other people. For instance, a person might be deciding whether to believe that someone else liked him. His trying to believe one way or the other might well influence the outcome of his research. James thought this exemplified the "cases where a fact cannot come at all unless a preliminary faith exists in its coming" (*WTB*, 27, 29).

This was so with any social organism. A republic, for instance, "is what it is because each member proceeds to his own duty with a trust that the other members will simultaneously do theirs. Wherever a desired result is achieved by the co-operation of many independent persons, its existence as a fact is a pure consequence of the precursive faith in one another of those immediately concerned" (*WTB*, 29). Any such hypothesis that depended on "our personal action" for realization and, hence, confirmation demanded that a person inform his activity with it before he was certain that it was true, even before he was reasonably certain. This was an important reflection for a thinker who understood the "religious hypothesis" as a perception of human destiny and always spoke of human destiny in social terms.

Finally, James argued that "the religious hypothesis" depended on personal action for confirmation. That hypothesis said, according to James, "that the best things are the more eternal things" and "that we are better off even now if we believe her first affirmation to be true" (*WTB*, 29). The suppressed assumption was that the consequences of pessimism made the hypothesis urgent enough to be acted upon immediately. The explicit assumption was that the hypothesis could never be realized without such action. If religious significance lay in the actualization of a social organism in which right was triumphant over might, then each person had to "proceed to his own duty with a trust that the other members will simultaneously do theirs."

James argued that *if* this hypothesis was live, it was forced and momentous. It was forced because not deciding to assent to it was tantamount to deciding not to assent to it: "It is as if a man should hesitate indefinitely to ask a certain woman to marry him because he was not perfectly sure that she should prove an angel after he brought her home" (*WTB*, 30). The hypothesis was momentous because even trying to believe it might generate a distinguishable pattern of behavior of great personal, private and social, importance.

Whether to believe the religious hypothesis, James argued, was a "living option which the intellect of the individual cannot by itself resolve," because available evidence was ambiguous. It was a living option that could be decided only by trying to believe *or* by not trying to believe *or* by trying not to believe. In any of these cases, James warned, "each must act as he thinks best; and if he is wrong, so much the worse for him" (*WTB*, 32, 33).

The Limitations of Philosophy and the
Search for Religious Facts, 1884–1898

"The Will to Believe" caused such a philosophical scandal in England and America that James was saddled with its defense for the last fifteen years of his life. The essay is still read as one of the few truly representative pieces that James wrote, a notion for which much could be said. But its reception and subsequent fame, or infamy, obscure the importance that James attached to it. While "The Will to Believe" summarized and solidified the philosophical position on religious faith that he had been constructing for twenty years, it also demonstrated the limitations of turning to philosophy alone as a cure for religious disease.

The essay was addressed to persons who neither suffered from religious melancholy nor believed the religious hypothesis; who could conceive of themselves in either position; and who were strenuous enough to act on their religiousness. For those who accepted James's argument, philosophy was sufficiently satisfying to motivate religious activity; but this was true only because they were "well-doers" to begin with—people who had the capacity to make efforts.

But as early as 1884, James was certain that it was mockery to suggest to a person suffering from religious disease that he *do well,* or try to believe. The theory of emotions that he had articulated that year militated against this strategy in some ways, and his analysis of the problems of religion in his introduction to *The Literary Remains of Henry James* clarified why.

There, James pictured his father's theology as a sort of "common-sense theism," according to which God was treated as a principle among others, *"primus inter pares,"* who had warmth and blood and personality. He was that "socius" or companion who could "rivet human regard" in his role as judge, but was also intimate enough with humanity to help individuals when they could not help themselves realize their own divine-natural humanity. As such, his father's theology remained "essentially faithful to pluralism," or the notion that salvation depended upon practical relations among "a collection of beings" (*LRHJ*, 114, 113). His God was more like the one popularly believed in than "The One and Only Being" of monistic philosophers and theologians. Most Europeans, James asserted, were pluralistic men. They were normally prepared to play their part in the battle against evil powers and in the militant struggle for righteousness, but also hoped to receive divine support when their efforts faltered. James claimed that his father's theology spoke for this attitude, if not to these men.

He also suggested that the most serious enemy to popular religion and his father's theology was "the philosophic pluralist," who maintained "a pluralism hardened by reflection, and deliberate; a pluralism, which, in the face of the old mystery of the One and the Many, has vainly sought peace in identification, and ended by taking sides against the One" (*LRHJ*, 116). These were moralists, humanists, and positivists who had given up the romantic quest for "multeity in unity" in order to turn to finite goals. They stood opposed to practical religious pluralism, which was still committed to ultimate and total harmony. James was a practical religious pluralist, not "the philosophical pluralist . . . hardened by reflection." To be sure, James argued that

> pluralism is a view to which we all practically incline when in the full and successful exercise of our moral energy. The life we then feel tingling through us vouches sufficiently for itself, and nothing tempts us to refer it to a higher source. Being, as we are, a match for whatever evils actually confront us, we rather prefer to think of them as endowed with reality, and as being absolutely alien, but, we hope, subjugable powers. Of the day of our possible impotency we take no thought; and we care not to make such a synthesis of our weakness and our strength,

57

and of the good and evil fortunes of the world, as will reduce them all to fractions, with a common denominator, of some less fluctuating Unity, enclosing some less partial and more certain form of Good. The feeling of *action*, in short, makes us turn a deaf ear to the thought of *being*; and this deafness and insensibility may be said to form an integral part of what in popular phrase is known as "healthy-mindedness." Any absolute moralism must needs be such a healthy-minded pluralism. [*LRHJ*, 117]

Such healthy-mindedness set the context for James's own message in "The Will to Believe." But, James continued, "healthy-mindedness is not the whole of life; and the *morbid* view, as one by contrast may call it, asks for a philosophy very different from that of absolute moralism. To suggest personal will and effort to one "all sicklied o'er" with the sense of weakness, of helpless failure, and of fear, is to suggest the most horrible of things to him" (*LRHJ*, 17).

Persons with morbid views crave consolation. But perhaps of more philosophical importance, because "the sanest and best of us are of one clay with lunatics and prison inmates," the achievements of "well-doing" lay constantly shadowed by the lack of "well-being." Well-being is the object of the *"religious* demand" and this demand is "so penetrating," according to James, "that no consciousness of such occasional and outward well-doing as befalls the human lot can ever give it satisfaction" (*LRHJ*, 118).

This was one of the lines of thought that led James to proclaim in the preface to *The Will to Believe and Other Essays* that a "science of religions" should be established to ascertain "articles of faith" that have "maintained themselves through every vicissitude, and possess even more vitality today than ever before" (*WTB*, 8). If religious history had witnessed the demise of one religious hypothesis after another, articles of religious faith remained that were vital enough to combat absolute moralism and hardened philosophical pluralism.

Indeed, the Will-to-Believe doctrine was a stopgap measure, to some extent. It allowed for "the freest competition of the various faiths with one another" until a science of religions could be sufficiently constituted to make its judgments on evidence for "the supernatural." "The Will to Believe" preached "courage weighted with responsibility" to academic audiences prone to "timorous *abulia*," an abnormality "brought about by the notion, carefully instilled, that there is something called scientific evidence by waiting upon which they shall escape all danger of shipwreck in regard to truth" (*WTB*,

8, 7). The "science of religions" could never displace the need to act out of trust. Its task was to discover distinctively religious facts from which religious conceptions and faiths were developed.

In 1895, when James gave his lecture "Is Life Worth Living?" to members of Harvard's YMCA, he had suggested three cures for pessimism. One could abandon metaphysical interests, believe in supplementary facts which permit a religious reading to go on, or actually discover such facts. By that time, he had already tried the first two cures. A year later, he announced his intention to attempt one of the last sort, by participating in a science of religions. He would try to verify or confirm his own religious hypothesis by demonstrating that his father was right: first, that religion began in despair; second, that it was sustained through encounter with divinity; third, that divine encounter was a nonlogical process which restored melancholics to vital emotionality; and fourth, that with such restoration came saintliness or the sort of sociality that exemplified the kingdom of heaven on earth. With this, the notions that became James's Gifford Lectures, *The Varieties of Religious Experience*, were born.

Imaginary Devils and Human Blindness, 1896–1900

James wrote his preface to *The Will to Believe and Other Essays* knowing that he would deliver the Gifford Lectures in the near future.[16] Indeed, a year before *The Will to Believe* was published, James had delivered eight lectures at the Lowell Institute in Boston on the topic "Abnormal Mental States." There, he made an attempt to discover some distinctively religious facts. His subjects were dreams and hypnotism, hysteria, automatisms, multiple personalities, demoniacal possession, witchcraft, degeneration, and genius. His aim, among other things, was to investigate religion at its worst, religion which epitomized narrow-mindedness and the sociality of coercion. When he read histories, James suggested, it became clear to him that religion "drips with blood." Christianity in Western European history tended to combine authority with feebleness of intellect. Its officers held power over life and death even when their mental makeups were "almost idiotic for [their] meanness, timorousness, and unmanliness." Religious inquisitions demonstrated that there was "no worse enemy of God and man than zeal armed with power and guided by a feeble intellect" (WJC, 4404–5).

Christians had always been ready to execrate, excommunicate, and curse enemies as satanic. One lesson learned from their history was "to keep power of life and death away from that kind of mind, the mind that sees things in the light of evil and dread and mistrust rather than in that of hope." Finally:

> What human life really has been and may be again if the best men do not keep up a constant fight against an imaginary satan but the real devil of intolerance and ignorance [are people] inflamed with the lust for power and the conceit that they alone can save the world, and getting all of the legitimate professional and legal authority into their hands. Strange as it may sound, there can be little doubt that a good-natured scepticism, and willingness to let the devil have his head a bit, is for public purposes a better state of mind than too exalted a notion of one's duty toward the world. [WJC, 4404–5]

James argued that the new psychology of the irrational was so significant because it made "the devil's sphere" less broad. Where people used to fear and shun those who were different, and even burn them, the new theories of the subconscious allowed humane treatment for hysterics, degenerates, and those suffering from multiple personalities. The result was to bring disease and health closer together. "Witchcraft," for instance, could be explained as a type of "demon possession," which was a kind of "hysteria," which could be classified as a sort of "hypnotism," for which there were known cures. The worst in Europe's religious history was that combination of narrow-mindedness and raw power which bred intolerance, lack of sympathy for the alien, and no respect for anything but one's own —in a word, "tribal instinct."

While completing the investigations that developed into the Lowell lectures of 1896, it became clear to James that his own country was as prone to tribal instinct as any other. Thus he began writing newspaper editorials and speeches bitterly opposing United States involvement in imperialist adventures. In his Lowell Lectures he warned his audience about zeal armed with power and a feeble intellect. A few years later, he warned the nation about President McKinley in precisely the same terms. As James understood McKinley's attitude toward the Philippines, America was saying: "We are here for your own good; therefore, unconditionally surrender to our tender mercies, or we'll blow you into kingdom come."[17] When American troops invaded Manila, James's response was religiously measured: "We are now openly engaged in crushing out the sacredest thing in this great human world—the attempt of a people long enslaved to attain to the possession of itself, to organize its laws and government, to be free to follow its own internal destinies according to its own ideals. . . . We are destroying down to the root every germ of a healthy national life in these unfortunate people, and we are surely helping to destroy for one generation at least their faith in God and man."[18]

Imperialists used the excuse that America was bringing civilization to a primitive and backward people that could not possibly civilize itself. From James's vantage point, this idea was self-contradictory because it assumed that civilization could be equated with pacification. If America were truly interested in civilizing Filipinos, James suggested, it would send saints, not warriors. It was safe to say, James wrote, that missionaries, whether primitive, Protestant, Catholic, Buddhist, Mohammedan, or Tolstoyan, "could build up realities, in however small a degree; we can only destroy the inner realities; and indeed, destroy in a year more of them than a generation can make good."[19]

James was bewildered when he saw a nation dedicated to life, liberty, and the pursuit of happiness "cold-bloodedly, wantonly, and abominably destroying the soul of a people who never did us an atom of harm in their lives."[20] The response that he recommended to overcome that confusion was quite specifically religious: let thinking men manifest saintliness by practicing peace and persuasion, methodically enough for the practice to become habitual. This might begin to remedy the situation by energizing "every American who still wishes his country to possess its ancient soul—soul a thousand times more dear than ever, now that it seems in danger of perdition."[21]

The "Philippine Tangle" contributed to a very significant change in James's views about America and about human order more generally. These imperialistic forays seemed to sanction James's worst fears about "the enemy within" America and made his Romantic religious views all the more republican. They also convinced James that laissez-faire human order was destitute. "The worst of it," he told his brother Henry, "is the complete destruction of the old belief in the *vox populi*. There is no doubt of collective attacks of genuine madness sweeping over peoples and stampeding them. And liberalism must slowly and sadly go to work against the possibility of them" (*TC*, 2:307–8).

This realization stimulated a number of activities for James. It resulted in his plea for Americans to return to their American Religion (*MS*, 43); in his participation in anti-imperialist organizations; in his urging educated people to become politically involved as a self-conscious intellectual class pitted against the "party of red-blood"; and, most important from the point of view of his religious investigations, in his development of the doctrine of human blindness.

James wrote a letter to the editor of the *Boston Evening Transcript* in 1899 noting that "for our rulers at Washington, the Filipinos have not existed as psychological entities at all. . . . We have treated them as if they were a painted picture, an amount of mere matter in our way. They are too remote from us ever to be realized in their inwardness." America was destroying "souls . . . even more than bodies."[22] Americans were blinded from the desires, wants, and goals of Filipinos and from the soul of their nation. Therefore, on the explicit assumption that the souls of nations are sacred, America should follow a policy of live-and-let-live. James tried to express this opinion more generally, if still rather informally, in his talk to students "On a Certain Blindness in Human Beings" (*TT*, 149–69).

James wanted to diagnose "the blindness with which we all are afflicted in regard to the feelings of creatures and people different from ourselves." Many opinions about aliens suffered from stupidity and injustice because of this blindness; even so, the blindness was normal. Because humans are practical beings, James argued, "each is bound to feel intensely the importance of his own duties and the significance of the situations that call these forth. But this feeling is in each of us a vital secret, for sympathy with which we vainly look to others. The others are too much absorbed in their own vital secrets to take an interest in ours." So long as a person stuck to his own personal "responsibilities," his ability to feel what aliens felt was undercut. In such cases, James suggested, "the subject judged knows a part of the world of reality which the judging subject fails to see, knows more while the spectator knows less; and wherever there is a conflict of opinion and difference of vision, we are bound to feel that the truer side is the side that feels the more, and not the side that feels the less" (*TT*, 149, 150).

If the world of practical relations in which people lived made them prone to blindness from the "more," however, there was a sort of "irresponsibility" that could open their eyes to the inner life of others sufficiently to catch sight of "the impersonal world of worths as such." If "the clamor of our own practical interests" made people blind and dead to "all other things," then it was necessary to "become worthless as a practical being" in order to be receptive. This was the task of philosophy in liberal education. It was also the message of Robert Louis Stevenson and Richard Jeffries and Whitman. James said that "only your mystic, your dreamer, or your insolent tramp or loafer, can afford so sympathetic an occupation" (*TT*, 159,

160). But these prophets and seers could constantly remind the rest that the "more" was there, sacred and acceptable as such.

Whenever one achieved this "higher vision of an inner significance," James said, "the whole scheme of our customary values gets confounded, then our self is riven and its narrow interests fly to pieces, then a new centre and a new perspective must be found." This claim prefigured one of the major themes in James's Gifford Lectures: the "more" constantly knocked persons off balance, once they noticed it. It displaced an old self-centeredness with a simple, but not simplistic, openness to humanity in its great and never-ending variety, an openness that "absolutely forbids us to be forward in pronouncing on the meaninglessness of forms of existence other than our own; and it commands us to tolerate, respect, and indulge those whom we see harmlessly interested and happy in their own ways, however unintelligible these may be to us. Hands off: neither the whole of truth nor the whole of good is revealed to any single observer, although each observer gains a partial superiority of insight from the particular position in which he stands" (TT, 156, 169).

James made the same point from another angle in his other "talks to students." In "The Gospel of Relaxation" and "What Makes a Life Significant," he warned against the dangers of moral materialism and puritanical nervousness. Imperialism abroad was matched by profligate concern for material comforts at home. Elsewhere, he declared that America's "bosom-vices are swindling and adroitness, and the indulging of swindling and adroitness, and cant, and sympathy with cant—natural fruits of that extraordinary idealization of 'success' in the mere outward sense of 'getting there,' and getting there on as big a scale as we can, which characterizes our present generation" (MS, 351).

The quest for material success no matter what was a spiritual disease that aided and abetted blindness to the world of "impersonal worths." Its most effective cure, James recommended, was asceticism, the voluntary acceptance of material simplicity, one of the traditional saintly methods and the quintessence of religiousness. James assumed that the great motive force behind idolization of "the bitch-goddess success" was fear and argued that Americans had much to learn from the James-Lange theory about displacing fear with acceptance. "American over-tension and jerkiness and breathlessness and intensity and agony of expression" were bad habits that accompanied fear of the environment and an all-consuming urge to control it. New Thinkers like Annie Payson were right (on the grounds of the James-Lange theory) to preach " 'Power through Repose,' a book that ought to be in the hands of every teacher and student in America of either sex" (*TT*, 139–40, 143).

With "the doctors, the Delsarteans, the various mind-curing sects, and such writers as Mr. Dresser, Prentice Mulford, Mr. Horace Fletcher, and Mr. Trine to help," Americans could let go of "fear-thought" in order to accept a simpler life. "The way to do it, paradoxical as it may seem, is genuinely not to care whether you are doing it or not. Then, possibly, by the grace of God, you may all at once find that you *are* doing it, and, having learned what the trick feels like, you may (again by the grace of God) be enabled to go on" (*TT*, 146, 148).

As Americans began to accept themselves, they might simultaneously break through their "ancestral blindness" and recognize a diversity of personal situations, problems, and solutions. This, James thought, was the message of "the religion of democracy," which made permanent gains the more people opened themselves to the "more" that humanity had to offer. Higher education could play its role in this religious mission by extending the human imagination. By humanistic study, James declared, "you divine in the world about you matter for a little more humility on your part, and tolerance, and reverence, and love for others; and you gain a certain inner joyfulness at the increased importance of our common life. Such joyfulness is a religious inspiration and an element of spiritual health, and worth more than large amounts of that sort of technical and accurate information which we professors are supposed to be able to impart" (*TT*, 178, 188).[23]

The Emergence of Pragmatism, 1898

James brought his humanism with him to Berkeley in 1898, where he delivered his lecture "Philosophical Conceptions and Practical Results." This piece initiated the public history of the pragmatic movement in American thought. By then James had expressed his opinion that religious disease was not only debilitating to individuals but depressing for the nation's ancestral faith, threatening to leave only its blindness. If the debate between theists and materialists had always been basically social, it took on increased importance in this regard for James after his loss of faith in the vox populi. He had grown up thinking that "without vision the people perish." By 1898 he was convinced that the people had to be given visions to follow, because "angelic interests and predatory lusts divide our heart exactly as they divide the hearts of other countries."

The times were such that persons devoted to American religion could demonstrate their commitment to the premises of the republic only by becoming absorbed into "the great international and cosmopolitan liberal party," the party opposed to "jingoism and animal instinct," the party that "believes in educational methods and in rational rules of right."

We are, James said, "only its American section, carrying the war against the powers of darkness here playing our part in the long, long campaign for truth and fair dealing which must go on in all the countries of the world until the end of time. Let us cheerfully settle into our interminable task. Everywhere it is the same struggle under various names—light against darkness, right against might, love against hate. The Lord of Life is with us and we cannot permanently fail" (*TC*, 2:313).

In Berkeley, James announced the core of his policy for "the long, long campaign for truth and fair dealing." He said he was seeking to define the most likely direction to start upon the trail of truth and the best way to deal fairly with diverse visions like materialism and theism. The clue or compass to follow, he asserted, was the "principle of practicalism" developed by Peirce. According to James, Peirce said that the production of belief motivated thought and that beliefs were rules for action; hence, "the whole function of thinking is but one step in the production of habits of action" (*Prag*, 259). James had made the same claims about thought, belief, and action since his earliest philosophical articles. The heart of Peirce's doctrine, according to James, was semantic:

> If there were any part of a thought that made no difference
> in the thought's practical consequences, then that part would
> be no proper element of the thought's significance.... To at-
> tain perfect clearness in our thoughts of an object, then, we
> need only consider what effects of a conceivably practical kind
> the object may invoke—what sensations we are to expect from
> it, and what reactions we must prepare. Our conception of
> these effects, then, is for us the whole of our conception of the
> object, so far as that conception has positive significance at all.
> [*Prag*, 259]

Traditional rationalists had claimed that the key to meaning lay in the relation of terms with one another. Traditional empiricists had claimed, to the contrary, that the key to meaning was objective reference. According to James's reading, Peirce subordinated the more traditional doctrines to his own. Sometimes the meaning of a term did lie in its relation to other terms, because the particular difference the term made was simply conceptual. Other times, it lay in its relation to some objective referent, because the particular difference it made outran the formation of conceptual habits to include practical ones. But in any case, meaning was intimately related to our conduct as thinking agents.

James argued that Peirce's principle should be deployed as a rule of method for philosophical disputes. On the assumption that philosophy ought to find out what definite differences "world-formulas" made to people, pragmatism was a fitting doctrine. It broke through the verbalisms that rationalism seemed prone to, as well as the recent positivists' verificationist theory of meaning, and it could restore philosophy to its proper social role. If most men had turned their backs on philosophy as nonsense because "logic has stepped into the place of vision, professionalism into that of life" (Prag, 265), the doctrine of pragmatism was suited to appreciate visions for the sake of life.

The crucial case in point, according to James, was the debate between materialism and theism. In the hands of divinity-school theologians, theism was "a set of dictionary-adjectives, mechanically produced," "a conglomeration of abstract general terms." Persons with religious needs received stones, not bread. In the hands of positive empiricists, materialism left people without hope. The debate between positivist empiricists and divinity-school theologians was idle because both sides articulated it within a retrospective context. Looking back, it made no difference whether Providence, on the one hand, or force and matter, on the other, governed the behavior of things. The world's history was one and the same on either ground. "Calling matter the cause of it retracts no single one of the items that have made it up, nor does calling God the cause augment them" (Prag, 265–66, 261).

The real difference between theism and materialism, James argued, lay in their visions of the future. Once a person stopped thinking of the world retrospectively and began assuming that it was "unfinished," the alternative between materialism and theism became intensely practical. According to the theory of mechanical evolution, "the laws of redistribution of matter and motion, though they are certainly to thank for all the good hours which our organisms have ever yielded us and for all the ideals which our minds now frame, are yet fatally certain to undo their work again, and to redissolve everything that they have once evolved." The problem was that matter ends in tragedy. That was the essence of "scientific materialism" (Prag, 263).

On the contrary, the conception of God meant that the best things are the final things. The idea of divinity, James argued, originated in concrete religious experience. It was an aftereffect of "conversations with the unseen, voices and visions, responses to prayer, changes of heart, deliverances from fear, inflowings of help, assurances of support, whenever certain persons set their internal attitude in certain appropriate ways." These experiences kept religion going, not the systems of logically concatenated adjectives of the faculties of theology. These "direct experiences of a wider spiritual life with which our superficial consciousness is continuous, and with which it keeps up an intense commerce, form the primary mass of direct religious experience on which all hearsay religion rests, and which furnishes that notion of an ever-present God, out of which systematic theology thereupon proceeds to make capital in its own unreal pedantic way. What the word 'God' means is just those passive and active experiences of your life" (*Prag*, 266).

Following the doctrine of pragmatism, James thought, the debate between materialism and theism could be adjudicated by investigating the varieties of religious experience. If the "passive and active experiences" out of which the conception of divinity developed confirmed the notion that there were powers at work to guarantee "an ideal order that shall be permanently preserved," the will-to-believe doctrine could be abandoned and the issue decided. Pragmatism did not establish any answers in the debate between materialists and theists, but it did define a way of establishing the requisite investigations for such answers. The principle of pragmatism made "God" something that was investigable, if it was anything at all. James was out to prove that it was.

In 1899, James wrote his friend Frances R. Morse that he was seeing his way clear "to a perfectly bully pair of volumes, the first an objective study of the 'Varieties of Religious Experience,' the second, my own last will and testament, setting forth the philosophy best adapted to normal religious needs" (*LWJ*, 1:112). The morbidity of the statement was not simply comical: James was worried about dying. In any case, four months later, he wrote the same woman, outlining the problem he had set himself.

> *First*, to defend (against all the prejudices of my class) "experience" against "philosophy" as being the real backbone of the world's religious life—I mean prayer, guidance, and all that sort of thing immediately and privately felt, as against high and noble general views of our destiny and the world's meaning; and *second*, to make the hearer or reader believe, what I invincibly do believe, that, although all the special

manifestations of religion may have been absurd, (I mean its creeds and theories), yet the life of it as a whole is mankind's most important function. A task well-nigh impossible, I fear, and in which I shall fail, but to attempt it is *my* religious act. [*LWJ*, 1 : 127]

So James, a religious philosopher, turned to a task few religious philosophers have attempted, the study of religion itself.

PART II

THE GIFFORD LECTURES,

1901–1902

CHAPTER 3

JAMES AND THE SCIENCE

OF RELIGIONS

James and the Science of Religions in 1900

James turned to the science of religions when he became convinced that neither personal tenacity nor philosophy alone could solve the problems of religion with which he had contended for thirty years. Unable to live either with orthodox theism or natural supernaturalism, on the one hand, or without his desectarian religious faith, on the other, he struck out to discover a set of distinctively religious facts around which to spin a web of religious belief.

As James diagnosed his situation, the theist-materialist debate had arrived at a stalemate, largely because each side continued to wrangle over the character of the "world" without much consideration for particular facts. While this debate limped on, a rift widened between the culturally dominant forms of thought—"religious thinking, ethical thinking, poetical thinking, teleological, emotional, sentimental thinking, what one might call the personal view of life" —and the "mechanical rationalism" that was coming to saturate the professional "scientific academic mind" (*WTB*, 239).

In light of this analysis, James searched for an academic enterprise to restore "continuity to history" by returning the category of personality to its rightful place in the human sciences, and he thought that the Society for Psychical Research was just such an enterprise. As he saw it, the proceedings of that society had "conclusively proved one thing to the candid reader; and that is that the verdict of pure insanity, of gratuitous preference for error, of superstition without an excuse, which the scientists of our day are led by their intellectual training to pronounce upon the entire thought of the past, is a most shallow verdict" (*WTB*, 239–40). The investigations of divinations, inspirations, demoniacal possessions, apparitions, trances, esctasies, and occult powers which the Society executed hardly ever corroborated the *theories* that spiritualists offered about their data. But they did confirm the data.

In James's estimation, the work of Edmund Gurney on hypnotism and Frederic Myers on "the subliminal self" in the proceedings of the society corroborated the hypothesis that, as Myers put it, "each of us is in reality an abiding psychical entity far more extensive than he knows—an individuality which can never express itself completely through any corporeal manifestation" (quoted in *WTB*, 233, from *Proceedings of the Society for Psychical Research* 7 [1891–92]: 305). Gurney and Myers documented "facts of experience" that justified "the chronic belief of mankind, that events may happen for the sake of their personal significance." The experiences that they located and specified had three characteristics in common: they were capricious or not easily controlled; they were the productions of peculiar people; and "their significance seems to be wholly for personal life" (*WTB*, 239, 240). Together, they provided a hefty counterweight to prevailing materialistic assumptions in academic circles.

Pointing to the new religions, James reported that there was an abundance of phenomena "generally called mystical." But orthodox science dismissed religious experience on the grounds that it was an "effect of the imagination" and historically aberrant. For instance, James said, "We suppose that 'mediumship' originated in Rochester, N.Y., [with the Fox sisters] and animal magnetism with Mesmer; but once look behind the pages of official history, in personal memoirs, legal documents, and popular narratives and books of anecdote, and you will find that there never was a time when these things were not reported just as abundantly as now" (*WTB*, 223).

Preternatural phenomena, James asserted, "are there, lying broadcast over the surface of history." Anyone acquainted with the history of religions, even in its infancy, could find plenty of precedents for the new religious movements that emphasized both mind over matter and experiences peculiarly suited to personal needs. Investigations in the history of religions not only cast doubt on orthodox science but lent support to the hypotheses of both natural and supernatural personality.

Indeed, by 1900, James had been studying essays in "the science of religions" off and on for thirty years. Between 1867 and 1872, he read two foundational works in religious studies, Friedrich Max Müller's "Essays on the Science of Religion" (1867) and Emile Burnouf's *La Science des religions* (1872).[1] During this same period he read David Friedrich Strauss's essays in the history of religion (in French) and Etienne Vacherot's positivist account of religion. By

1878 he was acquainted with E. B. Tylor's work, probably *Primitive Culture* (first published in America in 1874). By the turn of the century, he could comment on the work of Tylor's sometime-disciple Andrew Lang. Finally, among other works in his library were F. B. Jevon's *An Introduction to the History of Religion* (1896), C. P. Tiele's *Histoire comparée des anciennes religions de l'Egypte et des peuples sémitiques* (1882), and Daniel Brinton's *The Religion of Primitive Peoples* (1897). In a word, James was acquainted with the greater bulk of the first works in religious studies. Just as important, he knew intimately the works of Spencer, Darwin, and Comte, whose theories of culture and history set the context for most of those investigations.

No more than thirty years old in 1900, the discipline of the science of religions was tended by a relatively small group of individual scholars at disparate universities trained either in classics or in one of the new evolutionary sciences, either psychology, anthropology, sociology, or philology. Seen in broad perspective, work in the new field reflected the tensions of Victorian academic culture. Humanists like Max Müller tried to appreciate religion as a human achievement. Led by Tylor, anthropologists tried to demonstrate that and how religion was a holdover or "survival" from an older state of society or a primitive state of culture. Christians like Jevons aimed at demonstrating that Christianity bettered what was good in other religions while neglecting what was bad in them.

James followed the lead of Max Müller. The German-born scholar held out the promise of a discipline on the grand scale that could simultaneously reconcile science with religion and provide avenues of mutual understanding and encouragement between devotees of the world religions.

No less optimistic about the prospects for the new science was James himself. In his effort to wrest philosophical theology from the seat of intellectual authority in matters of religion, he called on philosophy to "frankly transform herself from theology into science of religions," to abandon a priori arguments for and against the supernatural for the sake of "interpretative and inductive operations, operations after the fact, consequent upon religious feeling, not coordinate with it, not independent of what it ascertains" (*VRE*, 455, 433).

James suggested that the science of religions should eliminate the local and accidental from definitions of the divine, remove historical "incrustations" from dogma and worship, and square "spontaneous religious constructions" with the results of natural science. It should sift out "unworthy formulations" and deal with the residuum as hypotheses, testing them according to standards of inquiry common to all the sciences. Far from construing the science as simply analytic, James suggested that it should establish a range of warranted religious thought and action and should even champion religious conceptions as they were verified or became verifiable. In consequence, James said, "she can offer mediation between different believers, and help to bring about consensus of opinion" (*VRE*, 456).

James's enthusiasm for his idea of religious studies was almost unbounded. He construed his Gifford Lectures as a "crumblike contribution" to its foundations and told his audience and readers that he did not "see why a critical Science of Religions of this sort might not eventually command as general a public adhesion as is commanded by a physical science. Even the personally nonreligious might accept its conclusions on trust, much as blind persons now accept the facts of optics—it might appear as foolish to refuse them" (*VRE*, 456). The science of religions, in other words, might do what philosophy had failed to do: settle beliefs about the supernatural and evaluate the role of the divine in the lives of men.

James's positions on the study of religion competed with those of Christian apologists and Comtean positivists. Whereas James established an attitude of pursuit of religious truths and left the just value of religious thought and action an open question, apologists like Jevons assumed the truth of Christianity and served it by diagnosing the causes of deficiency in other religions. Anthropologists like Tylor assumed the essential illegitimacy of traditional religious thought and action in a modern society and furthered their case by diagnosing the causes of the retention of religious life in the modern West.

No matter what position scholars took on the aims of the study of religion during this period, however, the triumph of the genetic sciences under the banner of "evolution" imbued the enterprise with a concern for history, economic fitness, origins, and mechanisms of transmission. To be sure, Max Müller desired to model the science along the lines of philology, still only vaguely historical. But if Max Müller was wary of the Darwinians, he fully accepted the evolutionary nature of the task of appreciation. He told students to trace a religion to its beginnings in order to evaluate it. There, a religion was devoid of the offensive characteristics that accrued as it developed into a complex institution. His focus on the descent of religions from simple and pure to complex and polluted enterprises was emphatic.

By the 1880s self-proclaimed Darwinians like Spencer and Tylor were claiming that religion was one of the keys to understanding primitive or uncivilized humanity. Assuming a broadly Comtean understanding of the course of history, they declared that religion and belief in the supernatural were outmoded, first by metaphysics and finally by the empirical sciences. According to Comte and those whom he influenced, religion had two damning strikes against it. First, religionists conceived and explained things in terms of personality (both natural and supernatural), whereas scientists conceived things systematically and explained them mechanistically. Second, religionists were close-minded and unable to make intellectual progress, whereas scientists were open-minded, able to respond to the challenges of new information.

From a Comtean perspective, it became important to ask why people maintained religious enterprises in a scientific world. Tylor responded by developing the doctrine of survivals. He argued that there are "processes, customs, opinions, and so forth, which have been carried on by force of habit into a new state of society different from that in which they had their original home, and they thus remain as proofs and examples of an older condition of culture out of which the newer has evolved."[2] Religion was a paradigmatic survival which both misfit its current social environment and involved massive amounts of human energy. It was carried on "by force of habit" and without sufficient reason.

Tylor's attempt to account for the vitality of religious enterprises in a society that no longer construed religious thought and action as legitimate ingeniously combined Comte's view of the stages of society with Darwin's understanding of historical retention and elimination from transmission. But James thought it rested too heavily on Comte's scheme and abused Darwin's theory of evolution. As early as 1878, he chided Tylor, along with Spencer, for invoking Darwin's authority for the notion that "whatever throws light on the origin of a conception throws light on its validity." Darwin hardly ever spoke about validity, but when he did (for example, in *The Descent of Man*), "validity" was associated with environmental success, not origins. James also pointed out that Tylor and Spencer missed both the spirit and the letter of Darwin's laws by constantly attempting to characterize a thing by its precursors. James argued the absurdity of this method by asking, "If the embryologic line of appeal can alone teach us the genuine essence of things, if the polyp is to dictate our law of mind to us because he came first, where are we to stop? He must himself be treated in the same way. Back of him lay the not-yet-polyp, and, back of all, the universal mother, fire-mist" (*EP*, 9–10). Darwin characterized things not by their precursors but as "spontaneous variations," whose historical transmission was governed by "natural selection."

On Darwinian grounds, James presumed that survivals met the demands of a society in specifiably suitable ways. Instead of assuming that religion was appended to modern society, he sought to identify the vital characteristics of various kinds of religious life, for example, the "new" religions or Calvinism, and to articulate the demands that these met. Instead of focusing on the links between religions and social structures that anthropologists and psychologists said preceded religions, for example, "fetishism and magic" (*VRE*, 30–31), he focused on the links between originating experiences—"direct personal communion with the divine"—and consequent religious life. In general, he pitted his own doctrine of *fit* survival against the anthropological doctrine of *mere* survival to describe and appreciate religion as a human achievement.

Great Men and Their Environment

When James went to Edinburgh to deliver his Gifford Lectures, he was already known for his Darwinian stances. His earliest efforts in philosophical psychology pitted Darwin against Spencer, and his influential theory of emotions was built up from and out of Darwinian themes and claims. His great work in psychology, the *Principles*, reconstructed the characteristics of human life to accommodate Darwin's organismic-environmental picture of things. He devoted the last chapter of that work to philosophical problems concerning "necessary truths and the effects of experience," couching his answers in ideas like mental variation and social selection. The Darwinian terminology was not coincidental.

James's aim in Edinburgh was to show that "the best fruits of religious experience are the best things that history has to show." He focused strategically on great religious men and women and their social environments and assumed, along with Max Müller and many other contemporary scholars in the field, that religions, at least the vital world religions, were founded and that "the *founders* of every church owed their power originally to the fact of their direct personal communion with the divine" (*VRE*, 259, 30). He went on to make specifically Darwinian moves, ones he had first articulated in his only developed work in the philosophy of social history, "Great Men, Great Thoughts, and Their Environment" (1880).

James had opened that lecture twenty years before with the assertion that "a remarkable parallel, which I think has never been noticed, obtains between the facts of social evolution on the one hand, and of zoological evolution as expounded by Mr. Darwin on the other" (*WTB*, 163). Darwin's method of getting at scientific truth, James argued, accounted for the role great men played in history in a way that Spencer's methods could not. Spencer, who had laid much of the groundwork for anthropological and sociological studies of religion of the time, assumed "the common platitude that a complete acquaintance with any one thing, however small, would require a knowledge of the entire universe" (*WTB*, 163). To accept this attitude, one must construe the universe as a "whole" and assume both that the whole was more than the sum of its parts and that the whole determined the nature of its parts. When these assumptions stood, it followed that the parts could not be understood in isolation from the whole; indeed, it followed that parts were governed by the whole. On these grounds, Spencer thought, one could claim that science admitted no accidents.

Yet James wanted to demonstrate that abnormal, supernatural events occurred, that parts of the universe could be sufficiently discontinuous to allow for invention and novelty and, therefore, for religious founders. So far as history went, Spencerian anthropologists and sociologists claimed that "changes are irrespective of persons, and independent of individual control. They are due to the environment, to the circumstances, the physical geography, the ancestral condition, the increasing experience of outer relations; to everything in fact, except the Grants and the Bismarks, the Joneses and the Smiths" (*WTB*, 164).

On these grounds, of course, religion was no human achievement, because there were no real human achievements. Every human masterstroke turned out to be an achievement by something else or, more accurately, no achievement at all. James thus saw Spencer as undercutting humanistic inquiry and argued that he had no sound warrant to do so. He asserted that Spencerians failed to identify or analyze the real causes of social historical change.

Spencerians held holistic assumptions that had more to do with Romantic philosophizing than scientific investigation. People might believe that "all things in the world are fatally predetermined, and hang together in the adamantine fixity of a system of natural law" (*WTB*, 165), but such claims were scientifically useless. If social historians aimed to identify distinctive human achievements, Spencer offered no help.

According to James, scientific investigation was a practical matter. Specific investigations were undertaken for determinate purposes, to reach conclusions that would help settle doubts about some area in human experience. Thus, scholars engaged in myth-making, not investigation, when they attempted to apply their analytic machinery to unlimited, nonspecific ranges of reference. Investigators, as distinguished from philosophers concerned with the "world," assumed

> *different cycles of operation* in nature; different departments, so to speak, relatively independent of one another; so that what goes on at any moment in one may be compatible with almost any condition of things at the same time in the next. The mould on the biscuit in the storeroom of a man-of-war vegetates in absolute indifference to the nationality of the flag, the direction of the voyage, the weather, and the human dramas that may go on on board; and a mycologist may study it in complete abstraction from all these larger details. Only by so studying it, in fact, is there any chance of the mental concentration by which alone he may hope to learn something of its nature. [*WTB*, 166]

Darwin stood on the side of scientific investigation in these re-spects and opposed to work like Spencer's. James argued in par-ticular that it was "the triumphant originality of Darwin" to distinguish two different cycles of operation in nature, one gov-erned by "causes of production," the other by "causes of mainte-nance." James wished to do something analogous in his study of religion. He would focus on the experiences of religious "geniuses" and ignore altogether the question of their "production," relegating that question to the philosopher until investigators found ways to handle it. Then he would characterize religious experience in its variety and ask what preserved various sorts of religiousness in social life.

Pre-Darwinians like Lamarck had failed to make that important distinction. James said that they had "also tried to establish the doctrine of descent with modification; but they all committed the blunder of clumping" the cycles of production and maintenance. They claimed, for instance, not only that "the giraffe with his pe-culiar neck is preserved by the fact that there are in his environ-ment tall trees whose leaves he can digest" but also that the presence of the trees "made his neck long by the constant striving they aroused in him to reach up to them" (*WTB*, 167). Spencer followed Lamarck in holding that "the environment" produced modifications in species by direct pressure.

James saw Darwin's achievement as twofold. First, he had demonstrated that while some directly adaptive changes did occur, their numbers were insignificant compared to the changes produced by "internal molecular accident" (*WTB*, 168). Second, by distinguishing causes of production from causes of maintenance and defining the historical problem as retention in and elimination from transmission, Darwin showed that the causes of production of animals, including human animals, were inaccessible to direct observation of any kind but compatible with any environmental conditions. Conversely, the variants themselves and their causes of maintenance were accessible to direct observation and varied according to environmental conditions.

According to James, the same relations held when it came to investigating social developments, including religious ones. Social evolution resulted, he argued, from the interaction of two wholly distinct factors: "The individual, deriving his peculiar gifts from the play of physiological and infrasocial forces, but bearing all the power of initiative and origination in his hands; and second, the social environment, with its power of adopting or rejecting both him and his gifts. Both factors are essential to change. The community stagnates without the impulse of the individual. The impulse of the individual dies away without the sympathy of the community" (*WTB*, 174).

He realized, of course, that the analogy between zoological evolution and social change was not exact. In the zoological case, the causes of production and of maintenance belonged to incommensurate cycles—one physiological, the other ecological. In society, however, the people who changed society were in part its products. Society, James said, "remodels" its individuals to some degree by its "educative influence" (*WTB*, 170). But he self-consciously neglected this aspect of the relation that holds between individuals and society in cases of social change, not for reasons of methodological principle but to emphasize the doctrine of interaction. He had to drive home the Darwinian point that *two* sorts of analytic variables were needed to account for historical change. By this means, he could undercut at its base the battle between individualists and holists. According to James, social change could be accounted for neither wholly by facts about individuals nor wholly by facts about collective entities or wholes. The analysis of social change depended on specifying interactions between individuals and the collective entities that they helped to constitute.

James thought that individualism was inadequate because "not every 'man' fits every 'hour.' " Change is determined, in part, by the practical possibilities present in a given society. Some thoughts and activities are so outlandish when set in contexts of particular societies or historical epochs that no individual who exhibited them or promoted them would be taken seriously. Hence, "the social surroundings of the past and present hour exclude the possibility of accepting certain contributions from individuals; but they do not positively define what contributions shall be accepted, for in themselves they are powerless to fix what the nature of the individual offerings shall be" (*WTB*, 172, 173–74).

Hard-and-fast holism was equally wrongheaded. Spencerians attacked the "great-man theory" of history largely on the grounds that the genius of a great man could be accounted for by examining his social environment. They argued that "before he can remake his society, his society must make him."[3] But James countered that Spencerians employed the term 'make' in a way that conflated the issues of production and retention. Physiological forces, not society, produced people who developed thoughts that were then retained or rejected by society.

For James, social environment was basically selective. It determined "what shall be only by destroying what is positively incompatible." From this perspective, Spencer's evolutionary philosophy was a "lapse from modern scientific determinism into the most ancient oriental fatalism" (*WTB*, 178, 183). Modern scientists claimed that once events had occurred, determinate accounts could be given of them. But Spencer's philosophy simply and constantly reasserted the dogma that people are caught in an inexorable process in which individual initiative is epiphenomenal.

On James's grounds, the historical development of societies was a vital transformation. He thought that "a community is a living thing," endorsing Clifford's claim that "it is the peculiarity of living things not merely that they change under the influence of surrounding circumstances, but that any change which takes place in them is not lost but retained, and as it were built into the organism to serve as the foundation for future actions."[4] But James argued that no necessary connection existed between the vital character of societies and metaphysical monism. Societies did possess lives of their own, but they were not determined in some fatalistic way, because "societies of men are just like individuals, in that both at any given moment offer ambiguous potentialities of development" (*WTB*, 171).

The subject of social investigation, then, was "the zone of formative processes, the dynamic belt of quivering uncertainty, the line where past and future meet." The purpose was to catch human achievements *"in the making."* To do this, investigators needed to focus on "the part not yet ingrained in the race's average, not yet a typical, hereditary, and constant factor of the social community in which it occurs. It is like the soft layer beneath the bark of a tree in which all the year's growth is going on. Life has abandoned the mighty trunk inside, which stands inert and belongs almost to the inorganic world" (*WTB*, 193, 194, 192).

Darwin had provided a mode of analysis geared for investigations of "particular cases of change." The mode was historiographic, because it allowed investigators not only to assert or name a developmental change but also to demonstrate its variables. But Darwin's theory neither assumed historical ascent nor entailed doctrines about the overall direction of any sort of development. It did not provide equipment for articulating a doctrine of cosmic progress—or, for that matter, of decline. Darwin differed from Spencer and many early anthropologists and sociologists who studied religion in abandoning Lamarck's assumption that the historical record can, by itself, reveal invariant norms of evolutionary advance. The principles of spontaneous variation and natural selection did not apply to issues of "inevitable" progression. Darwin deployed them once he had accepted descent as a fact and rejected both the hypothesis of independent origins and the unidirectionality of history. He shared hardly any of the prophetic ambitions of other evolutionists and brilliantly undercut their teleological pretensions.[5]

Darwin wished to understand how species, understood as modifiable populations, came to be as they are, not how things in general will be after everything else has happened. The latter question was metaphysical and had nothing to do with making scientific discoveries. Spencerians who addressed it served "an obsolete anachronism, reverting to a pre-darwinian type of thought" (*WTB*, 189). Darwinian analysis, to the contrary, provided tools for understanding specific social and intellectual problems and achievements.

Darwin, Religion, and Neurology

James's first Gifford Lecture was entitled "Religion and Neurology" and followed lines of thought established in his earlier work on great men and their environments. In it, James argued that *the causes of production* of religious genius were inaccessible to investigators and, more significantly, irrelevant to issues having to do with religion construed as a human achievement. His religious investigations, he suggested, were aimed at appreciating—in the sense of setting a just value on—religions, and that was best done by characterizing the experiences of great religious men and women in ways that made their religious genius stand out.

"Every religious phenomenon has its history and its derivation from natural antecedents." For James, religions originated when some variety of religious experience was selected by some social organism as depicting and evoking the ways of salvation. If the task was to reach both existential and evaluative judgments about religions, the strategy was to ask how religions came about, what their histories looked like, and what their importance amounted to, now that they were here. Neither an existential judgment nor a proposition of value was deducible "immediately from the other," because they proceeded from different intellectual preoccupations (VRE, 4). But both preoccupations were informed by Darwin's understanding of historical analysis.

James asserted that issues concerned with the "constitution" or "nature" of religion were "manifestly questions of historical fact" (VRE, 4). The varieties of religious experience presented the "spontaneous variations" that constituted religion, variations that were subsequently retained in or eliminated from historical transmission in specifiable ways. Establishing the selective factors in any religious enterprise—that is, the characteristics that made religions "fit" for historical retention—generated the bases for making spiritual judgments or criticisms of religion.

James's psychological inquiries about religious personalities were placed in this broadly Darwinian context. He made it clear that he was "neither a theologian, nor a learned scholar in the history of religions, nor an anthropologist" (VRE, 2). The contributions of these kinds of investigators were also needed. But the psychologist could investigate the feelings, impulses, and activities of religious geniuses or originals in ways that articulated the distinctiveness of religious life. And the philosopher could investigate the criteria for selecting and abandoning patterns of religious thought and action.

Certain investigators of religious personality did not adequately distinguish between "existential" and "spiritual" judgments. In Darwinian terms, they conflated the issues of "production" and "maintenance," as pre-Darwinians had been disposed to do. They evaluated the religious beliefs and activities of religious originals only by their causes of production. Two parties approached religious personality in this way: religious apologists, who wanted to confirm religious beliefs and actions as supernatural in origin, and investigators with some animus against religion, who wanted to show that religious beliefs and actions could be accounted for pathologically.

James assumed that persons listening to or reading his Gifford Lectures were mostly religious. He assured them that his division between existential and spiritual judgments was not meant to degrade or discredit the religious side of life. Undercutting religion was "absolutely alien" to his intentions. His aim was to appreciate religions. He said he was following the lead of biblical critics who first asked "Under just what biographic conditions did the sacred writers bring forth their various contributions to the holy volume?" and only subsequently asked "Of what use should such a volume, with its manner of coming into existence so defined, be to us as a guide to life and a revelation?" James suggested that scientists of religions could pursue their subject by investigating, not just the Bible, but *any* book which was "sacred"—that is, the literature "produced by articulate and fully self-conscious men, in works of piety and autobiography" which related encounters with the divine (*VRE*, 6, 4–5, 3).

On inspection, James asserted, religious geniuses appeared personally peculiar. Religious "pattern setters," as distinguished from people simply devoted to religious conventions, evidenced "symptoms of nervous instability." They displayed the same psychological characteristics that figured in personalities that were currently being labeled "psychic." They had capricious experiences, were subject to fits of depression and elation, and said and did things that seemed outlandish to others. "Geniuses who have brought forth fruits effective enough for commemoration in the pages of biography" had often experienced divided selves, melancholy, obsessions, or fixed ideas. Frequently, they heard voices, saw visions, and felt unseen bodies. All these peculiarities were "ordinarily classed as pathological" (*VRE*, 6–7). What is more, James asserted, the pathological features of their experiences had lent an aura of coerciveness to their influence as religious authorities.

Students of religion must not ignore the pathology of religious genius in religious studies. Even if they instinctively recoiled from associating religious genius with nervous disorder because of their religious commitments, the connection had to be named and described, disinterestedly. If students were interested in religion as a human achievement, they were duty-bound to expose it entirely. Indeed, from some vantage points, it could turn out that the concomitance of religious genius with nervous disorder would lead to higher respect and more humane treatment for persons suffering from psychological disabilities.

To be sure, people worried that "such cold-blooded assimilations threaten . . . to undo our soul's vital secrets, as if the same breath which should succeed in explaining their origin would simultaneously explain away their significance." The expression of this assumption was common among unprofessional diagnosticians, who claimed such things as "William's melancholy about the universe is due to bad digestion—probably his liver is torpid." Then, too, psychologists were tending to criticize the religious emotions by "showing a connection between them and the sexual life" (VRE, 10). James's own student E. D. Starbuck (a person whose work James admired and appropriated in many instances) had tried to demonstrate that conversion is a crisis of puberty and adolescence.[6]

The tie between "origins" and "significance" coincided with the polemics of medical materialists in various ways. Medical materialism tried to undercut the spiritual authority of religious geniuses by showing what odd people they were. James said that it finishes up "Saint Paul by calling his vision on the road to Damascus a discharging lesion of the occipital cortex, he being an epileptic. It snuffs out Saint Teresa as a hysteric, Saint Francis of Assisi as a hereditary degenerate" (VRE, 13).

He argued that it was possible to accept the hypothesis that "the dependence of mental states upon bodily conditions must be thorough-going and complete" (VRE, 13). His own *Principles* assumed that hypothesis. But medical materialists could not generate particular claims about the importance of religious geniuses from the general theory of mind-body dependence. If every mental state depends upon bodily conditions, whether healthy or morbid, then it is not very telling to claim that the mental states of religious geniuses are dependent upon bodily conditions.

More generally, James argued, neurophysiology had not remotely approached the point where its practitioners could explain in neurophysiological terms all the causal connections and influences that played a role in operations of the brain and nervous system. Even if practitioners of the science could explain things this way, they would want to take credit for their scientific discovery, *even if their scientific discovery could be accounted for neurophysiologically.* Either spiritual and existential judgments were noncompetitive, or "none of our thoughts and feelings, not even our scientific doctrines, not even our *dis-beliefs*, could retain any value as revelations of the truth, for every one of them without exception flows from the state of their possessor's body at the time" (VRE, 14). Medical materialists failed to arrive at any skeptical conclusion about their own claims. They gave no physiological theory of their own productions but simply attempted to discount mental states that, for quite other reasons, they disliked. They suppressed assumptions about the criteria for evaluating religious thought and activity and then went on to *diagnose* the pathology for what they presumed was diseased.

But a great gap existed in the structure of the reductive arguments employed by medical materialists like J. F. Nisbet and Max Nordau. They failed to work out "in advance some psychophysical theory connecting spiritual values in general with determinate sorts of physiological change" (*VRE*, 14). Without such a theory, which was developed by psychoanalysts following James's death, the medical materialist arguments or diagnoses undermining the authority of religious geniuses were weak at their base.

James suggested that medical materialism was simply one example of a prevalent, pre-Darwinian structure of argument shared by "dogmatic philosophies." These philosophies were all built on the analogy of a house with unshakable foundations. They were developed before intellectuals recognized the triumph of historical consciousness, and hence they construed the structures of mind, knowledge, and nature in static, immutable terms in pursuit of the dream of "some direct mark, by noting which we can be protected immediately and absolutely, now and forever, against all mistake" (*VRE*, 18). Typically, they attempted to specify the origin of belief as the requisite criterion of truth, though they argued about which origin was right. Some said that immediate intuition was the solid foundation for truth, but others suggested pontifical authority, supernatural revelation, direct spiritual possession, prophecy, or automatic utterance.

The medical materialists simply turned the tables on those who had been attempting to accredit truth from origins and began to discredit them. But both groups suffered from the same general problem. As positivists had pointed out, they were all programmed to reach philosophical impasse. No school of thought constructed persuasive arguments showing that, say, immediate intuition was the right foundation for truth while supernatural revelation was the wrong one, because it was difficult to inspect either of these things. But perhaps even more troubling philosophically, historically it proved nearly impossible to adjudicate claims among people who held the same "dogmatic" position. Immediate intuitions, it turned out, sometimes were contradictory, as were revelations, papal bulls, and automatic utterances.

Within the Darwinian matrix that James assumed, the investigation of "origins" had a good deal to do with understanding the "character," or "nature," or "constitution," of religious thought and action. But even in this respect, "origins" were not definitive in any privative sense. Like zoological populations or species, religions were historical entities that were accurately characterized by answering the question What provides their continuity and coherence despite all the real changes they have undergone? Addressing the constitutive issue this way, James thought, provided an effective alternative to the old essentialist approach to the question of definition, according to which philosophers asked What is the immutable reality underlying the apparent changes religion has undergone?

Once *continuity and coherence* displaced *essence* at the heart of existential judgments scholars had an easier way to distinguish propositions of value from them. Furthermore, the Darwinian notion of selection through fitness provided the analytic machinery to permit evaluation of the "spontaneous" religious variations presented by religious originals.

James was quick to point out that the man that he considered the cleverest rebutter of supernatural religion, Henry Maudsley, admitted that "it is the work that is done, and the quality in the worker by which it was done, that is alone of moment."[7] An adulterer or lunatic could reveal enduring truths and even depict and evoke ways of salvation for other people. So far as certifying religion was concerned, Maudsley said, the "last resort" was "the common assent of mankind, or of the competent by instruction and training among mankind."[8] James agreed.

James also asserted that the competent by training and instruction among mankind commonly assented to the claim that three general principles guided the selection of beliefs or rules of action, namely the principles of *"Immediate luminousness, . . . philosophical reasonableness, and moral helpfulness"* (VRE, 18). James said that if a theology could stand these tests, it would make no difference how psychologically peculiar its proponents were.

James clarified what he meant by saying that "it is the character of inner happiness in the thoughts which stamps them as good, or else their consistency with our other opinions and their serviceability for our needs, which make them pass for true in our esteem" (VRE, 15). In so doing, he was reasserting a position that he had established in his earliest articles on rationality, faith, and activity: perception, conception, and volition each had normative roles to play in the selection and retention of beliefs. In general, if something or some thought was intuitive, in the sense that it went without saying, it caused no perplexity; hence, it was immediately luminous or evoked inner happiness. If it cohered with other views already held, it caused no sense of disequilibrium. Finally, if it guided actions in ways that helped to actualize moral or practical objectives, it "passed for true."

To be sure, there were hard cases. Some intuitions aggressively challenged the total view by which persons usually judged conceptual coherency. Then, too, "What immediately feels most 'good' is not always most 'true,' when measured by the verdict of the rest of experience." These discrepancies led to the "sad discordancy of so many of the spiritual judgments of human beings," particularly in the appreciation of religious life that placed heavy emphasis on revelations. Revelations, James suggested, seldom came, and they did not come to everyone. Typically, they made no connections with "the rest of life," which contradicted more than confirmed them. "Some persons follow more the voice of the moment in these cases, some prefer to be guided by the average results" (VRE, 15–16). James did not evaluate either party in this first lecture, but he would do so before the series was through.

By the end of his first lecture, James had argued for the separation of issues having to do with the causes of production of religious originals and those having to do with their effectiveness as pattern-setters. On Darwinian grounds, he turned to the latter set of issues. If investigators wanted to know what difference religious experience made to humanity, they had to observe it when it was making the addition, not when it was already part of the more or less stable social scene. What is more, once religious experience was characterized by its variants, scientists of religions could select those patterns set by religious originals which were humanly fittest, or at least demonstrate to others how they could choose them on their own.

The Definition of Religion

The second time James met his audience in Edinburgh, he considered the "Circumscription of the Topic" of religion. Here, James addressed the vexing question of definition from his natural history point of view. Traditional philosophers of religion had attempted to uncover some one "essence" of religion underneath the rather chaotic diversity of religious phenomena. Recent students of religion, for example, the Swiss-born American psychologist James H. Leuba, had gathered various "essences of religion" discovered by sundry influential thinkers and had suggested the futility of attempting to adjudicate among them.[9] James agreed. From a Darwinian point of view, " 'religion' cannot stand for any single principle or essence," because it accounts for phenomena that resemble each other as much as, but no more than, the mutants in any population do. So "religion" is a "collective name" (*VRE*, 26).

Philosophers who allowed themselves to be governed by the aesthetic demands of theory, especially the demand to unify and simplify by means of associations and identifications, obstructed understanding of the diversity of religious life. Their quest for the one right essence of religion was "the root of all that absolutism and one-sided dogmatism by which both philosophy and religion have been infested" (*VRE*, 26). The search for essences was wrongheaded, at least the search for essences as essentialists understood them.

James had argued in *Principles* that the crux of the reasoning that went on in investigation or inquiry was analysis and abstraction. When an investigator was confronted with some complex fact or entity, he broke it up and identified one of its separate attributes as "the essential part of the whole fact before him." This "essence," James asserted, had properties or consequences which the "whole" was not known to have, but which, "now that it is noticed to contain that attribute, it must have" (*PP*, 2:330).

James developed his view of investigatory reasoning this way:

> Call the fact or concrete datum S;
>   the essential attribute M;
>   the attribute's property P.
> Then the reasoned inference of P from S cannot be made without M's intermediation. The 'essence' M is thus the third or middle term in the reasoning which a moment ago was pronounced essential. From his original concrete S the reasoner substitutes its abstract property, M. What is true of M, what is coupled with M, then holds true of S, is coupled with S. As M is properly one of the parts of the entire S, *reasoning may then very well be defined as a substitution of parts and their implications or consequences for wholes.* [PP, 2:330]

What is more, James asserted that essences "characterize *us* more than they characterize the thing" (*PP*, 2:334). They were those "parts" of whole entities or situations or enterprises that were most instrumental in solving relevant problems presented by the relevant data. People, James argued, are selective and emphatic in their observations of things, even if they typically suppress this information and the point of view from which their characterizations are made. Investigators distinguish themselves from ordinary thinkers, in fact, by attempting to make their points of view, selections, and emphases as explicit as possible.

This is the line of thought that governed James's circumscription of the topic of religion. James warned that he would not pretend to cover the whole field of religion. His lectures were limited to a fraction of the subject. Investigators divided up the enterprises of religion in varoius ways, for example, into institutional, conceptual, practical, and personal components. All of these components and more presented the fact or concrete datum, religion. James was going to "break" religion into its "essential part," to focus his investigation in a way that would give rise to solutions to his problem of religion.

He proposed to confine himself as far as he could to "personal religion pure and simple," preferring not to deal in any direct way with conventional religion or "the fully organized system of feeling, thought, and institution . . . of which this personal religion, so-called, is but a fractional element" (VRE, 29). From a Darwinian point of view, "rudimentary" elements in any historical entity provided the keys for its characterization. The "active ring" of any historical entity was "*elementary*," not "complex" or "differentiated." The study of the rudiments of social enterprises was "the highest of topics for the social philosopher" because the ups and downs and twists and turns of those enterprises were determined by "individual variations" (WTB, 194). If the problems of religion involved distinguishing religion from other sorts of enterprises and if its distinction was to demonstrate facts requisite to the support of his religious hypothesis, then, James reasoned, he needed to inspect religion in its "unorganized rudiment"—that is, "the zone of formative processes" that eventuate in full-blown religious life.

The part of religion that James isolated for investigation was "essential," in other words, because it would confirm or invalidate his thesis that religion, "on the whole," was "the most important of all human functions," even when "every several manifestation of it in turn have to be corrected and sobered down and pruned away" (VRE, 51). The investigation of "personal religion" would make or break James's religious reading of the course of events.

His definition of religion, therefore, characterized his own problem of religion (a problem he thought was widely shared) more than the phenomena in all of their complexity. "*The feelings, acts, and experiences of individual men in their solitude, so far as they apprehend themselves to stand in relation to whatever they may consider the divine"* (VRE, 31) were the things that required inspection if one was searching for evidence for the supernatural.

On historiographic grounds, James argued that personal religion was more fundamental than either theology or ecclesiasticism, the two main components of conventional religion. Churches lived at second hand, upon tradition, and tradition commemorated the lives of religious originals. So personal religion was "the primordial thing," even if it was an abstraction from the complex, concrete data of religion.

As anthropologists like Frazer and Jevons had pointed out, fetishism and magic may have preceded religious traditions. But these things could just as easily be considered primitive science as elementary forms of religious life. James was interested in the descent of current and competing religious options, and these were traditions or movements that originated when the religious experiences of religious geniuses were commemorated in specific ways. Methodism, for example, was born when John Wesley's religious experiences began to inform the way a certain group of Christians thought about salvation and tried to enact it. Experiences like Wesley's were paradigmatic and "acute." Investigating them caught religious sensibility in the making, before religious life took on characteristics shared by a host of other human enterprises and incidental to conventionalization.

The nub of religious experience, James argued, was divine encounter. He suggested that 'divinity' could be construed in ways that accounted as much for Buddhist and transcendentalist experience as for Christian phenomena, even though Buddhists and transcendentalists did not "positively assume a God," in the sense of a "superhuman person." When persons encountered divinity, they transacted with some object that ordered the world in a way that protected all ideal interests. An experience of divinity (or divine experience—sometimes it was difficult to distinguish neatly between "subject" and "object") was an experience of "first things in the way of being and power" which overarched and enveloped other things so completely that "what relates to them is the first and last word in the way of truth" (VRE, 31, 34).

Tragic Stoics and comic hedonists experienced things somewhat as religious originals did, because all three parties sensed "the whole residual cosmos as an everlasting presence, intimate or alien, terrible or amusing, lovable or odious." Each of these sensibilities was grounded in experiences that simultaneously cast the basic temperament of personal life and "the character of this universe" (VRE,

35). But the "total reaction" of the original Stoics and original Epicureans was different from total religious reactions. Religious originals neither cursed the world nor made it the subject of jest when they felt divinity. They thought it outlandish to say "Who cares?" or to claim any ultimate anguish. Unlike Epicureans, religious originals felt energized in divine encounter. Unlike Stoics, they felt deliverance, or its inception.

If James was accurate in his characterization of divine encounter (he had given no examples of it at this point), religious experience encompassed both the sense of *well-doing* that the moralist achieved when he set out seriously and solemnly to accomplish some objective and the sense of *well-being* that religious people demanded but moral activity could never guarantee. Such events permitted James's religious reading to continue by showing in positive ways how the supernatural functioned in the lives of men. Religious experience could not only stimulate energetic activity but also console the morbid-minded.

Even when an investigator clarified what he meant by "divinity," definition remained a problem because, James said, "we are dealing with a field of experience where there is not a single conception that can be sharply drawn." Just as in zoology, where subspecies and even species sometimes overlap descriptively, in the science of religions "the boundaries are always misty, and it is everywhere a question of amount and degree." This was the case as much because the events investigated were human as because they were religious. The way to manage this difficulty so far as definition was concerned was to initiate investigation by looking at the most exaggerated cases, "cases where the religious spirit is unmistakable and extreme" (*VRE*, 39). Instances of extreme social behaviors played the same methodological role for social scientists of any sort that microscopes played in a natural scientist's laboratory.

Morality and Religion

James had signaled to readers since the middle 1880s that he was a practical religious pluralist. He conceived of the universe as ordered and orderable by a plurality of powers, some of which were human. His "commonsense" religion was neither pessimistic nor optimistic about these powers; it was melioristic. James believed that the "best things" could become the "more eternal things" if the requisite powers played their part. But "shipwreck" was among the real possibilities.

Like his father and his father's Calvinistic fathers, James was convinced that no matter how successfully certain individuals or groups achieved their goals, humanity could not achieve salvation on its own. He thought that deliverance had to play a role in the life of humanity at large, because some people required it. Deliverance might not be possible for everyone, but anyone could suffer helplessly enough to need help when well-being was the desideratum. Either other powers helped the morbid when they could not help themselves or the moods of Schopenhauer, Nietzsche, and Carlyle were totally appropriate.

By the same token, James was convinced that he could not restore religion to its rightful place in the social economy by focusing on healthy-minded religious persons alone. The New Thought religions were packed with optimistic sorts, persons who had found the energy to work toward the actualization of both personal and impersonal worths. But too many of these believers were blinded to the experience of evil both within and without the human heart that Calvinism had made emphatic in American religious consciousness. If morbid-minded Calvinists needed their eyes opened to the differences that people made, and could continue to make, in the course of history, healthy-minded New Thinkers could also profit from the efforts of the religious investigator, for they failed to see the actuality of suffering, absurdity, and evil in the world.

His strategy, therefore, was to combat the healthy-minded pluralist "hardened by reflection," by developing his own religious and practical pluralism. Once again, the distinction between well-doing and well-being played a crucial role in his argument. He admitted that both absolute moralism and religion of any sort were total views. Both were concerned with the manner in which persons accepted the universe. The moralist, however, "accepts the law of the whole" which he "finds reigning, so far as to acknowledge and obey it, but [he] may obey it with the heaviest and coldest heart, and never cease to feel it as a yoke" (VRE, 41). James's youthful Stoic hero, Marcus Aurelius, was the exemplar. The keynote in Marcus Aurelius was resignation.

When typical religious imperatives were compared with Aurelius's recommendations, however, "the practically important *differentia* of religion" emerged. When James looked at such diverse Christian documents as the *Theologia Germanica*, the *Imitation of Christ*, or Mary Moody Emerson's diary, he noticed that Christian faith stimulated the same "energy" that was prominent in moralists, "even though that energy bring personal loss and pain." But unlike moralists, for whom life was a war to be endured, Christian saints found themselves acting energetically on behalf of both personal and impersonal worths or ideals, *without any sense of effort.* If both the Stoic and the saint spurned "the pinched and mumping sick-room attitude," the moralist held his breath and kept his muscles tense in order to attain his goals. But "the Christian spurning is the result of the excitement of a higher kind of emotion, in the presence of which no exertion of volition is required" (*VRE*, 45, 46). The typical moralist felt exhausted as a result of his efforts; the typical saint felt transported and elated as a result of his divine encounter.

At this point, James simply echoed the claim about religion that he had made in his introduction to *The Literary Remains of Henry James*: religion came to the rescue when people realized, on the one hand, that moralism depended on an "athletic attitude" and, on the other hand, that athletic attitudes inevitably broke down. In a religious state of mind, "the will to assert ourselves and hold our own has been displaced by a willingness to close our mouths and be as nothing in the floods and waterspouts of God." In religious consciousness, he claimed, *"the willingness to be"* displaced the willingness to do (*VRE*, 47, 248).

Indeed, reiterating his father's point of view on religious experience, James claimed that spiritual birthdays coincided with moral deaths. Religious experiences were classically spontaneous, not voluntary. A person could not will to believe them. Divine encounter added to life "an enchantment which is not rationally or logically deducible from anything else." It came as a gift and was "either there or not there for us" (*VRE*, 47).

These claims underscored James's departure from the point of view that philosophy alone could solve the problem of religion. They also placed his will-to-believe doctrine in broader context. James had once claimed that a simple process of reasoning solved the problem of religion. He had spent a great deal of effort clarifying the conditions under which reasons of the heart played a legitimate role in decisions about what to believe. But in his second Gifford Lecture, he made it clear that the most important religious facts were "non-logical" and that, for the paradigmatically religious, belief was generated not in any decision-making process but rather in states of possession. Divine "enchantment" occurred, and fortified those who were enchanted, but it was not simply the outcome of deliberation. If anything, it was the outcome of letting go of deliberation.

James asserted that, despite other important differences, morbid-minded revivalists and healthy-minded New Thinkers shared honors for recognizing the great role that letting go of deliberation could play in the formation of saintliness, especially the well-being felt by the saint. The saint's "enthusiastic temper of espousal, in regions where morality strictly so-called can at best but bow its head and acquiesce," occurred when and after he felt a Carlylean resistance to the world but happily acquiesced in his role in the world (VRE, 48). For some religious individuals, acquiescence meant inertia, quietism—but not for every religious individual. The happiness evident in the lives of saints was not ordinary, because it had little or nothing to do with relief. Saints no longer cared to find relief. Far from serving as opiates, their religious experiences left them actively falling on thorns and facing death.

Thus, the lives of saints proved why religion was so durable, according to James. He argued that, like the saints, "we shall have to confess to at least some amount of dependence on sheer mercy, and to practice some amount of renunciation, great or small, to save our souls alive." Religious individuals positively espoused "surrender and sacrifice" in a world whose constitution required them. Religion, therefore, made "easy and felicitous" what was existentially inevitable. "For when all is said and done," James argued, "we are in the end absolutely dependent on the universe; and into sacrifices and surrenders of some sort, deliberately looked at and accepted, we are drawn and pressed as into our only permanent positions of repose" (VRE, 51).

CHAPTER 4

RELIGIOUS FACTS

The Immediate Content of Religious Consciousness

As James understood it, the science of religions disciplined its contributors to recommend the humanly fittest religious beliefs and activities in light of investigations of distinctively religious facts. Scientists of religions differed from philosophical theologians because they drew their inferences and devised their imperatives on the basis of their appreciation of "the immediate content of the religious consciousness" (VRE, 12). They worked from a natural history point of view, not from either an ontological or an epistemological standpoint.

Within this context, James set the bounds for his particular contributions to the science of religions. He proposed to argue that religion was the most important function of mankind even if every manifestation of it had to be corrected. Humanity could neither live without religion nor live with it as it was. Without religion, the dreams of the sick-souled could never come true; they required supernatural help if they were ever to be well. But religion was prone to sectarianism, tribal instinct, absolutism—in a word, to coercion. The task that he set for himself was to demonstrate on the basis of distinctively religious facts that supernaturalism of some sort was conceptually fit and that saintliness was practically fit. Moreover, he wanted to show that neither supernaturalism nor saintliness was inevitably tied to the ways that coercive people thought and acted.

All of this was predicated on the explicit assumption that salvation, the "religious demand," lay in "well-being," an assumption that was part of James's Romantic inheritance. Like his father, James maintained allegiance to the Romantic cult of integrity. Indeed, he never seriously questioned his father's vision of perfect humanity, even though he did tinker with it. Henry James, Sr., maintained that the "artist" was perfect because he was mentally and physically "whole." The artist was whole because his action always made "the object fall *within* the subject." He never permitted "the object to lie out of or beyond the subject's self." This "spontaneity" of action distinguished the artist from both the "natural" and the "moral" individual. The conduct of natural and moral men exhibited "an exactly contrary order" (*HJS*, 136, 137). Their lives were fraught with heteronomy, bifurcation, and the yokes of physical and moral laws.

Henry James, Sr., had claimed the perfect man was constituted by "the relation of complete unity between his inward spirit and his outward body, or what is better, between his ideas and his actions." But this perfection was possible only within a social context. People were born into societies or fellowships, so that "no man can truly be himself so long as any inequality exists between him and his fellow" (*HJS*, 143, 144). Everyone must be well equally. The perfect man exhibited the sort of integrity only observed in individuals who are at one with themselves, their fellows, and their natural environments.

The son followed the father's line of thought by claiming that the beauty of the saints consisted in their ability to execute not only intentions but the best of intentions *without disease.* They did easily and felicitously what the best moralists did only with exhaustion. They escaped the yokes of physical and moral tension in order to participate actively in the suppression of evil or tragedy. James had written earlier that "the course of history is nothing but the story of men's struggles from generation to generation to find the more and more inclusive order" (*WTB*, 155). Now the task was to show the vital role that religious experience and consequent saintliness played in that story.

The key, James argued, was to investigate "the immediate content of religious consciousness." Contrary to much of the Western philosophical tradition, James had gone to great lengths in *Principles* to demonstrate that "the immediate contents" of consciousness were happenings that could be publicized and investigated. To be sure, they were "personal" happenings. The elementary psychic fact, James claimed, was not "thought" or "this thought," or "that thought," but "*my thought,* every thought being *owned*" (*PP*, 1:226). But whatever one person could specify as "owned" could be related to another person. In part, this was true because "men have no eyes but for those aspects of things which they have already been taught to discern" (*PP*, 1:443). They preperceive what they see in the sense that their perceptions are formed by standards of appropriateness they inherit through education;

hence, "the only things which we preperceive are those which have been labelled for us, and the labels stamped into our mind. If we lost our stock of labels we should be intellectually lost in the midst of the world" (*PP*, 1:444).

Persons, James argued, are born into languages that they must learn to speak and to speak about if they are to think. From this point of view, the immediate content of consciousness amounts to someone's thoughtful life as it is going on and before it becomes, in turn, the subject or topic of another thoughtful life. According to James, therefore, there is nothing in principle that one person can observe about himself that cannot be shared with others. People may not share pain or silent trains of thought, but one person can tell another as much about those things as he can tell himself. As James put it in his work on "human blindness," one can come to know others for the spiritual beings that they are, but coming to know them involves learning a good deal from the subjects themselves.

As he was careful to insist in his Gifford Lectures, the "spiritual attitudes" that informed personal experience were "as describable as anything else" (*VRE*, 500). But this did not imply that looking at the immediate content of the religious consciousness led to any easy discoveries about religious experience. He assumed that investigations of persons which did not require instruction by the subjects themselves were bound to be ethnocentric or egocentric or both. Investigators could not adequately describe, much less evaluate, the conduct of persons without understanding what the latter were thinking and doing from the standpoint of their own goals, desires, interests, standards of appropriateness, and feelings of achievement. James argued that while these things were initially mysterious in any given case, they were illuminated by articulating all the variables of personal experience.

These variables included "an objective and a subjective part": the objective part consisted in the things that people thought or felt; the subjective part was the "inner 'state,'" from which others were normally, but not terminally, excluded. A matrix of ideals, problems, and conceptual strategies provided the context for the things people thought, an orientation from which "thinking comes to pass" (*VRE*, 498, 499).

James argued that distinctively religious facts were personal facts, which demanded investigation of both objective and subjective parts. In order to appreciate religious experience, investigators had to describe not only what religious originals thought or felt, but also the spiritual attitudes from which those thoughts and feelings emanated. They had to pursue "full" facts. Full facts, according to James, were constituted by "a conscious field *plus* its object as felt or thought of *plus* an attitude towards the object *plus* the sense of a self to whom the attitude belongs" (*VRE*, 499).

These claims about full personal facts guided the formation of James's first series of Gifford Lectures. He attempted to indicate the "conscious field" of religious individuals in his circumscription of the topic of religion. The field was teleological and the goal was well-being, as specified in various ways. Religious persons were haunted by questions and problems connected with personal destiny, and they organized perceptions, conceptions, and rules of action in ways that facilitated answers and solutions.

Within this context or "conscious field," religious originals felt or thought of some "unseen reality," or encountered some sort of divinity. The encounter informed their sense of destiny and stimulated them to participate in the actualization of that destiny in distinctive ways. In James's third lecture, "The Reality of the Unseen," he investigated the psychological peculiarities associated with "belief in an object which we cannot see" (*VRE*, 53).

Illumination about religious experience remained distant, however, without investigation of temperamental attitudes toward unseen reality. In James's time and place, two such attitudes were prominent: the religious geniuses who originated "old-time" Calvinism as well as the revivalists whose messages descended from Calvinism were sick-souled or morbid, pessimistic about personal destiny; those who originated the new harmonial religions were healthy-minded, emphasizing the divine help that persons received more than the suffering, absurdity, or evil that necessitated that aid. In each case, the full facts of their religious experiences could be accounted for only by clarifying those emotions. James set out to do just this in his four lectures on the religions of the healthy-minded and the sick-souled.

Finally, the full facts of religious experience were rounded out by investigating "the sense of a self" to which religious attitudes belonged. James attempted to accomplish this inquiry in his three lectures on the divided self and the process of its unification, especially through conversion. These lectures ended his first series and prepared the way for his description of the consequences of religious experience as well as his appreciation of religion in light of those fruits.

Divine Encounters

The religious attitudes of religious originals were set, according to James, in encounters with divinity. Feelings or thoughts of some "unseen order" provoked religious optimism, pessimism, meliorism, and indifference. Each of these religious attitudes presented "the belief that there is an unseen order, and that our supreme good lies in harmoniously adjusting ourselves thereto" (VRE, 53). Religious originals believed not so much in *another* world as in a *wider* world than the ones that most naturalists, positivists, moralists, and materialists affirmed. They perceived real things that the irreligious did not perceive. This claim was bound to bother various sorts of investigators, of course, who challenged the notion that persons could perceive unseen orders, as well as the notion that religious persons were privy to certain realities to which the irreligious did not have access.

James responded to these challenges first by claiming that "all our attitudes, moral, practical, or emotional, as well as religious, are due to the 'objects' of our consciousness, the things which we believe to exist, whether really or ideally, along with ourselves" (VRE, 53). People's attitudes did not emerge as news from nowhere; they were responses to their perceptions of reality. But what was real? Since James's earliest speculative effort, he had argued that "the reality of a thought is proportionate to the way it grasps us" (EP, 21). If the only objective criterion of reality was long-run coerciveness over thought, then 'reality' varied as and when belief did.

This criterion of reality held whether or not 'things' were sensible. In either case, they elicited reactions. "Thoughts" without sensible reference provoked or evoked reactions that were notoriously stronger than those stimulated by "sensible presences." "The memory of an insult," for example, made people angrier than the insult itself. Then again, Christ never appeared to many Christians who, nevertheless, led intensely Christian lives. Their 'thought' of Christ polarized their lives through and through. Finally, certain imageless thoughts, like 'the best things are the more eternal things,' could saturate behavior in quite definite ways, even if, "for purpose of definite description," they were not very useful.

On top of these arguments, James asserted that "the whole universe of concrete objects, as we know them, swims . . . in a wider and higher universe of abstract ideas that lend it its significance" (VRE, 56). This evidenced James's commitment to conceptual

99

idealism—that is, the doctrine that analysis of human apprehension of the world was incomplete without reference to the standards of appropriateness that people brought to their experiences.

If idealists were right in this regard, then 'reality' did not coincide with the world of sensible objects. There was no simple way to associate 'reality' with the 'objective world' or 'unreality' with the 'subjective world.' Thoughts and things alike determined attitudes. Indeed, thoughts determined the way people perceived things.

But it was one thing to defend the reality of the unseen and quite another to defend a perception of such reality. James argued that certain psychical phenomena could be regimented to confirm *"a sense of reality, a feeling of objective presence, a perception* of what we may call *'something there,'* more deep and more general than any of the special and particular 'senses' by which the current psychology supposes existent realities to be originally revealed." Instances of hallucination collected by members of the Society for Psychical Research stood as "curious proofs" for the hypothesis that persons had "an undifferentiated sense of reality" (*VRE,* 58). Some individuals, for instance, felt something come into their rooms, but *nothing in particular.* Oftentimes, these feelings provoked perfectly definite attitudes, for example, happiness or fear.

Some of these perceptions of "residual presence" had no connection with religious life, but others did. In one case of hallucination, for instance, an individual felt "the close presence of a mighty person, and after it went, the memory persisted as the one perception of reality. Everything else might be a dream, but not that." Whether or not experiences like this were hallucinations was beside James's point; they grasped the individuals undergoing them so intensely that they were "believed in in spite of criticism." What is more, James noted, there was no paucity of such cases. Together, they presented "a well-marked natural kind of fact." Gurney in England and Théodore Flournoy in Switzerland were gathering a census of them. In light of their sifting of testimony, James was willing to claim with certainty that "in the distinctively religious sphere of experience, many persons (how many we cannot tell) possess the objects of their belief, not in the form of mere conceptions which their intellect accepts as true, but rather in the form of quasi-sensible realities directly apprehended" (*VRE,* 60–61, 58, 64).

Some encounters with divinity could not be classified without distortion as subjective (conceptual) or objective (sensible). They were affecting, no matter what other classifications they received.

They stimulated strong and quite specifiable patterns of conduct. Their effects were durable, not fleeting; discernible, not vague; tangible, not simply visible. To be sure, both divine encounters and their aftereffects were "conceptual." They marked changes in a person's thought. But that was just the point: no analytic ice was cut by interpreting them as either subjective or objective.

The sort of experience that James noted was a commonplace among contemporary religious persons. The Unitarian literary genius James Russell Lowell said that he "clearly felt the spirit of God in me and around me" one time when he saw the "whole system" of the universe rise up before him in a way that evoked calm and clear prophecy on his part. Others enjoyed "communication with God" in more conventional ways, either by enduring the magnificent beauty of the world or by engaging in or witnessing suffering service. Still others felt the *loss* of divinity on occasion, as when a person "groped mentally for the familiar sense of that higher mind of my mind which had always seemed to be close at hand as it were, closing the passage, and yielding support, but there was no electric current. A blank was there instead of *It*: I couldn't find anything" (quoted anonymously; *VRE*, 65).

James had encountered divinity himself in 1898. At least, his description in a letter from St. Hubert's Inn in Keene Valley, written on July 9, 1898, to his wife, closely resembled many of the cases of encounter he chose to include in his lectures. He had been hiking with friends, but had chosen to think alone during the evening and "got into a state of spiritual alertness of the most vital description" (*LWJ*, 2:76). He wrote his wife that

> the influence of Nature, the wholesomeness of the people
> round me, . . . the thought of you and the children, dear
> Harry on the wave, the problem of the Edinburgh lectures, all
> fermented within me till it became a regular Walpurgis
> Nacht. . . . It seemed as if the Gods of all the nature-mytholo-
> gies were holding an indescribable meeting in my breast with
> the moral Gods of the inner life. The two kinds of Gods have
> nothing in common—the Edinburgh lectures made quite a
> hitch ahead. The intense significance of some sort, of the
> whole scene, if one could only *tell* the significance; the in-
> tense inhuman remoteness of its inner life, and yet the intense
> *appeal* of it; its everlasting freshness and its immemorial an-
> tiquity and decay; its utter Americanism, and every sort of
> patriotic suggestiveness, and you, and my relation to you part
> and parcel of it all, and beaten up with it, so that memory and

sensation all whirled inexplicably together; it was indeed worth coming for, and worth repeating year by year, if repetition could only procure what in its nature I supposed must be all unplanned for and unexpected. [*LWJ*, 2:76–77]

James had felt ecstasy. More to the point, his catalog of contemporary encounters with divinity was little more peculiar than his Walpurgis Nacht. They were all examples of what he called "the human ontological imagination," in which "unpicturable beings are realized, and realized with an intensity almost like that of an hallucination." These encounters haunted those who had them as a lover is haunted by his lady: even when he cannot picture her, he cannot forget her; "she uninterruptedly affects him through and through" (*VRE*, 72).

As a matter of biographical and historical fact, James argued, the feelings that persons had of divinity in their religious experiences were as convincing as any direct sensible experience and more convincing than any "results established by mere logic ever are." He suggested that most of the people listening to him had probably endured similar experiences—that is, perceptions that, no matter how illogical, were strikingly intuitive. In such instances, James asserted, "your whole subconscious life, your impulses, your faiths, your needs, your divinations, have prepared the premises, of which your consciousness now feels the weight of the result; and something in you absolutely *knows* that the result must be truer than any logic-chopping rationalistic talk, however clever, that may contradict it" (*VRE*, 72, 73).

Once again, as a matter of historical fact, religious attitudes emerged out of encounters that provided a compact symbol for "your whole subconscious life, your impulses, your faiths, your needs, your divinations." They did not emerge from logically regimented arguments based on "observations" or on "the meaning of terms" about the order of things in general.

Interestingly enough, James characterized the *convincingness* of the feelings or thoughts of divinity in a religious encounter as *mystical*. The surety that was provoked in religious experience was groundless, especially given traditional philosophical specification of "grounds." Such grounds, James asserted, consisted of four things: "(1) definitely statable abstract principles; (2) definite facts of sensation; (3) definite hypotheses based on such facts; and (4) definite inferences logically drawn" (*VRE*, 73). Religious originals did not justify their belief that divinity existed on any of these grounds.

But James argued, as he had in "The Will to Believe" and elsewhere, that empiricists, as opposed to rationalists, should not care whether beliefs originated from philosophical or even logical processes of thought. Religious conviction was suspect not because it emerged from a kind of vague experience but insofar as it was found unsuited to the management of difficulties and the solution of problems that it was geared to address.

Indeed, he continued, construing warrants for belief as "grounds" was pointless because the architectural metaphor systematically distorted the shape of mental life. Persons were born into webs of belief. They did not and could not "build" their beliefs from "foundations" up, because they never started from scratch and could not decide to do so with any effectiveness. The "epistemological" search for incorrigible foundations of belief was fruitless from a natural history point of view because no matter what epistemology achieved, "it will fail to convince or convert you all the same, if your dumb intuitions are opposed to its conclusions" (*VRE*, 73).

"Dumb" intuitions went without saying, so it took more persuasion than rationalists could deliver to challenge those intuitions, much less force their neglect. If philosophical theology was wedded to rationalist "grounds," James suggested, it was outmoded as a form of religious reflection. Indeed, the association between philosophical theology and the pursuit of "foundations" accounted for the dearth of interest in the traditional literature or divine "proofs." "Our generation," James said, "has ceased to believe in the kind of God it argued for" (*VRE*, 74).

In sum, the perception of unseen reality in religious experience carried with it the same sort of psychological certainty that other dumb intuitions did, no matter how "groundless" they were. A person who had undergone religious experiences not only demanded well-being but was sure he had encountered "something there" that guaranteed, at least, the chance of salvation and, at best, its actualization.

Religious Attitudes

On the basis of his data, James argued that persons who thought or felt divinities reacted by developing certain attitudes. They evinced patterns of "sadness and gladness" in particular, though the precise complexion of these emotions depended in large part on "the sense of the kind of object" to which religious self-surrender was made. Some encounters with divinity provoked intense convictions of sin when the gap between divinity and personality was revealed. This led to sadness. Other encounters provoked feelings of release from conviction and practical union with divinity, the gladness of deliverance. Still others unleashed a gladness in persons who knew no need for release from sin. James noted that the most complex religious attitude was the sense of well-being actualized in deliverance from fear. On the principle that "the more complex is also the more complete," he claimed that a man's religion "involves both moods of contraction and moods of expansion of his being" (VRE, 75).

Whatever principle James deployed to make his point, however, it was polemical. "Constitutionally sanguine" persons in positions of power preached their own brands of religious gladness without any sense of self-criticism: President McKinley was the paradigm. In such persons, there was "no tendency to flexion, no bowing of the head" (VRE, 77). Instead, they were gross sectarians. When McKinley and his fellow travelers both in America and in Europe preached the religion of "civilization," they preached it against the " 'lower' races" and inflicted it on them "by means of Hotchkiss guns, etc." (VRE, 77). James found it practically impossible to live with this simply sanguine religious attitude. Religious optimism was a natural result of religious experience, and those who maintained it had much to teach nay-sayers. But it permitted human blindness of the grossest sort. To demonstrate this understanding, he turned to his investigation of the "religion of healthy-mindedness."

But even before he delivered his lectures on the predominant religious attitudes or emotions, he had executed a remarkable clarification of his theory of emotion. James's 1884 theory had seemed reductively physiological to many of his readers, and that had been the subject of vigorous debate from the moment that the work appeared. But no matter what interpretation people placed on James's essay, he had argued in 1884 that without bodily changes, all that would remain of psychological life was dispassionate spectral judgment.

In 1901, his conception of "full" personal facts highlighted the connections between "beliefs" and "emotions." Religious happiness and religious contrition were responses to "objects of consciousness" or "things believed to exist." There was an inevitable judgmental or cognitive variable in the constitution of emotions (at least of religious emotions), along with the variables of bodily change and subsequent disposition. Without objects of consciousness or things believed to exist, then, bodily changes would be

unemotional! Emotions were not reducible to physiological specifications alone and, indeed, resembled "worldviews" more than
sheer sensations, like tickles. Religious emotions were "total"
views, which depended on experiences of divinity. Religious optimism and religious pessimism were the two most prominent contemporary cases in point. They issued from encounters with different gods, even with different sorts of gods.

Though James tried in his lectures on the religion of healthy-
mindedness to clarify the connections between belief and emotion,
the lectures had a more expansive aim. He wanted to appreciate
the success of such religious movements as liberal Protestantism,
transcendentalism, and the various sorts of New Thought and experimental religions, but in ways that permitted criticism of them
insofar as they blinded devotees to the demands of the sick-souled.

To achieve these ends, he claimed that the systematic cultiva-
tion of optimism was consonant with important "currents in human
nature" (VRE, 90). Normally, he suggested, religious persons di-
verted their attention from suffering and evil enough to concentrate on the actualization of their ideals and interests. This accounted, in part, for the advance of liberal Protestant movements
like Unitarianism, Universalism, and even Andover's Progressive
Orthodoxy. Preachers in these movements seemed devoted to making as little of sin as possible, rather than magnifying consciousness of it.

Then, too, the doctrine of progress or general meliorism, which
fit the normal tendency to work toward the best and to forget the
worst, accounted, in part, for the rise of Spencerian evolutionism
as a religious doctrine. Along with liberal Protestants, Spencerians
construed the "continual preoccupation of the old-fashioned Christian with the salvation of his soul as something sickly and repre-
hensible rather than admirable; and a sanguine and 'muscular'
attitude, which to our forefathers would have seemed purely hea-
then, has become in their eyes an ideal element" of character
(VRE, 91).

"Muscular" Christianity was encouraged by the preachers of
progress, whose world was "a poetic fiction far handsomer and
cleaner and better than the world really is." In some cases, this sort
of optimism manifested a "contentment with the finite," which en-
cased an individual "like a lobster-shell and shield[ed] him from
all morbid repining at his distance from the Infinite" (VRE, 90,
93).

The mind-cure movements, or New Thought, also encouraged a
deliberately optimistic scheme of life. These were doctrinally de-

scended from such diverse sources as the Gospels, New England transcendentalism, Berkeleyan idealism, spiritism, evolutionism, and Hinduism, and their leaders believed intuitively in the powers of positive thinking as such. Mind-cure was a reaction "against all that religion of chronic anxiety which marked the earlier part of our century in the evangelical circles of England and America" (*VRE*, 95). The gospel of realization preached by such people as the Dressers, Henry Wood, Horace Fletcher, Annie Besant, and Trine persuaded masses of eager listeners that the "misery-habit" and the "martyr-habit" associated with Anglo-American Calvinism emerged out of an attitude of fear that was in turn based on egotistical attempts to appropriate and control the surrounding world.

Trine, whom James respected more than some other New Thinkers, coined the term "fear-thought" in order to attack old-guard Christianity. Fletcher declared that happiness was found in forethought minus fear-thought. Dresser cribbed Bradley's notion of an "unearthly ballet of bloodless categories" in order to characterize diverse fears. And Wood wrote that the historical course of religion in America was such a "perpetual nightmare" of cramped, limited, and depressed mentality that "nothing but the boundless divine love, exuberance, and vitality, constantly poured in, even thought unconsciously to us, could in some degree neutralize such an ocean of morbidity."[1]

The great message of the New Thinkers was that "one need remain in hell no longer than one chooses to; we can rise to any heaven we ourselves choose; and when we choose so to rise, all the higher powers of the Universe combine to help us heavenward."[2] The point, as Trine suggested, was to get "in tune with the Infinite." The movement resembled Hegelianism, James noted, especially as enunciated by Edward Caird in his Gifford Lectures of 1890–92 on the evolution of religion. Both Hegelianism and New Thought played on the doctrine of the oneness of man and God. Caird's lectures clearly suggested that optimism leads to power, whereas pessimism leads to weakness.[3]

But these "second-order" articulations of the new optimism were matched by "spontaneous" religious exclamations of well-being. Indeed, James argued, the success of the new movements had more to do with "experimental" results than with theological persuasion. James reported various cases of mind-cured neurasthenia and added that self-deception was possible in such cases. Yet the numbers of regenerated characters were too large to allow one to deny that the New Thought movements had "general tonic effects on public opinion." Even when investigators overlooked "the verbiage of a good deal of the mind-cure literature," its blinded optimism and its vague theories, "the plain fact remains that the spread of the movement has been due to practical fruits, and the extremely practical turn of character of the American people has never been better shown than by the fact that this, their only decidedly original contribution to the philosophy of life, should be so intimately knit up with concrete therapeutics" (*VRE*, 95, 96).

H. H. Goddard had demonstrated to James's satisfaction that "the cures by mind-cures exist," even though many cases showed self-deception and fraud. In his dissertation in psychology at Clark University, Goddard documented, among others, cases of disease in which doctors failed and mind-curers succeeded. To Goddard it was "hardly conceivable that the large body of intelligent people who comprise the body known distinctly as Mental Scientists should continue to exist if the whole thing were a delusion." The cures were neither fleeting nor isolated, and if the therapists used strategies "in no respect different from those now officially recognized in medicine as cures by suggestion," what the therapists were suggesting effected relief in "many a sufferer of ills that the ordinary physician cannot touch."[4]

The key to the success of mind-cure, James argued, was a set of methods which New Thinkers shared with older religionists, not all of whom could be considered "healthy-minded." He found striking psychological similarities, for instance, between New Thought and both the Lutheran and Wesleyan movements, inasmuch as all three deployed "anti-moralistic" methods of "surrender," according to which "passivity, not activity; relaxation, not intentness, should now be the rule." Each of these religious movements developed ways of giving "your little private convulsive self a rest, and finding that a greater Self was there." This was the heart of Lutheran justification by faith, Wesleyan acceptance of free grace, and New Thought regeneration by relaxing. No matter whether the phenomena were given theistic, pantheistic, or materialistic causal explanations, they remained "firm facts of human nature" (*VRE*, 110, 111).

To suggest that mind-cure worked by methods of "suggestion" was not very telling, according to James. The term "suggestion" threw "a wet blanket on investigation." The point of inquiry was to establish *what* suggestions worked and why. "Suggestion" was only "another name for the power of ideas, *so far as they prove efficacious over belief and conduct.*" If the ideas of Christian churches were efficacious in this sense at one time, James claimed, they were no longer so. In the contemporary world, "popular Christianity" did absolutely nothing therapeutically successful "until mind-cure came to the rescue." Mind-cure worked for people whose ears were deafened to the Gospel as it was preached in Protestant churches. The New Thought movement, indeed, was original because it found a channel, "until then sealed up," through which "springs of higher life" were set free in a distinctive "group of human beings" (VRE, 112, 113, 114).

Among other things, James argued, New Thought was significant for the same reasons that psychical research was important: it beat materialists at their own scientific game. Survival theorists argued largely on the assumption that "science . . . has proved that personality, so far from being an elementary force in nature, is but a passive resultant." They claimed that "science" supplanted "primitive thought" by "the strict use of the method of experimental verification" (VRE, 119).

But mind-cure set up an opposite claim and corroborated it experimentally. Whether or not an investigator considered the patients to be "deluded victims of their imagination" made no difference, according to James, so long as "they seemed to *themselves* to have been cured by the experiments tried" (VRE, 121), because they were themselves authorities when it came to the issues of their own pain or lack of it. Their cures were startling enough to themselves to make them converts.

To be sure, not everyone proved susceptible to the therapies of mind-cure. But there was no a priori argument for holding that those cures should be universally applicable. The world might be complex enough that both "religious" and "medical" or "scientific" therapies were "genuine keys for unlocking the world's treasure-house to him who can use either of them practically. Just as evidently neither is exhaustive or exclusive of the other's simultaneous use." In the meantime, "numbers of educated people" still found "primitive thought" at least as powerful as "scientific" thought. Very few individuals stopped construing much of their experience in terms of "individualized personal forces" (VRE, 122, 123).

But if James thought New Thought was so successful because it united healthy-mindedness with a readiness for regeneration by letting go, he was just as convinced that some of its influential spokesmen fostered human blindness by declaring that evil was unreal. He warned that "nothing can be more stupid than to bar out phenomena from our notice, merely because we are incapable of taking part in anything like them ourselves." Preachers of healthy-mindedness like Whitman might leave many readers feeling simply sanguine, but thoughtful people should beware: not everything people called evil was "due entirely to the way men take the phenomenon" (*VRE*, 109, 88). A philosopher, at least, intent on unblinding persons to one another, could not chide the sick-souled for their "dumb" intuitions of evil the way Whitman did when he compared them unfavorably to "placid and self-contained animals."[5]

Healthy-mindedness, of course, was not born with New Thought. James noted that very influential historical figures had been optimistic in a sort of congenital way: Saint Francis, the young Rousseau, Spinoza, Diderot, and de Saint Pierre were like this. So far as religious traditions went, optimism was more prominent in the history of Catholicism than in that of Protestant Christianity. Catholic confession and absolution was a systematic method for keeping healthy-mindedness "on top" (*VRE*, 128). But, then, according to James, so was Luther's conception of repentance.

The various sorts of religious optimism, however, were matched by a "radically opposite" religious attitude "based on the persuasion that the evil aspects of our life are of its very essence, and the world's meaning most comes home to us when we lay them most to heart" (*VRE*, 130–31). On the American scene, of course, the attitude was associated with orthodox theism or Calvinism. Even if New Thinkers and liberal Protestants thought the attitude totally outmoded, it survived to compete with their healthy-mindedness in revival movements led by leaders like Moody and in the traditional churches whose devotees still outnumbered those in heterodox movements.

Religious individuals expressed different levels of pessimism. But every sort of religious pessimist thought that healthy-minded consciousness was "a bell with a crack; it draws its breath on sufferance and by accident" (*VRE*, 136). Religious pessimists were of two types: once and twice born. Once-born pessimists thought that evil meant a maladjustment with things in their environment and sought "natural" strategies of assimilation and accommodation to correct disorder. Twice-born pessimists thought evil was a wrongness or vice in their own nature. They pictured the wrongness as so divisive that no "superficial rearrangement" of the self could cure it; evil required a supernatural remedy.

James, of course, had signaled allegiance to the twice-born position on evil since 1884. Failure was a pivotal human experience; escape from it was "just a lucky chance." But failure was only the first stage of the "world-sickness." Persons reached the second stage when they realized that the purely naturalistic look at life was sure to end in sadness. Then, momentary successes were struck against an "evil background," against a future when "the skull will grin in at the banquet" (*VRE*, 136, 140, 141).

Naturalism pictured man as "living on a frozen lake" that was both inescapable and melting. Those bounded by it demanded a sort of well-being that it could not satisfy. This "unreconciled contradiction" sometimes led to the third stage of world-sickness, where "there is a pitch of unhappiness so great that the goods of nature may be entirely forgotten" (*VRE*, 144). This state of *anhedonia* brought either an incapacity for joyous feeling or, more positively, active anguish and constant exasperation, especially about oneself. When *anhedonia* provoked querulousness, it tended toward irreligion. When it stimulated some effort for relief, it was often characterized as religious melancholy.

According to James's reading, the religious melancholiac not only experienced his world as alien but experienced a need to have its strangeness overcome. Religious melancholiacs like Tolstoy sometimes found "objective conditions" alien because they were utterly capricious, not purposive. Others, like Bunyan, found their own selves alien because they could not maintain purity of heart or single-mindedness. Still others found anything and everything alien—self, world, and all. If the vanity of mortal things brought Tolstoy to despair, and a sense of sin provoked melancholy in Bunyan, a fear of the universe haunted others to the point of inertia. This "worst kind of melancholy" was the sort sustained by James thirty years before, and expressed when he wrote as the "anonymous French correspondent."

All these religious melancholiacs cried for help when they could not help themselves. All demanded deliverance "in as strong a form as the complaint." Together, James assertd, they revealed "the real core of the religious problem: Help! Help!" Their sick souls provided reasons why "the coarser religions, revivalistic, orgiastic, with blood and miracles and supernatural operations, may possibly never be displaced" (*VRE*, 162).

Indeed, the actual experiences of sick souls demonstrated the inadequacy of healthy-mindedness "as a philosophical doctrine, because the evil facts which it refuses positively to account for are a genuine portion of reality" (*VRE*, 163). Systematic healthy-mindedness was formally less complete than systems that tried to give some positive account of evil. Thus, the New Thinkers outstripped the bounds of philosophical propriety when they eliminated traditional Christian emphasis on evil. Christianity and Buddhism were the "completest" historical religions because both gave constructive analyses of natural wrongness and of deliverance from it.

James's line of reasoning echoed his father's: the varieties of Christian and post-Christian liberalism lacked religious vitality because they failed actively to attend to "sorrow, pain, and death." However religious thinkers chose to transform their traditional Christian inheritance, they were constrained to retain Calvinism's insistence that "there is something wrong about us as we naturally stand." Without it, they were bound to be "unspeakably blind and shallow" (*VRE*, 165, 162).

The Self in Transformation

On James's reading of religious consciousness, religious persons were occupied with questions and problems of personal destiny. They sought to resolve those questions and problems in light of divinities encountered or remembered as encountered. The answers and solutions they revealed varied according to temperament, the intensity of their complaints, and the sorts of power they experienced when they encountered divinity.

But the heart of James's analysis of religious experience was his investigation of the sort of self to which religious attitudes belonged. He claimed that religious attitudes belonged to selves in transformation, to divided selves becoming integral selves, to world-sick selves becoming well as never before. Once again, of course, he was talking about religious originals, not just any devotee of some religious way of life. He was particularly interested in the transformation of selves who experienced "new birth," because the *difference* religion made for people was observable there as nowhere else.

E. D. Starbuck had published *Psychology of Religion* in 1899. James thought Starbuck's book, among other things, demonstrated beyond the shadow of doubt that "the psychological basis of the twice-born character seems to be . . . an incompletely unified moral and intellectual constitution." Given James's own work on self-consciousness in *Principles*, this came as no surprise to him. He had argued there that "the normal evolution of character" mainly consisted in "the straightening out and unifying of the inner self" (*VRE*, 167, 170). Normally, the maturation of thought amounted to relief from mental division and the emergence of a mind whose parts were accommodated to one another (cf. PP, 2:309–29).

An accompanying sense of conviction made some divided selves religious. Divided selves who were religious both tried to overcome the divisions they felt within themselves and failed in the attempts. So their unhappiness took the form of "moral remorse and compunction, of feeling inwardly vile and wrong, and of standing in false relations to the author of one's being and appointer of one's spiritual fate" (*VRE*, 170). Augustine was exemplary, but numerous cases could be found in contemporary evangelical literature, including the testimony that Starbuck had collected from Methodist preachers and laymen and Christian soldiers in the Women's Christian Temperance Union.

According to James, religion was only one of many ways to attain a unified self. Some persons had experienced new birth away from religion into unbelief or incredulity; others had been converted from divisive moral scrupulosity to single-minded license. In every sort of self-unification, religious or otherwise, a "firmness, stability, and equilibrium" succeeded "a period of storm and stress and inconsistency" (*VRE*, 176).

But several qualities distinguished the self-unification of religious originals from irreligious transformations. First, religious transformation brought a sense of release from conviction. Second, religious originals escaped the sadness of division as a result of their "firmer hold upon religious realities" (*VRE*, 189)—that is, upon encountered divinities. Third, the "new identity" of religious originals, born of religious experience, was indefinite, conservative enough to sustain interest in personal destiny at the center of consciousness but revolutionary enough to displace fear and anxiety as the basic motive for conduct with assurance of well-being and love for the other as it lives for itself.

The third quality of religious self-transformation was the most crucial and the most vexing. As a scientist of religions, James aimed both to discover facts that would make the supernatural more evident and to demystify distinctively religious events by developing psychological accounts of these happenings. He focused on conversion for two reasons: first, psychologists gave no adequate causal account of the radical identity-transformations that occurred in conversion; and, second, conversion was manifestly similar to other psychic events for which researchers accounted as "subliminal activity." The key to James's program was to legitimize the supernatural reading of conversion while locating the psychic mechanism that permitted conversion to occur.

James developed a model of religious transformation that turned on issues of avowal, not of belief. He noted that alterations of character were normal, but that "transformations" were extraordinary. Transformations occurred "whenever one aim grows so stable as to expel definitively its previous rivals from the individual's life. Whenever transformation occurred, an individual avowed his identification with a new and particular group of ideas. Thus, James reasoned, "to say that a man is 'converted' means, in these terms, that religious ideas, previously peripheral in his consciousness, now take a central place, and that religious aims form the habitual centre of his energy" (VRE, 194, 196).

Rational psychologists had never been able to account for any particular religious transformation. They had described *what* went on, but not *how* or *why* transformation occurred. All they knew, according to James, was that "there are dead feelings, dead ideas, and cold beliefs, and there are hot and live ones; and when one grows hot and alive within us, everything has to recrystalize about it." In a general way, of course, psychologists had employed "the hackneyed symbolism of a mechanical equilibrium" to account for transformation, noting variables that retarded changes of mind and variables that accelerated them. "New information," for instance, accelerated mental alterations, while "formed associations of ideas and habits" retarded change (VRE, 197).

But these variables were tied to a picture of mind as both conscious and self-conscious. Their explanatory power lay in a subject's ability to tell an investigator what associations of ideas and habits informed his view on things, and what new information strained that view. Many conversions, however, were striking precisely because, if there was any "new information," it seemed to the subject to be ineffable and also because the convert's "new identity" seemed utterly disassociated with ideas and habits that had previously informed his view on things. The "stress and strain" of the self-conscious mind did not account for these "sudden" and radical transformations.

But, James suggested, psychologists did not have to abandon the model of mechanical equilibrium. They could modify their view of mind to include levels of consciousness, including subliminal or subconscious levels. Then it would be possible to postulate that variables of acceleration and retardation were at work, that mental equilibration was the product of these variables, and that people were, at least on occasion and to some degree, unaware of their own mental processes.

Psychologists and psychical researchers had succeeded in corroborating the hypothesis of subliminal mental activity, especially through experimentation in hypnosis. Starbuck had distinguished conscious and voluntary religious conversions from unconscious, involuntary ones, calling them, respectively, the volitional and self-surrendering types of religious conversion. Volitional conversion proceeded as education did: gradually, self-consciously, and in piecemeal fashion. Self-surrendering conversion proceeded as recollection of a forgotten name sometimes did: sometimes the forgotten name was "*jammed*, and pressure in its direction only kept it all the more from rising. And then the opposite expedient often succeeds. Give up the effort entirely; think of something altogether different, and in half an hour the lost name comes sauntering into your mind" (*VRE*, 205).

In self-surrendering conversions, according to James, "some hidden process" was started in people trying to escape conviction of sin, "which went on after the effort ceased, and made the result come as if it came spontaneously" (*VRE*, 205). So long as someone suffering from religious melancholy made efforts to escape his natural wrongness, the identity he avowed was still the "imperfect self," so that the more perfect self he longed to be was jammed. Starbuck suggested, and James agreed, that relaxation of the will of an avowed imperfect self permitted subconscious forces to take the lead. Supposing that the group of ideas which constituted the convert's born-again identity were among those forces, they could only rise to consciousness when the convert "let go" of his avowedly imperfect self.

This psychological account of sudden conversion in terms of disavowal and avowal of selves provided James with a theoretical link connecting his science of religions with another "natural" science. It articulated religious transformation in terms of a "well-accredited" theoretical mechanism, but without inevitably reducing spontaneous religious discourse to something else. No matter whether an investigator described religious crisis theologically, physiologically, or psychologically, the event was distinctively religious, because, "*in any terms*, the crisis described is the throwing of our conscious selves upon the mercy of powers which, whatever they may be, are more ideal than we are actually, and make for our redemption" (*VRE*, 210).

James concluded that psychology and religion "both admit that there are forces seemingly outside of the conscious individual that bring redemption to his life" (*VRE*, 211). Admitting this did nothing to adjudicate disputes between theologians and nontheological psychologists concerning the *location* of the "ideal forces" that brought redemption. Christian theologians insisted that these forces transcended the individual's personality; atheological psychologists implied that they did not. But, according to James, much of the force of this dispute depended on conceptual ambiguity: theologians and psychologists tended to mean different things by 'personality' and 'the transcendence of personality.'

Aiming to make the supernatural more evident, James tried to break the deadlock between theologians and atheological psychologists. First, he noted that religious melancholics could not possibly will to believe their own religious transformation. A person could make himself more faithful to beliefs of which he had "the rudiments," but he could not "create a belief out of whole cloth" when his perception actively assured him of the opposite. So long as a person avowed identification with imperfection, "the better mind proposed to us comes in that case in the form of a pure negation of the only mind we have, and we cannot actively will a pure negation" (*VRE*, 212). On these grounds, and assuming no great difference between "personality" and "the only mind we have," the power to transform an old person into a new one, a convicted person into a regenerated one, transcended "personality."

Second, he specified two ways for anxiety-ridden persons to become well and willing to be. Either the "willingness to be" had to "overpoweringly break over us," or anxiety-ridden persons had to become indifferent to their own imperfection. When a religious melancholiac became indifferent to his imperfection and avowed that he was saved, he was converted.

The logic of the matter was peculiar, of course, because 'self-transformation' was one of those notions in which 'self' was construed both actively and passively (like 'self-deception'). The self was transforming, but the self was also transformed. James thought it fruitless to analyze self-transformation as a process of the development of beliefs, because the beliefs of the old and new selves in a conversion experience were discontinuous: the one set negated the other.

Third, James suggested that radical changes of heart might be understood as a "strictly natural process, divine in its fruits, of course, but in one case more and in another less so, and neither more nor less divine in its mere causation and mechanism than of any other process, high or low, of man's interior life" (*VRE*, 230). If investigators assumed what he had argued in *Principles*, namely, that the unit of mental life was a field of consciousness, not a single idea, that the bounds of any particular field were indefinite, not determinate, and that fields of consciousness succeeded one another continuously, they could lay the psychological groundwork for understanding regeneration as a natural process.

James argued that "the important fact which this 'field' formula commemorates is the indetermination of the margin" of consciousness. "Fields" had centers of interest or attention, which were connected link by link to "objects of which we are less and less attentively conscious." Each link played some role in determining behavior and "the next movement of our attention," so that the field's margin "lies around us like a 'magnetic field,' inside of which our centre of energy turns like a compass-needle, as the present phase of consciousness alters into its successor" (VRE, 231, 232).

On this view, voluntary conversion was simply a matter of ordinary field-succession—that is, actively making some marginal object of consciousness more and more central. But involuntary conversion was another matter. James noted that "ordinary psychology" had taken it for granted that "what is absolutely extra-marginal is absolutely non-existent, and cannot be a fact of consciousness at all" (VRE, 232). But to some converts, their "new" selves had been extramarginal for their "old" ones: their "old" ones had paid their "new" ones absolutely no attention.

Myers's discovery in 1886 of extramarginal objects of consciousness recovered under hypnosis threw "a wholly new light upon our natural constitution" (VRE, 235). Since his discovery, researchers like Pierre Janet, Jean Charcot, and Sigmund Freud had deployed knowledge of the unconscious to heal the insane and neurotic, while others, including James, Flournoy, Carl Jung and Myers himself, had pondered the possibility that the subliminal mind transcended the senses and perceived some noumenal reality.[6]

James argued that the most important consequence of having "a strongly developed ultra-marginal life" was that "one's ordinary fields of consciousness are liable to incursions from it of which the subject does not guess the source" and which, therefore, took the form of "automatisms." The simplest instance of an automatism was posthypnotic suggestion. But, "interpreting the unknown after the analogy of the known," the presumption was that *any* instance of automatism indicated subliminal activity, whether it be "motor impulses, or obsessive idea, or unaccountable caprice, or delusion, or hallucination" (VRE, 233, 235).

His point was that the source of these things was to be sought in the subject's subconscious life, not that the subject was the source of these things. In hypnotic cases, the suggestion promulgated by the hypnotist was the source of automatisms. In certain hysteric cases, lost memories were the source of automatisms. The question that faced scientists of religion was this: given the assumption that involuntary conversions were automatisms and that the sources of automatisms were to be found connected with the subject's subconscious life, how could the source of involuntary conversion be identified?

James was not sure. The question involved "a vast program of work to be done in the way of verification, in which the religious experiences of man must play their part." In many cases, he was prepared to claim that "the accumulation of vestiges of sensible experience (whether inattentively or attentively registered)" was the source of involuntary religious conversion. But, he said, "there are occasional bursts into consciousness of results of which it is not easy to demonstrate any prolonged subconscious incubation." In such cases, the "result" might be ascribed either to "a merely physiological nerve storm" or, "in case it was useful and rational, . . . to some more mystical or theological hypothesis" (VRE, 236).

The "subliminal" mind linked science with religion, but it did not reduce religion to irreligion, because, as James employed the notion, the subliminal was construed as a region, not a source. 'Subconsciousness' identified a universe of mental activity, not a cause of automatisms. Theological hypotheses addressed 'causal' problems; 'subliminality' indicated lack of explicit awareness. For James, this meant that divinity and human subliminality might be connected, so that theology and psychology might become reconciled in some fashion or other.

But even if religious changes of heart were strictly natural processes, James argued, the consequences might be divine. "The real witness of the spirit," he asserted, "is to be found only in the disposition of the genuine child of God, the permanently patient heart, the love of self eradicated." If investigators studied the masses of conversions in the "fully evolved Revivalism of Great Britain and America," that is, if they considered only the "usual run of 'saints,'" they would find that "no splendor worthy of a wholly supernatural creature fulgurates from them, or sets them apart from the mortals who have never experienced" the favors of methodistic revivals. Nonetheless, the "spiritual grubs and earth-worms" who participated in contemporary revivals were better off for their experiences because these "Crumps and Stigginses" had still found their own "highest centre of energy," so they were literally saved (VRE, 237–38, 239).[7]

Great or small, James argued, salvation did occur in conversion. Some persons did not need to pass through any crisis in order to be saintly; some of them were even found "outside of Christianity altogether" (*VRE*, 239). These individuals did not require salvation. But many more did. Some of the latter were willing to be their best selves as a result of conversion.

With other American investigators working on religious conversion, especially Starbuck, George A. Coe, and Leuba, James reasoned that the test of the religious value of conversion was its achievements, not "how it happens." Religiously transformed selves attained a distinguishable "faith-state" characterized by a loss of worry, a willingness to be one's best self despite the consequences, a perception of truths, especially about oneself, not known before, a perception of objective changes in the world, especially a sense of the beauty of the thing once feared, and sustained happiness. The duration of the faith-state was variable, James noted, but "the point of serious interest" was "not so much the duration as the nature and quality of these shiftings of character to higher levels" (*VRE*, 257). Persons who experienced divinity in conversion avowed themselves as being well, as having been delivered from an anxiety that had saturated their lives previously.

Saintliness

As James understood "full" personal facts, "that unshareable feeling which each one of us has of the pinch of his individual destiny as he privately feels it rolling out on fortune's wheel may be disparaged for its egotism, may be sneered at as unscientific, but it is the one thing that fills up the measure of our concrete actuality, and any would-be existent that should lack such a feeling, or its analogue, would be a piece of reality only half made up" (*VRE*, 499).

In light of this, James spent much effort at the beginning of his second series of Gifford Lectures characterizing "regenerate" religious characters as they were *for themselves*. His three lectures on saintliness were intended to execute a "general natural history of the regenerate character" in ways that would demonstrate that "the best fruits of religious experience are the best things that history has to show" (*VRE*, 268). But his demonstration depended on the assumption that "the best things" history revealed were often disconnected with contemporary understanding of what was best.

For "us," James asserted, both contemporary regenerates and historical exemplars of saintliness were peculiar and often offensive. But one could "never fathom an emotion or divine its dictates by standing outside of it" (*VRE*, 325). The piety and the charity of saints "fit" a different universe of discourse and especially of practice from the contemporary workaday world of "lusts and fears." Religious emotions formed "another centre of energy altogether" from the emotions of the prudent intellectual yoked with responsibilities, exhausting himself in order to do the right thing. So "the only sound plan" for "us" was to observe "as well as we are able" those who felt religious emotions and to "record faithfully what we observe" (VRE, 235). By so doing, we might cast critical light on our own sensibilities.

Saints often looked like "monstrous aberrations from the path of nature," according to James, because they appeared to have no inhibitions. Like mothers caring for newborns, the inhibitive power of pain in them was extinguished by some " 'expulsive power of a higher affection' " (VRE, 261, 262). Normally, moral and practical attitudes resulted from an equilibration between impulses and inhibitions, but saints appeared compelled. Where "the previous carnal self" merely wished he was his better self, the man who lived "in his religious centre of personal energy" was driven to be his better self (VRE, 267).

James worried that his mechanical analogies were "delusive" because no one knew just why or how intense spiritual excitement came about in one person rather than another. No one knew, for instance, why or how some drunkards got reformed at the Jerry MacAuley Water Street Mission in New York, while others did not. No one knew why or how the infamous Colonel Gardiner was cured of his sexual vice, but others continued to philander. But these "small men" were now willing to be their best selves, after they abandoned "self-responsibility." The regenerates in America and Great Britain responding to noonday revivals and social calls to the Gospel exemplified a religious sensibility that they shared with the "classic" saints: they found themselves at home in a world wider "than that of this world's selfish little interests" (VRE, 272). In their new earth, they felt befriended by their best selves enough to surrender to them. Surrender melted down their selfish interests and encouraged the love of others, the acceptance of their claims, and the pursuit of their happiness.

Living in this world, according to James, had characteristic practical consequences. The saints who were accommodated to this unseen reality typically exemplified observable patterns of conduct. They were ascetic, patient, single-mindedly intent, and charitable or tender. These dispositions did not derive one from another, nor could they be deduced somehow from religious belief. The "faith-state" carried all these dispositions with it by "organic consequence." They provided, together, the pragmatic meaning of living in the "presence of a higher and friendly Power" (*VRE*, 274).

Investigating historical records, James claimed that these "saintly methods" antedated theologies and were independent of philosophies. They were, indeed, reshaped by every speculative creed that they accompanied. Hence, for instance, the asceticism of a medieval Catholic saint was found to carry physical flagellation with it, because his best self demanded punishment of the body, but the asceticism of a Romantic pantheist was not. Both demanded poverty, even physical poverty, of themselves. But for the Romantic, that meant simplifying life, not scarring one's back.

James realized, of course, that any form of saintly conduct looked suspicious to persons who thought they were no longer called upon to live with energy, though energy bring pain. He even assumed that his own contemporary Anglo-American culture prized the instinct to seek the easy and the pleasant, thus making saintliness appear abnormal in any instance. Typical Anglo-Americans were driven by a need to *have* things, to own or control them. But this was because they lived in a material world, where the only alternative to having was being had. The "spiritual grounds" for the apparently unnatural conduct of saints rested on the ideal of being, not having. Saints did not identify their "essence" with possessions. Possessions stimulated private interests, but "only those who have no private interest can follow an ideal straight away" (*VRE*, 319). Saints followed their impersonal worths in order to be or become children of their gods.

If saintly sentiments looked alien and extravagant to a culture informed by demands for power and concerns for material, they began to make sense as their "wider world" was revealed, according to James. Following the assumptions of his "Certain Blindness" argument, James claimed that "in all these matters of sentiment one must have 'been there' one's self in order to understand them" (*VRE*, 325). Just as "no American [could] ever attain to understanding the loyalty of a Briton towards his king" until he placed himself at the center of the Britisher's view of the world, no prudent and responsible moralist at the turn of the century could understand any saint without realizing that saints lived in worlds befriended by saving powers. Understanding *who* any particular saint was inevitably involved determining *what* power saved him from *what* natural wrongness in order to avow the particular identity he had.

The power that saved Gautama from natural attachments and desires so that he could avow his Buddhahood differed from the power that saved George Whitefield from his sins so that he could do or suffer the will of Jesus. Saintliness was even pluralistic within traditions: the power that befriended Jonathan Edwards's world regenerated Edwardsian saints so that they might delight in the execution of sinners, among other things; this appalled Romantic Christians, who had been trained into cultures that avoided or voided issues of radical sin and saw themselves able to regenerate or rehabilitate the natural "rightness" in men. But whatever the powers, wrongnesses, and salvations looked like, they revealed the "sentiments" that oriented religious geniuses, and that distinguished religious geniuses from their irreligious brothers.

When James delivered these lectures on saintliness, of course, the saint was still a noticeable "character" in England and America. Those people who attended the lectures probably had no more difficulty thinking of exemplary saints than they had pointing to great explorers or brilliant warriors. But the character of saintliness already seemed old-fashioned and, in most cases, outlandish. By giving saintliness the aura of historical precedent, James hoped to sustain that character as an optional and attractive model of conduct. But sustaining that character meant avowing identification as a particular sort of self, with particular sorts of attitudes, provoked by particular and peculiar objects of consciousness. If people in England and America wanted saints to show them who to be, they needed to admit that encounters with divinity provoked the faith of transformed selves. When they admitted these "full" religious facts, they provided bases for developing a case for supernaturalism of the "crass" or miraculous sort.

CHAPTER 5

THE APPRECIATION OF RELIGION

AS A HUMAN ACHIEVEMENT

When James finished his lectures on saintliness, he announced that he was taking a new direction that required a new attitude. He had established both the "spontaneous variations" of religion—the "full facts" of religious experience—and the fruits of those facts. He was ready to ask "whether the fruits in question can help us to judge the absolute value of what religion adds to human life" (*VRE*, 326).

In other words, James turned to the task of "appreciation," not in the contemporary sense of sympathetic sensitivity, but "in the older sense in which it means the thoughtful setting of a just value" on a subject of investigation.[1] Sympathetic sensitivity to the thoughts, feelings, and activities of religious people played a crucial role in the descriptive or existential elements of James's study. Without it, he did not think he could possibly describe religious life adequately. His "Certain Blindness" argument had convinced him of that. But investigation, as James understood it, did not end in sympathy. Investigation was geared to establish conclusions about what to believe. It was meant to fix beliefs based on criticism. Hence, criticism was the purpose of James's lectures on the value of saintliness.

The task was complex for several reasons. First, James's Darwinism committed him to the assumption that everything investigable was some sort of historical entity. This, in turn, led him to claim that, a priori, there was no one standard of human achievement against which to measure the saintly methods of devotion, purity, charity, and asceticism. Within the empirical setting that his Darwinism permitted, according to James, "we have merely to collect things together without any special a priori theological system, and out of an aggregate of piecemeal judgments as to the value of this and that experience—judgments in which our general philosophical prejudices, our instincts, and our common sense are our only guides—decide that on the whole one type of religion is approved by its fruits, and another type condemned" (*VRE*, 327).

Second, James's "appreciation" had two levels. He not only subjected saintliness to his brand of criticism but also attempted to persuade his listeners that his methods of criticism were better than both the "mystical" methods of criticism that were associated in various ways with revivalism and transcendentalism and the "philosophical" methods that were associated with dogmatic college theologians and religious thinkers professing modern idealism at places like Edinburgh and Harvard.

Third, the kind and magnitude of James's "appreciation" complicated his work. From one angle, of course, James contributed to a debate among intellectuals about the legitimacy of religious thought and activity in modern culture. But James assumed that intellectuals participated in debates of this sort for great social stakes. If they were university professors engaged in liberal education, they trained both leaders and an influential part of the franchise that elected those leaders. Thus they, indirectly at least, set the tone and direction of nations! From this angle, James's effort to establish a Darwinian science of religions was fundamentally ideological in that sense of the term which implies a battle for the mind of "the people."

Fourth and finally, James's perduring commitment to the Romantic norm of inclusive integration or the 'harmony out of many' principle inclined his criticism in ways that provided room for both diversity of religious thought and action and enough mutuality to encourage equilibrium. He tried to develop a method of appreciation that did not sacrifice religious particularity to demands for religious unity, but also that did not permit religious particularity to become religious sectarianism.

In the long run, the way that the Romantic vision of "distinctions without division" shaped James's appreciative venture gave the lie to Santayana's influential claim that James "did not really believe; he merely believed in the right of believing that you might be right if you believed."[2] James made it crystal clear in his lectures on the value of saintliness that he believed. He believed in specific *principles of salvation* and that certain truths held concerning man and his situation which credited those principles. But he distinguished between *principles* of salvation, which federated religious peoples, and religious *opinions*, which differentiated them. He did this in order to retain the intellectual creations of "spontaneous" religious experience and to perfect them by denying their pretensions to absolute liberty. He tried to provide the diversity of religions with principles of cooperative liberty—English liberty, Mill's liberty, the liberty that he thought was more at home in the first new and non-monarchial nation than in the land of its birth.

In sum, James's Darwinism, its historicism and its opposition to predominant modes of religious appreciation or criticism; the ultimately ideological context in which he placed his appreciation; and his overriding commitment to the norm of inclusive integration— all made "spiritual judgment" of religion in James's lectures a very complex affair.

James's Darwinism: The Survival of the Humanly Fittest

James set out to decide which types of religion were approved and which types condemned. He claimed that his approach to this set of decisions was piecemeal, not systematic. The standards that he used to judge the various sorts of religion consisted of "our general philosophical prejudices, our instincts, and our common sense" (VRE, 327), although he felt sure that this approach seemed "form-less" to many, and worse, totally "illogical" to many more.

To begin with, orthodox minds, of whatever religious opinion and of whatever institutional affiliation, were bound to claim that James was wrongheaded when he made conduct the primary target of appreciation. Sectarians asserted that one could not measure the worth of types of religion "without considering whether the God really exists who is supposed to inspire them." They were also inclined to claim that if a god really exists, "then all the conduct instituted by men to meet his wants must necessarily be a reasonable fruit of his religion" (VRE, 327).

On paper, James suggested, this "epistemological" approach to the problem of religious appreciation appeared convenient. But this appearance of facility evaporated when it was put into practice because there was no widely accepted method for adjudicating relevant disputes about the existence and nature of gods. The approach, James asserted, did not work, because it led to impasse: it inevitably ended in a sort of debate in which proponents placed beyond criticism precisely those claims that opponents sought to place in jeopardy, or submit to doubt. This made the task of appreciation interminable: when the quest for divine knowledge served as propaedeutic to the evaluation of religious life, the former enterprise never stopped and the latter one never started.

So James turned the standard "epistemological" approach to the problem of religious appreciation on its head. He subordinated issues concerning beliefs to issues concerning practice and made the evaluation of theological theses a subsequent and consequent (but *not* trivial) step dependent on the appreciation of religious conduct.

James appeared, however, to be trying to have his cake and eat it too when it came to the problem of appreciation. On the one hand, he announced that he was not going to play according to his competitor's rules, because they inevitably led to impasse. In this regard, he claimed that his method of appreciation was not strictly dependent on, or opposed to, the truth-claims of various and diverse theologies. But, on the other hand, he proposed to evaluate religious conduct according to "prejudices," "common sense," and "instincts," concepts that were both theologically relevant and partial. What is more, they were standards that he *brought* to his investigation of religions and, hence, a priori standards in a fairly classical connotation of that term.

James, then, did not derive his appreciation of religions from a consideration of observations of religious conduct alone, but from such an inspection *as informed* by beliefs or standards of appropriateness that were, for the most part, inherited and assumed by his "age." Thus, he appeared to be arguing *with* theologians by pitting the a priori claims of "common sense" *against* the a priori claims of religious schools and sects. In a limited way, in fact, James admitted vulnerability here: he said that "if disbeliefs can be said to constitute a theology, then the prejudices, instincts, and common sense which I chose as our guides make theoretical partisans of us whenever they make certain beliefs abhorrent" (*VRE*, 328).

But James did not think this admission placed him in any great jeopardy. According to him, his criteria for the evaluation of religions were held prior to any specific investigation of religion and, hence, were relatively a priori in character. But unlike those who measured the worth of religions against "revelations" that were purportedly "eternal" and, hence, beyond the range of criticism, James claimed that his relatively a priori criteria were "themselves the fruit of an empirical evolution." He claimed that his common sense was "begotten out of the drift of common life. It is the voice of human experience within us, judging and condemning all gods that stand athwart the pathway along which it feels itself to be advancing" (*VRE*, 328, 330).

Thus, James thought that while commonsense standards were relatively a priori, their genesis was empirical in the sense that it was historically specifiable. Further, they were subject to correction, modification, or even neglect by experience, both present and future. James argued that theological modes of appreciation led to impasse because they placed all the weight of their procedure on beliefs that were themselves the focus of dispute. He thought that his mode of appreciation escaped this problem, first, because common sense was constituted by beliefs that were not currently disputed and, second, because his "philosophical prejudices" disposed him to organize evaluation in ways that permitted equilibrium between contending religious parties, not impasse. His criteria were developmental, he argued, because they constantly, if slowly, could adapt to and accommodate novel circumstances. He reasoned that if these points were sound, the formal inconsistency that theologians might charge against his methods of appreciation was "immaterial, and the charge may be neglected" (VRE, 331).

Thus, James proceeded to claim that if the saintly methods commend themselves, then "any theological beliefs" that might inspire them "in so far forth will stand accredited" (VRE, 331). If, for example, a certain sort of asceticism was commendable, then so was belief in the powers that helped to engender it (no matter how those powers were specified) so long as the specification of those powers was not deployed to authorize condemnable conduct as well.

In its particulars, James's method of appreciation was modeled on Darwin's doctrine of natural selection: "It is but the elimination of the humanly unfit and the survival of the humanly fittest, applied to religious beliefs" (VRE, 331). James asserted that religions approved themselves when they met "vital needs" and, thus, stood in need of no apology. But when they violated other needs too strongly or when competitive religions served the same needs better, they were, or at least they should have been, eliminated from historical transmission.

As a matter of historical fact, James claimed, "no religion has ever yet owed its prevalence to 'apodictic certainty.'" In every historical instance, he argued, "the gods we stand by are the gods we need and can use, the gods whose demands on us are reinforcements of our demands on ourselves and on one another" (VRE, 331–32). However, this line of thought was open to a major objection. James appeared to be establishing the reasons *why* religions had achieved success. But even if his analysis was adequate, giving the "causal" reasons why something was achieved was hardly tantamount to giving reasons *for* retaining or selectively reforming this or that sort of religion now. Darwin's model might serve to account for natural selection—that is, telically blind selection—but it did not, on its surface, account for *rational* selection, the sort of selection a scientist of religions ought to be interested in.

But James argued, in turn, that Darwin's model could be harnessed to the uses of rational selection because humans were *agents* of historical change and, more specifically, because some human agents of change systematically and methodically deployed relevant problem-solving instruments to bring their transformations about. Darwin's model was genuinely adaptable to questions of rational selection because it avoided the genetic fallacy and made the verisimilitude of beliefs or theories subordinate in importance to their function.

According to James, the key notions of rational assessment were 'demand' and 'satisfaction', not 'logical form' and 'truth'. The rationality of religious beliefs or total views was ascertained by appreciating the activities inspired by them. This conduct, in turn, was appreciated by judging the extent to which it solved outstanding problems that stood in the way of satisfying demands that were claimed by actual persons.

James argued that if saintliness overcame problems or managed difficulties that a person had, it was an instrument of progress: it helped to satisfy certain specifiable needs. He argued further that if it was practically impossible for saints to exemplify the saintly methods without crediting unseen powers for helping them or if giving up the feeling or thought of divinity made the saintly methods negligible, then it was irrational to give up the feeling or thought of divinity! On the other hand, when we no longer approved what the definition of a god implied insofar as conduct was concerned, "we end[ed] by deeming that deity incredible" (*VRE*, 329). If a god reinforced illegitimate demands, he was himself illegitimate.

James gave this illustration. Once his Calvinist ancestors construed their deity as a coercive monarch. Many of their beliefs about this deity were implications of his all-powerful sovereignty and absolute liberty to coerce his subjects to do this or that—in arbitrary ways. Edwards, for instance, was able to persuade himself that the arbitrary doling out of salvation and damnation to select individuals was a doctrine "exceeding pleasant, bright, and sweet." But if people were committed to the ideals of a federal republic, they did not need such a deity to help them when they could not help themselves to live in light of those ideals. In fact, they needed to abandon a god who turned out, from their perspective, to represent evil (coercion) more suitably than good (persuasion).

They had no use for a god who was simply a more powerful and cunning exemplar of the sovereign monarchs that they had emigrated to escape. If there were good reasons to believe that the premises of the republic were better than others with which they competed, there were also good reasons to find an absolutely sovereign deity "sovereignly irrational and mean" (*VRE*, 330).

This illustration clarified James's Darwinian position on the problem of rational appreciation. Some beliefs were rational for some persons and irrational for others. This made no sense when verisimilitude, "objective truth," or "apodictic certainty" was a sine qua non for rationality. But it made good sense when rationality was analyzed in terms of demands, satisfaction, and problems that stood in the way of satisfaction. The definitions of these three things were infamous for their variability across cultures and for their mutability over time, but they were not either fruitless or arbitrary. When rational judgments were analyzed according to demands and satisfactions, they were bound to be set historically, to be comparative in force, and to be subject to correction in light of new information. The question was never simply What is the rational value of this activity or that belief? The question confronting the "rational" agent of transformation was Does this activity or that belief solve a problem that people have lived with (historically) better than its predecessors and contemporary competitors (and in ways that clarify both the adequacies and inadequacies of other attempts at solution)? In sum, for James, persons were rational when they made progress, not progressive when they were rational (a doctrine typically held by rationalists in James's day).

The saintly methods were habitual ways of doing things for the sake of salvation or well-being, which was *the* religious problem in Western culture as James understood it. To appreciate them was to judge their suitability to the task. Of course, specifications of the task had changed as culture reached for "the more inclusive order." But these changes, whatever their origins, had been subjected to the tests of trial and error, tests that were themselves transforming. To appreciate the saintly methods from James's admittedly selective and corrigible perspective, they had to be tested by their "economical relations" (*VRE*, 374).

Darwin's doctrine of natural selection was predictive: if there were variations, if these were inherited, if one variant was more suited to some task than another, and if success in accomplishing that task affected the ability of the organism to survive in whatever happened to be its environment, then natural selection would produce an evolutionary change. James's method of appreciation was more prescriptive than predictive. Nonetheless, it was conditional and modeled fairly rigorously on Darwin's understanding of historical transmission. James claimed that if there were variations in social activities, and if these had been organized methodically by social groups, and if one of these variants was more suited to some task than were other variants, and if the success in accomplishing that task affected the ability of the society to satisfy its own demands, then "rational" agents should dispose themselves to it and, hence, effect an evolutionary change in social activity (including social thought).

In these regards, James followed the path that he had pioneered in "Great Men and Their Environment" and laid out even more specifically in "The Moral Philosopher and the Moral Life" (1891). There he had claimed that when social life was sanguine, persons measured the value of their activities as they fit standards of appropriateness shared by their group. But history demanded open-mindedness. Sometimes persons questioned shared standards of appropriateness. Then the connections between rationality and allegiance to systems of spiritual judgment broke down, and the relations between rationality and objectives or demands became apparent. Darwin's introduction of the notion of *spontaneous variation* gave social thinkers a way to analyze revolutionary change without sacrificing recognition of historical continuity. His model of interaction between variations and selection made the notion that rationality was a matter of open-minded progress defensible (cf. *WTB*, 157–58).

With these doctrines of rational appreciation in hand, James inspected the saintly methods of devotion, purity, charity, and asceticism. Given "the religious demand" for well-being, James queried, should saintly conduct be retained, abandoned, or readjusted? He asked whether saintly conduct better achieved a task or set of tasks than competitive sorts of conduct, in ways that affected the abilities of humanity to achieve the salvations that persons sought.

The question, James admitted, was vague, and the answer required by it was imprecise. What is more, James claimed that any critic who asked the question was "too close to the struggle not to be to some degree a participant, and he is sure to approve most warmly those fruits of piety in others which taste most good and prove most nourishing to him." In other words, James admitted that both personal tenacity and social inclination inevitably played roles in the appreciation of any human conduct, including religious conduct. But this did not mean anarchy so far as rational selection was concerned. Far from assuming that there was one right sort of religious conduct, James, with his philosophical prejudices, was committed to the presumption that there must be many right sorts because there were "different functions in the organism of humanity allotted to different types of man," hence, for instance, "religions of consolation and re-assurance" for some and religions of "terror and reproof" for others (*VRE*, 333–34).

Then too, the question of appreciation was made more complex because of varying conceptions of cultural desiderata. Religion competed with moral materialism. Religionists of whatever stripe contrasted saintly methods with those of "strongmen," whether characterized in either economic or military terms, whereas Nietzsche approved the methods of the latter and ridiculed those of the saints. As James understood him, Nietzsche thought that saintly methods were literally dangerous, weakening the race and making perfection less possible. According to Nietzsche, saints were "sophisticated" invalids, degenerates, men of "insufficient vitality" (*VRE*, 372).

James construed Nietzsche as representing moral materialism and took the feud between that attitude and moral idealism very seriously. He saw it as revolving around two points: first, "shall the seen world or the unseen world be our chief sphere of adaptation?" and, second, "must our means of adaptation in this seen world be aggressiveness or non-resistance?" If the sensible world alone set demands on human conduct, then unseen realities were irrelevant to the task of appreciation. But if the material world was set within a "wider" spiritual one, then both material and ideal requirements played their roles in evaluation. In light of these debates, James asked, how was success to be measured absolutely "when there are so many environments and so many ways of looking at the adaptation." He asserted quite simply, though not simplistically, that success "cannot be measured absolutely; the verdict will vary according to the point of view adopted" (*VRE*, 373, 376).

If this was so, then any appreciation of saintliness was ultimately conditional, dependent on goals that persons set for themselves and on problems that they met when they attempted to actualize those goals. If people were idealists and imagined the "millennium" as a society "in which there should be no aggressiveness, but only sympathy and fairness, then the habitual love of saints appeared entirely adapted to it." In such a social environment, still ideal and yet to be actualized, the saint's "peaceful modes of appeal would be efficacious over his companions, and there would be no one extant to take advantage of his non-resistance." Then the saint would be "adapted to the highest society conceivable, whether that society ever be concretely possible or not" (*VRE*, 375). Nietzsche's superman, to the contrary, would undercut its order. But, James warned, if people estimated saintly conduct, say charity, from the vantage point of this "concrete world" and not simply from a millennial point of view, the "just value" of religious conduct was bound to change.

Perfect human conduct, James claimed, was "a relation between three terms," not simply a matter of measuring the fit between two independent variables, say, organism and environment. Conduct was not perfect when an agent successfully executed an intention or materialized an idea. Human conduct was inevitably *social* conduct. The three variables of conduct included "the actor, the objects for which he acts, and the recipients of the action" (*VRE*, 355). In perfect conduct, James claimed,

> intention, execution, and reception should be suited to one another. Thus no critic or estimator of the value or conduct can confine himself to the actor's animus alone, apart from the other elements of the performance. As there is no worse lie that a truth misunderstood by those who hear it, so reasonable arguments, challenges to magnanimity, and appeals to sympathy or justice, are folly when we are dealing with human crocodiles and boa-constrictors. The saint may simply give the universe into the hands of the enemy by his trustfulness. He may by non-resistance cut off his own survival. [*VRE*, 355]

Thus, so far as the actual, as opposed to either the material or the spiritual, world was concerned, both strongmen and saints might be required, the former to assure the survival of culture, the latter to signal and activate the premises or ideals that animated it.

"Let Us Be Saints"

Within the context of his Darwinian mode of appreciation, James argued that neither total retention nor total elimination of the saintly methods was in order. Readjustment was. As he saw it, the religious tradition in the West was multistranded and fraught with paradox. On the one hand, the tradition presented various salvific visions of heaven on earth which informed and animated social, political, economic, and personal life. On the other hand, Western religious history was soaked in blood shed by those who were orthodox, zealous, and intellectually feeble or mean.

The distinction that James had made between personal piety and institutional religion was *diagnostic*, an attempt to divide religion as it appeared to him into its healthy and diseased elements. James made the distinction between "religion as a personal function, and religion as an institutional, corporate, or tribal product" in order to solve the problem of religion as he understood it. He did so to recommend retention of what was vital both to personal well-being and to his nation's ideals while eliminating the sociality of coercion that inevitably undercut somebody's well-being and corrupted American religion.

James argued that piety or the saintly habits were distinguishable from religion's "wicked partners," corporate and dogmatic dominion, just as an elixir was distinguishable from poison. Friedrich von Hügel to the contrary,[3] James's argument did not pit the personal and the private against the social experience—on James's grounds both individuals and their religions were inevitably social. James pit the sociality of persuasion—the sociality of friends and compatriots—against the sociality of coercion—the sociality of sovereigns and subjects. Indeed, nothing could be clearer than the sociality of James's vision when he rhapsodized on behalf of saintliness. James warned that

> were the world confined to . . . hard-headed, hard-hearted, and hard-fisted methods exclusively, were there no one prompt to help a brother first, and find out afterwards whether he were worthy, no one willing to drown his private wrongs in pity for the wronger's person; no one ready to be duped many a time rather than live always on suspicion; no one glad to treat individuals passionately and impulsively rather than by general rules of prudence; the world would be an infinitely worse place than it is now to live in. The tender grace, not of a day that is dead, but of a day yet to be born somehow, with the golden rule grown natural, would be cut out from the perspective of our imaginations. [*VRE*, 356]

Specified this way, saintly conduct was not culpable for "the baiting of Jews, the hunting of Albigenses and Waldenses, the stoning of Quakers and the ducking of Methodists, the murdering of Mormons and the massacring of Armenians" (*VRE*, 338). But religious people had done all of these things—and out of inspirations they understood as religious.

No matter how these religious executioners understood themselves, James could analyze their atrocities social-psychologically as the result of certain compulsions. Tribal instincts made them blind to the spiritual lives of their victims. Their coercion was a product of that "aboriginal neophobia, that pugnacity of which we all share the vestiges, and that inborn hatred of the alien and of the eccentric and non-conforming men as aliens" (*VRE*, 338). Piety often masked these compulsions, and dogmatic religious formulas often rationalized them, but spiritual blindness caused by tribal instinct was basically to blame for these horrors, not either transaction with divinity per se or the devotion, purity of heart, charity, and asceticism that were characteristic of the best results of religious experience.

But if this was the case, James asked rhetorically, why did persons find the lives of saints so inappropriate, so contrary to the norms of conduct associated with "science, idealism, and democracy"? They tended to praise saints for their devotion, humility, poverty, and singleness of purpose, and they admired the passion with which saints accomplished their tasks. But saints appeared both too excessive and too extravagant for mass imitation. Besides, many saints celebrated as heroes of religious history were disposed to religious objects and objectives that contemporary persons no longer admired.

The saints of history seemed to suffer generally from two diseases: "error by excess" and the intellectual limitations of their age. James argued that these diseases were not unrelated. Saints were likely to behave pathologically whenever "other interests [were] too few and the intellect too narrow" (*VRE*, 340). But this typical intellectual feebleness was probably absorbed from the narrow mind-set of their time and place.

According to James, if saintly conduct were readjusted in ways that abandoned close-mindedness, the diseases of religious coercion might be cured. Whether close-mindedness was imputed to the individual alone or to the corporate structures that partly organized his life, it was the culprit that was responsible for the elements of saintly conduct that had to be eliminated to solve James's problem of religion.

James's notions of open- and close-mindedness were bound up with the normative ideal of inclusive integration. In previous work, he had made it clear that the genius of the philosopher lay in his synoptic abilities. The philosopher was able to put his own thought, conditioned as it was by time and place, in perspective and to attempt to harmonize it with differing and conflicting perspectives of other people, even those from other times and other places. When and insofar as the saints suffered from close-mindedness, they were not philosophical. They did not put their own thought into broad perspective, and they did not even attempt to harmonize their thought with differing and conflicting perspectives. To the contrary, close-minded people, including saints, attempted to either absorb or expunge differing and conflicting perspectives and, hence, to maintain the supremacy of thought through strategies of exclusion.

In the extreme, the strategies of close-minded saints resulted in inquisition, execution, and anathema. This sort of behavior, James warned, as well as any belief that legitimized it, had to be eliminated from historical transmission in order to solve his problem of religion. If people committed to "science, democracy, and idealism" admired the felicity, purity, charity, patience, and self-severity of the saints that dotted religious history, they deplored their "holy excesses—fanaticism of theopathic absorption, self-torment, prudery, scrupulosity, gullibility, and morbid inability to meet the world." Their inferior intellect was typically inspired by "paltry ideals" and, as such, "can be even more objectionable and damnable than a superficial carnal man would be in the same situation" (VRE, 370).

But both "narrow intellect" and "paltry ideals" could be abandoned for more synoptic views and a driving concern to harmonize as many human ideals as possible. Animosity toward intellectual imbalance and provincialism should not force anyone to abandon admiration for "the saintly impulses in their essential nature," because they could be informed by the philosophical mentality and redirected toward other and better objectives.

Indeed, James thought that in view of Anglo-American cultural objectives, it was practically unthinkable to consider how the golden rule could become natural without the lives of saints. He argued that the conduct "we" accused saints as exemplifying was dependent upon particular beliefs and doctrines, not bound to the saintly methods as such—beliefs and doctrines that could be eliminated from historical transmission, or transformed, without eliminating religious life. If saintly methods were associated with "superior intellectual sympathies," like "science, democracy, and idealism," religious devotion or piety should bear "useful human fruit."

Informed by republican ideals, methodical purity or love of God included the love of humanity and, indeed, of any man; salvation became reassociated with social responsibility. If charity often led to the preservation of the unfit, the principle of individual human sacrality from which this charity was derived stood at the heart of the doctrine of English liberty. So even if the nonresisting saint was ill-adapted to the world as it stood, "he makes converts, and the environment gets better for his ministry. He is an effective ferment of goodness, a slow transmitter of the earthly into a more heavenly order" (*VRE*, 360).

James claimed that charity and asceticism were the most useful saintly methods for treating the problems of the culture as he saw them. The extravagant tenderness of the saint might spell disaster if widely imitated in a world still populated by human "crocodiles and boa-constrictors." But, limited to religious geniuses, the disposition was socially creative. They struck at the heart of materialism and imperialism and, in the doing, served as "practical proof" that private interests could be transcended. Because they were individuals devoted to the spiritual lives of others, they were harbingers of "a more heavenly order." The saints presented a "magic gift to mankind" as exemplars of "the golden rule grown natural."

James argued that asceticism was the most distinctively religious of the saintly methods and that it was the most effective bulwark against encroaching moral materialism. On James's reading, it was the element of saintliness that had most to teach "the modern imagination." He suggested that, of course, "the general optimism and healthy-mindedness of liberal Protestant circles today makes mortification for mortification's sake repugnant to us. We no longer sympathize with cruel deities, and the notion that God can take delight in the spectacle of sufferings self-inflicted in his honor is abhorrent" (*VRE*, 362).

But to identify asceticism with mortification for its own sake was to equate a kind of conduct with a subspecies of it. Ascetic conduct at its most general and inclusive level expressed "the belief that there is an element of real wrongness in the world, which is neither to be ignored nor evaded, but which must be squarely met and overcome by an appeal to the soul's heroic resources, and neutralized and cleansed away by sufferings" (*VRE*, 362). This, James suggested, was the heart not only of twice-born religion but of religious consciousness per se. Asceticism was simply another name for religious heroism. A religious individual who was both optimistic and methodically ignorant of evil might reject the significance of this sort of heroism. But on the grounds of inclusive integration, his attitude must be rejected as a solution to the religious demand for well-being because it failed to take account of tragic, melioristic, and pessimistic sensibilities. Once persons sympathized with the plight of the pessimistic and the melancholic, pure optimism and the studied ignorance of evil had to be deprecated as so much self-deception.

If this was so, ascetic discipline had to be renovated in ways that would make it "objectively"—that is, publicly and socially—useful. In Victoria's era, he suggested, methodical asceticism was associated with militarism. The character who exhibited ascetic discipline, who was severe with himself in his service, was the warrior. But his motive for self-severity was battle effectiveness. His inspiration was the opposite of the saint's desire to live and let live. His interest was not harmony, and his principle of conduct was not persuasion. Rather, his interest was destruction, and his principle was coercion. His profession was, therefore, a "wholesale organization of irrationality and crime." What moderns needed to discover then, "in the social realm," was "the moral equivalent of war." On the assumption that materialism was republican society's most debilitating internal disease, voluntarily accepted poverty was the moral equivalent of war. Asceticism was the only sort of strenuous life to which moderns could devote themselves that did not involve "crushing weaker people" (VRE, 367). It was just "the spiritual reform which our time stands in need of," marked as the age was by the bloodstains of the bitch-goddess success and imperial armies.

Convinced that his culture could be served neither by irreligion nor by dogmatic or imperialistic religion, James set himself the task of articulating ways to retain the piety inherited by his society but to eliminate the close-mindedness associated with it. Sectarians were, once again, subordinating their heads to their hearts, whereas educated people were slipping back into the sort of Enlightenment thinking that subordinated heart to head. The optimal solution was to show that head and heart were not effectively dissociable and that broad-minded people were big-hearted and vice versa.

The first step in this campaign was to overcome materialism, or that "spirit of capitalism," in the English-speaking world that encouraged its citizens to despise "anyone who elects to be poor in order to simplify and save his inner life." Anglo-Americans, James said, found it difficult if not impossible to imagine the ancient ideal of poverty. "The liberation from material attachment, the unbribed soul, the manlier indifference, the paying our way by what we are or do and not by what we have" all seemed rather inappropriate to those who led the republic and set its tone (VRE, 368).

Thus, James called up historical precedents of asceticism to challenge the emerging assumption of materialism in the English-speaking world. He declared that it was time for thinking men to protest and to criticize "so unmanly and irreligious a state of opinion." He warned that the "prevalent fear of poverty among the educated classes is the worst moral disease from which our civilization suffers" (VRE, 368). Moreover, he suggested that this fear would be overcome only when materialism was overcome and that materialism would be overcome only when the educated classes began adapting themselves to the unseen or ideal world that animated their civilization, instead of to the seen and material one. Educated persons would do this when they realized that they must adapt themselves to an unseen world in order to solve the wrongness about them as it naturally stood. In other words, they would do this by disposing themselves to a religious attitude.

With this line of thought, James's appreciation of saintliness came to a—not *the*—conclusion. He claimed that his criticism of saintliness by "practical common sense and the empirical method" had left it "in possession of its towering place in history. Economically, the saintly group of qualities is indispensable to the world's welfare." Without asceticism, charity, and devotion to "a more heavenly order," the world's well-being and peace were simply the dream of sick men yearning for a cure. Whatever their opinions, dogmas, doctrines, and formulas, influential men must exemplify these principles of salvation in their lives. Mankind had to dispose itself to cooperation with unseen powers in order to build a universe strong enough to withstand the chaos that constantly threatened it. Hence, James announced a rather conclusive recommendation: "Let us be saints . . . whether or not we succeed visibly and temporally" (*VRE*, 377). James's appreciation of saintliness, the best consequence of the most distinctive sort of religious performance, issued in a definite and positive order. He thought that a just value had been set. If "we" became saints, "we" would herald and leaven a more heavenly order. He exonerated us to try to make saintliness habitual, for without the saintly methods, establishment of the sociality of persuasion was practically unthinkable.

Much of the force of this plea, of course, had to be read as directed to a particular sort of person. "We" had to be saints if "we" could. "We" were *thinking* or *philosophically minded* Anglo-Americans, confronted with irreligion, on the one hand, and an array of conflicting religious sects and schools, on the other. If "we" could be saints, then faith would complement open-mindedness and the atrocities of religion might become a thing of the past. If and when philosophical men became religious in the active sense of saintly or religious men realized the indissoluble link between broad and open minds and big hearts, the historical breach between "religion" and "science" could be healed, with religion restored to its rightful place in the social economy.

James's imperative, to be sure, was conditional. Educated Anglo-Americans should become saints *if they could*. Saints acted out of kinds of inspiration that few persons experienced. Their habits were formed out of religious experiences that were strong enough to overcome "natural" and "prudent" inhibitions inevitably felt by most. If educated men were able to become saints, they would be enabled by powers that surpassed their ordinary and deliberate ones. Hence, educated men should accept cooperative powers that came their way when and if they came. Consummate religious experience could not be deliberately engineered; it was simply a matter of chance. James felt certain that if historical precedent proved anything, it proved that people realized saintliness as much despite as in light of their best efforts.

So James's recommendation urged thinking men who received the requisite sense of inspired well-being to accept the new energies that they were given and to dispose themselves to the sociality of total persuasion if and when those modes of conduct became options for them. Thinking men should dispose themselves to saintly methods if they could, despite manifest failures to achieve the more heavenly order that lured them. Religiousness was always a gamble that, as James once put it, no insurance company would cover. But from the vantage point of James's practical religious pluralism, the only alternative to such gaming was bankruptcy, which was no honorable alternative at all.

James did not recommend any sort of religious uniformity, though he was urging basic unanimity on the most general outlines of religious methods of life, as well as the form and principle of salvation. He sought common agreement on the methods that people used when they were saints, on the sort of order that was heavenly —one constituted out of necessity by many—and on the principle of order that assured that form—the principle of persuasion. But he thought that reaching agreement on these issues left room for religious particularity by leaving the questions of specific belief alone.

James argued, in sum, that readjusted to meet current theoretical and practical needs, the general policies of piety were better for "handling the gift of existence" than was moralism—which was operative, not cooperative—militarism—which was destructive and coercive, not integrative and persuasive—or materialism, which turned everything into a commodity to be used or abused. From James's religious perspective, moralism, militarism, and materialism undercut the promise of humanity.

James's call to become saintly brought his religious investigations to their most practical conclusions. He had described "full" religious facts in their variety and had investigated the habits that saints had committed themselves to in order to "decide how far the religious life commends itself as an ideal kind of human activity." As a harbinger and leavener of the more heavenly order that Anglo-Americans in his class yearned for, it more than commended itself, James claimed.

But the point that James reached was penultimate because the ultimate purpose of the investigation was to make a persuasive case for "the supernatural." His recommendation to be saintly carried this case with it, but only implicitly. The case for the supernatural had to be explicated. Before James did this, however, he had to persuade his audience that his Darwinian mode of appreciation was better than the revelatory modes of appreciation employed by mystics and philosophers.

Mystical Experience and Mystical Appreciation

If James's opponents were right, the best way to appreciate religions was to establish the veracity or the verisimilitude of the theological claims that informed them. Hence, James admitted that "the plot inevitably thickens upon us, we cannot escape theoretical considerations" (VRE, 377). The issue that James faced was whether the two prominent varieties of theological appreciation in his intellectual world were better suited to the task of evaluating religious thought and action than was his own humanism.

James suggested that the three methods that competed for the allegiance of thinking men who were concerned with suitably transforming religion were personal tenacity, philosophical speculation, and experimental inquiry. Mystics made a virtue of personal tenacity. They held a doctrine of religious appreciation that made the value of religious life a function of the veracity of religious testimony, just as many philosophers did. But their position was distinguished from the philosopher's, in that mystics claimed that the testimony of religious witnesses—that is, people who had encountered divinity—was intellectually authoritative. Mystics claimed that religious truth was revealed to individuals in events that were totally private. They claimed that the religious testimony that emerged from religious experiences was self-validated and that whatever people *did* in consequence of such experiences was legitimized by revelation.

As James characterized the mystic, his faith was steady and immovable. He was a throwback to a prescientific age, when sensible evidence was subordinated to the testimony of witnesses and the

authority of books. Mystics based their opinions on their own witness and on the authority of their own books reporting revelation.

Of course, James meant two different things when he inspected
and criticized "mysticism." On the one hand, mysticism was a profession that truth could be "seen" in a "special manner." On the
other, it was a distinctive state of consciousness. James himself
depended on the actuality of mystical states of consciousness to initiate his investigations of religious experience. But the whole point
of his inquiry was "to keep the testimony of religious experience
clearly within its proper bounds" (VRE, 378, 526). This involved
curbing the mystics' pretensions to intellectual—and ultimately
practical—authority.

Mystical states of consciousness stood at the "root and center" of
personal religious experience, according to James (VRE, 379). But
describing religious experience as totally informing for religious
geniuses did not warrant affirming revelations as true for everybody. So mysticism as a psychologically compulsive state of mind
had to be distinguished from mysticism as a doctrine about the
authorization of particular religious thoughts and activities. Both
revivalists and Romantics were right to insist on the occurrence of
nonrational revelations, and even to presume their significance or
importance. But the very things that made these mental states special—a combination of their privacy and their compulsiveness—ultimately bankrupted them as ways of settling dispute and doubt.
When mysticism was taken as intellectually authoritative, it became
a hindrance to persuasive order. James thought that this was so
because if mystics were honest in their reports about mystical experience, they literally were unable to help believing as they did.
But the process of persuasion was suited only to people who actively
sought opinions in an ordered way or, in other words, who helped
themselves decide what to believe.

Mystical states of consciousness were distinguished from "ordinary," "deliberate" consciousness. They were ineffable because they
eluded articulation during and after their occurrence; "noetic," or
qualitatively cognitive, because they included "objects of consciousness"; and transient. Moreover, they were passive because those
undergoing them experienced a surrender of their selves to some
thing or some other.

Characterized this way, mysticism was in direct competition with
scientific inquiry as a way of thinking. Although inquiry and mysticism did share a claim to cognitivity, they were at odds in almost
every other respect when the fact of a mystical experience was used
to justify a doctrine of criticism. Inarticulateness and mystery bat-

tled discourse and clarification; transiency fought cumulation; compulsiveness stood at odds with informed selection. Finally, and perhaps most importantly, the witness of men and the authority of books confronted experiment and experience.

As James characterized it, mysticism was no marginal religious phenomenon. Reports of "illumination" dotted both religious and secular histories. The most rudimentary sort of "illumination" occurred whenever some "deepened sense of the significance" of something swept over one (VRE, 382). Certain déjà vu experiences and trance states were more complex forms of the same phenomenon. In each of these instances, persons felt rational, as they found themselves being transported from some sort of disturbance to a sense of mental ease, peace, and rest. Mystics were struck by these experiences precisely because they clarified what before was shadowed by darkness.

The same sort of transition occurred in experiences of intoxication, according to James: both alcohol and nitrous oxide experiments had stimulated mystical consciousness "to an extraordinary degree" (VRE, 387). Whatever the veracity of the assertions made in their wake, these experiences gave notice to various forms of consciousness. All that was required for discovery was the requisite stimuli.

The question that James raised, then, was not *whether* mystical states of consciousness existed but "how to regard them . . . for they are so discontinuous with ordinary consciousness" (VRE, 388). Mystical states were not states in which reasoning of any sort went on, but they determined attitudes and opened regions of experience not accessible to ordinary modes of thought. As such they could be "metaphysically significant." They might signal something about the meaning of experience that was not discovered in any other way.

Indeed, when James investigated contemporary mystical literature, he was struck by the references in practically all of them to experiences of deliverance. This deliverance corroborated the Romantic vision in which spirit soaked up and absorbed nature into itself, overcoming chaos in a climacteric production of harmonious order. But the question was whether this revelation was a cultural derivative of natural supernaturalism or some independent warrant for it. Many Romantics, for example, Wordsworth, placed the "illuminated moment" at the center of their imagination. They sought or found apocalyptic visions that effaced personal consciousness and rendered it "cosmic" and bestowed a selfless perspective from which they could view the world of impersonal worths.[4]

Among the important historical precedents for the Romantic moment, followers of the *Yogic* tradition in India, Hindus seeking *samadhi*, and Buddhists seeking *dhyana* cultivated "consciousness of illumination." So did the *Sufis* among the Moslems and, closer to home, the medieval Christians in their spiritual exercises.

Mystics justified their claims to religious knowledge by virtue of their achievement of it through revelation or illumination. This, of course, was an argument from origin. They claimed that their deliverances carried the one requisite mark which made them incorrigible: they were illuminated or revelatory deliverances. According to mystics, this made them intuitive; they went without saying. Indeed, they claimed that because their deliverances were intuitive, they were not open to dispute. They were declarations based on evidence, but privileged evidence, evidence shared by the mystic and God alone. Thus, James said, "mystical truth exists for the individual who has the transport, but for no one else." Because its form was "intuitive," it had been "constructed more after the pattern of what in ourselves is called immediate feeling, than after that of proposition or judgment" (*VRE*, 405).

Mystics claimed to know something intuitively. By this they did not mean that they had merely inferred what they claimed to know from other things that they knew. Nor were they simply claiming to have a hunch about something. They were claiming to know something indubitably that could not possibly be inferred from other things they knew. James drew analogies with first-person reports about feelings or sensations, because he assumed that it was never irrational to believe that a person had a feeling once it was known that he believed that he did, even if other, sophisticated investigators doubted his report. But James also assumed that it was not inevitably irrational for sophisticated investigators to challenge such reports either. In these cases, as in mystical ones, justified belief was accompanied by a lack of procedures for settling doubt. Indeed, James suggested, in the face of the doubts of others, the mystic might systematically suppress reasons that could persuade him to change his mind. His own proclamations of helplessness were, in fact, at least rhetorical deflectors of any reasonable debate.

As James understood them, mystical claims were like claims about rock-bottom data of perception, which depended upon privileged access for articulation, much less evaluation. But James thought it was one thing to have an intuition and quite another to construe it as self-certified. Like his mentor Peirce, James thought that this self-certification process amounted to "personal tenacity," a method for fixing belief that he had used as a young and desperate man. So long as this method of tenacity worked, according to James, it was strong, simple, and direct. Persons who used it did not waste time trying to deliberate about what to think. They dismissed reason. But problems arose when other persons began to report contrary or even contradictory rock-bottom observations. The mystics who delivered their illuminations did not come equipped with any acceptable way of adjudicating issues arising from competition. They asserted that their claims were indubitable. But James argued that if plenty of people actually doubted the illuminations of mystics, their claims were quite dubitable. The problem was that mystical claims permitted disputes that were nonadjudicable along accepted lines of resolution.[5]

James argued that people could not assume that mystical claims were indubitable simply because they could not point to any existing method for settling disputes about them. But he also argued that his science of religions provided ways to settle disputes about mystical claims that mystics had no way to settle themselves. James's aim was to appreciate the mystical states of consciousness that generated those claims as well as to inspect religious conduct informed by them. When he turned to the practical consequences of mystical consciousness, he found, not surprisingly, that they recapitulated the range of results from religious experience more broadly conceived. They ran the gamut from utterly passive to utterly energetic sorts of behavior. They were sometimes informed by close-mindedness, sometimes by synoptic vision. Thus, he argued that the possibility of appreciating mystical consciousness "in general" was as hopeless as treating any other part of religious life that way.

To be sure, mystical states of mind might result in the most energetic inspiration, but on the mystics' own grounds, "this could be reckoned an advantage only in case the inspiration were a true one. If the inspiration were erroneous, the energy would be all the more mistaken and misbegotten." But here, James suggested, mysticism as a tradition of religious appreciation reached impasse. In light of the great diversity of "illuminations," the problem of religious appreciation was not solved but redoubled. The crucial question for James was whether "mystical states establish[ed] the truth of those theological affections in which the saintly life has its root" (VRE, 415).

In response to this question, James argued, first, that the beliefs that mystics thought were true were justified in some sense, but the sense was psychological, not epistemological. Just as an individual was warranted to claim that he was in pain once he believed he was, because his feelings of pain were things to which he had privileged access, so mystics were justified in making their rock-bottom claims, once they believed them, because they were "intuitive." It was "vain for rationalism to grumble about this." Rationalists could throw a mystic into a prison or a madhouse, but they "cannot change his mind—we commonly attach it the more stubbornly to its beliefs" (VRE, 423).

As a matter of historical fact, James asserted, rationalists were mocked by mystics when they tried to persuade them to change their minds. Indeed, as a matter of logic, James said, "our own more 'rational' beliefs are based on evidence exactly similar in nature to that which mystics quote for theirs." Just as investigators relied on rock-bottom perceptions for their claims, so mystics relied on "face to face presentations of what seems immediately to exist" (VRE, 423, 424). As such, mystics escaped "our jurisdiction." The only motive for investigation was to overturn doubt and settle belief. Hence, anyone that did not share the doubt that spurred the inquiry escaped its jurisdiction. If the "illumination" of mystical experience brought real and living doubt to an end for someone, he simply had no motive for further investigation, no demand for a change of mind. The mystic simply asserted that his claims were not governed by the logic of inquiry. His experiences resulted in confession, not profession. Indeed, because the mystic's beliefs were confessional, because he could not help believing what he did, he was invulnerable to criticism.

But second, James argued that mystics were not legitimately authoritative for anybody else. Indeed, his declaration of the mystic's right to believe was a backhanded denial of his right to participate in religious investigation. Mystical states might put out the burning doubts of particular individuals, but that did not make mystical claims true. In fact, if mystical claims were confessional, they were not warranted at all. Reasons warranted beliefs, but reasons played no role in confession. Reasons played a role only in cases in which people did not confess but had to decide which, among competing things, to believe. Religious investigators were among those people.

On James's reading, mystics did not typically deal in reasons. Mystics revealed things. They did not, insofar as they were mystics, try to convince themselves or others that their beliefs were more adequate than competing ones according to normal rules of inference. Thus, the utmost that they could ask investigators to do was "to admit that they establish a presumption." To be sure, mystics tended to form a consensus, and their revelations displayed a certain "unanimity." But "unanimity" appealed only to numbers, and "an appeal to numbers has no logical force. If we acknowledge it, it is for suggestive, not for logical reasons. We follow the majority because to do so suits our life" (*VRE*, 424).

In sum, the mystic could not participate in religious investigation and had no procedure to overcome the doubts of people who disputed his declarations. No reasons could change his mind about men, gods, and the world. If others accepted the mystic's claims on mystical grounds, they did so not from force of persuasion but from some sort of purportedly divine coercion that they felt as mystics. So whether mystical experience led to presumptive truths or not, the mystic presented no "infallible credential."

Mystics tried to evaluate religions by the veracity of their beliefs. But they had no way of convincing those who stood in need of it. So their strategy for appreciating religions failed. However, James argued that mystics might well have some things to teach religious investigators. This led to his third claim about mystical consciousness: its very existence toppled the notion that the only sort of consciousness was self-consciousness or reflective consciousness. Mystics did not offer effective arguments that might overcome intellectual impasse, but this failure did not undercut their interpretation of the causes of their beliefs per se; nor did it establish their claim as necessarily false.

Indeed, James suggested, mystical experience served as evidence of abilities to signal events *unreflectively*. In any case, many of the claims that were purported to result from religious experience "point in directions to which the religious sentiments of nonmystical men incline. They tell us about the supremacy of the ideal, of vastness, of union, of safety, and of rest." If investigators were not mystics themselves because they did not confess truths but rather pursued them, the mystics could still "offer us hypotheses, hypotheses which we may voluntarily ignore, but which as thinkers we cannot possibly upset. The supernaturalism and optimism to which they would persuade us may, interpreted one way or another, be after all the truest of insights into the meaning of life." But if these things were the truest of insights, James argued, humanistic appreciation, not mysticism, would demonstrate why. Mystical claims had to be "sifted and tested, and run the gauntlet of confrontation with the total context of experience. . . . Its value must be ascertained by empirical methods so long as we are not mystics ourselves" (*VRE*, 428, 426–27).

In other words, mysticism did not "stamp a warrant of veracity upon the religious man's sense of the divine." It was not a solution to the problem of religion that educated men like James faced; it was part of the problem. As such, it was something to be investigated, something from which religious investigators could selectively reconstruct their own religiousness. But because mysticism did not establish the veracity of any theological claim made by any religion, it failed to fulfill its promise as a tradition of religious appreciation. Mysticism was "too private (and also too various) in its utterances to be able to claim a universal authority" (VRE, 430).

Philosophy as a Tradition of Religious Appreciation

In James's view, the social impulse ultimately bankrupted mysticism as a doctrine of criticism. In the absence of disputes, or disputes taken seriously by mystics, in any case, mysticism worked fine enough for mystics. But persons generally aimed to establish truths that could be shared, and mysticism offered no canons for the establishment of intersubjective truths. The other dominant tradition of religious appreciation did. Philosophy, as represented by Christian theology and modern idealism, diagnosed mysticism as too private and individualistic to settle religious disputes and offered to cure the disease of mysticism by establishing uniform criteria for the adjudication of truth-claims. Philosophers traditionally published "results which claim to be universally valid if they are valid at all" (VRE, 430).

Like mystics, philosophers held a doctrine of religious appreciation that made the value of religion a function of the veracity of religious truth-claims. But unlike mystics, they did not find face-to-face presentations of divinity self-certifying. The various exemplars of "philosophy" tried to ground their evaluations on certain intellectual intuitions, rather than on perceptual ones. They argued ultimately from the meaning of terms or from structures of thought purported to be universal, invariant, and publicly acknowledgeable. Their aim, James asserted, was to construct "religious objects out of the resources of logical reason alone, or of logical reason drawing rigorous inference from non-subjective facts" (VRE, 433). Their method of appreciation was to affirm any belief agreeable to reason and to value any sort of conduct informed by such belief.

The question that James posed in his Gifford Lectures about the philosophical tradition was not epistemologically technical. He did not bring any arguments to bear against any specific doctrine articulated by dogmatic theologians or post-Kantian idealists. He simply questioned whether philosophy had made good on its promise to displace the discordant voices of individual religious geniuses with one universal creed, by establishing universal theological truth. James thought that the answer was an undisputed no.

James was as careful in his discussion of philosophical "rationalism" as he had been in that of mysticism to distinguish the objects of his criticism. His aim was not to criticize rationality per se, or even the intellectual constructions of religious thinkers. His aim was to point out the inadequacies of "rationalism" as a method of settling religious opinions, especially ones about the role of the supernatural in human life. Kant had already asked whether the schools of metaphysicians had ever articulated a method for the adjudication of disputes among themselves and had answered no. Now James asked the question again, only this time he included Kant and post-Kantians among those who suffered from the metaphysicians' disease.

He asserted that the rational task—as distinguished from the rationalist task—was to redeem religion from "unwholesome privacy," to make it something more than the willful adherence to a belief. He said that "it would be strange if I disputed this, when these very lectures which I am giving are (as you will see more clearly from now onwards) a laborious attempt to extract from the privacies of religious experiences some general facts upon which everybody may agree" (*VRE*, 432–33). James asserted the need to moderate and mediate religious disputes and said that his investigations aimed to do just that.

But philosophical rationalism, or "intellectualism" as James began to call it, operated in an a priori way and, quite apart from judging the rationality of religious thought and action, claimed to warrant the veracity of certain religious beliefs. Intellectualists promised to "convince men universally" (*VRE*, 435). Indeed, that was why intellectualists thought their program was superior to mysticism. They aimed to overcome the bifurcations of sect and school and to free religion from subjective sentiment, personal caprice, and waywardness.

James thought he did not need to "discredit philosophy by laborious criticism of its arguments," because "as a matter of history it fails to prove its pretensions to be 'objectively' convincing" (*VRE*, 436). Philosophers themselves formed sects and schools, the very diversity they proposed to cure. The problem with the philosophical tradition, including philosophical theology, was that it promised something that it never delivered. Like the mystical tradition, it operated according to ground rules that inevitably led to intellectual impasse and dispute.

In part, the philosophers aimed for too much. They let their objective be formed by the demands of radical skepticism. In other words, they were motivated to think not by real and living doubts but by any conceivable doubt. Hence, philosophers sought certainty and assumed that their claims had to come to rest on absolutely indubitable propositions, on unshakable "foundations."

But James was convinced that historical inspection demonstrated that philosophers had never succeeded in persuading one another, or anyone else, that the foundations that they argued for withstood the radical skepticism that they intended to overcome. They never constructed epistemological edifices sound enough to please one another, much less to settle the doubts of the doubter who doubted not for his own sake but for doubt's sake.

As James analyzed the enterprise, traditional philosophy or a priori speculation was diseased in a number of ways. By pursuing certainty, and not simply the settlement of opinions of actual people who had real and living doubts, philosophers aimed for something that eluded achievement. Moreover, this pursuance vitiated the force of intellectual authority by making intellectual life a sport in which points were argued for the sake of argument, not for the sake of resolving the problems of men.

When it came to the appreciation of religions, philosophy, like mysticism, cut across sectarian lines. But James asserted that whether philosophers were Protestant, Catholic, idealist, or pagan, they were all committed to the doctrine, actually enunciated by John Caird, that "it is by the content or intelligent basis of a religion, and not by feelings, that its character and worth are to be determined" (VRE, 434). James readily admitted, of course, that any defensible appreciation of religions took into account their "intelligent basis." But he wanted to undermine the philosophers' pretension to secure otherwise doubtable beliefs on the basis of this ploy. He thought that if philosophers could not secure their beliefs the way they promised, they could not "stamp a warrant of veracity upon the religious man's sense of the divine"; and if they failed to do this, their claim to superiority as evaluators of religion was worthless.

With this in mind, James inspected examples of dogmatic theological proofs for the existence and characteristics of God. He claimed that these proofs only corroborated views that dogmatic theologians were inclined to believe in the first place. Dogmatic theologians, on James's reading, clarified the implications of beliefs, an exercise which was not indefensible. Among other things, it amplified, defined, dignified, and articulated ideas that people were already inclined to believe. Thus, philosophical analysis lent plausibility to theology. But, nonetheless, according to James, "it finds arguments for our convictions, for indeed it *has* to find them" (*VRE*, 436).

James asserted, in fact, that the arguments that philosophers found for their convictions hardly ever convinced anybody who really doubted to begin with. Rational men came away from a demonstration of the ontological argument, for instance, as opposed to each other as they ever were on religious issues, including the issues of divine existence. James thought that the reason why this was so was fairly clear: to prove that something must conceptually be so did not prove the actuality of anything. As he saw them, all the proofs for the existence of God ended up demonstrating that if there is one, it exists. If the arguments for divine existence proved this, then, James suggested, "if you have a God already whom you believe in, these arguments confirm you. If you are atheistic, they fail to set you right." This was so much the worse for the college theologians who disciplined their students to prove God's existence this way and to appreciate religions on the basis of the proofs. According to James, their arguments failed to convince otherwise rational people who entertained real doubts. Indeed, he suggested that college theological arguments were nothing but the "shuffling and matching of pedantic dictionary-adjectives, aloof from morals, aloof from human needs, something that might be worked out from the mere word 'God' by one of those logical machines of wood and brass which recent ingenuity has contrived as well as by a man of flesh and blood" (*VRE*, 446).

To be sure, James argued, theological systems articulated a priori were valuable. But they were not valuable as adjudicators of religious dispute in any direct sense. Their value was aesthetic. They made "bare piety" richer by adding "exulted and mysterious verbal additions" to it, additions that contributed "to their hold on human nature" (*VRE*, 458). James warned empirical humanists not to forget aesthetic motives when they appreciated the inevitable intellectualization of religious experience. But this aesthetic appeal made theologies the subjects, not the instruments, of appreciation. Theology was testimony of a sort and reiterated the problems inherent in making testimony intellectually authoritative that James had reviewed in his critcism of mysticism.

As James saw them, the most important difference between mysticism and rationalism was that rationalism intended to present public testimony, not private. But in the end, according to James, the cash value of this difference was plain: mysticism was constituted by individuals willfully clinging tenaciously to beliefs; rationalism was constituted by communities, schools, and sects clinging tenaciously to beliefs. Like his mentor Peirce,[5] James argued that a priori methods for fixing beliefs ultimately boiled down to an "appeal to numbers" (VRE, 424).

But, James argued, numbers did not establish the objective and indubitable basis for the appreciation of religions that rationalism promised. Rationalists reached impasse when their basic definitions and "necessary truths" began to contradict one another: they had no widely accepted methods according to which disputes about these things could be adjudicated.

Then too, according to James, the "modern idealism" presented by important university professors like Harvard's Josiah Royce suffered from the same difficulty, even though it emerged in response to and in denial of dogmatic theology and metaphysics. Modern idealism had much to teach, but in one crucial respect it was a variety of a priori speculation. Like dogmatic theology, modern idealism relied "on her poor self for witness" (VRE, 448)—that is, it failed to subject its testimony to the evidence of things accessible to anybody.

James thought, in particular, that "the Hegelian school, which today so deeply influences both British and American thinking," was guilty of confusing the conceivability of some things with their actuality. The school ran on two principles, he said: First, thought was dialectical, so that "every object which our thought may propose to itself involves the notion of some other object which seems at first to negate the first one"; and second, thought realized itself progressively, so that "the mere asking of a question or expression of a dissatisfaction proves that the answer or the satisfaction was already immanent; the finite, realized as such, is already the infinite in posse" (VRE, 449).

James thought that as an alternative to philosophies based on the logic of identity, the Hegelian program was "excellent" because "the universe is a place where things are followed by other things that both correct and fulfill them." What is more, Hegelians provided a metaphysic that made sense of religious experience. They uttered "what the mystic felt but was unable to communicate; and the saint in hearing them, recognizes his own experience" (VRE, 450, 453). In these ways, nothing could be more unlike dogmatic theology than Hegelianism.

Hegelians might adequately account in a descriptive way for the development of meanings and opinions. Their methods might provide an effective way for individual thinkers to clarify to themselves how they arrived at the opinions that they held. But like dogmatic theology and mysticism, Hegelianism offered no procedures for settling disputes between individuals whose thoughts had developed from different experiences, interests, and problems. Perhaps most telling, Hegelianism offered no principles for settling metaphysical disputes about meaning outside its own universe of discourse.

According to James, these problems with Hegelianism led to a situation in which "a majority of scholars, even religiously disposed ones, stubbornly refuse to treat" Hegelian arguments as convincing (VRE, 454). Far from establishing uniform beliefs about anything, Hegelians had formed themselves into several competing schools. Their claims to have established the veracity of theological beliefs had fallen on the deaf ears of otherwise rational men, and historically speaking, they had done no more to establish religious harmony than had the mystics and sectarians that they had promised to replace.

Cribbing from his Berkeley address "Philosophical Conceptions and Practical Results," James suggested that the impact of intellectualism on the philosophy of religion had been decisive and disastrous: "Verbality has stepped into the place of vision, professionalism into that of life" (VRE, 446). The problem with rationalism was not its emphasis on thought. James himself was a rationalist in the weaker sense of holding that thought can and must perfect what observations and feelings initiate. But rationalism was problematic because it misconstrued the function of thought by making it an end in itself.

James claimed that Scottish and English thinkers were more careful than those on the continent to connect thought with conduct. They construed intelligence in terms of observation-inference-action. Moreover, some Americans were continuing this tradition, Peirce foremost among them. Peirce's principle of pragmatism was a method for settling philosophical disputes that escaped the pitfalls of a priorism by submitting testimony to the evidence of things (or what Peirce called "reality"). According to pragmatists, James said, thought's only function was to dispel doubt by producing beliefs or establishing standards of habitual conduct. By defining concepts according to our conception of their real effects or practical consequences, pragmatism emphasized thought as a faculty for making *ordered interventions*. Thought functioned well, according to pragmatism, only when the ordered practical interventions that it generated redounded to our welfare in some specific and conceptually relevant way.

On these grounds, James argued that "the best method of discussing points of theory is to begin by ascertaining what practical differences would result from one alternative or the other being true" (VRE, 443) *not* initially ascertaining whether they are true as both mysticism and philosophy attempted to do. Neither of these two traditions succeeded in demonstrating the truth of theological claims. Mysticism was not successful as a method for fixing belief, because it denied the social impulse. Rationalism or traditional philosophy, employing a priori methods, was not successful either, because it had no way to contend with a diversity of basic beliefs. So far as James was concerned, the only other challenging competitor in the field of religious appreciation was the science of religions, and philosophical pragmatism not only underwrote it but established the outlines of its organization.

As James understood it, the genius of pragmatism lay in its ability to adjudicate disputes that personal tenacity and a priori methods could not. Pragmatism committed its adherents to a reality principle that evaded many of the problems inherent in the mystical and rationalist traditions: according to pragmatists, intellectual impasse would occur so long as investigators attempted to warrant beliefs simply by other beliefs. But when investigators attempted to warrant beliefs by the consequences that followed from holding them, they deployed a standard *over which they had no control.* Testimony could be manipulated; real effects or practical consequences could not. On pragmatic grounds, the question whether divinities played a crucial role in the world depended on there being real effects of divinity in the world. James's "thoroughly 'pragmatic' view of religion" assumed that "the world interpreted religiously is not the materialistic world over again, with an altered expression; it must have, over and above the altered expression, a *natural constitution* different at some point from that which a materialistic world would have. It must be such that different events can be expected from it, different conduct must be required" (VRE, 518). In his conclusions to the Gifford Lectures, James argued that he had demonstrated that facts confirmed a religious reading of the world.

CHAPTER 6

RELIGION AND A CASE FOR

THE SUPERNATURAL

James concluded his Gifford Lectures with a theory of religion, a solution to his modern problem of reforming religion, and an argument for what he called "crass" or "piecemeal" supernaturalism (*VRE*, 520). He had urged thinking men to become saints if they could. They could do this only if they had religious sensibilities, were open to the possibility of divine encounter, and, hence, admitted that the world was "wider" than naturalisms pictured. His theory of religion specified what he thought it meant to have religious sensibilities. His solution to the problem of religious transformation defended the right of thinking men to see the world religiously enough to make divine encounter a live option. His argument for crass or piecemeal supernaturalism rested on his ability to turn the mass of religious testimony that he had gathered into evidence for divine and supernatural power at work in the world.

James's Theory of Religion

In many books on religion, James noted, three things were represented as its most essential elements: sacrifice, confession, and prayer. This ordinary view of essential religion rested on the theory that religion was a complex social system with certain more or less significant functions or parts. James did not deny that sacrifice, confession, and prayer played important roles in religious life. Indeed, they were the most significant characteristics of the complex social organizations that had descended from a variety of original religious experiences: confession was the formalized expression of "rottenness"; prayer the ritualization of encounter; and sacrifice the codification of personal self-surrender and new identity. But these three formal behaviors characterized religion already made up, not in the making. Besides, they did not account for religious personali-

ties who maintained a religious sensibility, avowed a religious identity, and conducted themselves accordingly, but did not associate
with any "church." Confession, prayer, and sacrifice were not, therefore, religion reduced to "its lowest admissible terms" (VRE, 503).

Indeed, if "rudimentary" religion was religion reduced to its lowest admissible terms, then James's investigation of it revealed that
religion "carries on her principal business" between certain *feelings*
or *sensibilities* and certain *modes of conduct*. He claimed that while
theologies were variable and secondary, "the feelings on the one
hand and the conduct on the other are almost always the same, for
Stoic, Christian, and Buddhist saints are practically indistinguish-
able in their lives" (VRE, 504). Naive as it now seems, this claim
was vindicated by works on alien religions that James had read. It
prepared the way for his explicit theory of religion, his claim that
every religion "consists of two parts":

1. An uneasiness; and
2. Its solution.
1. The uneasinesss, reduced to its simplest terms, is a sense
that there is *something wrong about us* as we naturally stand.
2. The solution is a sense that *we are saved from the wrongness* by making proper connection with the higher powers.
[VRE, 508]

Every religion, according to James, was informed by perceptions
of human imperfections, divine encounters, and human regenera-
tions. Buddhism, Stoicism, and Christianity each articulated its
own "uneasiness" and its own "solution." But knowing what these
were for each was to know about each.

On these grounds, theologies and ecclesiasticisms formed "loop-
lines which may be perfections and improvements . . . but . . . are
not to be regarded as organs with an indispensable function, necessary at all times for religious life to go on" (VRE, 504). As James
understood them, Jesus, Gautama, and, for that matter, most other
religious originals, lived religious lives without theologies or ecclesiasticisms. To be sure, they engaged in "spontaneous" intellectual
constructions—that is, they reported their religious perceptions—
but they made no effort to systematize their perceptions or codify
their conduct. They had felt both something wrong about themselves as they naturally stood and saved from the wrongness by
making proper connections with the higher powers. These feelings
were the determinants of their conduct, which was characteristically saintly. Religious originals talked and acted religiously, but
they did not necessarily "do" theology. Persons who did theology

might talk and act religiously as well, but when they did theology, they talked *about* religious perceptions and actions without necessarily engaging in them.

James meant it, of course, when he said that religion's "short circuit" of feeling and conduct might be perfected and improved by engaging in theology and in the construction of religious codes of behavior. Indeed, he assumed that "the varied world of concrete religious constructions" included both these pursuits. Feelings of wrongness and solution, on the one hand, and saintly conduct, on the other, simply established a "nucleus . . . on which it may be hoped that all religious persons may agree" (*VRE*, 503). Once religious persons agreed that they shared certain sorts of perceptions and interests, they could add "ruddier" beliefs on and around the things they all shared.

Thus, James's theory of religion provided for connections between religious feeling and conduct, on the one hand, and theology, on the other, without making theology the crucial element of religion that distinguished it from other human enterprises. From the vantage point of his own religious investigations, this was important. First, it made good on his intention to defend " 'experience' against 'philosophy' as being the real backbone of the world's religious life." But second, it provided a way for him to base his own "high and noble general [view] of our destiny and the world's meaning" on his perceptions of the varieties of religious experience. James had been constructing a religious metaphysics for over a quarter of a century by the time he finished his Gifford Lectures and thought of his world view as a "religion," a way of "fronting life, and worth fighting for" (*LWJ*, 2:127, 122). In his view, his conclusions about religion in *Varieties* did nothing to dilute his "high and noble" pursuit. To the contrary, he thought his conclusions provided data for it.

In James's synthesis, religious philosophy or theology perfected or improved spontaneous religious constructions when it mediated among varying religious sensibilities, connected knowledge of divinity with knowledge of other things, and articulated a more complete picture of things than rudimentary divine encounter provoked. Religious metaphysics or theology was quite specifically an aesthetic pursuit, according to James. Yet the complex pictures that it fashioned formed ways of life and set the bounds for interpretation, meaning, and even evidence. Moreover, it could enrich the "bare piety" generated in religious experience and address the needs of the imagination by offering compact images to clarify and simplify the complex significance of divine encounter.

Thus, its promulgation was a "religious act," a reflective sort of religious conduct.

Informed by the norm of inclusive integration, James saw his own task in the science of religions as having essentially to do with "balance," itself an aesthetic category. By investigating the stories of eccentric religious persons, he had charted the range of religious sensibilities that required some measure of inclusion in any religious universe. By isolating the excesses of religious thought and action, he enabled himself to ask: "What are the dangers in this element of life? and in what proportion may it need to be restrained by other elements, to give the proper balance?" (*VRE*, 486).

His explicitly Romantic assumption was that "the divine can mean no single quality, it must mean a group of qualities, by being champions of which in alternation, different men may all find worthy missions. Each attitude being a syllable in human nature's total message, it takes the whole of us to spell the meaning out completely." No two individuals had the same difficulties, nor should they seek the same solutions or deliverance. To be certain, "some men have the complete experience and the higher vocation, here just as in the social world; but for each man to stay in his own experience, whate'er it be, and for the others to tolerate him there, is surely best" (*VRE*, 487, 488). This language of statesmanship revealed James's understanding of his own religious vocation more clearly than any other. The scientist of religions engaged in the *religious* task of unblinding religious persons to one another and of clarifying the interests they shared, even when they pursued them differently.

Tradition and Modernity

The very idea of a science of religions, of course, undercut the assumption, held by many of James's colleagues in the study of religion, that religion misfit modern culture or consciousness. The British intellectualists, Frazer and Tylor especially, had maintained that religion was a component of culture that had failed to evolve in certain ways and, hence, was a sort of living fossil. They assumed that religion was basically an explanatory enterprise, an attempt to account for both ordinary and extraordinary events. On their reading, religion was a rational enterprise precisely because it pursued explanations. But it was a case of arrested cultural development because it was not informed by philosophical skepticism in the way that science came to be and because it was animistic.

Religions did not allow adherents to place any of their tenets in jeopardy. According to the intellectualists, that was the reason that religious beliefs were held as sacred. Moreover, religions located the most important forces in the universe in personal characteristics and categories: they never developed their explanations to the point where "impersonal" cause-and-effect played a crucial role.

In one important respect, James's science of religions challenged the notion that religion was an explanatory enterprise. If his analysis was adequate, the "nucleus" of religion was diagnostic and therapeutic, not explanatory. Religious life had continued, and perhaps would continue, to pursue human interests in well-being, to diagnose the natural divisions and bifurcations that prevented well-being, and to promote strategies for self-transformation through self-surrender without ever developing a "necessary" theological branch.

But as a religious metaphysician bent upon developing his own supernaturalism out of his religious investigations, James's view of religion was in direct competition with the intellectualists. They claimed that religion was necessarily both precritical or close-minded and bound to personal categories of explanation. He claimed, to the contrary, that religion had fostered narrow-mindedness in infamous instances, but that it had not in every instance, and need not promote it now. He also claimed that religion had accounted for some events that were more adequately accounted for impersonally, but that its personal explanations of salvation experiences were better than impersonal accounts.

In other words, James accepted the intellectualist claim that religious explanation was cast in a personal idiom but rejected the intellectualist claim that religious thought was necessarily close-minded. The one fundamental fact in the world of religion, James asserted, was personality. Indeed, "the pivot round which the religious life, as we have traced it, revolves, is the interest of the individual in his private, personal destiny." This was the case for "savages" and "men disciplined intellectually" alike (*VRE*, 491). The worlds of religious individuals were imbued with the presence of some "thou," some power that met them on the basis of their personal concerns. Belief in divinity was conserved from age to age, not as a fossil, but as revitalized by the religious experiences of religious originals in every age in every great culture.

James argued that science and religion had not been in conflict until the seventeenth century. Both enterprises had been articulated in dramatic language. But since the seventeenth century, science had repudiated "the personal point of view." It was no longer doxological and constructed its "theories quite careless of their bearing on human anxieties and fates." For science, "private selves" were "epiphenomena. . . . Their destinies weigh nothing and determine nothing in the world's irremediable currents of events." From this vantage point, the dramatic and personal accounts of human life that religionists gave were anachronisms "for which deanthropomorphization of the imagination is the remedy required." If it was scientific to assume that "universal" terms had to be "impersonal," it was illegitimate to "mix the private with the cosmic" (*VRE*, 491, 495, 498).

Insofar as the scientific attitude was impersonal, as distinguished from being impartial, he continued, it was shallow. Especially when scientists accounted for human affairs in such terms, they presented only "symbols of reality." Only when they dealt "with private and personal phenomena as such" did they handle "realities in the completest sense of the term." If scientists wanted to account impartially for human events, in other words, they needed to use dramatic and personal categories of thought. At least when it came to accounting for persons, idealist doctrine was right: "The only meaning we can attach to the notion of a thing as it is 'in itself' is by conceiving it as it is *for* itself; that is, as a piece of full experience with a private sense of 'pinch' or inner activity of some sort going with it" (*VRE*, 498, 499).

But if James was right about full personal facts, then orthodox scientists were narrow-minded when it came to religious investigations. Scientists were "absurd" when they said that "the egotistic elements of experience should be suppressed." By doing so, they failed to address genuine questions having to do with personal destiny. However such questions might be answered, according to James, persons became profound by "living in the sphere of thought which they opened up. . . . But to live thus is to be religious; so I unhesitatingly repudiate the survival-theory of religion, as being founded on an egregious mistake." Religion was a fit survival, not a mere survival, because it occupied itself with personal destinies and thus kept in contact with "the only absolute realities which we know" (*VRE*, 499, 500, 503).

To be sure, "our ancestors made so many errors of fact and mixed them with their religion" (*VRE*, 500), but that was no permit for abandoning religion; it was a warning to reform it. James had argued since his earliest essays that religious thought was not inevitably credulous, false, or dogmatic. In "The Will to Believe" he had attempted to show that both religious and scientific belief could and should be held as corrigible; neither religious nor scientific belief exemplified simple commitment or utter detachment.

On James's diagnosis, of course, religions had suffered from tribal instinct and narrow-mindedness. But viewing religions through his Darwinian spectacles, he was able to consider mechanisms for the elimination of these things from historical transmission. His own science of religions was one such mechanism. To be sure, espousal of "the science of religion as our own religion" was wrong-headed because knowledge about a thing was not the thing itself. "The best man at this science might be the man who found it hardest to be personally devout." But good religious persons could participate in and learn from the science. If they did, they would cultivate that habitual "nervousness" associated with "scientific verification" because "the cultivator of this science has to become acquainted with so many groveling and horrible superstitions that a presumption easily arises in his mind that any belief that is religious is probably false" (VRE, 488, 489, 490).

James saw his science of religions, therefore, as a mechanism for the solution of his own religious problem. Interlocked with other natural historical sciences and potentially connected with philosophy and theology, his science of religions was an enterprise that disciplined its participants to maintain an open mind about the determinants and consequences of religious experience. It also demanded philosophical reflection on the part of its adherents, thus making inclusive integration of religious interests the superordinate consideration. If James was convinced that neither he nor his culture could live without the personal consolations and social additions that religious life brought, he was just as certain that credulousness and tribal instinct had to be displaced by a willingness to respond to new information with an open mind and by a strenuous toleration of tolerant peoples. He thought participation in his science of religions *required* training in these dispositions.

The Case for the Supernatural

In his 1898 address "Philosophical Conceptions and Practical Results," James had argued that the promise of theism was its claim that some persons were enabled by it to become their best selves when they were unable to do so on their own. On pragmatic grounds, the word 'God' meant those concrete passive and active religious experiences "of a wider spiritual life with which our superficial consciousness is continuous. This pragmatic analysis of the word 'God' set up the crux of his religious investigations later pursued in *Varieties*. He assumed that if he discovered the sort of experiences "which furnishes the notion of an ever-present God" (*Prag*, 266) then his crass supernaturalism was rendered evident.

James concluded in *Varieties* that he was, in fact, successful in his attempt to render crass supernaturalism evident. He had discovered cases of self-transformation that kept the promise of his theism. He summarized the type of experience that he had discovered this way:

> The individual, so far as he suffers from his wrongness and criticizes it, is to that extent consciously beyond it, and in at least possible touch with something higher, if anything higher exist. Along with the wrong part there is thus a better part of him, even though it may be but a most helpless germ. With which part he should identify his real being is by no means obvious at this stage; but when stage 2 (the stage of solution or salvation) arrives, the man identifies his real being with the germinal higher part of himself; and does so in the following way. *He becomes conscious that this higher part is conterminous and continuous with a MORE of the same quality, which is operative in the universe outside of him, and which he can keep in working touch with,* and in a fashion *get on board of and save himself when all his lower being has gone to pieces in the wreck.* [VRE, 508]

James claimed that this description accurately accounted for the divided self and its struggles, the change of personal center and a disavowal of "the lower self," the appearance both of the exteriority of "the helping power" and of union with it, and religious feelings both of security and strenuousity. In any case, religious originals had given testimony to this effect, testimony rendered plausible by conduct not only subsequent to religious experience but, as analyzed psychologically, consequent to it as well.

To be sure, James realized that deception and self-deception were possible in any particular report of religious experience. But he argued that *only in case nothing was actually transacted* must religion be classed as "rooted in delusion altogether, just as materialists and atheists have always said it was" (*VRE*, 465). James had never intended to execute any historiographic vindication of any particular case of religious experience. In no case did he check religious testimony against particular eyewitnesses or more general character witnesses or critical historical evaluation of all this relevant material. He relied, instead, on biographies that he thought were received as indisputably saintly in character by educated men. Whatever "elements of delusion" such biographies contained, they were not "rooted in delusion altogether," inasmuch as everyone admitted the requisite self-transformation in them.

In other words, James assumed that he was reflecting on the personal stories of religious originals whose conduct was commonly accepted as saintly and whose attitudes were known to be faithful. Assuming that religious originals were telling the truth (that is, being honest or not deceptive in any basic way) and that they acted more saintly subsequent to their religious experiences than prior to them, James thought he had a mechanism for transforming the subsequent relation between religious feeling and religious conduct into a consequent relation. Just as psychologists could point to mechanisms that made people irritable when they had headaches, James thought he could point to a mechanism that made people faithful and saintly when they had religious experiences: the process of self-transformation articulated in his chapters on the divided self and conversion *made* faithfulness and saintliness consequent upon divine encounter, or encounter with that " 'MORE of the same quality' with which our own higher self appears in the experience to come into harmonious working relation" (*VRE*, 510).

In the doing, James thought he was transforming testimony into evidence in one specific sense, but not another. He was showing how religious conduct was consequentially related to religious feeling in a way that rendered the religious original's account of his divine encounter *plausible*. He was not demonstrating the *actuality* of any particular divine encounter per se. The most he could do, he warned, was to offer an hypothesis about the process of religious self-transformation "that may fit the facts so easily that your scientific logic will find no plausible pretext for vetoing your impulse to welcome it as true" (*VRE*, 511).

His task was to give a "definite description" of "the MORE," and of personal "union" with it, without taking sides in any particular theological debate. He said that all theologies agreed that the "more" really existed and acted in ways that made life better. Showing psychologists definite facts for which the "more" and "union" with it stood would lay the groundwork for reunion between science and theology. From this angle, the task was to establish connections between spontaneous religious constructions and psychology, on the one hand, and theology, on the other.

"The *subconscious self*" was "the mediating term required" to connect psychology with the findings of the science of religions, according to James (*VRE*, 511). It was "a well-accredited psychological entity" that *both* accounted for the salient characteristics of religious experience *and* left the door open for theological (not to mention physiological) speculation. The term 'subconscious self' was an invitation to theological speculation, because nobody had developed an adequate theory to establish any particular correspondence between subconscious mind and body or an adequate answer to the question of mental individuation. Psychologists granted that subliminal activity went on, but they could not begin to say whether or how 'subconsciousness' was parcelled. All psychologists knew was that 'subconsciousness' was 'more' mind and, incidentally, more of this or that mind. If 'subconsciousness' was treated essentially as something general enough for individuals to participate in, theological speculation easily arose.

In any case, "starting thus with a recognized psychological fact as our basis" and, hence, preserving "a contact with 'science' which the ordinary theologian lacks," James vindicated the theologian's contention "that the religious man is moved by an external power." Whether or not 'subconsciousness' was individuated per human body, the language of subliminal activity was a language of invasion and control, not only for subjects but also for clinical investigators. So, James argued, his hypothesis that "whatever it may be on its *farther* side, the 'more' with which in religious experience we feel ourselves connected is on its *hither* side the subconscious continuation of our conscious life" was "not merely apparently, but literally true" (*VRE*, 512–13).

If this was so, then the reports of religious originals about their own encounters became plausible: their testimony was not self-evident, but it was rendered evident by a psychological entity that most of them had never heard of. To be sure, James warned, his hypothesis was only "a doorway" into the subject. Theoretic difficulties abounded as soon as investigators stepped through it and asked "how far our transmarginal consciousness carrie[d] us if we follow[ed] it on its remoter side" (*VRE*, 513). But the difficulties invited religious scientists to pursue their investigations and to connect them with metaphysical or theological enterprises.

James thought that the most productive way to pursue theoretical problems concerning the "more" was to raise the issue of "union." He suggested that if every theology accepted the existence and activity of the "more," each theology was distinguished from the others on the basis of conceptions of union. This was the point, he thought, over which "pantheism and theism, nature and second birth, works and grace and karma, immortality and reincarnation, rationalism and mysticism" carried on their disputes. His psychological theory permitted him to claim that *"the fact that the conscious person is continuous with a wider self through which saving experiences come"* was *"literally and objectively true as far as it goes."* His challenge was to develop finer-grained analyses of the "continuity" involved in such events and of the "farther limits of this extension of our personality" (*VRE*, 510, 515).

He addressed these challenges by issuing an "over-belief," or a belief worth further probing. "The whole drift" of his education led him to believe two things. First, human-divine continuity was *transactional*—that is, salvific events were codependent on the operations of both human and nonhuman agents. Second, the wider selves who cooperated with humans to bring about well-being had experiences of their own that "have a meaning for our life also" (*VRE*, 519).

On the issue of continuity, James commended investigators to probe the notion that "we and God have business with each other; and in opening ourselves to his influence our deepest destiny is fulfilled" (*VRE*, 516–17). "We and God" were not necessarily continuous in the sense of consubstantial or numerically identical, but were "continuous at certain points" in the sense of sharing certain objectives and acting in concert to bring them about. If and when "orthodox" theists pictured salvation as bestowed by grace or saw well-being achieved solely by divinity, not cooperatively, they differed from James. When pantheists argued that *no particular* transaction between a person and his God brought about well-being and when moralists argued that well-being depended solely on the works of men, they differed from James. James pictured well-being as the outcome neither of divine action alone nor of human action alone but of business between them—particular business.

The psychologists' task was to suggest specific mechanisms that could permit such transactions. The metaphysicians' task was to clarify how "we" and "God" could be both discrete agents *and* continuous. The logic of identity regnant among metaphysicians assumed discontinuity among identifiable entities. Two things might produce one other thing, but two things could not be one thing; either they were two things or one thing. James suggested that "we" and "God" were *both* discontinuous and continuous. But he needed to persuade philosophers that anything, much less God and man, could be both two and one.

On the issue of "wider selves," James urged investigators to probe the notion that "the further limits of our being plunge . . . into an altogether other dimension of existence from the sensible and merely 'understandable' world," a dimension where ideal impulses originated, an unseen region or "higher part of the universe" which placed demands on persons the fulfillment of which guaranteed an "ideal life." James warned that if divinity was taken simply as the thing that entered into the religious man's sense of union, it fell short of being a "useful" hypothesis. A good hypothesis had "other properties than those of the phenomenon it is immediately invoked to explain, otherwise it is not prolific enough" (*VRE*, 515, 517–18).

Religious persons were not justifiably sanguine about the best things being the more eternal things unless the 'God' hypothesis successfully predicted "remote objective consequences." God needed to "enter into wider cosmic relations in order to justify the subject's absolute confidence and peace." In other words, religion had to be more than "a mere illumination of facts already elsewhere given, not a mere passion, like love, which views things in a rosier light." Religion was that, but it had to be more than that to make the chance of salvation an intellectually responsible notion. If there were wider selves that experienced things for themselves and were not reducible to experiences for "us," then the world "must be such that different events can be expected from it, different conduct must be required" (*VRE*, 517, 518). If divine miracles were "interpolated into the field of nature," things not only *looked* rosier; *events over which people had no arbitrary control made them look rosier*. The point of further religious investigation was to specify the sorts of events that would tend to confirm the chance of salvation, and then to discover whether these occurred.

This, James suggested, was a "thoroughly 'pragmatic' view of religion," a view that demanded discovery of "characteristically divine facts." What these were, "apart from the actual inflow of energy in the faith-state and in the prayer-state," James did not know. But he commended his audience to accept the possibility that "their own poor over-beliefs" might "help God in turn to be more effectively faithful to his own greater tasks" (*VRE*, 519).

Unresolved Problems

The work that James did for his Gifford Lectures made important differences for his own religious investigations. First, he demonstrated to his own satisfaction that pragmatism was an effective method for setting issues and settling disputes. Second, he suggested mechanisms for the solution of his problem of religion, by not only *naming* a science of religions but also analyzing its functions and relations to religious experience, other sciences, and religious philosophy or theology. Third, he challenged the very logic of materialism and presented evidence for events that materialists could not readily account for. Fourth, he demonstrated that disconsolate persons were transformed into their best selves, when they could not rationally transform themselves. Fifth, he argued persuasively that these conversions could not be accounted for without reference to selves that were "wider," because they eluded consciousness, and that were "super," because they accomplished things that rational and responsible behavior had failed to accomplish. Sixth, he suggested that such evidence improved the chance of salvation. Finally, he refined his thought on divinity by making it clear he could be neither an orthodox or scholastic theist nor a mainline pantheist. His psychological account of divine encounter made divinity too intimate to suit the claims of Old Lighters; his emphasis on the interpolation of divinity in the natural world made divinity too executive for refined or natural supernaturalists.

But James left many issues unresolved in his conclusions to the Gifford Lectures. If he was neither an orthodox theist nor an orthodox pantheist, what exactly was crass or piecemeal supernaturalism? In the short run, James characterized it in contradistinction to "refined" or "natural" supernaturalism—that is, Romantic pantheism. Crass supernaturalism was like Romantic pantheism in that it pictured natural and supernatural united in or through human beings; crass divinity was "intimate" and "friendly," not "foreign" and "magisterial." But crass supernaturalism was unlike Romantic pantheism in that it was an interpretation of particular events in the world, not of the "whole" world, and it pictured divinity as executing judgments in the world, hence, performing miraculous and providential deeds, not simply arriving at some "bare academic verdict or platonic appreciation" of the whole world (*VRE*, 522).

When Romantics called nature divine, they meant that the whole world was full of soul. But James could not square that claim with those parts of the world that were simply brutal. What is more, he was not ready to overthrow the logic of identity altogether. He had asserted that persons were continuous with wider selves through which saving experiences come, but he had not worked out any logical argument supporting this sort of union. Even if he could present such an argument, the only thing that the variety of religious experiences testified to was "that we can experience union with *something* larger than ourselves and in that union find our greater peace." Religious experience alone did not permit James to "'pass to the limit'" as philosophers and mystics bent on satisfying their craving for unity had. There were probably many gods, not one. When the testimony of religious experience was kept "clearly within its proper bounds," James suggested, "polytheism" returned upon us. But, then again, James was unsure what sort of polytheism he found probable. He simply suggested that "anything larger will do, if only it be large enough to trust for the next step. It need not be infinite, it need not be solitary. It might conceivably even be only a larger and more godlike self, of which the present self would then be a collection of such selves, of different degrees of inclusiveness, with no absolute unity realized at all" (*VRE*, 525, 526). James knew this was vague and meant to work out his own theology if health permitted.

But vague as they were, James's theological suggestions made it clear that his old problem of the one and the many was still haunting him. If he took experiences of salvific union at face value, he could not be either a strong monist or a strong pluralist, for in some crucial cases selves were both discrete and continuous. If things were neither one nor many but possibly one and many, then monism and pluralism did not exhaust the metaphysical possibilities. *Varieties* posed problems for the problem of the one and the many, but did not reach any solutions.

If his immediately subsequent work was any indication, James was intent on finding ways to dissolve the problem of the one and the many. The essays in radical empiricism that he began to publish the year after he returned from Edinburgh to Cambridge pursued strategies to do this, among other things. But in concert with work on this issue, James's essays in radical empiricism were geared to construct and defend a metaphysics of "full" facts, constituted by complex experiences. Again, *Varieties* was organized by James around his assumption that "the motor currents of the world run through" personal experiences (*VRE*, 499). But apart from his important instantiation of this claim by reference to the varieties of religious experience, James's Gifford Lectures gave no defense of it. He still had to develop a metaphysics of experience without encountering the pitfalls of traditional idealism.

Finally, James made it clear to readers of *Varieties* that the problem of religious truth was left unresolved. Sometimes, James had employed the term 'truth' to mean "bare value for life." Other times, he had meant "something additional," namely, cognitive value for life (*VRE*, 509). He still had to give a general theory of truth which sustained *both* "subjective" and "objective" connotations of it, but he had no clear way to do this given the traditional philosophical understanding of subjectivity and objectivity. His essays in radical empiricism began to address this problem along with the others.

Each of these outstanding issues indicated James's intention to engage in theological segments of religious investigation. Many critics heard James's message that the core of religious life was religious experience, not theology. But too many of these failed to follow the connections between *Varieties* and the works that James wrote afterward, and were left with the impression that James thought theology was not only secondhand but also second-rate. Their impression was mistaken.

PART III

RELIGION IN A WORLD OF

PURE EXPERIENCE, 1902–1910

CHAPTER 7

THE PLACE OF RELIGIOUS

FACTS IN A WORLD OF

PURE EXPERIENCE

James lived for eight years after he delivered his Gifford Lectures. During that time he was extremely productive, pursuing various interests including, though of course, far exceeding, his religious investigations. In 1904 he began publishing his essays in humanism and radical empiricism. Some of these were metaphilosophical, others metaphysical, and still others concerned with the meaning of truth. Many of them were edited by Perry as *Essays in Radical Empiricism* in 1912, two years after James died.

In 1906, James began delivering his lectures on pragmatism. The book *Pragmatism* appeared in 1907. He continued to publish articles clarifying his pragmatic theory of truth until 1909, when he collected a series of them as *The Meaning of Truth*. In 1908 he delivered his Hibbert Lectures on the present situation in philosophy. He published these in 1909 as *A Pluralistic Universe*. There, James developed his pluralistic pantheism and dissolved the philosophical problem of the one and the many.

For the last year of his life, James accomplished exacting and technical philosophical work, especially on the problems of the infinite and of novelty. He made this work the keystone to his unfinished *Some Problems of Philosophy*, posthumously published in 1911. In all, James published more than eighty pieces during this last period, articles that not only explored or established philosophical positions but expressed cultural criticism, defended pacifism, gave tribute to influential thinkers, reviewed literature in psychology and psychical research, and suggested ways to understand mysticism. The emergence of his pluralistic pantheism in *A Pluralistic Universe* coincided with some of the most sophisticated work that James ever produced.

James's philosophical work from 1903 to 1910 intersected his continued religious investigations at various points. Religion was hardly the center of his attention in much of his philosophical work, though *A Pluralistic Universe* is a clear exception and *Pragmatism* is at least a borderline case. But James's essays in radical empiricism, pragmatic method, and theory of truth, as well as his work on the logics of identity, infinity, and novelty, were central to the continuation of his religious investigations. They clarified many positions that James established in *Varieties*, pursued the resolution of philosophical problems that remained in James's conclusions to that work, and served as crucial conduits from it to the pluralistic pantheism of *A Pluralistic Universe* and, even beyond, to his suggestions about mysticism and his declaration of faith attached to *Some Problems of Philosophy* in 1910.

Full Personal Facts and the Charge of Subjectivity

James's Gifford Lectures had concluded that the full personal facts of religious experience vindicated the hypothesis that religion was mankind's most important function by demonstrating that "the conscious person is continuous with a wider self through which saving experiences come" (*VRE*, 515). Salvatory events occurred, no matter how people accounted for them.

Many critics challenged James's right to draw this conclusion from his investigation. Some argued that these "saving experiences" were subjective, not objective. Others added that the notion that individuals could become continuous with some other individual was nonsense.[1] These related problems of "subjectivity" and of "conjunctive relations" received James's full attention during the years immediately following his return from Edinburgh.

Leuba, in particular, charged that James's description of religious experiences robbed them of all cognitive import. He noted that on James's own grounds, these experiences were feelings; and, Leuba added, feelings per se played no role in cognitive questions. If Leuba's contentions were right, James's religious investigations were in trouble. James had announced in "Philosophical Conceptions and Practical Results" that he could specify the "original" of the God-idea by turning to "spontaneous" religious experiences. He had concluded that the reports of religious experience that he collected for *Varieties* lent plausibility to the idea of divinity—of gods, if not God. But he was also satisfied that his contention that religious experiences were felt experiences was basically sound. He simply differed from Leuba, and a host of other dualists, over the nature of feeling and its role in cognitive processes. Indeed, this difference was so general that it marked his allegiance to a particular metaphysical position at odds with the dualisms of both common sense and psychology.

Dualists like Leuba assumed two basic kinds of entities in the world, physical and mental ones. Physical scientists studied physical states of one sort or another; psychologists studied mental states. On dualistic grounds, the two sorts of investigation were not inevitably parallel. But while physical scientists were clear about how to analyze physical states into composite elements, psychologists were unclear about how to analyze mental states in the same way. Every time a psychologist analyzed a mental state into "something else," its elements turned out to be more mental states. But, in any case, dualists assumed that *feelings were mental entities*, something James had challenged as early as 1884. Dualists assumed, further, that mental entities were essentially different from physical entities and that these two sorts of things were not inevitably related. Finally, dualists assumed that if mental entities like feelings did relate to physical ones, they did so because they somehow transcended themselves.

According to James, the "epistemological problem" emerged out of this dualistic view. "Epistemologists" were trying to specify the relation that allowed mental entities to "know" physical ones: that was the "cognitive relation," the relation according to which a "subjective" feeling, or idea or perception or conception, was given an "objective referent." No matter how dualists conceived the cognitive relation, according to them no "feeling" could have cognitive status unless it were in relation to some objective referent, essentially different from itself. Indeed, even when a "feeling" achieved cognitive status, the problem remained how to distinguish true cognitions from false ones: feelings could relate to objects to which they did not really correspond.

In sum, on dualistic grounds, feelings per se did not count for anything cognitively. They counted only when they essentially transcended themselves. So, for dualists, to feel divinity was merely subjective because the experience was constituted by psychical material that might or might not have any corresponding objective referent.

Since writing *Principles*, James had realized the enormity of the task in challenging the dualism of common sense and of contemporary psychology. He also realized that the magnitude of the problem was increased by his unwillingness to toe any normal idealistic line on solutions to the epistemological problem generated by metaphysical dualism. But he could not shirk the task. He wrote Leuba that he

> found it preposterous to suppose that if there be a feeling of
> unseen reality shared by large numbers of best men in their
> best moments, responded to by other men in their 'deep' mo-
> ments, good to live by, strength-giving—I find it preposterous,
> I say, to suppose that the goodness of that feeling for living
> purposes should be held to carry no objective significance, and
> especially preposterous if it combines harmoniously with our
> otherwise grounded philosophy of objective truth. *You* say we
> must consider it a purely subjective affection. But this opens
> the whole subject of what the word "truth" means, and I can-
> not enter that except to say that if inferences from "good for
> life" to "true" were on principle forbidden, not religion but the
> whole notion of truth would probably have to be the thing
> overhauled and revised. [*TC*, 2:350]

James was not speculating idly here. He did revise the notion of truth in order to legitimate the inference from "good for life" to "true" in certain instances. In light of his religious investigations, he found it nonsense to claim that "the best fruits that history has to offer" were untrue or deceitful. But his work on the meaning of truth was part of a grander task that he worked on after his Gifford Lectures, the task of elaborating a world view he first called "humanism" and later named "radical empiricism." Either of these specifications denoted a world view that was meant to displace the dualism of thoughts and things embedded in common sense.

James had no qualms with the ways ordinary people used the notions of thoughts and things. He was critical of ways that philosophers deployed the distinction to adjudicate disputes about such things as the role of feelings in the thoughtful life of men and the significance of the categories of personality in accounts of human life. Criticisms like Leuba's about the cognitive emptiness of feelings were illustrative of the scientific prejudice that "personality" had no independent role to play in the investigation of human life. In order to demonstrate otherwise, James developed a metaphysical point of view which not only permitted but demanded analysis in terms of personal categories whenever possible. His "principle of pure experience" furthered the gains he had made in *Varieties* toward articulating a plausible religious picture of things by vindicating the cognitive role of personal experience as well as the actuality of "conjunctive relations" between persons of lesser and greater powers attempting to order the chaos and reorder the orders around them in various satisfactory ways.

Indeed, James had been in the midst of formulating his new humanism when he wrote *Varieties*. He had decided to articulate his full vision, particularly its most controversial religious aspects, empirically or by transforming testimony into a kind of evidence. *Varieties* presented those active and passive experiences that gave meaning to the notion of divinity that James was willing to defend as part and parcel of his total view. Once the Gifford Lectures were over, he turned to the consideration of a general view of things which complemented his religious conclusions and set the stage for further discussions about the chance or possibility of salvation.

From the point of view of his religious investigations, then, the essays that James wrote during 1903–7 secured the philosophical nuts and bolts that *Varieties* begged for and that his 1908 Hibbert Lectures, published as *A Pluralistic Universe*, depended upon. James had written in his preface to *Varieties* that he wanted to write a metaphysical treatise supporting and elucidating his conclusions in the twenty Gifford Lectures. He was a sick man when he wrote this preface and might well have figured on writing only one last piece of work. Death was surely on his mind. But, in fact, he wrote no one metaphysical treatise aimed at further vindication of his contentions that religion was mankind's most important function, that persons are sometimes helped when they cannot help themselves to realize their ideals, and that the chance of salvation was made plausible in light of certain actual relations that persons experienced. Many of the eighty-five essays and lectures that James published between 1903 and 1910 bear directly on these issues, as does *Some Problems of Philosophy*, published posthumously in 1911. The man who wrote "The Energies of Men" in 1907 had himself experienced an explosion of new energy after his Gifford Lectures that provided him with the wherewithal to work out much of his position on the satisfaction of man's religious appetites through philosophy.

The Metaphysics of Humanism

James recognized that his own new humanism was simply one wave in a greater sea change that Western philosophy was undergoing. In 1903 he took special notice of the personal idealists in Britain and America, and in 1904 he gave appreciative acknowledgments to John Dewey's "Chicago School." The personal idealists protested the tendency among Hegelians to construe individual personalities as "phenomenal adjectives" or mere appearances of the absolute, as simple expressions of the one Real Person. But at the same time, they wished to maintain an idealistic metaphysical position, largely out of respect for its solution to the problem of knowledge. They argued that reality was an eternal republic constituted by persons linked to one another through Mind or God. This view denied naturalism as did absolute idealism, but without undercutting individuality. James thought it suffered from vagueness on the question of God's relation to the selves that he created.

But James saw himself aligned with much of personal idealism. He aimed, with them, to defend the irreducibility of human personality to lower terms, the theoretic and practical originality of human individuals, and a view of the universe "re-anthropomorphized" enough to make his religious thought not only intelligible but sound. James said that personal idealism was "a new departure in contemporary thought, the combination, namely, of a teleological and spiritual inspiration with the same kind of conviction that the particulars of experience constitute the stronghold of reality as has usually characterized the materialistic type of mind" (CER, 442–43).

James was simply reasserting his 1902 contentions about "full" personal facts when he claimed in 1903 that a radical empiricism assumed that "the only fully complete concrete data are . . . the successive moments of our own several histories, taken with their subjective personal aspect as well as with their 'objective' deliverance or 'content.'" Both radical empiricism and personal idealism led "to the assumption of a collectivism of personal lives (which may be of any grade of complication, and superhuman or infrahuman, as well as human), variously cognitive of one another, variously conative and impulsive, genuinely evolving and changing by effort and trial, and by their interaction and cumulative achievements making up the world" (CER, 443–44).

James saw radical empiricism and personal idealism as varieties of "empirical evolutionism." Dewey's school in Chicago was developing yet another variation on this theme. James sympathized with Dewey's work, which, like his own, was radical because it postulated "no real, whether being or relation between beings, which is not direct matter of experience. There is no Unknowable or Absolute behind or around the finite world. No Absolute either, in the sense of anything eternally constant; no term is static, but everything is process and change" (*EP*, 103).

James noted that Dewey differed from personal idealists by construing 'consciousness' as functional, not substantial or constitutive. He made biology and psychology continuous and always analyzed 'experience' according to two variables or factors, the way Darwinians should. According to James, Dewey construed every situation in terms of an "E" (environment) and an "O" (organism). These factors interacted and developed each other "without end; for each action of E upon O changes O, whose reaction in turn upon E changes E, so that E's new action upon O gets different, eliciting a new reaction, and so on indefinitely" (*EP*, 103). Dewey called this process "reconstruction," and claimed that it was the process of which all reality consisted.

Panpsychism separated Dewey's group from the personal idealists. The personal idealists wanted to claim that the stuff of reality was conscious—all of it, any of it, each constituent of it. They contended that a tree experienced its own falling when no one else was in the forest to witness the event; hence, "trees" were psychic. Dewey did not align himself with panpsychism. Instead, he tried to reconstruct idealistic problems in ways that avoided idealistic solutions. He assumed that consciousness was an instrument of order the use of which was required by the continual appearance of disorder. James said that Dewey gave "no positive account of the order of physical fact" per se (*CER*, 105). Dewey only gave an account of physical fact as informed by human thought. He demonstrated that environments lent themselves to human concerns: they were both malleable to some extent and intelligible. But the intelligibility of physical things did not make them intelligent for Dewey.

James wavered between the panpsychism of the personal idealists and a naturalism of a Deweyan sort for the rest of his life. He was attracted to panpsychism for basically religious reasons, for he wanted to speculate on the role that physical things might play in the course of salvation. But to the extent that he was attracted to the dissolution of ontology as a distinctive philosophical pursuit, his interest in panpsychism waned. Whenever he urged philosophers to devise metaphysics without ontologies and to construe metaphysics as aesthetic, cultural, and critical instead of ontological, panpsychism in any full-blooded sense became irrelevant.

In any case, panpsychism played no crucial role in James's articulation of the world view that he thought was general enough to share with *both* Deweyans and personal idealists. The new humanism pictured things in general. It was a "shifting of perspective," he wrote in 1904, "like one of those secular changes that come upon public opinion overnight, as it were, borne upon tides 'too deep for sound or foam,' that survive all the crudities or extravagances of their advocates, that you can pin to no one absolutely essential statement, nor kill by any one decisive stab" (*MT*, 39).

James said that humanism was a shift away from formalism in philosophy, away from the cult of systematicity, analogous to and complementing changes from "aristocracy to democracy, from classic to romantic taste, from theistic to pantheistic feeling, from static to evolutionary ways of understanding life" (*MT*, 39).

Various events and movements led to the abandonment of the vision of nature, mind, and knowledge as static and invariant structures. James said that the three most important influences that conspired to dissolve the old perspective were (1) the emergence of logicians like John Mill, Rudolf Lotze, and Christoph Sigwart who "emphasized the incongruence of the forms of our thinking with the 'things' which the thinking nevertheless handles" (*CER*, 448–49); (2) the doctrine of evolution which viewed the world as plastic and any human function including intellectual ones as adaptive and modifiable; and (3) the recognition that natural scientists had abandoned the quest for certainty in favor of statistical analysis and the generation of probability statements.

Historical events like these motivated a variety of philosophers to align themselves with a humanism that assumed that "it is impossible to strip the human element out from even our most abstract theorizing." The new philosophies were tied together by their commitment to the claim that "all our mental categories without exception have been evolved because of their fruitfulness for life, and owe their being to historic circumstances, just as much as do the nouns and verbs and adjectives in which our languages clothe them" (*CER*, 451).

James warned that humanism suffered from incomplete definition because it was still in the midst of formation. But its "essence" was perfectly plain to James by 1905: humanists claimed that experience has no transempirical supports. To the contrary, they claimed that "tho one part of our experience may lean upon another part to make it what it is in any one of several aspects in which it may be considered, experience as a whole is self-containing and leans on nothing" (*ERE*, 99).

James knew that his abstract description of the essence of humanism "also expresses the main contention of transcendental idealism" (*ERE*, 99). But he claimed that the contention could be supported without relying on the notion of self-transcendence assumed by idealists of any stripe. Like Dewey, and as he himself had argued in earlier work, James argued that "experience is a process that continually gives us new material to digest." People managed the new material intellectually "by the mass of beliefs of which we find ourselves already possessed, assimilating, rejecting, or rearranging in different degrees" (*MT*, 42). Thought went on, in other words, just as all historical entities did, constantly assimilating and accommodating the environmental conditions surrounding it.

Playing on Peirce's phenomenological terminology, James tried to solidify his humanistic position by construing it as three leveled: the first layer of our experience was not fully characterized—it "sets us questions"; the second layer amounted to "the common-sense traditions of the race" or the "fundamental categories, long ago wrought into the structure of our consciousness and practically irreversible, which define the general frame within which the answers must fall"; the third layer involved the "assimilating, rejecting, and re-arranging" of tradition and "gives the detail of the answers" to questions which pure experience set "in the shapes most congruous with all our present needs" (*MT*, 43).

James thought this description secured a metaphysics without ontology. During the years 1904–5, anyhow, humanism left untouched the question "whether the Other, the universal That, has itself any definite structure, or whether, if it have any, the structure resembles any of our predicated *whats*" (*MT*, 431). Ontologically minded philosophers, including transcendental idealists, were engaged in the very questions that "humanism leaves untouched." To be sure, James thought he had to characterize "our" experience in a way that denoted a question-setting *that*. But his characterization left *that* without definite description, on purpose.

As James understood humanism, it was capable of sustaining a variety of submovements precisely because it left the characterization of the "other" an open question. He thought, for instance, that Shadworth Hodgson was a materialist but also a humanist. Dewey was a naturalist and Henri Bergson a panpsychist or vitalist but, according to James, they too were humanists. He read his own humanism "theistically and pluralistically" (*ERE*, 99) and elaborated his position in 1905 as follows:

> If there be a God, he is no absolute all-experiencer, but simply the experiencer of widest actual conscious span. Read thus, humanism is for me a religion susceptible of reasoned defence, tho I am well aware how many minds there are to whom it can appeal religiously only when it has been monistically translated. Ethically the pluralistic form of it takes for me a stronger hold on reality than any other philosophy I know of—it being essentially a *social* philosophy, a philosophy of 'co,' in which conjunctions do the work. But my primary reason for advocating it in philosophical journals is its matchless intellectual economy. It gets rid, not only of the standing 'problems' that monism engenders ('problem of evil,' 'problem of freedom,' and the like), but of other metaphysical mysteries and paradoxes as well.
>
> It gets rid, for example, of the whole agnostic controversy, by refusing to entertain the hypothesis of trans-empirical reality at all. It gets rid of any need for an absolute of the bradleyean type (avowedly sterile for intellectual purposes) by insisting that the conjunctive relations found within existence are faultlessly real. It gets rid of the need of an absolute of a roycean type (similarly sterile) by its pragmatic treatment of the problem of knowledge. [*ERE*, 99]

James had concluded *Varieties* with the claim that persons actually experienced salvation when their selves became conjoint with wider selves in specific ways. He also issued a promissory note to work out a theistic interpretation of things that complemented his claims about the experience of salvation by assenting to an overbelief in crass supernaturalism. Humanism set the context for defending the "reality" of conjunctive relations between people while avoiding both the dilemmas of determinism and the paradoxes involved in absolute idealistic attempts to square the finite with the infinite.

James thought humanism committed him to a doctrine that experience was neither infinite nor finite but (as Bergson was to point out) indefinite.[2] He thought it satisfied man's religious appetites without interfering with the self-denying ordinances of philosophical-mindedness. His humanism presented a picture of things that accommodated actual wrongness, conflict, bifurcation, error, and disease, as well as salvation, reparation, unification, truth, and personal well-being. It held out the possibility of complete world-reparation and transformed the question of the agency of world-integration from a formal one into an empirical one. James executed his key strategic moves for the development of this "religion" in two articles published during 1904: "Does 'Consciousness' Exist?" and "A World of Pure Experience."

The Principle of Pure Experience

The most startling conclusion to *Varieties* was James's contention that people *experienced* conjunctive relations. The reports of divine encounter that he had investigated testified to experienced relations conjoining people and divinities. As James understood them, classical empiricists and rationalists alike disputed the very idea of directly experiencing conjunctions. James challenged this position shared by classical empiricists and rationalists in "Does 'Consciousness' Exist?" On the issue of subjectivism in particular, James's strategy was to develop a position on 'thoughts' and 'things' that would salvage what was important about rationalism and empiricism without generating their paradoxes. James began his essay on consciousness with a historical introduction. He suggested that 'consciousness,' or 'the spiritual principle' maintained by Western philosophers, had lost its personal form after Kant had undermined 'the soul' and introduced his 'transcendental ego.' Ever since Kant, 'consciousness' was construed as "a bare *Bewusstheit* or *Bewusstsein uberhaupt*" (*ERE*, 3)—that is, as noting that the content or material of experience was known.

But James thought that Kant had gone too far. He agreed with Kant that 'the soul' caused more trouble than it was worth when it was employed as a substantial spiritual principle, but he argued that Kant created untold numbers of philosophical puzzles when he threw out the "personal form and activity" traditionally associated with thinking.

James claimed that when 'consciousness' was employed in post-Kantian ways, it named a nonentity. 'Consciousness', he said, does not exist; 'thoughts' do. He claimed that 'consciousness' stood for a function, not an entity. 'Consciousness' was the function which thoughts performed; that function was knowing. But there was no "stuff" out of which thoughts were "made."

Various critics thought that James was claiming that while 'matter' exists, 'consciousness' does not. But they did not understand the force of James's claim. James claimed that 'matter' existed no more than did 'consciousness' (*ERE*, 271). 'Things' existed: 'things' were experiences that got classified as both forceful and stable. 'Mere thoughts' existed also: they were experiences that got classified as practically indifferent and evanescent. 'Things' and 'thoughts' were classification labels for sorts of experience, not distinctive entities or substances.

According to James's post-Kantian opponents, 'consciousness' was the logical correlative of 'content', the notation that something was witnessed. On this view, consciousness was not simply a psychological function; it was an 'epistemological necessity'; it was something that must obtain "even if we had no direct evidence of its being there" (*ERE*, 5). But according to many post-Kantians, consciousness could actually be distinguished by subtracting the content from thought and looking at the remainder. G. E. Moore and Paul Natorp, for instance, held this position.

James contended, to the contrary, that the separation of experience into consciousness and content or into 'thoughts' and 'things' was achieved by addition, not subtraction. He preserved the dualism connoted by 'experience', but reinterpreted the distinction to signal functions, not entities.

His first attempt to demonstrate his claim about thoughts and things focused on perceptual cases. He suggested that if someone began with his actual field of vision, the things that he saw were not situated in two different places simultaneously (for example, "out there" and "in the mind"). A person simply perceived things "there." Working from dualistic assumptions, some philosophers developed "representative" theories of perception to account for this phenomenon. But James argued that their introduction of an "intervening mental image" violated common sense unnecessarily. He argued, to the contrary, that persons subsequently divided their experiences into "subjective" and "objective" ones because perceptual experience was "a place of intersection of two processes" (*ERE*, 8). One of them was the viewer's personal biography; the other was the history of the situation presented in the field of vision. Taken as part of the perceiver's personal history, things were true of the experience which were false when it was treated impersonally.

James argued, further, that conceptual cases could be treated in the same way as perceptual fields. Taken in their "first intention," concepts were bits of pure experience—that is, material to receive further classification, either through connections with the biography of the conceiver or through connections with impersonal or ideal worlds. In other words, on reflection, a person could treat concepts either as instruments of personal discourse or as syntactic and semantic items. In the first instance, James argued, concepts were treated as consciousness; in the second, as content. If this was the case, then subjectivity and objectivity were functional attributes only, realized when experience was "talked-of" twice. Experience as pure was "plain unqualified actuality or existence, a simple *that*"; consciousness, or the subjective aspect of experience, connoted an external relation, not a special stuff or way of being.

On James's grounds, a dreamer first actually experienced a golden mountain; then discovered that it failed to connect with anything outside his dream world; and, hence, classified it as "subjective." This account clarified James's understanding of "pure experience." No general stuff composed pure experience. There were "as many stuffs as there are 'natures' in the things experienced" (*ERE*, 14). Pure experience was no residual experience; it was not preconscious experience. The purity of an experience had no reference to "ontological" issues; it simply classified an experience as not-yet-reflected-upon.

James's view of pure experience had far-reaching consequences for his investigation of religious experience, because he presented those experiences as unqualified observations that persons had made. As they happened, in other words, religious experiences were neither subjective nor objective. They were just actual. Whether religious experiences got classified as subjective or objective or, as James would soon urge, neither subjective nor objective but "affectional," was a matter of further experiences, just as specifiable as the unqualified observations that religious witnesses originally made.

In other words, James thought that if his analysis of experience was adequate, then the charge of subjectivity that haunted his religious investigations was vitiated somewhat. If experiences of conjoint relations with unseen realities, whether conceptual or quasi-sensible, were not inevitably subjective, then neither were religious experiences.

But, James realized, a dualist might contend that the attributes of thoughts and things made them heterogenous: thought, for instance, was absolutely unextended; things were extended. If this were the case, it made no sense to analyze 'thoughts' and 'things' as "the self-same piece of pure experience taken twice over" (*ERE*, 15).

He responded to this objection by claiming that it was false that thoughts and things shared no attributes. Thoughts and things alike were "beautiful, happy, intense, interesting, wise, idiotic, focal, marginal, insipid, confused, vague, precise, rational, casual, general, particular, and many things besides." In fact, James claimed, it was impossible to tell just what sensations contributed to experience as distinguished from thought: "Sensations and apperceptive ideas fuse so intimately that you can no more tell where one begins and the other ends, than you can tell, in those cunning circular panoramas that have lately been exhibited, where the real foreground and the painted canvas join together" (*ERE*, 16). Pure experience came already humanized. Its purity did not reside in its absolute nonhumanity; it resided in its being the first order of any particular experience.

As James construed subjectivity and objectivity, objective fires always burned sticks, whereas subjective fires might or might not burn subjective sticks and, normally, did not burn physical sticks. But their "natures" were identical. The crucial distinction between experiences separated the forceful from the inert. Objective experiences were those that "*act*." Subjective experiences were those "whose members, having identically the same natures, fail to manifest themselves in any 'energetic' way" (*ERE*, 17).

On these grounds, a religious experience became merely subjective when it was shown to be *demonstrably inactive* over the long haul. Critics like Leuba had challenged James's right to ground "objective" claims on "subjective" experience, assuming the traditional, unreconstructed distinction between objectivity as attributable to extended material stuff out there and subjectivity as attributable to unextended spiritual stuff nowhere. On the dualistic view, religious experiences were precluded from playing a role in the adjudication of claims about "objective content" as a matter of principle. But according to James's way of thinking, the question whether religious experiences were merely "subjective" or "objective" was a question of fact, not of principle, a question that was answered by observing the connections between religious experiences and other, subsequent experiences that persons had. Some religious experiences might be "subjective." But the subjectivity of religious experience was demonstrated by specifying its ineffectiveness on the whole, *not* its lack of reference to material objects. Reference played no general role in the subjective/objective distinction, even though it played a *special* role in a particular sort of verification procedure, namely the verification of a particular class of conceptual claims by a particular class of observation reports.

The place of religious facts in a world of pure experience was clarified even further when James distinguished affectional facts from both subjective and objective ones. Critics had complained that it was impossible to tell whether James was talking about divine experiences or experiences of divinity in his Gifford Lectures. Once again, the complaint depended on the traditional dualism of consciousness and content. According to the critics, if experiences of relations with unseen agents were divine experiences, then James was simply specifying certain feelings, certain psychological entities, that some persons had had. But if experiences of relations with unseen agents were experiences *of* divinity, then James was specifying not only feelings but something to which those feelings referred objectively.

James did not raise the problem of divinity specifically in "Does 'Consciousness' Exist?" But he did raise the more general issue about feelings. Certain feelings, particularly *appreciations*, appeared to withstand classification as either subjective or objective. The ambiguities of ordinary language reflected this problem. For instance, experiences of painful objects were also painful experiences: "The adjective wanders as if uncertain where to fix itself." Pain simultaneously connoted an emotion and an objective value. Thus, he said, "Both in the mind and in the thing these natures modify their context, exclude certain associates and determine others, have their mates and incompatibles. Yet not as stubbornly as in the case of physical qualities, for beauty and ugliness, love and hatred, pleasant and painful can, in certain complex experiences, coexist" (*ERE*, 18).

The Place of Affectional Facts

This radically empirical theory of feelings fleshed out the new thought about emotion that James had articulated in *Varieties*. He no longer construed emotion either as a psychological state or as a physiological one. James followed up the contentions that he had made about feeling in "Does 'Consciousness' Exist?" in "The Place of Affectional Facts in a World of Pure Experience." The point of this essay, written in 1905, was to demonstrate how emotional behavior supported the doctrine of pure experience. The commonest objection to the argument for pure experience was that "affections" are made of consciousness exclusively. James admitted that it was possible to imagine a universe of experiences where there were two discrete groupings of experience, one active and the other inactive. Here the physical and mental status of any piece of experience would be unequivocal.

But James claimed that the classification of experience as either mental or physical depended on specific purposes, and further, that emotional or appreciative experiences did not consistently suit the uses to which people put either 'thoughts' or 'things.' He claimed that if the debates about the James-Lange theory of emotions proved anything, they proved that emotions were ambiguous as regarded the psychological/physical distinction.

James's claim was telling, of course, because it charged that a purely physiological account of emotions was inadequate. His new argument was twofold. First, if persons attempted to rigorously classify feelings, affections, or appreciations as subjective or objective, "language would lose most of its esthetic and rhetorical value. . . . The man is really hateful; the actions really mean; the situation really tragic—all in themselves and quite apart from our opinion" (*ERE*, 72). Second, investigators had shown that there was "a primitive stage of perception in which discriminations afterwards needful have not yet been made" (*ERE*, 73). For instance, some people perceived motion-in-general before they associated motion with, say, their own bodies or something else in their situation. The paradigm was the experience of motion people had looking out the window of trains at other objects. James claimed that

> something like this is true of every experience, however complex, at the moment of its actual presence. Let the reader arrest himself in the act of reading this article now. Now this is a pure experience, a phenomenon, or datum, a mere *that* or content of fact. '*Reading*' *simply is, is there*; and whether there for someone's consciousness, or there for physical nature, is a question not yet put. At the moment it is there for neither; later we shall probably judge it to have been there for both.
> [*ERE*, 73]

Affectional experiences maintained this relatively pure condition. James claimed that there was no urgent need to decide whether affectional facts were rigorously mental or physical. To the contrary, they remained equivocal because it was convenient to maintain them as open-textured.

For James's radical empiricism, the bottom metaphysical line was "experience," and "experience was already a fusing of two orders of life," conceptual and sensational. Within this context, emotions and appreciations could be first-order judgments, responses to situations that were spontaneous in the sense that they went without saying, not in the sense that they occurred without training.

Even when affections or appreciations were the subject of rigorous analysis, James argued, there was no unambiguous way to classify them as objective or subjective when those qualities denoted activity or the lack of it. This was so, he reasoned, because "although they are inert as regards the rest of physical nature, they are not inert as regards that part of physical nature which our skin covers. It is those very appreciative attributes of things, their dangerousness, rarity, utility, etc., that primarily appeal to our attention. . . . The 'interesting' aspects of things are thus not wholly inert physically, though they be active only in these small corners of physical nature which our bodies occupy. That, however, is enough to save them from being classed as absolutely non-objective" (*ERE*, 75).

This argument makes no explicit reference to religious experience, but it played a crucial role in bridging James's conclusions about religious facts in *Varieties* and his own religious metaphysics, as he articulated it in *A Pluralistic Universe* and elsewhere. It bolstered his analysis of religious observation reports by demonstrating their lack of peculiarity. Some had argued that James was guilty of treating religious experiences with special gloves, allowing them the privilege to glide between subjective and objective experience. But, on this 1904–5 analysis, a larger class of experiences maintained this status: religious experiences did not differ from other appreciative or affectional experiences in this regard; they exemplified both the privileges and the vagaries of their class.

Others had argued that James had created an artificial distinction between first-order religious experiences and second-order intellectualizations of these more immediate encounters. But, on James's analysis of affectional facts in a world of pure experience, the peculiarity of religious experience in this regard was also dispelled.

Indeed, the very occurrence of religious experiences served, from James's new angle, to impugn the dualistic assumptions on which his critics' positions depended. On the grounds that James established with his 1904–5 radical empiricism, his claim that religious experiences had a quasi-sensible character contained nothing untoward. The new assumption was that experience, whenever "pure," was "objective" in the sense that it was an encounter of something there. If religious persons had encountered divinity this way, the purity of their experiences was indicated, and little else besides.

On James's grounds, there was no inevitable requirement to redescribe religious experience as either objective or subjective. So far as religious experience was affectional, rigorous reconstruction of religious experience as either objective or subjective generated tortured interpretations. On the other hand, James's own assertions about the *authority* of mystical experience received support from his new theory of emotions. If mystical experiences were "inert as regards the rest of physical nature" but active as regarded that part of physical nature which the skin of the mystic covered, they were not unambiguously either objective or subjective. They were powerful enough to compel the mystic to think and do this or that, but they lacked the power to persuade nonmystics to assent to the mystic's claims without further support. They were worth investigation on the nonmystic's part to the extent that he observed active relations between the mystic's affectional experience of divinity and subsequent experiences.

According to James's line of thought, although the first-order experiences of mystics might not affect anything in the nonmystic's experience, and, hence, be classified as subjective, they might effect something more in the mystic's experience that was demonstrable to the nonmystic, and, hence, be classified as objective. Within this context, the crucial question was not whether the religious experiences of mystics were subjective or objective. The crucial question was whether the mystic's religious experience led to other experiences.

To be sure, James's analysis challenged many traditional claims made by religious persons about their own experiences, for instance, all of those persons who claimed that their divinity was utterly objective. But to his credit, James's theory accounted for the predilection on the part of religious persons to insist on the objectivity of divinity. When "objectivity" was analyzed according to "activity" instead of "picturability" or "objective reference," it was sustained for the agent who had been motivated to do things inspired by religious experience. But it was sustained in a way that did not undercut the nonmystic's claim that those experiences were inert for him.

In a world of pure experience, the religious facts that James gathered and distinguished in *Varieties* played a demonstrable role. As affectional, they were neither subjective nor objective. Previous thinkers tortured religious facts by trying to shape them in dualistic molds. Like other affectional facts, "their equivocality is one of their great conveniences" (*ERE*, 73).

James did not think, however, that religious experiences were important simply because they were affectional. He thought that they were important because they were distinctive agents of change. They were agents of change from physiological disease to health, from psychological division to integration, and, most important if most complex, from social conflict to social equilibrium. As such, they were among those "original" experiences from which the very idea of rationality descended: experiences in which people felt a transition from a state of puzzlement and perplexity to a state of continuous or stabilized order of the most all-encompassing sort.

But these claims depended on that one assumption that both rationalists and empiricists agreed was false: the assumption that relations, particularly conjunctive relations, could be experienced. It was one thing for James to have argued successfully that religious experiences should be classified as affectional facts and quite another to argue that religious experiences of relation were even possible.

Chaos and Orders

James had never seriously questioned the communitarian idealism of his father's generation of Romantic religious thinkers. His allegiance to republican ideals largely accounts for his attraction to the new humanism. Both personal idealists and Deweyans emphasized the idea that perfection would be won when complete social order was achieved. The parties to this new world of humanism differed slightly when it came to speculating on the agencies of transformation. But what attracted James to thinkers as diverse as Friedrich Paulsen, F. C. S. Schiller, Harald Höffding, Gustav Fechner, Henri Bergson, and John Dewey was their parallel efforts to make plausible pictures of "the world" as reparative, as becoming more ordered and less divided. This rather vague normative picture tied together parties that otherwise bickered about most philosophical problems. James laid the outlines of a world view that accommodated this "social philosophy" in his essay "A World of Pure Experience."

"A World of Pure Experience" opened with James's typical notice that philosophy was changing in light of the recognition that life was confused and superabundant. Transcendental idealism was "inclining to let the world wag incomprehensively, in spite of its Absolute subject and his unity of purpose"; Berkeleyan idealism was "abandoning the principle of parsimony and dabbling in panpsychic speculations"; empiricism was flirting with teleology; and natural realism was emerging once again. James's radical empiricism competed with these metaphysical positions. He said it was an empiricism, as opposed to a rationalism, because it accounted for things by parts and made "the whole a being of the second order" (*ERE*, 22). But it was more radical than Humean empiricism because it counted conjunctive as well as disjunctive relations as directly experienced.

Ordinary empiricism had emphasized disjunctive relations alone.

Hume had established its major premise when he claimed that "all of our distinct perceptions are distinct existences, and that the mind never perceives any real connection among distinct existences." Empiricism's emphasis on disjunction had motivated rationalism's efforts to correct empiricism's view of a disjointed world by adding a transempirical agent of unification. Radical empiricism, to the contrary, investigated and discovered experiential agents of unification. Radical empiricism, therefore, claimed that it overcame the incoherencies of classical empiricism, while it simultaneously obviated the motivation for rationalist thought about transexperience.

The paradigm for "conjunctive relations," according to James, was "the change" experienced in personal histories or biographies. Personal histories were

> processes of change in time, and the change itself is one of the things immediately experienced. 'Change' in this case means continuous as opposed to discontinuous transition. But continuous transition is one sort of a conjunctive relation; and to be a radical empiricist means to hold fast to this conjunctive relation of all others, for this is the strategic point, the position through which, if a hole be made, all the corruptions of dialectics and all the metaphysical fictions pour into our philosophy. [ERE, 25]

On James's view, no especially enlightened consciousness was required to perceive or feel the change or the continuous transition of one's own personal history. The point, he claimed, was to take this experience "at its face-value, neither more nor less" (ERE, 25).

James had clarified what he meant by the continuity of personal history fourteen years before in his chapter on self-consciousness in *Principles*. There, he had introduced various analogies, including that of "the stream" employed in his analysis of the way thought goes on. But perhaps the most telling analogy he gave compared the continuity of personal history to "Sir John Cutler's pair of black worsted stockings." The identity "which the I discovers, as it surveys this long progression, can only be a relative identity, that of a slow sifting in which there is always some common ingredient retained." This "relative identity" was like Cutler's black worsted stockings "which his maid darned so often with silk that they became at last a pair of silk stockings." These socks were slowly reconstructed until "there was not perhaps one thread left of the first pair of stockings" (PP, 1:372), but at any given time they retained enough of their character for Sir John to think of them as "the same."

The key characteristics of this analogy had to do with its simultaneous emphasis on permanence and change. Just like the stockings, personal histories could cohere, even given all their vicissitudes. From an ahistorical, logical point of view, a pair of worsted stockings could not be identified with a pair of silk stockings. But from an historical point of view that assumed *selective maintenance and elimination from transmission*—that is, from a Darwinian point of view—there was no formal problem in charting relative identity.

Neither personal histories nor stockings were necessarily or inevitably coherent in this historical way. James was fully aware of the phenomena of divided selves, multiple personalities, and self-destructive forms of psychosis. His point was to show that the *normal* experience of persons was an experience of continuity, and hence of constant conjunction among experiences: "Continuity here is a definite sort of experience; just as definite as is the *discontinuity-experience* which I find it impossible to avoid when I seek to make the transition from an experience of my own to one of yours" (*ERE*, 25).

Classical empiricists admitted the discontinuity-experiences; so did classical rationalists. But in failing to admit continuity-experiences on an equal footing (indeed, on any footing), they failed to observe "the originals of the ideas of continuity and sameness, to know what the words stand for concretely, to own all that they can ever mean" (*ERE*, 26).

Personal history, of course, was a particular sort of conjunctive relation: the most "intimate" sort, according to James. Biography illustrated, at its best, the continual achievement of integrity, not simple permanence but a sort of coherence adaptive and accommodating enough to thrive in equilibrium with other persons in surrounding environments. Personal history, and hence personal identity, stood at the apex of a hierarchy of experienced conjunctions. This hierarchy, governed by the norm of inclusive integration, formed variously graded universes for James:

> Merely to be with one another in a universe of discourse is the most external relation that terms can have, and seems to involve nothing whatever as to farther consequences. Simultaneity and time-interval come next, and then space-adjacency and distance. After them similarity and difference, carrying

the possibility of many inferences. Then relations of activity, tying terms into series involving change, tendency, resistance, and the causal order generally. Finally, the relation experienced between terms that form states of mind, and are immediately conscious of continuing each other. . . . The universe of human experience is, by one or another of its parts, of each and all of these grades. Whether or not it possibly enjoys some still more absolute grade of union does not appear upon the surface. [*ERE*, 23–24]

Intimacy was the principle of order in James's hierarchy of universes from 1904 on. But the "self-relation" did not encapsulate the meaning or nature of perfect intimacy, because the "self-relation" might not be fully social. The self-relation was still too privative. Because "my experiences and yours" were, for the most part, simply with one another, the "self-relation" was an example of imperfect intimacy. Perfect intimacy, to the contrary, was achieved in a state of distinctions with no divisions—that is, in the state of well-being that James had investigated in his Gifford Lectures.

James's argument required a social analogy to clarify what he meant by perfect intimacy. But no social analogy was forthcoming until 1908, when he argued that the perfectly intimate universe could be construed as analogous to a federal republic. But that was four years away. In "A World of Pure Experience" the social analogy that he was seeking was simply not specified.

Around the same time that James was writing "A World of Pure Experience," however, he started a metaphysical treatise which established the outlines of his last views on the relations between people, divinity, and the world. The treatise, never finished as such, was called "The Many and the One." In it, James said that "the chief patterns in this world-picturing industry of mine are drawn from the mental and social spheres." Both minds and nations, James suggested, were open-textured enough to be modified "to suit events which interfere with the original plan, and although when one looks back upon a certain finished cycle in either it is possible to trace lines of fulfilment, these are always general and abstract." On this analogy, James was willing to believe that "there may be larger souls than my own, whether connected or disconnected with the larger material aggregations. . . . But I do not believe, picturing the whole as I do, that even if a supreme soul exists, it embraces all the details of the universe in a single absolute act, either of thought or of will." Minds and nations struggled too deeply for James "not to suspect that hindrance and experiment go all the way through" (*TC*, 2:379).

This vision set the context for James's understanding of knowledge as another sort of experienced conjunction. Inquiry was incidental to struggle, both mental and social. James had argued as much since his earliest articles, but now he gave an account of knowledge in strictly social terms. James's early position on knowledge had been criticized as solipsistic. But beginning with his essays in radical empiricism, his position simply assumed "the social situation." It seemed to him "really fantastically formal to ignore *that* much of the truth that is already established, namely, that men do think in social situations. The externality and independence of our 'objects' means primarily that even if *we* be annihilated they are identifiable with objects that are still there for other people" (*TC*, 2:510).

James was analyzing knowledge now as a social historical enterprise in which experiences got conjoined in fruitful ways. His sometime paradigmatic instance of perceptual knowledge or knowledge by acquaintance of some 'thing' by some 'one' was now subordinated to a more basic structure of inquiry that was utterly social in character. He now saw 'cognition' as a relationship between experiences. What counted was the analysis of that relationship, not the attribution of it to individual minds. On radically empirical grounds, cognition occurred when one experience satisfactorily answered questions put to it by other experiences. How these experiences were individuated was beside the point: the solutions that were promulgated were social recommendations—things we ought to believe.

James argued in his section on the cognitive relation that "every conjunction" required to make the cognitive relation intelligible was fully given in finite experience, whether of individuals or groups. For instance, to know that Memorial Hall was a ten-minute walk from his home amounted to a conjunctive relation between a sign and certain experiences related to it externally or as a matter of fact. When James claimed that he knew the hall, he claimed that he could lead others to it, tell them about its history and present uses, and so on. He thought this illustrated the more general fact that knowledge of sensible realities was made by certain relations that unrolled themselves in time. All that knowing of this sort was known-as was the fulfillment of an expectation, of a sign in some object.

James suggested that classical rationalists and empiricists might object that his analysis failed to answer the crucial questions about how one thing can know another. They were bound to argue that "mere intermediaries, even tho they be feelings of continuously growing fulfilment, only separate the knower and the known." But on his analysis, the 'otherness' assumed to exist between knower and known "itself was an illusion" so that the question of how 'one' thing could know 'another' ceased to be a real one. 'Knowledge about' Memorial Hall, for instance, "consists in intermediary experiences (possible if not actual) of continuously developing progress, and finally, of fulfilment, when the sensible percept which is the object is reached" (*ERE*, 29, 31). On these grounds, strictly formal questions about knowledge were irrelevant.

James's critics had argued that his conclusions about religious experience were, at best, empirical generalizations about subjective reports, not 'truths'. The critics depended explicitly on the assumption that 'truth-claims' had to meet certain formal conditions—that is, certain nonobservable conditions like epistemological self-transcendency. But James thought his "Memorial Hall" example demonstrated that one need not ascend from the actual to the formal in order to understand the logic of perceptual knowledge.

In his section on the notion of 'substitution', he gave a radically empirical account of conceptual knowledge that relied on the assumption of experienced conjunctions. Once again, his account was geared to halt the philosophical move from observation to formal "epistemology" in matters of knowledge. He claimed that the importance of conceptual knowledge lay in its substitutive function—that is, the fact that "an experience that knows another can figure as its representative, not in any quasi-miraculous 'epistemological' sense, but in the definite practical sense of being its substitute in various operations, sometimes physical and sometimes mental, which lead us to its associates and results" (*ERE*, 31).

James reasoned that if experience was construed along empirical evolutionary lines, then, "as a whole," it was a process in time. He suggested that the two basic sorts of events that happened in such a world were transitions and arrivals: in a characteristically human world, the important transitions were attempts and the important arrivals were achievements. If this was so, then "the only function that one experience can perform is to lead into another experience; and the only fulfilment we can speak of is the reaching of a certain experienced end" (*ERE*, 32).

On these grounds, the function of thought was to "outstrip the tardy consecutions of the things themselves, and sweep us on towards their ultimate termini in a far more labor-saving way than the following of trains of sensible perception ever could." To be sure, many thoughts were not substitutes for anything actual or virtual. When signs were wholly nonsubstitutional, they ended "outside the real world altogether, in wayward fancies, utopias, fictions, and mistakes" (*ERE*, 32). But where signs substituted for objects, they were normally employed to achieve certain things better and more easily than otherwise. Signs were more manageable commodities than the objects for which they stood.

But here again, James recognized that classical rationalists and empiricists were likely to see the "epistemological chasm" rearing its ugly head. He said he faced the most important step "in the development of a philosophy of pure experience." He had to show that the dispute over "self-transcendency," which generated the distinctive enterprise of *erkenntnistheorie*, was "a pure logomachy" (*ERE*, 33, 36). "Epistemologists" tried to establish the formal grounds for any claim to knowledge, given the chasm assumed to exist between mind and reality. But as James saw things, the notion of 'self-transcendency' derived from the experience of substituting signs for objects, and hence, from perfectly empirical events.

James argued that anyone who was operating on signs that substituted for objects was having an experience "that reaches beyond itself" in empirically specifiable ways. The inference, for example, from 'smoke' to 'fire' was successful because observations of smoke were, all things being equal, followed not only subsequently but consequently by observations of fire. James's view of knowing admitted that the notion of self-transcendency counted for so much. But the more traditional views of knowing went on to claim that knowledge occurred if and only if thoughts *referred to reality*.

As James saw it, the challenge thrown to the radical empiricist by the traditionalist was How could the radical empiricist account for the fact that things thought to be true turned out to be false without invoking the notions of correspondence and objective reference? James's answer to this challenge depended on making a distinction between actual and virtual knowledge. He argued that people virtually knew things long before they were certified as actually knowing them. Their assertions were virtually true before they withstood the tests of experience and the demands of critics.

Within this framework, "objective reference" was not a special relationship between mind and reality. It was simply "an incident of the fact that so much of our experience comes as an insufficient and consists of process and transition" (*ERE*, 35). In the traditional view, either "our ideas are self-transcendent and 'true' already, in advance of the experiences that are to terminate them," or knowledge was impossible. But when James unpacked 'self-transcendence' pragmatically, the difference between claiming that ideas are true despite their justification (the traditional view) and claiming that ideas would be found to have been true (the radical empiricist view) was trivial. The fruits for inquiry were the same.

On these grounds, there were no good reasons to construe knowledge in terms of formal or static relations. Assertions warranted in the short run sometimes failed to maintain their warrants in the long run. Hence, things thought to be true turned out to be false. But nobody had to leave the theater of empirical observations to account for this.

James's "knowledge" joined hands with his notion of "pure experience" and, more generally, his "social" philosophy of work getting done conjointly. Consciousness did not exist. Knowledge functioned to resolve the theoretical and practical problems of men by substituting signs for objects in effective ways. James thought he had accomplished this in his conclusions to *Varieties*. He had substituted thoughts about religious experience which outstripped "the tardy consecutions of the things themselves" in order to break the deadlock between materialists and theists over the significance of religious experience and, hence, in order to vindicate the "economic" importance of religion for human life.

More generally speaking, James construed knowledge in ways that made it part of his religious picture of things: knowledge helped to order (and reorder) the physical and social sorts of chaos that constantly threatened humanity. It was man's way of cooperating with the world for the sake of well-being. Knowledge was essentially social. Inquiry proceeded through shared procedures, regulations, and conclusions. Once this experimental view of knowledge was accepted, James thought it was impossible to "subscribe to the idealism of the English school." For Berkeleyan idealists, individual experiences of 'Memorial Hall' were discontinuous. Even if both experiences were perceptual, they were "wholly out of connexion with each other" (*ERE*, 37). For Berkeley, God had to join what experience put asunder. James said that because idealists held this view, radical empiricists were closer to natural realists. But radical empiricists differed from both these schools by construing the problem of shared knowledge as empirical, not formal.

James argued that "if the reader will only allow that the same '*now*' ends his past and begins his future; or that, when he buys an acre of land from his neighbor, it is the same acre that successively figures in the two estates . . . he will also in consistency have to allow that the same object may conceivably play a part in . . . any number of otherwise entirely different minds. . . . *It is therefore not a formal question, but a question of empirical fact solely*" (*ERE*, 39–40).

Both English idealists and natural realists were empirically refuted, idealists because they asserted that what was actual was impossible, realists because they carried shared knowledge too far. According to James, people may share some knowledge. When he and Royce looked at Memorial Hall, for instance, they were looking at the same *place*. At least, "there is no test discoverable, so far as I know, by which it can be shown that the place occupied by your percept of Memorial Hall differs from the place occupied by mine" (*ERE*, 41). But there were plenty of tests capable of demonstrating that perspectives on Memorial Hall differed, depending on the orientations that persons took toward it. In general, persons shared the same knowledge if they answered the same questions about the same subject matter. But this made the problem of shared knowledge empirical: Persons could share the same knowledge and often did. "Epistemologists" might spin wheels on questions about how they could possibly do this, but only on the assumption of the old dualism.

Knowledge thus retained its importance in James's radical empiricist view, but not "epistemology" or the search for the formal conditions of knowledge. Knowledge was important because it played a crucial role in the invaluable business of increasing the "unity" of the world. For James, "the universe continually grows in quantity by new experiences that graft themselves upon the older mass; but these very new experiences often help the mass to a more consolidated form" (*ERE*, 43).

James clarified his position on shared knowledge in subsequent articles written during 1905. In "How Two Minds Can Know One Thing," James argued that a unit of pure experience could enter into an indefinite number of consciousnesses. First, he reminded his reader how, for instance, *that pen* becomes part of consciousness initially. When *that pen* is construed retrospectively as a percept, it figures as a fact in conscious life. *That pen* had to be used a particular way in order to be classed as a psychical fact. But *that pen* "stands, throughout the operation, passive and unchanged" (*ERE*, 64).

If this was so, *that pen* became a piece of shared knowledge or consciousness when "a second subsequent experience, collateral and contemporary with the first subsequent one" appropriated it. Thus, "the paradox of the same experience figuring in two consciousnesses seems thus no paradox at all." On the grounds of the doctrine of pure experience, experience-as-it-happened could be "postulated with any amount whatever of span or field" (*ERE*, 65, 66). If this was so, somebody could have a pure experience of somebody else's conscious experience. For instance, William could experience *that pen*. Henry could witness William experiencing *that pen*. Alice could witness Henry witnessing William reporting *that pen*. Even if their three orientations toward *that pen* differed, it was the same pen.

If this was so, there were fewer reasons to doubt James's analysis of religious experience as coconscious experience, especially when he insisted that the more God-like self, the wider self, inherited the thought of the older, narrower self in order to complete it. *Varieties* made the possibility of coconscious experience come to life through the documentation of actual cases. Thus, it is little wonder that James concluded his remarks on shared knowledge with the claim that "speculations like Fechner's, of an Earth-soul, of wider spans of consciousness enveloping narrower ones throughout the cosmos, are, therefore, philosophically quite in order, provided they distinguish the functional from the entitative point of view, and do not treat the minor consciousness under discussion as a kind of standing material of which the wider ones consist" (*ERE*, 67).

A New Pantheism Emerges

From the vantage point of his religious investigations, James's radically empirical analysis of knowledge was important for a number of reasons. First, it took his view of "full personal facts" seriously. Second, it clarified the reasons for initiating the scientific investigation of religion by considering first-order, relatively 'pure' observation reports about divine encounter. Third, it corroborated his picture of the deliverances of religious experiences as true for religious persons so long as those deliverances solved relevant, living problems for those persons without their becoming overly problematic or infirm in light of other beliefs they held. Finally, it provided a view of things that made talk about coconsciousness, even coconsciousness between humans and infra- and super-humans, sensible (if not sound).

On James's view, of course, organized inquiry was not the only sort of activity that served to "consolidate" the universe. Indeed, his analysis of knowledge depended on a defense of the notion of activity, and particularly the notion of cooperative activity. The latter notion was particularly crucial for his religious investigations, given his claim that religious experiences were, first and foremost, cooperative.

The survival theorists of religion had assumed that scientific progress had displaced analyses of human affairs as personal activity with impersonal causal explanations. James attacked the philosophical assumptions of their strategy in "The Experience of Activity," published in 1905. There, James turned the tables on the positivists. He argued that, in fact, the original experience of 'causality' was most likely the experience of motivated, purposive, successful action characteristic of persons.

James argued that much of the debate over 'activity' resulted from jumbling three different questions together: the psychological question concerning the perception of activity, the metaphysical question whether there was a *fact* of activity, and the logical question how people knew activity. He attempted to introduce the pragmatic principle to hash these issues out.

By the principle of pure experience—the principle that everything real must be experienceable and everything experienced must be real—either 'activity' was a meaningless term or "the original type and model of what it means must lie in some concrete kind of experience" (*ERE*, 81). James suggested that there were more and less specific senses of the term 'activity.' In the broadest and vaguest sense, 'activity' meant "something going on" or "life" or "change taking place." Even if no more specific meaning could be given, this made Bradley's contention that "there is no original experience of anything like activity" preposterous.

But "bare activity" was distinguishable from activity in the most full-blooded sense. James argued that the psychological question about activity was answered by observing those complex experiences in which something was going on, but with *definite* direction, accompanied by desires and a sense of goal, complicated with resistances which were overcome or succumbed to. Here, "the notions of distinct agents, and of passivity as opposed to activity arise. Here also, the notion of causal efficacy comes to birth" (*ERE*, 83).

Whatever investigators might claim about the facts of activity, and whatever they might claim about the criteria for distinguishing activities from other sorts of events, full-blooded personal activity provided the subject matter for their work. Whether activity was attributed to mental agents or physical causes, and whether activity was directed or aimless, resistance complicated the situation. If some tendency continued despite resistance, 'effort' made its appearance, and 'will' appeared when 'effort' was sustained. On the other hand, when a resistance to any tendency was too great, 'tension' or 'succumbing' appeared. If activity did go on outside of our experience, according to James, people had to suppose it to be "something sustaining a felt purpose against felt obstacles, and overcoming and being overcome" (ERE, 85).

But some philosophers, for example, Arthur Lovejoy, Bradley, Hugo Münsterburg, and G. F. Stout, claimed that merely to feel, perceive, or experience activity was not activity 'itself', because neither the 'agents' nor the 'resistances' nor the 'effects' said to be part of activity-situations were real. Thus, they broached the metaphysical question. These philosophers claimed that the experience of activity was simply the record of it and that more basic questions had to do with 'activity' before a record of it got made.

James argued that three metaphysical positions on activity competed for philosophical attention. Absolute or transcendental idealists took "a consciousness of wider time-span than ours to be the vehicle of the more real activity. Its will is the agent, and its purpose is the action done." Associational psychologists claimed that " 'ideas' struggling with one another are the agents, and that the prevalence of one set of them is the action." Medical materialists claimed that "nerve-cells are the agents, and that resultant motor discharges are the acts achieved" (ERE, 89).

James noted that if the transcendentalists were right, then he was lecturing for a wider thinker who was the agent of the lectures. If people took the wider thinker in a religious way—that is, as someone supportive of his own intentions—then "he does not derealize my activities. He tends rather to corroborate them so long as I believe both them and him to be good" (ERE, 89).

But if ideas were the agents of the lecture, James claimed, then they achieved it for him, but might or might not satisfy the intentions that he seemed to himself to have in mind. Finally, he claimed, if nerve cells were the agents of the lecture, then "the gross resultant, as I perceive it, is indifferent to the agents, and neither wished or willed or foreseen. Their being agents now congruous with my will gives me no guarantee that like results will recur again from their activity." What made the metaphysical problem interesting was the relation that held between "long-span" or "teleological tendencies" and "short-span actions summing themselves 'blindly.' " The important question was "Are the forces that really act in the world more foreseeing or more blind? As between 'our' activities as 'we' experience them, and those of our ideas, or of our brain-cells, the issue is well defined" (ERE, 90, 91).

In fact, James argued, the metaphysical question about activity boiled down to the old question of creation. Real activities were causal. They effected things otherwise not. The experience of activity seemed to be the experience of creation. But when philosophers claimed that the experience of activity was merely a subjective impression, they inferred that the experience of creation, of causing something to be brought into being, was "only a shadow of another fact" (ERE, 92).

Assuming the doctrine of pure experience and the principle of pragmatism, James argued that naive experience established the *quality* of activity. The empirical sciences were geared to establish answers to questions about the *conditions* of activity. So that, from a radical empiricist point of view, "the greater sublimity traditionally attributed to the metaphysical inquiry . . . entirely disappears." The traditional metaphysicians, the ontologists, were guilty of "grubbing underground for what effects effectuation, or what makes action act" (ERE, 94). The healthy thing for philosophy to do was to stop this sort of inquiry, which depended upon an unnecessary appearance/reality bifurcation.

From a radical empirical point of view, James argued, naive experience and empirical investigation delivered "the whole butt and being" of activity. He commended philosophers to "try to solve the concrete questions of where effectuation in this world is located, of which things are the true causal agents there, and of what the more remote effects consist" (ERE, 94). But these were empirical pursuits, neither "epistemological" nor "ontological."

James was not issuing any positivist call to arms in this work on activity, but various philosophers, like Walter Pitkin, took James's attack on "ontologists" this way.[3] Pitkin reasoned that if, as James claimed, "experience is self-supporting (in *any* intelligible sense)," then it was impossible for there to be something *not* experienced *and* impossible for there to be any relation between or interactions between things seen and things unseen. But James replied that the radical empiricism that he maintained did not preclude the possibility of either unexperienced things or interactions between seen and unseen things. James simply remarked: "How could it?" Radical empiricism, particularly the doctrine of pure experience, amounted to a methodological postulate for metaphysical debate, *not* an ontological conclusion "supposed to flow from the intrinsic absurdity of transempirical objects." Thus, James said that he was "perfectly willing to admit any number of noumenal beings or events into philosophy if only their pragmatic value can be shown" (ERE, 123).

The point of James's methodological postulate was not to preclude speculation about unseen realities but to insist that such speculation must be developed to account for things or events that were observed or observable. No one had observed atomic particles when James articulated his position, but he did not wish to insist by his doctrine that atomic theory should not be considered in debates about physical behavior. He developed his doctrine in order to insist that, say, atomic theory was introduced to account most specifically for manifest phenomena. More to the point, James declared that his humanism was theistic and sought to confirm the "unseen realities" evidenced in *Varieties*. He just insisted that theism account specifically for religious and other manifest experiences. These theoretical nuts and bolts accorded religious speculation about first and last things a place in intellectually defensible thought.

James's work in radical empiricism, especially his work on 'activity', provided the keys to understanding the place of religious experience in the world. Once the old dualism was displaced by radical empiricism, religious experiences could be classified as affectional facts, neither "subjective" nor "objective" in any unreconstructed sense, but *active* in specifiable ways, *inactive* in others. Their function as organizers of personal integrity and harbingers of social harmony or equilibrium could be clarified within this philosophical context, which James thought was a satisfactory answer to the *formal* criticism of subjectivity.

What is more, James's new view overcame many of the qualms that he had maintained about construing his religious position as a sort of pantheism. His inability to accept pantheism had been threefold: He could not believe that, if there was a God, nature was his adequate expression, because nature per se was all plasticity. Second, he could not accept the deterministic character of absolute idealistic pantheism, because moral judgments of regret were nonsense on those grounds. Third, he was convinced that allegiance to the logic of identity precluded acceptance of absolute pantheism, which entailed identification of the one with the many.

But once James accepted humanism or radical empiricism, an unhumanized nature became an abstraction and the logic of identity became a conceptual tool with a limited range of reference. Moreover, James realized he could speculate that divinity was in the making. It occurred to him that a pantheistic God might be an "Ultimate," not an absolute, an "extract" from experience, not "the whole" (*Prag*, 142). James had concluded in his Gifford Lectures that the varieties of religious experience supported a kind of intimate theism, a theism in which gods were more and people were less of the same sort of power—the power to overcome the diseases resulting from social-psychological bifurcation. This theism departed entirely from what James called orthodox philosophical theology; its "intimacy" coupled it with the pantheism of the Romantics in one crucial respect.

Now, James thought, if the problem with pantheism of a Romantic sort is simply that it is an abstraction or a "saltatory" reconstruction of some ongoing process, then it could be resolved by reconstructing pantheism once again in order to restore the "ambulatory" character of divinity—that is, the process of world-unification. James's lectures on pragmatism, delivered in 1906, continued his religious investigations by clarifying what he meant when he talked about world-unification. He shed light on this issue in his lecture on "the most central of all philosophical problems," the problem of the one and the many. There, he demonstrated his self-consciousness about the vagaries of the notions of "unification" and "continuity." He distinguished various sorts of unity and continuity, once again attempting to establish a hierarchy of "universes." To begin with, he posited universes of discourse and universes of operation and argued that the claim that "the world" presented a universe of discourse simply announced an intention to talk about everything, to leave nothing out. But he also argued the existence of various specific, operative universes: for instance, mechanical, electrical, chemical, and social ones. These "systems" resulted "in little worlds, not only of discourse, but of operation, within a wider universe" (*Prag*, 67).

According to James, the universe of discourse, the intention to talk about everything, was "wider" than any of the universes of operation, and all of them together. Nobody could claim on evidence that the world had any unity of purpose. Oneness might mean aesthetic union, but here again, the hypothesis that the world was unified "outstrips the evidence." It followed that "whoever says that the whole world tells one story utters another of those monistic dogmas that a man believes at his risk." If absolute idealists like Royce insisted on teleological and aesthetic unity, they "brought us no farther than the book of Job did—God's ways are not our ways, so let us put our hands upon our mouth" (*Prag*, 71, 70). Pantheism of an absolute sort ended in mystery, or in a failure to clarify adequately the relationship between the knowledge, purposes, and histories of persons and "infinite" knowledge, purpose, and life.

On pragmatic grounds, the philosophical problem of the one and the many dissolved. So far as "the world" could be given specification, it was "neither a universe pure and simple nor a multiverse pure and simple" (*Prag*, 73). Thus, the formal inquiry generated by Parmenides' question whether one real world lay behind its many appearances was superfluous. What mattered were material or factual questions about coherence. From James's perspective, the task was to order things "economically" for nations and the people who constituted them so that the problems which stood in the way of realizing personal and impersonal worths could be resolved as adequately as possible. But, here, contingency was the important consideration.

James's discussion of world-unification brought him closer to specifying his ideal universe in completely social terms. When he got around to articulating his hierarchy of universes this time (1906), a full-blown vision of society rested at the pinnacle. The unity of the ego, or personal integrity, demonstrated a higher order of things than any world which lacked persons. But altogether "private" minds were less powerful agents of purposive organization than minds with "social life." Interestingly enough, when James graded sorts of social life, the life of friends, of simple love, did not come out best. James asserted, instead, that the best sort of universe was one in which customs and institutions systematized love. This marked a development from the vision of salvation articulated in the Gifford Lectures four years before, in which James had taken his father's line that the perfect life was the life of friends. He now reasoned with Royce and Peirce (and after Hegel) that institutions and customs stabilized relationships that were otherwise too spontaneous to be depended upon for economic order. They conserved orders of the highest quality, so they were agents of world-unification. They were "those systems of connexion . . . which human energy keeps framing as time goes on" (*Prag*, 77, 76). They illustrated what a perfect universe would look like. Not least important, they were evolved in consequence of specific human needs.

James's line of thought on social institutions led him to declare that

> with the whole of past eternity open for our conjectures to range in, it may be lawful to wonder whether the various kinds of union now realized in the universe that we inhabit may not possibly have been successively evolved after the fashion in which we now see human systems evolving in consequence of human needs. If such a hypothesis were legitimate, total oneness would appear at the end of things rather than at their origin. In other words, the notion of the 'Absolute' would have to be replaced by that of the 'Ultimate.' The two

notions would have the same content—the maximally unified content of fact, namely,—but their time relations would be positively reversed. [*Prag*, 77–78]

If human systems—that is, institutions and customs—were agents of order in the universe, James thought it was surely possible to speculate that the universe might possibly achieve more and more economic order of that sort.

But James was asserting something more than this. He was claiming that every sort of order might have evolved as human institutions developed: to fulfil a need. If this were so, then every order might be the result of intelligent intelligence. Everything as ordered might participate in some purposive enterprise. If this were so, a kind of pantheism might be defensible (but not the kind defended by absolute monists). In other words, everything as ordered might participate in some divinity or providence or power to satisfy personal needs.

The problem with the pantheisms of the absolute idealists was that they "brooked of no degrees." "The independence, however infinitesimal, of a part, however small, would be to the absolute as fatal as a cholera germ" (*Prag*, 78). From an absolute idealistic point of view, chaos or disorder was, if not illusory, not "ontologically" real either. James wanted to articulate a pantheism that admitted real *chaos* on the one hand but real *reparation* of chaos on the other. In order to do this, he thought he had to show that while elements of the universe were chaotic, the world was constituted in ways that admitted, perhaps even promised, effective management of difficulties. He tried to do this in his lectures "Pragmatism and Humanism" and "Pragmatism and Religion."

In his lecture "Pragmatism and Humanism," James endorsed Lotze's contention that the nonhuman universe could rationally be construed as stimulating sorts of intelligent activity that made value-enhancing additions to reality. According to the view that James was commending, "the world stands really malleable, waiting to receive its final touches at our hands. Like the kingdom of heaven, it suffers human violence willingly. Man *engenders* truth upon it" (*Prag*, 123). His world, in other words, was *not* securely divine and, as it stood, everything in it was *not* full of soul. So far as James's pragmatism claimed this, of course, it was no longer simply a method for adjudicating metaphysical disputes or a genetic theory of truth. It was a cosmology from which the method and the theory were derived.

James was prepared to argue that from historical evidence that was specifiable, "salvation" or deliverance from chaos was a warrantable hope. He said that "nothing outside of the flux secures the issue of it," but that persons could "hope salvation" from the "promises and potencies" that they have already experienced. Persons could point not only to their own deliberate activities as ordering otherwise chaotic situations but also to their participation in events divine enough to solve problems that deliberation failed to resolve.

James pursued this line of thought on salvation in his lecture "Pragmatism and Religion." There his desideratum was to show that the pragmatist took perfection or salvation as a possible *terminus ad quem*. Within theology the pragmatic difference between rationalists and empiricists revolved about "the notion of the world's possibilities." For James and other empiricists, "the world *may be* saved." For absolute idealists like Royce, "the world must and shall be saved" (*Prag*, 135). In other words, while idealists like Royce maintained a doctrine of optimism, claiming that the salvation of the world was inevitable, James (along with both personal idealists like George Howison and naturalists like Dewey) continued to hold a doctrine of meliorism, claiming as he had in *Varieties* that the chance of salvation was sufficient for the religious consciousness to live on, and far more rational because far more probable than idealist optimism.

James was not prepared to defend the commonsense notion of 'possibility' if that meant "a sort of third estate of being, less real than existence, more real than nonexistence." But 'possibility' was used in two philosophically respectable ways, according to James: to signal the absence of real grounds of interference and to signal the actuality of requisite conditions. On this analysis, he argued, "salvation" was a grounded possibility because every cherished ideal that became realized was "one moment in the world's salvation" (*Prag*, 136, 138). Human activities created the world's salvation so far as they made room for themselves.

To be sure, James asserted, as things actually are, "the wishes of the individual are only one condition. Other individuals are there with other wishes and they must be propitiated first. So Being grows under all sorts of resistances in this world of the many, and from compromise to compromise, only gets organized gradually into what may be called secondarily rational shape." From this view, the business of salvation was "a social scheme of co-operative work genuinely to be done. . . . It is a real adventure, with real danger, yet it may win through." That it might was enough for some to respond to the challenge, especially those healthy-minded enough to withstand the inevitable tragedies involved. That it might not made some practically inert. The danger made "their teeth chatter, it refrigerates the very heart within their breast" (*Prag*, 139, 140).

But James did not construe the disjunction between absolute idealism and humanistic meliorism as equivalent to one between religion in the sense of self-surrender and moralism in the sense of self-sufficingness. If the world "existed distributively and were made up of a lot of eaches, it could only be saved piece-meal and *de facto* as the result of their behavior," and it could only be saved at some expense. But a specifiable sort of harmony could be achieved. James asserted that he could maintain this view of "a drastic kind of universe" without being either an atheist or a self-sufficing moralist because there might be suprahuman forces promoting human welfare. He thought his book "on men's religious experience, which on the whole has been regarded as making for the reality of God" (*Prag*, 143) demonstrated as much.

In *Varieties*, certain events made the distinction between self-surrender and self-sufficingness an inadequate tool for clarifying the role that persons played in the realization of their most cherished ideals. If saintly conduct looked for all the world to epitomize self-sufficingness, it felt like self-surrender to the self-sufficing saint who avowed a new self when she or he encountered "more" than the old self and experienced something powerful enough to achieve what the old self found practically impossible. The saintly methods made it plain that if "personal acts" are "the workshop of being" (*Prag*, 138), where the facts of world-unification are caught in the making, those "personal acts" depend upon the cooperation of unseen powers personal enough to share intentions but superhuman enough to realize them when deliberation fails.

James believed that of all the sorts of theology, pantheism gave the best account of the human drive toward harmony because it permitted a construal of divinity as a pattern of behavior in which an indefinite number of discrete agents could participate. What he could not abide, out of allegiance to experience, was a pantheism "through and through," a pantheism that made everything inevitably full of soul, rational, in equilibrium, saved, delivered, or perfected. His task was to develop a "concatenated" pantheism, a really adventurous theology that speculated that gods helped men achieve their ideals but that the chaos or disorder or evil that men faced might prove too difficult for even god and man together to manage.

This theological venture was one of James's pursuits during 1908–9, as he prepared and delivered his Hibbert Lectures, "The Present Situation in Philosophy," subsequently published as *A*

Pluralistic Universe. But before James developed his final theological vision, he made good on his promise to Leuba by attempting to reconstruct the meaning of 'truth' in order to safeguard the inference from 'good for life' to 'true' under special conditions.

CHAPTER 8

PRAGMATISM AND THE

PROBLEM OF RELIGIOUS TRUTH

The Charge of Capriciousness

James had argued in *Varieties* that the humanly fittest religious beliefs should survive and that the fitness of religious belief was analyzable by dispositions connected with it. He had argued, as well, that "epistemological truth" played no role in the appreciation of religious belief, though truthfulness in the sense of trustworthiness did. But if footnotes mark afterthoughts, James had realized after he finished delivering his Gifford Lectures that he had waffled between two meanings of 'truth', one connoting "bare value for life" and another connoting "something additional," or cognitive value (*VRE*, 509).

From a contemporary perspective, James's challenge to *erkenntnistheorie*, or the formal and distinctive discipline of epistemology, appears incredibly presumptuous. Today the history of philosophy is often written from the point of view of philosophers interested in charting the development of contemporary, competing epistemological theories, but when James wrote his essays on truth, this tendency was just beginning to emerge. The major philosophical figure in America who lent full support to the drive to turn philosophy into *erkenntnistheorie* was Royce. In his 1882 article "Mind and Reality,"[1] Royce had written that "ontology is play, the theory of knowledge is work. Ontology is the child blowing soap-bubbles, philosophical analysis is the miner digging for gold." He urged "the return to Kant," and, moreover, to the Kant who figured in an important way in the development of philosophy understood as epistemology. James was a lot more like Bradley than Royce with respect to "epistemology." Bradley claimed that he was "not competent to give any opinion as to what is to hold good within epistemology" (1900). For James, knowing was one very important external relation which linked experiences, and it was understandable without ascent to the formal questions of *erkenntnistheorie*.

Royce was the first philosopher to develop any major criticism of James's pragmatism insofar as it was relevant to issues in the theory of knowledge. His paper "The Eternal and the Practical" was delivered as the Presidential Address before the American Philosophical Association in 1903 and was largely based on a view of James's position as articulated in the essays collected in *The Will to Believe*.

The position that Royce took was that Jamesean pragmatism accounted fairly well for the historiographic process of evaluation or judgment, but failed to distinguish this process from the objective conditions that made it possible. Royce claimed, in other words, that Jamesean pragmatism confused a social-psychological process with a set of logical or epistemological conditions. In consonance with his view of James, he was ready to admit that "everything finite and temporal is practical." But he argued that if James believed this, he ought also to believe that "all that is practical borrows its truth from the eternal."[2] In other words, he argued that a sound pragmatic theory of justification logically depended on the epistemology of Roycean absolute idealism. This was why Royce called himself an absolute pragmatist.

To be sure, Royce acknowledged that his 1903 argument was as much an argument against his own early, James-inspired pragmatism as anything else. Royce's first important article had expressed a theory of truth "wholly in terms of an interpretation of our judgments as present acknowledgments." Since this theory of truth "made these judgments the embodiment of conscious attitudes that I conceived to be essentially ethical, and to be capable of no restatement in terms of any absolute warrant," Royce argued, it was "pure pragmatism" (117). But Royce subsequently modified that pragmatism when he became convinced that philosophical moves could be made to show that judgments require absolute warrants.

It was important that Royce was arguing against his own earlier brand of pragmatism. Royce's pragmatism shared only *some* elements with the theory of truth that James was articulating simultaneously, in 1903. Royce said as much in his article, but then went on to argue against "pure pragmatism" as if it were the core position shared by James, Dewey, and F. C. S. Schiller. His argument had seven steps. First, he characterized pragmatism as claiming that "every judgment, whatever else it may prove to be, is the expression of a present activity, determined by a consciousness of need, and is such as this need determines" (141). In other words, he characterized pragmatism as claiming that judgments are responses to present situations, and not copies of external objects. He endorsed this claim.

But, second, he argued that one need that persons aimed to satisfy in their constructive responses to situations was the "need that our judgments should not only be ours but true" (141). And third, he analyzed this need as the need for corroboration of our response from other points of view—first, our own other points of view; next, the points of view of other persons.

Royce was prepared to accept all three points. But at this place in his argument, he criticized certain pragmatists for arguing their theory of truth from the theory of evolution propounded by Darwin. Surely James was among those he had in mind. Royce claimed that "the evidence for pure pragmatism, if there is such evidence, must rest on what you can now observe as to your present thought and its objects." But "the evidence for the doctrine of evolution must rest upon beliefs that relate to vast numbers of objects such as are supposed somehow to have existed long before you or I or any other human being could have been there to acknowledge their existence" (128). In other words, he challenged the capacity of pure pragmatism to account for historical knowledge, or for historiographic conditions allowing historical knowledge to occur.

Royce assumed that the pure pragmatist was a psychological individualist, who had no way to account for shared knowledge, either synchronically or diachronically. He also argued that those pragmatists who defended their position in light of the doctrine of evolution either executed viciously circular arguments or depended on some nonpragmatic understanding of truth when it came to Darwinian theory. They either established the authority of Darwin's theory on pragmatic grounds and then derived the authority of pragmatism from his theory, or they assumed that his theory was really or absolutely true and derived the authority of pragmatism from this nonpragmatically warranted source.

In fact, Royce suggested, pragmatists did not simply need to believe in the doctrine of evolution; they supposed that they *ought to need so to believe.* But, according to Royce, pure pragmatists had no way to account for the 'ought'. The deployment of an 'ought' depended on the assumption of a social or intersubjective situation, but pure pragmatism was solipsistic. "Modified pragmatists" like James might appeal to "well recognized objective truths,—to evolution, to common sense, to whatever is likely to seem universally valid" (129, 131), but they had no way to account for universal validity on their own grounds. Pragmatists should feel lonesome, but they do not, because they do not systematically apply their doctrine. Royce said they appealed to objective grounds as much as anyone else, but they did not notice that judgments were not only constructive responses but social *resolves*. So, Royce concluded, the pragmatist is caught in the following dilemma: "If the pragmatist has taught us a truth, then he has done something more than assume his inner needful attitudes. But if he has merely adjusted himself to his conscious environment by means of his own inner mental reconstruction, then he has instructed nobody and refuted nobody; and has said nothing that has genuine meaning for anybody but himself" (134).

This conclusion led to Royce's fourth step: in order to correct the deficiencies of the pragmatic position on truth, philosophers must assume that other points of view, including an objective point of view, belonged to and were included within "a single self, whose partial functions these various selves are, and whose common conscious purpose defines the ought to which each of the various judgments is to conform." The needful responses of individuals were partially adequate representations of the needs and satisfactions of one self who (fifth) could not be mutable and still determine a "genuine ought." So (sixth), the self whose point of view was objective must be invariant and inclusive of all mutable points of view. Thus, finally, the self that conditions cognitive statements, whether true or false, "is of course complete at no moment of time," but eternal (141, 142).

Religious Truth in the Gifford Lectures

The brunt of Royce's criticism was the charge of capriciousness. "The Eternal and the Practical" was written after *Varieties*, but without reference to it. So the question arises whether Royce's criticisms apply to the methods of appreciation that James used in *Varieties* to generate his truth-claims. As a matter of fact, Royce's 1903 essay presented all eight "misunderstandings" of pragmatism that James was to catalog in 1908. As Royce understood the modified pragmatic position which borrowed support from such things as the doctrine of evolution and common sense, it was (1) like positivism, agnosticism, and skepticism because it suggested that *real* truth was inaccessible to people; (2) a sort of individual voluntarism, construing truth in terms of individual needs; (3) incapable of warranting claims which transcended present experience; (4)

subjectivistic, equating truth with satisfaction; (5) inconsistent, either absolutely true or not true at all; (6) guilty of clumping psychological issues together with logical ones; (7) guilty of ignoring theoretic interests, or any interest beyond that of the present moment; and therefore, finally, (8) solipsistic.

In the Gifford Lectures, however, James had gone out of his way to distinguish his pragmatism from positivism, agnosticism, and skepticism. The very idea of a science of religions cut against these movements. It was predicated on the assumption that persons could overcome real and living doubts through inquiry. So far as one was agnostic, one did not participate in such enterprises.

James's methods of appreciation were also articulated in direct competition with both positivism and skepticism. Positivists, especially the survival theorists, equated the unseen with the unreal. But James's pragmatism permitted speculation about unseen things, so long as their relations to seen things made some difference that could be experienced.

Skepticism, the approach to intellectual problems that involved a methodical refusal to conclude, stood at the very opposite end of the spectrum from pragmatism, which geared a person to reach adequate conclusions under conditions of uncertainty. James meant it when he said that "to admit one's liability to correction is one thing, and to embark upon a wanton sea of doubt is another." He argued that the investigator who "acknowledges the imperfectness of his instrument, and makes allowances for it in discussing his observations, is in a much better position for gaining truth than if he claimed his instrument to be infallible" (VRE, 332). James's fallibilism committed him to the position that no interpretation of the facts is self-warranting, not to the position that truth was inaccessible.

Then too, the pragmatism of Varieties was not a kind of individual voluntarism. James had emphasized from the start that investigators must be able to distinguish short- from long-run satisfactions. He was prepared to claim that "the gods we stand by are the gods we need and can use." But the criteria for selection in this regard were not themselves selected to suit the desires of any one person. The pragmatic investigator committed himself to methods of inquiry that were pragmatically warranted. This distinguished him from others who simply and simplistically willed to believe— that is, from those who did not inquire but clung tenaciously to their beliefs no matter what.

James's pragmatic investigator committed himself to certain

methods which were "tried and true." For instance, he judged beliefs in terms of "immediate luminousness," "moral helpfulness," and "philosophical reasonableness" because these criteria had proven to be successful indicators of trustworthy claims both past and present. Pragmatism conceived this way—methodologically— was fallibilistic to be sure, but it committed individuals to justify their beliefs, not only in the context of traditionally held beliefs but also in that of the evidence of things. The language of *tribunals* played a large part in the pragmatism of *Varieties*; it played no part in voluntary individualism.

According to Royce (and, of course, a host of others), James's pragmatism had no way to account for historical knowledge, knowledge of other minds, or knowledge of the future, because all these things exceeded claims about present observables. But the method that James employed in *Varieties* permitted current observations about past claims made, in turn, by persons about experiences of other minds. James's entire effort had been geared toward establishing what was plausible about the religious testimony historically given by religious persons. If James himself did not observe the divinities that certain religious persons experienced or even observe those persons, "intermediate experiences" linked religious geniuses to observations that he did make.

James treated the historical problem in his religious investigations unexceptionally. The experiences of religious geniuses and James's own were historically discrete, but events corroborated the veracity of some of the geniuses' claims, events that connected James with his religious past in some ways while disconnecting him from it in others. The testimony of religious geniuses was rendered plausible for James, and hence transformed into a kind of evidence, in part by their subsequent conduct, observed and noted by other persons. Sustained corroboration of the consequential relation between divine encounter and saintliness made original testimony trustworthy, insofarforth.

James realized that when religious testimony was taken literally and metaphysically, historical criticism might uncover the cultural and epochal relativity of its articulation. But such discoveries exhibited certain discontinuities of thought without undercutting the distinctiveness of religious facts. On James's grounds, it was no more difficult to confirm experiences of divinity than it was to confirm headaches. Both were "affectional facts." He was prepared to admit that "some day" or "even now somewhere in the larger life of the universe, different men's headaches may become confluent or be 'co-conscious' " (*MT*, 98). But, here and now . . . headaches do transcend each other and, when not felt, can be known only conceptually. My idea is that you really have a headache; it works well with what I see of your expression, and with what I hear you say; but it doesn't put me in possession of the headache itself. I am still at one remove, and the headache 'transcends' me, even though it be in nowise transcendent of human experience generally. But the 'gulf' here is that which the pragmatist epistemology itself fixes in the very first words it uses, by saying there must be an object and an idea. [*MT*, 98]

Just as declarations of pain accompanied by grimaces, super-sensitivity to light, grumpiness, and the like, "confirm" that some-one claiming to have a headache actually does, declarations of divine encounter and salvation accompanied by increased energies, psychological and physical well-being, and the saintly methods of conduct "confirm" that somebody has had a religious experience. Testimony to this effect was always open to suspicion, not because it was religious testimony, but simply because it was testimony. But so long as expectations established by the testimony were realized, the burden of proof was on the doubter.

In this regard, it is important to remember that James only trans-formed into evidence those elements of religious testimony that were supported by subsequent saintliness witnessed by contempo-raries and sustained not only by tradition but by psychological the-ory and responsible criticism (for example, his own). He was pre-pared to argue that there was a chance of salvation and that persons were saved from dissolution by wider selves when their own narrow selves were going to pieces because persons who did not and could not help themselves realize or achieve their own best intentions found themselves achieving them anyhow as a result of *felt* help.

The charges that James's methods of appreciation were (1) sys-tematically irrelevant to questions about "real" truth, (2) primar-ily a sort of voluntarism, and (3) incapable of handling issues having to do with knowledge about things beyond the present, ob-servable situation all rested on the assumption that James was a subjectivist in matters of evaluation. If he was committed to the claim that value was equivalent to satisfaction and that each indi-vidual differed when it came to questions of need, then, so critics reasoned, no objective guidelines for evaluation of any sort could be established. Objectivity depended on shared asumptions, among other things.

Critics easily read *Varieties* as a subjectivist tract. After all, James went out of his way to demonstrate that the varieties of religious temperament—pessimism, optimism, meliorism—were relative to certain personal needs. He also argued that religious movements ordered social life in light of those temperamental emotions. And he argued, as well, that persons evaluated religious ways of thinking and acting in light of their own interests, intuitions, and beliefs.

Confronted with the rise of sociology and anthropology, James wanted to keep the individual person at the center of religious studies. Thus, he emphasized the great extent to which persons were blinded to each other's needs, especially religious needs. He also demonstrated the importance of privacy in religious matters. In general, he pictured religion as the most significant human enterprise geared to searching for solutions to personal problems. As he put it in his theological school lectures of 1902, religion was the one sort of organized social life in which the desideratum was to be "recognized for what I am." Religion was the enterprise in which people asked whether there were realities beyond the individual which were pertinent to him only, and which welled up within him, not without him (WJC, 4479:sheet 25).

But in *Varieties* James tried to highlight the role of subjectivity in religion without committing himself to subjectivism. The key to realizing this lay in distinguishing James's second-order, normative methods of appreciation from the ways in which the subjects of his study evaluated things. James went out of his way to distinguish the science of religions from the religious life per se, even if he saw some continuity or overlap. The scientist of religions was to the religious populace what the republican statesman was to the people who constituted his nation. His interests were, in the broadest sense, religious, but his tasks were to lend dignity to religious variety, to find ways to enhance tolerance among religious groups living together, and to safeguard the rights to religious privacy and difference. All of this made for "the necessary predominance of subjective language in our analysis" (*MT*, 130).

But at the same time, the scientist of religions attempted to establish objective grounds for making religious claims and to square religious facts with other facts confirmed by other sorts of science. He also attempted to make "economic" evaluations of religious conduct, both diagnosing certain diseases associated historically with religions and recognizing the therapeutic impact of religious experience on individuals and of saintliness on societies. These evaluations were admittedly conventional and fallible, but they were not subjectivist in any hard sense: they were not constructed in light of any denial of reality independent of human thought, whether individuated or in general; they were constructed in order to better approximate "final realities"—that is, what was really the case for any one.

Far from being solipsistic, then, the methods of appreciation that James deployed in his Gifford Lectures assumed that persons thought and acted in social situations. Indeed, James's reliance on common sense was nearly pervasive. To be sure, James's understanding of common sense was left obscure in *Varieties*. But James could not be a conventionalist of any sort and a solipsist simultaneously.

Of course, Royce and others never denied that James depended on conventions. They denied that James had any right to be a conventionalist in light of his views on knowledge. They claimed that if knowledge were analyzed according to satisfactions, then James would have no way to break away either from the moment or from the individual.

James was, in fact, fond of saying that if an individual was faithful to his own light, he was intellectually responsible. But since his earliest philosophical efforts he had argued that the claims of individuals, no matter how peculiar or idiosyncratic, must be construed as social recommendations. The very idea of a Darwinian science of religions made strong individual voluntarism silly because social, national, and even racial "economies" set the bases for selection and transmission of religious thought and action. James's allegiance to Darwin also made short-run satisfactions rather unfit as criteria for evaluating anything besides short-run interests. His emphasis on the survival of the humanly fittest and his demand that claims and activities be tested by the rest of experience, "on the whole" and over "the long run," indicated his commitment to the position that things were better evaluated the more they were tested and the more various the tests.

In part, of course, the criticism of capriciousness emerged from the vagueness of James's writing. But it also emerged from obvious misunderstandings. When, for instance, James located evaluation in the present, some critics inferred that he was committed to a position that the range of reference of any evaluation was limited to the present. It did not occur to them that some thought or action might *now* be satisfactory precisely because of its historical record of success. Instead, they construed the use of 'the present' privatively, systematically excluding reference to either past or future. Their reading failed to do his argument justice. James had argued, for instance, that the exercises of the new religions were valuable not simply because they *worked now* but because they satisfied certain human interests in ways that had stood the tests of time. In each case, James's point was to distinguish aspects of current religions that satisfied enduring religious interests, and satisfied them over the long run of experience.

Hence, Royce's disjunctive way of viewing James's methods simply did not fit James's work in *Varieties*. Royce claimed that either Jamesean pragmatism assumed absolute truth for itself or was simply a current expression of need. But James claimed that his methods avoided the pitfalls of its competitors (for instance, medical materialism, positivist anthropology, mysticism, and philosophical theology), accounted for those pitfalls, and met satisfactorily the need for mediation that it was geared to fulfill. Hence, his methods were a "current expression of need," though not just that. But his methods did not assume any rock-bottom foundational or trans-empirical supports and, hence, did not assume absolute truth for themselves. Indeed, 'the truth' of formal epistemology was systematically irrelevant to the program that James established.

Royce was accurate in his criticism that Jamesean pragmatism ignored theoretical interests, but in this sense: *Varieties* ignored *erkenntnistheorie* on purpose. On the other hand, *Varieties* exhibited the sort of theoretical concern that Jamesean pragmatism could have. *Varieties* established the rudiments of a theory of religion and laid the groundwork for further research on religious experience by commending a psychological theory of identity transformation precisely in order to square religious testimony with the most basic assumptions and the most general conclusions of "the natural sciences," especially psychology.

From the standpoint of *erkenntnistheorie*, James was guilty of mistaking questions about psychological processes for questions about logical conditions in *Varieties*. Like traditional idealists, he had been committed to a theory of knowledge in which judgments were the focus of analysis, not "propositions." Thus, in *Varieties*, he was concerned with showing how religious beliefs came to be held and, once held, were found reasonable as rules for action. His issue was, quite precisely, social-psychological.

To be sure, James distinguished reasons *why* persons held certain religious beliefs from reasons *for* holding. From the start of his lectures, he was careful to insist on the distinction between the causes of belief and the warrants for belief. But he was convinced that warrants could be understood and even adjudicated "empirically," without succumbing to relativism or fatalism. These convictions, among others, led to his program on the pragmatic meaning of truth.

On the basis of his investigations in *Varieties*, James had concluded that religion at its best had been mankind's most important function because it provided motives, methods, and emotions for strenuously enacting community in ways that overcame debilitating anxieties and offered acceptance to those who were other and different: People were better off, even now, believing that the best things were the more eternal things, even when they could not verify that belief. But James had also concluded that the varieties of religious experience tended to confirm the religious belief that the best things are the more eternal things by demonstrating the experience of divinity.

James's efforts in *Varieties* exemplified what he called "the marriage function" of new truth in *Pragmatism*. His psychological theory of identity-transformation "preserved the older stock" of religious truths "with a minimum of modification, stretching them just enough to make them admit the novelty, but conceiving that in ways as familiar as the case makes possible" (*Prag*, 35). James's theory of "the wider Self" maintained the dualism manifested by traditional, common, or crass supernaturalism, but widened the natural world in order to do it. His theory of religious experience transformed the ontological distinction between natural and supernatural into a functional one, one accountable in terms of distinct behaviors. His crucial conclusion in *Varieties* was that the upshot of traditional supernaturalism—the chance of salvation—was both vindicated and made more intelligible by his analysis of religious experience.

James's account of religious experience in the language of subliminal behavior led him to believe that he had helped heal the historical breach that had left a gap between science and religion. As he put it in his theological school lectures in 1902, his theory gave dignity and backbone to reports of religious experience, rehabilitated the 'individual' as the locus both of religious problems and solutions, and left room for general science by opening up avenues of understanding and explanation of religious phenomena.

His work in *Varieties* left James satisfied that present information supported the notion that salvation was a grounded possibility because there were actually superhuman forces promoting human welfare: In point of fact, James concluded, "the conscious person is continuous with a wider self through which saving experiences come" (*VRE*, 515). This opinion was not true for James because it was convenient, because it brought him satisfaction, or because he wanted to believe it. It was true for him because events accountable within the limits of current theory made it so.

The Pragmatic Meaning of Truth

As critics were quick to point out, however, James's conclusions about religious truth in *Varieties* landed him in an apparent theoretical conundrum. On the view that he had established there, events accountable in terms of current theory warranted his assertion that "the conscious person is continuous with a wider self through which saving experiences come." But James admitted that there was room for error in his theory and, hence, in his account of religious experience and his conclusions drawn from their inspection.

If, as James claimed, the truth of an assertion was tantamount to its vindication as justified, then "the conscious person is continuous with a wider self through which saving experiences come" might be "true" even though it were not actually the case. On these grounds, critics as diverse as Royce, Bertrand Russell, Moore, John E. Russell, and Dickinson Miller contended that James was confusing the justification of an opinion with its truth or falsity.

James's critics also argued that James was wrong to analyze justification according to expediency or convenience. They pointed out, for instance, that the meaning of the statement that " 'God exists' is justified" did not coincide with the meaning of the statement that " 'God exists' is convenient or expedient." Hence, they claimed that James not only confused truth with justification, but undercut the meaning of 'justification' as it had come to be used by contemporary investigators.

His critics focused particularly on the theory of truth that James had articulated in his lectures on pragmatism. Indeed, the brunt of the attacks on his theory focused, rather naturally, on the one lecture that James had called "Pragmatism's Conception of Truth" (*Prag*, 95–113). James made ambiguous and slippery statements there that subsequently received much derision. He said, for instance, that the pragmatist asked for the "cash-value" of truth and that the 'true' was only the expedient in the way of our thinking. Ironically, such claims led critics to laugh at James's "pragmatic truth" as something fit for capitalist adventurers in America. The outspoken critic of the "bitch-goddess success" must have been appalled.

But James's theory of truth was developed throughout his lectures on pragmatism, and other journal articles besides. James's famous sixth lecture, "Pragmatism's Conception of Truth," did not encompass it. He began to develop it to safeguard the inference from "good for life" to "true." He became heartened when he found scientists of the rank of Sigwart, Ernst Mach, Wilhelm Ostwald, Jules Henri Poincaré, and Pierre Duhem claiming that

> *ideas (which themselves are but parts of our experience) become true just in so far as they us to get into satisfactory relation with other parts of our experience,* to summarize them and to get about among them by conceptual short-cuts instead of following the interminable succession of particular phenomena. Any idea upon which we can ride, so to speak; any idea that will carry us prosperously from any one part of our experience to any other part, linking things satisfactorily, working securely, simplifying, saving labor; is true for just so much, true in so far forth, true *instrumentally.* [*Prag,* 34]

The fact that James generalized from the way scientists settled into new opinions provided another connection between his Gifford Lectures and his subsequent work. The theory of truth that he elaborated in *Pragmatism* and *The Meaning of Truth* was the one he had used in *Varieties,* where he pitted scientific methods of fixing belief against personal tenacity and the a priori methods employed by philosophical theologians.

For James, to ask whether some new opinion, for instance, his opinion about a salvific wider self, was true was tantamount to asking whether investigation vindicated it. 'The truth' was a sort of event because an opinion became true the more vindication it received. 'Vindication' pragmatically meant solving what he called "the problem of the maxima and the minima"—that is, demonstrating "a minimum of jolt, a maximum of continuity" in one's total view of things (*Prag,* 35).

As James saw it, the question of truth never arose unless and until something challenged somebody's total view. Persons used the term 'true' to engage in disputes about the compatibility of certain opinions and the applicability of certain judgments to certain ways of the world. Thus, for instance, the discovery of radium seemed to contradict the principle of the conservation of energy, but the further discovery of helium as radiation's outcome solved the problem of the maxima and the minima, "so Ramsey's view is generally held to be true, because, although it extends our old ideas of energy, it causes a minimum of alteration in their arrangement" (*Prag,* 36).

The same conditions held for religious investigation, according to James. Thus, for instance,

> since . . . darwinism has once for all displaced design from
> the minds of the 'scientific,' theism has lost [its] foothold;
> and some kind of an immanent or pantheistic deity working
> in things rather than above them is, if any, the kind recom-
> mended to our contemporary imagination. Aspirants to a philo-
> sophic religion turn, as a rule, more hopefully nowadays to-
> wards idealistic pantheism than towards the older dualistic
> theism, in spite of the fact that the latter still counts able
> defenders.
>
> But . . . the brand of pantheism offered is hard for them to
> assimilate if they are lovers of facts, or empirically minded. It
> is the absolutistic brand, spurning the dust and reared upon
> pure logic. It keeps no connexion whatever with concreteness.
> [*Prag*, 39–40]

From the view established in *Pragmatism*, neither Roycean nor Bradleyan idealism solved the problem of the minima and the maxima for empirically minded thinkers bent on constructing a philosophic religion. Their "absolute" minds undercut theological tradition, thus minimizing continuity, and accepted any and every fact as part and parcel of divinity, thus maximizing jolts. On these grounds, absolute idealism failed to perform "the marriage function" and thus was not "true."

James did not argue simply from illustration when it came to his theory of truth. He developed a general theory which aimed not so much to overturn opposing theories, for example, correspondence and coherence theories, as to show that these were special instances of a more general theory that could accommodate various sorts of discourse and practice, including science and religion.

Put negatively, the heart of James's general theory was an attack on any sort of foundational knowledge. James had argued in *Varieties* that both mystics and philosophical theologians depended on foundational epistemologies which failed to persuade doubters. But he had avoided technical epistemological argument in the Gifford Lectures. By 1906, however, he was deeply engaged in the technical issues. He claimed that both classical empiricism and classical rationalism depended on the same epistemological strategy: both attempted to build knowledge claims on foundations more solid than rock. Empiricists tried to specify basic truths of observation or introspection. Rationalists tried to specify truths *ex vi terminorum*. Both these great traditions spent much effort attempting to locate things that could be known without inference from anything else that was known. Incorrigible knowledge without inference was construed as the only sort of knowledge strong enough to be foundational.

Both classical empiricists and rationalists were motivated to construct their foundational epistemologies, according to James, out of respect for radical skepticism. Their aim was to specify the sort of knowledge that could wrench the radical skeptic out of his pyrrhonistic position. Their strategies ultimately led to the construal of "epistemology" as a discrete, prior, and premier philosophical enterprise. As a result, many philosophers began to view the specification of foundational truths as the point of philosophy, where "foundational truths" were as distinguishable from the garden variety of truths as *scientia* was different from *opinio* for the medieval scholastics.

James thought that the problem with the "foundations" metaphor shared by empiricists and rationalists lay in their shared motivation: concern for skepticism of the most radical sort. The history of the empiricist and rationalist traditions was strewn with wrecked foundations. Philosophers in these traditions could not even decide among themselves what could count as foundational and what could not, much less ward off or convert radical skeptics. Even when "epistemologists" appeared to share beliefs about "foundations," they ran into "construction" difficulties that led to impasse; the classical problem of induction was paradigmatic in this respect.

James's strategy was to turn certain classical assumptions on their head in an effort to establish that the broadest outlines of the classical epistemological programs were misguided. He argued that philosophers were bound to spin their wheels so long as they took radical skepticism seriously, but could make real progress if they would assume that people did know things and if they would begin to ask how.

But more positively, the core of James's general theory could be stated thusly: truth forms itself out of the life of opinion (cf. *MT*, 45). With James, *opinio* completely displaced *scientia* as the seat of intellectual authority. James thought that "truth and knowledge are terms correlative and interdependent" so that "wherever knowledge is conceivable, truth is conceivable, wherever knowledge is possible, truth is possible, wherever knowledge is actual, truth is actual" (*MT*, 158). But when James spoke of "knowledge," he meant the knowledge of those who simply assumed that *opinion* was the coin of the knower's realm, the sort of knowledge that triumphed only as the clinical and evolutionary sciences achieved professional and intellectual supremacy.

According to the view of truth James was constructing, "the real force that works against skepticism" was not any bulwark of incorrigible beliefs but "the train of experience, which makes belief more convenient" than its suspension (WJC, 4506). On these grounds alone, radical skepticism was not worth rebuttal. From the standpoint of the natural historian of intelligence, radical skepticism simply fostered incapacity. In any case, the premises from which radical skeptics drew their conclusions permitted other, more reasonable conclusions.

The radical skeptics played on the corrigibility of opinion. They claimed that if a person believed something, there was some chance that the person's belief was false. But they did not stop there. They went on to infer that if this was always so, then the person had no sufficient warrant to claim to know anything. James accepted the radical skeptic's premise that if some person believes something, there is some chance his belief is false. But he inferred from this that a person may or may not know what he thinks he does. He was just as convinced as was the radical skeptic that epistemic certainty was a sham, but he developed a view of knowledge in light of this conviction, rather than an agniology.

Far from denying 'truth', the first thing that James did was to insist that 'truth' was an object of investigation and to affirm "the regulative character in his own thinking of the notion of absolute truth." He claimed that "to admit, as we pragmatists do, that we are liable to correction (even tho we do not expect it) *involves* the use on our part of an ideal standard. . . . What is challenged . . . is the pretense on anyone's part to have found for certain at any given moment what the shape of that truth is" (MT, 142–43).

'Truth' was not known as anything independent of knowledge. So, for instance, when James claimed that "the conscious person is continuous with a wider self through which saving experiences come" was literally and objectively true, he meant that if he knew that this was the case, it was the case! 'Truth' was not a condition of knowledge that had to be satisfied before people could claim to know. 'Truth' was part of an analysis of knowledge, hence a condition of knowledge that was satisfied when people know. This was why James complained to "the anti-pragmatist" in his final essay on the meaning of truth, that "where you see three distinct entities in the field, the reality, the knowing, and the truth, I see only two. Moreover, I can see what each of my two entities is *known-as*, but when I ask myself what your third entity, the truth, is known-as, I can find nothing distinct from the reality on the one hand, and the ways in which it may be known on the other" (MT, 158). On these grounds, truth was a relation that held between knower and known, or more accurately, between certain statements and things for which they accounted.

Circular Reasoning in James's View of Knowledge

James's arguments about truth were actually twofold. Some of them had to do with something philosophers now call the theory of justification. Others concerned the theory of truth proper. As a matter of historical fact, philosphers in James's time called theories of justification theories of truth. Thus, for instance, both coherence and correspondence "theories of truth" were geared to answer questions about justification. A coherence theorist specified why a belief was true: because it cohered with a system of accepted statements. A correspondence theorist specified the same sort of thing, only he answered: because it corresponds to a matter of fact.

Philosophers now say that theories of justification address the 'because' questions. But philosophers in James's time did not. James was engaged in this sort of debate concerning 'justification'. But he was concerned with more than that. He took the current dictionary definition of truth—that is, the agreement of ideas with reality—and asked what 'agreement with', 'ideas', and 'reality' meant pragmatically. In other words, he not only asked why some ideas were vindicated as true but also analyzed what an idea was, or more accurately, did, when it was true.

When James asserted that "empiricists think that truth in general is distilled from single men's beliefs; and the so-called pragmatists 'go them one better' by trying to define what it consists of when it comes" (*MT*, 141), he indicated the difference between the theory of justification and the theory of truth. Empiricists were accurate, he thought, when they placed truth within the realm of *opinio*, but none had actually given a theory of truth. When he analyzed truth, he found that it meant the act or process of assimilation, validation, or corroboration.

But the thing that challenged critics more than anything else was James's claim that "we plunge forward into the field of fresh experience with the beliefs our ancestors and we have already made; these determine what we notice; what we notice determines what we do; what we do again determines what we experience; so from one thing to another, altho the stubborn fact remains that there *is* a sensible flux, what is true of it seems first to last to be largely a matter of our own creation" (*Prag*, 122).

This "humanism" was clearly circular. James pictured persons as justifying opinions against standards that they or their forebears had made, doing things within the limits allowed by those warranted opinions, and correcting their understanding of experience according to the consequences of those acts. Critics like Royce had condemned James for arguing in circles, but on the grounds that James was laying, the best thought was propitiously circular (cf. MT, 144).

Four assumptions shaped James's claims about the normative circularity of inquiry. First, he assumed that 'reality' was ascertained *at the end of inquiry*. Second, apart from "absolute" truth, which was regulative—that is, apart from the truth about reality at the end of inquiry—the truths persons sought to justify were presumptive, not demonstrative. Third, any inquiry inherited 'truths' from its traditions and was required to eliminate some, transmit others, and innovate still others on the grounds of their suitability to the tasks of the inquiry. Fourth, *the consequences of actions* and not the conclusions of thought per se closed the circle of inquiry.

As James understood the structure of inquiry, then, Royce and others were right to point out that pragmatism as a theory of truth depended upon a Darwinian picture of the ways of the world, but they were wrong to construe the dependence as vicious (cf. MT, 131). Darwin's view of the ways of the world made James's pragmatic theory of truth possible. Moreover, the successful consequences of James's pragmatism would, in turn, vindicate his initial Darwinian picture of man, knowledge, and the world. James thought his circle was rendered propitious by making practical effectiveness the final arbiter of theoretical coherence. The reactions of environments disposed of actions that investigators proposed, forcing adjustments in their points of view, sometimes even basic ones. James's circular reasoning, in other words, was dynamic not static. He assumed 'the ways of the world' in order to generate methods to investigate 'the ways of the world'. But he also assumed that his investigations could readily modify portions of his initial position and transform its very shape.

James's religious investigations worked in this circular way. To begin with, for instance, he assumed a broad view of things in which 'reality' was constituted by a plurality of independent powers, including human beings who pursued well-being as well as other things that brutalized human effort. He began with a picture of men as *normally* active, reasonable, and responsive to environmental changes and challenges. He also assumed that people normally lived in traditional communities, with enduring goals and methods of attainment. Finally, he assumed that the natural world in which communities were situated was partially malleable, partially resistant to human intervention, generically orderable and, hence, neither totally brutal nor totally compromising as regards the goals of human communities and the individuals who constituted them.

Within this context, James asked whether there was a chance of salvation and, assuming man's limited abilities to achieve well-being on his own, whether divinity played a role in human experience in ways that vindicated belief in the possibility of salvation.

But also on the basis of his metaphysical picture, he developed a procedure for answering these questions. His principle of pragmatism—the principle that he employed to establish the subject of investigation in his science of religions—"depended from" his world view in the same way that earrings were said to depend from ears in turn-of-the-century parlance. The principle of pragmatism conformed to his world view in ways that left its own mark. His focus on the consequences of action as determinative of meaning and his insistence on the linkage between 'success' and 'truth' both "depended from" a view of thought as having to contend with capricious environments that made the long-run employment of false beliefs either damaging or fatal.

James employed the pragmatic principle in order to specify what 'God' meant. When he did, he claimed it meant superhuman forces that promoted human welfare. His pragmatic analysis of 'God' set the program for his Gifford Lectures, in which he demonstrated, to his own satisfaction, that people were helped to attain well-being when they could not help themselves by powers greater than they were. Events over which humans had no manipulative control vindicated supernaturalism. They also led James both to reendorse his initial metaphysic and to modify it by issuing an over-belief in pantheistic divinity. Clearly his line of thought was circular: his metaphysics generated his religious problem and the procedures for establishing ways to solve it; the conclusions that he reached when he used those procedures vindicated the metaphysics from which the procedures depended. But he thought his circle solved several religious issues and set further issues to be resolved.

Indeed, if the whole function of inquiry was to resolve conceptual problems which kept human enterprises from attaining their goals and if the world was the way that James pictured it, thought was normally circular or dialectical. The point of thinking was to patch and tinker with views of things until those views were accurate enough to facilitate beneficial environmental transactions. On these grounds, 'reality' stood at the end of "the long run" (cf.*MT*,

88–89). Standing reality was the ultimate terminus of investigation, James postulated, and thus not deployable to warrant beliefs or rules for action in medias res.

Of course, if reality—that is, standing reality—could only be ascertained or discovered in the long run, then so long as the current dictionary definition of truth was held, the "truths" that people actually depended upon for guidance could not be construed as demonstrative. Arguing from an analysis of conceptual change, he noted that "the world" was "incomplete" in at least one respect: people did not know all about it yet, even as they knew more and more. Investigators kept their old knowledge, prejudices, and beliefs as unaltered as they could. When they found themselves in some situation that challenged the adequacy of their prejudices and beliefs, they altered their total view. Out of any competing pool of new concepts, beliefs, or methods, they selected those that maintained as much continuity with common sense as they could, disturbing their tried and true standards of appropriateness as little as possible. There were natural and social selective reasons why this was the case: commonsense ways of thinking were habits that conserved and stabilized behaviors that permitted adequate management of circumstances.

"In the changes of opinion today," James argued, new truths resulted from new experiences and old beliefs combining and "mutually modifying one another" (*Prag*, 83). Since this was the case, he reasoned,

> there is no reason to assume that it has not been so at all
> times. It follows that very ancient modes of thought may have
> survived through all the later changes in men's opinions. The
> most primitive way of thinking may not yet be wholly ex-
> punged. Like our five fingers, our ear-bones, our rudimentary
> caudal appendage, our other 'vestigial' peculiarities, they may
> remain as indelible tokens of events in our race history. Our
> ancestors may at certain moments have struck into ways of
> thinking which they might conceivably not have found. But
> once they did so, and after the fact, the inheritance continues.
> When you begin a piece of music in a certain key, you must
> keep the key to the end. You may alter your house *ad libitum*,
> but the ground plan of the first architect persists—you can
> make great changes, but you cannot change a Gothic church
> into a Doric temple. [*Prag*, 83]

James, of course, realized that this argument was speculative. He did not think that anybody could actually check to see whether commonsense categories of thought were discovered the way new truths were, but it provided a line of thought which clarified what he had meant in *Varieties* when he asserted that the common sense that people brought to the appreciation of religious experience was itself the result of sifting experience. His argument for the historicity of common sense also awoke "a presumption favorable to the pragmatistic view that all our theories are instrumental, are mental modes of adaptation to reality, rather than revelations or gnostic answers to some divinely instituted world-enigma" (*Prag*, 94). Most important, his argument made more plausible the notion that like the Latin language or the common law, "the truth" was a result of graft upon graft of satisfactory developments.

James argued that philosophers who sharply divided beliefs about the forms of thought that condition experience from beliefs about experience let the *remoteness* of some conceptual discoveries get the better of their historical heads. Many post-Kantian critical philosophers suffered from this malady. Like laws and grammatical forms, truths might become so entrenched that they took on the aura of eternity or invariance. But entrenchment did not undercut the assumption of historicity: the assumption that 'truths' were introduced into traditions of thought at (or during) specific times and were subject to modification or elimination at other times. If the historicity of 'truths' was accepted, then 'truths' must be considered presumptive, no matter how long they survived in relevant ways. Though not known to be 'true' in any demonstrative sense, they must be regarded as having some claim to being considered true.

The charge of capriciousness that confronted James fixed squarely on the problem of justifying truths that were admittedly presumptive. He was less than careful when he argued that, in general, "satisfactory beliefs" were presumptively true. There was a great deal of difference beween arguing, on the one hand, that the true is the expedient in the way of thinking and, on the other hand, that the true is what expedites whatever it is that someone wants to think or do. James spoke both ways, and critics gave him the criticism that he deserved. Vagueness hovered over a distinction between the satisfaction of individuals and groups of persons, on the one hand, and the satisfaction of expectations or standards of justification, on the other. He was not clear in his writing about justification whether truth was what satisfied any demand or what satisfied reasonable ones.

But when James actually specified criteria for presumptive truth, some of the vagueness of his more general claims was dispelled. To

begin with, he was careful to note that people do not verify or corroborate facts so much as events do. For James, neither 'I' nor 'you'
nor 'he' makes or breaks a truth-claim so much as 'it' does, where
'it' refers to some objective state of affairs. To be sure, 'people' justified beliefs by vindicating them with reasons. But this meant that
people articulated the states of affairs which corroborated claims.
This is particularly what he had done in *Varieties* in his quest for
religious knowledge: he specified states of affairs, for example,
saintliness or salvation-experiences, which corroborated religious
testimony about supernatural powers supporting and promoting
human welfare.

James, to be sure, was no ordinary correspondence theorist. He
claimed that "we humanly make an addition to some sensible reality, and that reality tolerates the addition. All the additions 'agree'
with the reality; they fit it while they build it out." But he said that
this claim did not vindicate the "popular notion . . . that a true idea
must copy its reality." The popular notion followed the analogy of
the most usual experiences—that is, unambiguous perceptual observations. But it did not account for the significant role that interpretation played in any observation or for terms that could not be
pictured adequately, like 'divinity' (but also 'infinity', 'because', and
so on). Beliefs, theories, and methods did not necessarily have to
copy anything to be presumptively true; copying was simply one
way of accounting. But accounting was the important operation,
according to James, so that a person could not "play fast and loose
with the order which realities follow in his experience." Any conceptual instrument that played fast and loose with the order of
things would "lead him nowhere or else make false connexions"
(*Prag*, 121, 99).

James's understanding of 'agreement' between 'ideas' and 'reality'
was distinctive on two counts. First, 'agreement' was understood as
a sort of conduct or practice for him, as a sort of logical relation
for the devotees of *erkenntnistheorie*. A conceptual instrument
agreed with a reality when it allowed its employer to contend with
reality better than did other instruments. Second, he articulated
what people meant when they used the term 'reality'. 'Reality' meant
either 'matters of fact', 'logical relation', or 'inherited truth'. The extent to which viewpoints were wedged between matters of fact and
common sense, on the one hand, and logic, on the other, depended
on the enterprises in which they were located and the interests and
ends to which they were relevant. But in any case, for James, if beliefs were presumptively true, they were wedged, whatever the degree of pressure.

The Faith Ladder

As early as 1905, James began to talk about justifying religious over-beliefs. As ever, he argued that under certain conditions, investigators had the right to believe "in things for the truth of which complete objective proof is yet lacking" (*MT*, 138–39). He constructed his faith ladder as part and parcel of his overall position on the structure of knowledge, but it had obvious applications to his religious investigations. *Varieties* had ended with both conclusions and over-beliefs, both settled opinions and hypotheses worth pursuing in light of settled opinions. James's faith ladder served to organize his strategy of pursuit.

Perhaps the most interesting rendition of James's faith ladder come in his 1906 address to the Unitarian Club of San Francisco, cribbed from his Stanford lectures in philosophy that year. There, he asked rhetorically whether the facts of natural experience forced men's reason to religious conclusions and answered:

> Certainly men having every other appearance of possessing reason have been led to irreligious conclusions by the facts of the world. Men will always probably conclude diversely in this matter, as they have concluded diversely up to this hour. Some will see in moral facts a power that makes for righteousness and in physical facts a power that geometrizes and is intellectual, that creates order and loves beauty. But along side of such facts there are contrary facts in abundance; and he who seeks *them* can equally well infer a power that defies righteousness, creates disorder, loves ugliness and aims at death. It depends on which kind of fact you single out as the more essential. If your reason tries to be impartial, if she resorts to statistical comparison and asks which class of facts tip the balance, and which way tends the drift, she must, it seems to me, conclude for irreligion, *unless you give her some more specific religious experiences to go by*, for the last word everywhere, according to naturalistic science, is the word of Death, the death sentence passed by Nature on plant and beast, and man and tribe, and earth and sun and everything that she has made.[3]

His audience knew, of course, that James thought he had discovered the requisite religious facts in his Gifford Lectures. His religious investigations had widened the "natural world" by adding "religious facts" to it. His *Varieties* not only cataloged but suggested a plausible account of events in which the hopelessness of particular lives was robbed of its sting, undone, and displaced by a "willingness to be" or personal integrity that was saintly in character.

But unresolved questions remained concerning the agencies and significance of religious experience. James was particularly concerned with pursuing the difference that religious experiences made for "the *character* of the world" (*SPP*, 115); he was concerned with reconstructing theology in light of his religious investigations. He claimed that, whenever "the character of the world" was at issue, the following steps should be taken to decide whether a view was presumptively true:

1. There is nothing absurd in a certain view of the world being true, nothing self-contradictory;
2. It *might* be true under certain conditions;
3. It *may* be true, even now;
4. It is *fit* to be true;
5. It *ought* to be true;
6. It *must* be true;
7. It *shall* be true, at any rate for *me*.

Obviously this is no intellectual chain of inferences, like the *Sorites* of the logic-books. Yet it is a slope of good-will on which in the larger questions of life men habitually live. [*SPP*, 113]

James's 1902 over-belief was that "the world of our present consciousness is only one out of many worlds of consciousness that exist, and that those other worlds must contain experiences which have a meaning for our life also; and that although in the main their experiences and those of this world keep discrete, yet the two become continuous at certain points, and higher energies filter in." More succinctly, James said: "We and God have business with each other; and in opening ourselves to his influence our deepest destiny is fulfilled," *because* "where God is, tragedy is only provisional and partial, and shipwreck and dissolution are not the absolutely final things" (*VRE*, 519, 516–17).

Vindication of this over-belief was the key to James's religious characterization of "the world." He contended that "the world" held out the promise of salvation, but not its absolute guarantee. Absolute idealists like Royce were too optimistic, because they thought salvation was inevitable. Pessimists like Schopenhauer and Eduard von Hartmann thought the salvation of the world was impossible. James's own "meliorism" meant that salvation was a grounded possibility. The requisite powers could make good on the promise inherent in a universe constituted as "a social scheme of co-operative work genuinely to be done," but only if persons were helped to attain well-being when they could not help themselves. While the varieties of religious experience made short-run and partial salvations *evident*, they hardly decided issues about salvation "on the whole" and in "the long run."

Still, James claimed, his meliorism was the "most *probable* hypothesis" (*SPP*, 112). He was employing a particular, but hardly idiosyncratic, notion of probability, which played on ambiguities in meaning between 'chance' and 'credibility'. He claimed that his meliorism was rendered probable by passing the steps of his faith ladder successfully; hence, 'probable' meant credible. But he also claimed that his religious investigations had rendered 'salvation' 'probable'. In this regard, 'probable' meant chance. Matters were further complicated because, as James understood things, crediting melioristic faith, thus informing actions with it, increased the chances of salvation, which in turn rendered the vision more credible.

This was an instance of James's view that the best reasoning was circular. Credibilty and chance were joined together by "events" which proved a person either wise or foolish in his decisions about what to think and do religiously. He could make his decisions responsibly by climbing his faith ladder. To be sure, the faith ladder was no argument in any strong sense of the term. The 'rigor' of religious philosophy was different from the rigor of geometric sciences. Hence, according to James, the religious philosopher should not offer conclusions beyond the shadow of a doubt.

As James constructed it, the faith ladder resulted in imperatives, not conclusions. Its point of departure was a broad compendium of beliefs about things in general, and its steps engaged investigators in logical, psychological, historical, aesthetic, moral, and practical judgments about the suitability of the most general sorts of policy. In other words, it demanded every sort of judgment that traditional Western philosophers made, and demanded that each sort of judgment be made in conjunction with the making of every other. This was no task for anyone not well-informed or broad-minded.

Certainly, his faith ladder could be abused. It might admit the loosest sorts of relativism and voluntarism. But, viewed formally, so could every other extant decision procedure. Its very liberality tended toward the control of abuse because it was a thought process that forced an exit from thought by establishing dispositions that "must remain . . . practical, and not . . . dogmatic, . . . must go with toleration of other faiths, with the search for the most probable, and with the full consciousness of responsibilities and risks" (*SPP*, 113).

James concluded his lectures in *Pragmatism* with another rendition of his theistic over-belief of 1902. He claimed that he could not "start upon a whole theology at the end of this last lecture" but reminded his audience that he had "written a book on men's religious experience, which on the whole has been regarded as making for the reality of God" (*Prag*, 143). He hinted that a "melioristic type of theism" could steer a course between the Charybdis of "crude naturalism" and the Scylla of "transcendental absolutism" and urged his audience to believe that gods existed and "are at work to save the world on ideal lines similar to our own" and, indeed, to believe this on the strength of "the proofs that religious experience affords." But these assertions brought forth no new arguments and sidestepped James's 1902 insistence that "only when . . . faith concerning God is taken, and remote objective consequences are predicted, does religion, as it seems to me, get wholly free from the first immediate subjective experience, and bring a *real hypothesis* into play." 'God' had to have "other properties than of those of the phenomenon it is immediately invoked to explain" in order to vindicate a believer's "absolute confidence and peace" (*VRE*, 517, 518). By the end of *Pragmatism*, James had still not regimented arguments for these "other properties."

But if the arguments for cooperative and friendly powers were as yet insufficient, so were arguments against their assumption. Along with religious experience, James thought this was enough to assure the believer that crass supernaturalism might be true, and he could point to the sort of well-being achieved in religious experience when critics challenged him to show them what confirmation would look like in this regard. His detractors, however, were far from convinced that his defense of any faith, much less his own melioristic one, was satisfactory.

Transatlantic Criticism

In response to James's arguments about the right to believe certain things under conditions of uncertainty, John McTaggart wrote in *Some Dogmas of Religion* that "when the reality of a thing is uncertain [James's] argument encourages us to suppose that our approval of a thing can determine its reality. And when this unhallowed link has once been established, retribution overtakes us. For when the reality is independently certain, we [then] admit that the reality of a thing should determine our approval of that thing. I find it difficult to imagine a more degraded position."[4]

This rendering was unjust and missed the point of James's argument, which distinguished events, which could be conditioned, if not enacted, by what individuals did, from "independent realities," which escaped arbitrary control by men. James's pragmatic method of semantic analysis depended upon a metaphysic that postulated "something in every experience that escapes our arbitrary control" (*MT*, 45).

Critics like McTaggart continually read James's faith ladder as implying that a person could take part in the production of gods by desiring them. But James had just as continually claimed, to the contrary, that a person could take part in the venture of salvation, even if he lacked sufficient power to guarantee that enterprise, which might be guaranteed only if there were gods.

But other critics focused on the issue whether pragmatists could "discriminate sincerity from bluff," or proof from truth (*MT*, 46). Idealists like Bradley, A. E. Taylor, and Royce joined realists like Russell and Moore in questioning whether James's theory of truth provided any standard rigid enough to sanction justified beliefs as really true.

Russell summed up James's theory of truth in the definition: "A truth is anything which it pays to believe."[5] This definition seemed misleading to Russell, "chiefly in regard to religion." For instance, James had specified certain utilities in believing that there was an Absolute Mind. He had said that such a belief sanctioned certain "moral holidays" for disconsolate individuals on pitiful enough occasions to warrant them. Russell argued that on James's own grounds, if consequences useful to life flowed from the hypothesis of the Absolute, it was "insofarforth" a true hypothesis. Russell thought the problem was that while pragmatism "persuades us that belief in the Absolute is 'true' " because it is a trustworthy device for disconsolate people or their defenders to employ on certain occasions, James did not "persuade us that the Absolute is a fact." To the contrary, James tried to persuade people that the Absolute was probably not a fact. But "in ordinary logic, if the belief in the Absolute is true, it follows that the Absolute is a fact." So Russell charged James with holding that " 'A exists' may be true even if A does not exist" (124–25, 123). Thus, Russell contended, people could not *generally* infer "true" from "good for life."

James was infuriated by this analysis, but it motivated him to be more discriminating and circumspect in further articulation of his theory. In his annotations of Russell's article, he noted that he never meant to equate truth with utility (though he obviously had on occasion): "The true means not 'the useful' but 'the useful in the way of leading to a reality.' Many beliefs are useful, but not in that sense. And true beliefs are useful in *that sense* only when the realities are useful only" (*MT*, 307).

Even granting the ambiguities of "Pragmatism's Conception of Truth," however, James thought that Russell's charge was a total misrepresentation. 'A exists' could not possibly be true if A did not exist in light of the "pragmatist postulate" that truth is a relation between statements and facts. In response to Russell's criticisms of his position on the Absolute, he wrote: "All this is rubbish. The coincidence of the true with the emotionally satisfying becomes of importance for determining what may count for true, only when there is no other evidence" (*MT*, 309).

Royce made the same sort of criticism: pragmatists could hold that the idea of something was true even if it was not so. James argued that his critics were making two mistakes, one having to do with the distinction between truths and facts, another having to do with the distinction beween declarations of truth and reflection on declarations of truth. On the one hand, critics chose examples in which incompetents believed what competents had infirmed. On the other, they claimed that James construed beliefs and the function of beliefs as semantic equivalents.

James argued that his critics fostered confusion by making propositions the basic epistemological unit. Propositions were neither judgments nor realities, at least unambiguously. The inevitable 'that' of propositions sometimes meant the fact that and sometimes the belief that. On pragmatic grounds a person could believe that Caesar was alive when in fact he was no longer living. He could be justified in believing that Caesar was alive when in fact he was no longer living. But it was not true on pragmatic grounds that a person could believe that Caesar was alive when he was justified in believing that he was no longer living. Nor was it true on pragmatic grounds that Caesar could in fact be alive when he was no longer living.

A person could be justified in believing that Caesar was alive when in fact he was not if, on the basis of his present information, everything indicated that he was, even though on the basis of information not available to him at the time it turned out that he was wrong. Once again: "the long run of experience" turned out to be the linchpin in James's theory. James's point was that when further information turned up that impugned the shorter-run claim, no other formal condition than that of justification would be achieved. Quite simply, more material information would be achieved in the long run. Thus, justification in the long run carried the very same payload that 'truth' did in inquiry.

In response to his critics' charge that he confused justification with expediency, James argued that they were confusing levels of discourse. On pragmatist grounds, James argued, justified beliefs are convenient. But beliefs are not justified simply because they are convenient (without further specification). In response to his critics' charge that if the truth of an idea were constituted by its workings, then one could not account for truths that were never known, James argued that his critics confused 'truth' with 'reality'.

According to the antipragmatists, if James admitted the existence of truths that were never known, he would have to surrender his theory; if he claimed there were none, he would fly in the face of common sense. But James argued that if the 'propositions' of *erkenntnistheorie* were displaced by his variables, 'ideas' and 'reals', the problem would dissolve. On pragmatist grounds, numerous *facts* and *reals* were never known, but not 'truths': reals were construed as varying independently of statements in James's theory, but truths were construed as a function of both statements and reals varying independently of each other.

Royce, for one, was not convinced. The problem, as he saw it, was that James postulated certain things that could never be verified in order to launch his theory of truth. Abandoning most of his 1903 criticisms, Royce centered on James's crucial postulate that there was a tendency towards epistemic consensus in the long run of experience. In "The Problem of Truth in the Light of Recent Discussion" (1908), Royce argued that three things motivated recent theories of truth: the success of the historical sciences, "the longing to be self-possessed and inwardly free,"[6] and the love of objectivity. He said that the difference between his own theory of truth and James's was not that his was "intellectualist" while James's was "pragmatist." "It is the contrast between two well-known attitudes of the will—the will that is loyal to truth as a universal ideal —and the will that is concerned with its own passing caprices" (232–33).

According to Royce, James responded adequately to the first two motives but, try as he might, did not adequately satisfy the demands incumbent on the lover of objectivity. James correctly defined "the nature which truth possesses insofar as we ever actually verify truth"; but by making epistemic credit "relative to the creditor," without determining his "absolute form," James was incompetent when it came to determining real truth (224, 229).

But James's postulate about "the long run of experience" depended on a picture of things that permitted the employment of regulative principles that were no more like constitutive truths than mechanical rabbits were like hot-blooded bunnies. James did not dogmatize the postulate that there is "an ideal set of formulations towards which all opinions may in the long run be expected to converge." As he saw it, a pragmatist need only postulate that the future will "probably contain more of truth than anyone's opinion now" *because* the principle of absolute truth was *aufgegeben*, not *gegeben*: it was an expression of the way things should turn out if everyone relevant turned to the task in appropriate ways, not a reflection of the way things are or will inevitably be (*MT*, 143, 145).

James thought that Royce's mistake was thinking that he construed all statements as verifiable in the same way and in the same sense. The "long run" postulate was not governed according to the same rules of confirmation that, say, the claim "it is raining outside" was governed by. People went outside to check whether it was raining. No one checked on "the long run" in the same way. To the contrary, the postulate was confirmed the better it helped to organize and stabilize the achievements of inquiry. The 'reality' to which it led or for which it accounted was 'inquiry', not the subjects of inquiry.

From the standpoint of a Roycean world view in which divinity encompassed anything and everything, investigators searching for the truth presumed to be looking for something bounded or systematic, not open-ended. But from James's standpoint, in which divinity was extracted if ultimate, the search for "bounded totals" was instrumental, not relevatory. James's "world" boiled over from time to time, making the best efforts of the best investigators capricious by way of an acoustical illusion. The partly human-built world surrounding investigators dated the most finely honed instruments.

Recognition of the crucial role that metaphysics played in adjudicating the differences between pragmatism and its rivals led James to claim that

> the alternative between pragmatism and rationalism . . . concerns the structure of the universe itself. On the pragmatist side we have only one edition of the universe, unfinished, growing in all sorts of places where thinking beings are at work.

On the rationalist side we have a universe in many editions, one real one, an infinite folio, or *edition de luxe*, eternally complete; and then the various finite editions, full of false readings, distorted and mutilated each in its own way.

So the rival metaphysical hypotheses of pluralism and monism here come back upon us. [*Prag*, 124]

The world that James discovered in one edition was without end; it admitted ordering but just as certainly demanded reconstruction and reparation. Thinking beings were competent to attend to these tasks. If their anxieties often got the better of them, crippling their transactions, especially undercutting their capacity to realize their best intentions, the varieties of religious experience demonstrated that persons had actually seen hopelessness displaced by energies pointed in harmonial directions. Persons had known salvation sufficiently to thirst for more and had received enough help when they were helpless to believe that they were not alone, either in their desire for peace or in their ability to satisfy it.

In light of this reasoning, James turned to religious speculation. He was self-conscious about the strictures that he had laid on the doing of theology in his Gifford Lectures. The point of philosophical theology was to liberate new avenues of inquiry, to set questions that observation might answer. Responsible religious thought was secondary or reflective, but it could also mold new experiences to the images it drew. Theology was basically temperamental and aesthetic in character. But the very fact that James executed a theology in his Hibbert Lectures "The Present Situation in Philosophy" in 1908, executed it rigorously and in line with his over-belief in 1902, lends credence to the notion that James construed temperamental, aesthetic theology as utterly serious work for anyone broadminded enough to be considered philosophical.

CHAPTER 9

RELIGIOUS THOUGHT IN A

PLURALISTIC UNIVERSE

Pluralistic Pantheism in James's Last Works

James wrote his Hibbert Lectures, subsequently published as *A Pluralistic Universe*, during a period when people first began to imagine total war. The more world-wide war became probable, the more time he devoted to pacifist concerns. Before fellow pacifists he proclaimed a devout belief in the reign of peace and in the gradual advent of some sort of socialistic equilibrium. He commended nations to find "a moral equivalent of war," some set of tasks to train "societies to cohesiveness."

In this regard, James asserted that history was a bath of blood. He said that fear was the condition from which humanity needed to be emancipated in order to bring the reign of the sword to an end. "The fear of emancipation from the fear-regime . . . fear regarding ourselves now taking the place of the ancient fear of the enemy" kept nations from encouraging the sociality of persuasion among themselves. For centuries, fear of the enemy had motivated the moral life, the life of "fidelity, cohesiveness, tenacity, heroism, conscience, education, inventiveness, economy, wealth, physical health and vigor" (*MS*, 281, 280). Now people feared that these virtues would atrophy if the life of well-being ever displaced the life of well-doing, and if compromise and acceptance superseded righteousness and supremacy as national ideals.

But James pointed out that a "peace-economy" need not be a "pleasure-economy." If nations would, for instance, gather together to accommodate nature to the interests they shared, peace might ensue without debilitating pleasure. In general, James suggested, what "the whole community comes to believe in grasps the individual as in a vice. The war-function has grasped us so far; but constructive interests may some day seem no less imperative, and impose on the individual a hardly lighter burden" (*MS*, 289).

But, as James saw things, the community was not mature enough to engineer such a transformation without special help. Vox populi had run its gamut and failed. Ever the liberal, he believed that men's opinions were the predominant influence on social and historical change. But especially after the turn of the century, he became convinced that the educated classes must lead national opinion. "The notion that a people can run itself and its affairs anonymously is now well-known to be the silliest of absurdities. Mankind does nothing save through initiatives on the part of inventors, great or small, and imitation by the rest of us—these are the sole factors active in human progress. Individuals of genius show the way, and set the patterns, which common people then adapt and follow" (MS, 319).

On James's view, the function of the college bred was to steer the nation "amid the driftings of democracy." Their aim was to warp the world in the direction of pacific equilibrium by ceaselessly whispering "the more permanent ideals." They had to contend with "affections for old habit, currents of self-interest, and gales of passion," not by extinguishing these inevitable forces, but by channeling them toward the best things (MS, 320). The college bred had to play a role analogous to aristocracy in Britain, ensuring traditions in a class-conscious way. But they had to do so without the "corporate selfishness" of aristocracy and without wielding powers of corruption. Only when they came to understand themselves as "Les Intellectuels" might they overcome the parties of "every stupid prejudice and passion" and gain acceptance in the arena of public opinion.

Philosophy played a special role in this scheme, according to James, because it was the one discipline that explicitly sought to expunge one-sidedness by encouraging a synopsis of data, a search for truth in the views of opponents, an appreciation of old and outmoded thoughts and activities, and the criticism and cracking of "caked prejudices." Philosophy, James said, was "only a compendious name for the spirit of education which the word 'college' stands for in America" (SPP, 10). Without philosophy, citizens were "cads," unable to seek emotionally valuable results by hard reasoning.

James's assertions about war and peace, universities, philosophy, and social breeding demonstrated his continuing allegiance to a religion of the republic, a vision of many and various children of light constituting a "democracy stumbling through every error till its institutions glow with justice and its customs shine with beauty" (MS, 318). These concerns came together with many more technically philosophical ones in A Pluralistic Universe, where James defended the claim that the world or universe was "more like a federal republic than like an empire or a kingdom" (*PU*, 145).

James asserted, in other words, that whatever order or coherence or harmony the universe had, it was constituted by independent powers inhabiting it. This hypothesis, of course, recapitulated his father's emphasis on the form of polity enunciated in the motto of his country: *E pluribus unum*, one out of many. It set the stage for James's articulation of a strikingly new pantheism.

A Pluralistic Universe provided James with an opportunity to present a retrospective on his own development, especially on his development from an inchoate form of theism to a more choate form of pantheism. In his retrospective, he made it clear that his federal republican claim about the order of things was hard-won because the pluralism that he had held for roughly thirty years disallowed his making it. He had wanted to make it because of his religious attitudes. He had needed to make it in order to square speculative beliefs about the order of things with practical beliefs that he held about thought and action. But his claim that the world was like a federal republic was costly for him because he thought it meant giving up allegiance to a rule of thought basic to his philosophic tradition: the rule of numerical identity.

James was finally enabled to make his claim about the federal republican order of things when he realized that his radical empiricism was radical enough to overturn the authority of the logic of identity in speculative matters. According to the logic of identity, one thing, say, the United States of America, may be produced by many things, say, the individual states. But one thing cannot be many things, or vice versa.

But James thought he had to defend the latter claim in order to articulate his theology of the ultimate. That theology promised salvation, but unlike its transcendental competition, it promised salvation in the same way that James promised absolute truth—at the end of effort. Salvation was *aufgegeben*, not *gegeben*, a task, not a condition of moral life. But James thought even this meant demonstrating the grounded possibility that persons were not alone in their quest for well-being, that other things in the universe at least permitted and at best forcefully championed the survival of the humanly fittest.

In *Varieties*, he had stated his over-belief in a God whose "existence is the guarantee of an ideal order that shall be permanently preserved," a God that made tragedy "only provisional and partial." But he had not executed any argument on behalf of the hypothesis. In his essays in humanism and radical empiricism that followed publication of *Varieties*, James made the moves necessary to warrant the logical possibility of investing the world with soul, of making the world more and more orderly according to the shared intentions of cooperative agents. In *Pragmatism*, he specified what the world would look like if it were invested with soul.

Finally, in *A Pluralistic Universe*, James argued that the "objective part" of his religious hypothesis was a better grounded possibility than its chief competitors. On grounds of both "vision" and "justification," a pluralistic pantheism was more rational than any sort of materialism or the two other sorts of spiritualism with which it competed, orthodox theism and absolute idealism.

Philosophy and the Problem of the One and the Many

The emergence of James's argument for pluralistic pantheism was a process that covered most of James's philosophical career. James freely admitted that he had grown up under a "monistic superstition," even if it came packaged in the peculiar theology of the kingly commons of Henry James, Sr. But until James finished his Gifford Lectures and executed his essays in radical empiricism, he had thought two things stood in the way of arguing for any sort of pantheism. First, he assumed that applying the 'one out of many' principle to metaphysical discourse resulted in the claim that the 'one', or the divine, was consubstantial with the 'many', or the phenomenal world. On the grounds of the logic of identity, this was absurd. But second, even if he waived the logical objections, James thought the moral objections were insuperable: even if the world *could* be pantheistic, in other words, it would be damned if it were. For if the divine was consubstantial with the phenomenal world, harmony was consubstantial with discord, good consubstantial with evil, truth consubstantial with error. If this was the case, moral judgment—indeed, any sort of judgment—was either a sham or an impossibility. Even when Royce tried to persuade him that knowledge, not being, was the key to the problem of inclusive integration, James found the very same problem: the logic of identity and moral scruples stood in the way of characterizing the world of man as the object of thought of an Absolute God.

In the face of these difficulties, James had maintained an allegiance to theism, as against pantheism, until the turn of the century. The first sign of a break came in his Ingersoll Lecture, "The Immortality of Man," delivered in 1897. There, James made two points designed to challenge "the puritanism of science" on the issue of human immortality. First, the materialist premise that thought was a function of the brain did not necessarily entail the materialist conclusion that thought was expunged when the brain died. Second, the "aristocratic" premise that "immortals . . . were always an elite, a select and manageable number" was untenable because the issue of spiritual immortality was irrelevant to arithmetical questions.

On the first issue, James argued the existence of a number of ways to analyze the notion of function, only one of which led to materialist conclusions. Functional dependence could be analyzed as production, permission, or transmission. If thought was a function of the brain like steam was a function of a teakettle, then the brain was the condition without which thought could not occur; the brain was productive of thought. But if the brain released thought like the trigger of a crossbow released an arrow, then the brain was the condition that permitted thought to occur. Finally, if thought depended on the brain the way particular sounds depended on both air and the keys of an organ, then the brain simply had a transmissive function. James argued that investigators were not required to construe the functional dependence of thought on brain as a matter of production. Investigators could also consider permissive and transmissive functions because "we can frame no more notion of the details on the one hypothesis than on the other." The production of consciousness in the brain was an "absolute world-enigma." On the grounds of science positively understood, "function can mean nothing more than bare concomitant variation" (*HI*, 21, 20).

Opposing the materialist view, James argued that the relation of thought to brain was disanalogous with the production of steam in a teakettle in a crucial respect. In the latter case, the terms that changed were physically homogeneous; but in the former case, the terms were heterogeneous. Water and steam were generically the same; material and consciousness were not. All the problems in brain physiology emerged from the disanalogy, not the analogy. In support of the theory of transmission, James pointed out that (1) it did not break the principle of continuity; (2) it complemented general idealistic philosophy; (3) it also complemented Fechner's "new psychology," which pictured consciousness as dependent on a certain "threshold" whose height varied under certain circumstances; (4) it made sense of those "odd bits of knowledge" observed in "religious conversions, providential leadings in answer to prayer, instantaneous healings, premonitions, apparitions at time of death, clairvoyant visions or impressions, and the whole range of mediumistic capacities, to say nothing of still more exceptional and incomprehensible things"; and, finally, (5) the theory did not conflict with the notion that there was continuity of thought "hereafter" (*HI*, 25, 28). On all these grounds, the speculative notion that individual consciousness was "continuous with a mother-sea" seemed credible enough for investigators to pursue.

Moreover, if investigators supposed with both common sense and idealistic philosophy that physical analysis did not do justice to human experience, then they could consider the possibility that "the genuine matter of reality, the life of souls as it is in its fullness, will break through our several brains into this world in all sorts of restricted forms, and with all the imperfections and queernesses that characterize our individualities here below" (*HI*, 17).

James's first point denied materialists' claims against the possibility of pantheism and drew constructive connections between the hypothesis of "cosmic consciousness" and other salient features of the intellectual world that he and his audience shared. His second point drew attention to connections between pantheism and the political ideals that he espoused. Against pantheism, Christian theists had argued that it supposed heavenly life for everyone and everything—surely a heretical view. Christians who thought of "the hereafter" as a place populated by bodies found it difficult to imagine every thoughtful thing crammed into a heavenly city. Besides, from a sectarian point of view it was impossible to find any justification for providing "alien human creatures"—for example, "Chinamen"—with immortality, because aliens were "grotesque" and "repulsive."

James turned aside these concerns as remnants "of the old narrow-hearted aristocratic creed." The sort of pantheism that credited the theory of consciousness that James backed was democratic, one in which "paltry exclusions play[ed] no regulative part." So long as individuals participated in the quest for ultimate integration, they were "so many diverse channels of expression" of "the eternal Spirit of the Universe" affirming and realizing itself. Indeed, on the grounds of "transmission" that James provided, his pantheism broke "the monistic pattern" by providing a way to "conceive the mental world . . . in as individualistic a form as one pleases" (*HI*, 43, vii). The orthodox pantheist viewed the many as constituted by the one. His pantheism, as early as this lecture on human immortality, viewed the many as constituting the one.

The conclusions to James's *Varieties* that emphasized relations between selves and wider selves added an actual base for his pantheistic speculations, but as late as 1905 he wrote to Schiller complaining that he could not "yet get over the difficulty of seeing how a wide-span consciousness can be entitatively *constituted* of smaller consciousnesses" (*TC*, 2:588). The complaint demonstrates the extent to which James did not know his own mind on the issue because the break from commitments that precluded pantheism came with the publication of his premier essays in radical empiricism, written in 1904.

Until 1904, James thought that pantheism and "discontinuous experience" were incompatible. He thought, in other words, that if everything participated in divinity, then nothing was actually independent of anything else. But common sense insisted on such independence for many things. He realized in "A World of Pure Experience," however, that while idealism and discontinuous experience were incompatible, pantheism and discontinuous experience were not. So he developed a pantheism that was not an idealism!

As James understood them, the absolute idealists were committed to an appearance/reality bifurcation in the world which his radical empiricism did not tolerate. Their pantheism was a "two worlds" theology, which distinguished the reality of God from the appearance of his finite expressions. Absolute idealists "passed to the limit" on the issue of the continuity of consciousness. Whether they were Bradleyans or Royceans, they claimed that either there was complete continuity or there was none; looking for a transempirical "connection" made this conclusion inevitable. But for James, commitment to radical empiricism brought the search for a transempirical "connection" to an end. Idealists were correct to insist that human experience was informed experience, but vicious in their claim that 'disorders' in the universe were ordered and even overcome because 'disorders' played a role in some semantic system.

James's crucial move in the development of his pantheism was to insist on the historicity of things, including divinity. If reality was not made but was in the making, then 'things' were not self-identical entities; they did not behave like numbers. Things, like zoological populations, might constantly surpass any given definition of them. They were both 'themselves', in the sense of the definition given to them at any particular time, and 'something else', in the sense of the mutations that might lead to revisions in their definition. If things in general were like this, the logic of numerical identity was not applicable to metaphysical speculation.

What is more, if 'things' were historical entities, then they were almost inevitably 'conjoined' with other things. This claim complemented the commonsense notion that people observed such things as shoals of mussels, beehives, and the United States Senate. But it flew in the face of both classical rationalism and empiricism. James well knew that historical things were both one and many. He knew, for instance, that individual giraffes did not produce the species of giraffes but that they were the species and the species was them. Thus, at least some things were constituted one out of many.

James argued, further, that because people were historical beings in the process of coming to grips with historical environments, talk about all of the universe was ultimately unwarranted. But if each and every thing that could be observed turned out, on close inspection, to be simultaneously one and many in the same way that species were, he had grounds for claiming that the universe was constituted like a federal republic, *e pluribus unum*.

James used this tactic in his essays in radical empiricism. He argued that persons saw activity when they pointed to experience and that activity was "an affair of relations." If activity seemed chaotic at first, this was due to a superabundance of relations, not a paucity of them.[1] When persons saw activity, they particularized it and defined it. They took pure experience and stabilized what was really going on—and their stabilizing of it was one of the ways that they themselves went on successfully. Their classifying and attending—in a word, their thinking—about "that" was part and parcel of what was going on. Hence, thought was one sort of external relation between parts of experience.

James's line of thought implied that each time people experienced something unreflectively, they experienced much-at-once. Just as individual persons together did not produce the species *Homo sapiens* but 'were that species and it them,' so the superabundant relations that "made up" any activity did not produce the activity but 'were the activity and it them.' Ungrammatical as that sounds, it clarifies what James meant when he claimed that each experience was constituted one out of many.

If each experience was constituted one out of many, then it was thinkable to consider persons and things as both independent and part of divinity, especially when "one out of many" was understood diachronically. Once the logic of identity was overthrown in this fashion, James found it much easier to accept pantheism. The fact that radical empiricism did not require abandonment of 'discontinuity' once it admitted 'continuity' made its acceptance easier still. People and gods might be conjoined but still have to overcome social, psychological, and natural bifurcations surrounding them.

James's Pluralistic Universe

According to the position that James had articulated in *Varieties*, the business of salvation included transactions between persons and superhuman agents who became "continuous" with them under certain conditions, allowing those persons to be well in ways they were not able to achieve on their own. The metaphysical position that James developed in *A Pluralistic Universe* bolstered this religious thought. James called it "pluralistic pantheism."

Early on in *A Pluralistic Universe*, James set the direction of his argument by asserting that "the vaster vistas which scientific evolutionism has opened, and the rising tide of social democratic ideals, have changed the type of our imagination, and the older monarchial theism is obsolete or obsolescent. The place of the divine must be more organic and intimate" (*PU*, 18).

James began by characterizing the speculative philosophical enterprise in which his work on pantheism was located. He drew a picture of speculative philosophy as consisting of two parts: reasons and visions. Harking back to *Varieties*, he insisted that speculative visions were based largely on temperament, on whether or not one's most general attitudes were optimistic, melioristic, pessimistic, or indifferent. Recalling the strictures that he had placed on philosophy in 1902, he commended a view of philosophical speculation as aesthetic: there were all sorts of reasons that counted in philosophical debate, but when all was said and done, points of contention boiled down to the question of how harmonious and illuminating synoptic visions were.

Within this context, James claimed that so far as reasoning was concerned, the two competing sorts of philosophy were rationalism and empiricism. Both rationalists and empiricists were committed to the assumption that explanation had to do with the relation between wholes and parts. But rationalists explained parts by their wholes; empiricists explained wholes by their parts.

On the topic of visions, James claimed that the two sorts of philosophy competing for attention "in the present situation" were materialism and spiritualism. Materialists were cynical, temperamentally pessimistic or indifferent. They painted a picture of the world "so as to leave man's soul upon it as a sort of outside passenger or alien." Spiritualists, to the contrary, were sympathetic, either optimistic or melioristic, and insisted that "the intimate and the human must surround and underlie the brutal" (*PU*, 16). Meliorists differed from optimists on the meaning of "must." Meliorists claimed that the intimate and the human 'had better' surround and underlie the brutal. Optimists claimed that the intimate and the human 'inevitably does' surround and underlie the brutal.

James rigged the sort of philosophy that was worth pursuing by claiming three things. First, stealing thunder from his spiritualistic opponents, he invoked Hegel's assumption that "the aim of knowledge is to divest the objective world that stands opposed to us of its strangeness, and as the phrase is, to make us more at home in it." Thus, materialist visions were misguided: they missed the point of inquiry. Second, most people were sympathetic, and sympathy was healthy while cynicism was debilitating. Thus, materialist visions were symptomatic of disease. Third, no philosophical vision "can ever be anything but a summary sketch; a picture of the world in abridgment, a foreshortened birds-eye view of the perspective of events." Thus, any speculative vision was empirical to this extent: "We can invent no new form of conception, applicable to the whole exclusively, and not suggested originally by the parts" (*PU*, 109). The paradigms that rationalists and empiricists alike employed to talk about "wholes" were extrapolated from particular experiences.

Given these three assumptions, James's conclusion was almost inescapable: the best sort of reasoned vision was some sort of empirical spiritualism—precisely the sort of speculative philosophy that James was offering. If, James reasoned, Hegel was right about knowledge, then whatever investigation actually accomplished, speculation ought to respond to the motives for knowing by picturing the possibility of finding the "home" that persons sought.

But, according to James, there were two competing forms of spiritualism, and one promised more intimacy than did the other. Theism was less intimate than pantheism, especially in its orthodox, monarchial articulation, because it construed God and man and the world not only as externally related but as alien to one another. The God of theism affected people but not vice versa. He was not a friend but a magistrate or a potentate, and had no *social* relation with people. Social relation was the true mark of possible intimacy. Hence, James said that "the theistic conception, picturing God and his creation as *entities distinct* from each other, still leaves the human subject outside of the deepest reality in the Universe" (*PU*, 16).

Pantheism was the more intimate form of spiritualism because it construed humanity as "part," in some sense of that term, of the deepest reality in the universe. Moreover, it suited "scientific evolutionism" better than did theism because it allowed for historical development of divinity. And it better fit "social democratic ideals" because it imputed no essential inequalities between basic things.

But then again, according to James, different pantheisms could be less or more intimate. Pluralistic pantheism (variously articulated by Henry James, Sr., the early Dewey, Bergson, Howison, Schiller, and now by James himself) was more intimate than monistic pantheism (or most other pantheists' pantheism). The pantheism of absolute idealism especially was less intimate, because absolute idealists claimed that persons were locked into a relative vantage point and locked out of God's absolute vantage point. This radical discrepancy in vantage points made for as much foreignness, according to James, as monarchial theism ever did because it meant that "the eternal's ways are utterly unlike our ways" (*PU*, 23).

James's pluralistic pantheism, to the contrary, collapsed the radical discrepancy in vantage points by construing divinity distributively instead of collectively. In other words, James was "willing to believe that there may ultimately never be an all-form at all, that the substance of reality may never get totally collected, that some of it may remain outside of the largest combination of it ever made, and that a distributive form of reality, the each-form, is logically as acceptable and empirically as probable as the all-form commonly acquiesced in as so obviously the self-evident thing" (*PU*, 20).

James argued, in other words, that the hypothesis of an ultimate union constituted by the many agencies that 'were the universe' was logically as acceptable as absolute idealism and at least as empirically probable. By insisting that the federating of agencies would probably always go on without ever collecting or systematizing each and every interest as its own, James drew his analogy with a federal republic more closely, not less. James had learned from Thomas Davidson that the "best commonwealth" was the one that left the most room for "residual interests," interests too private to be systematized (*MS*, 102–3).

Once James had characterized the present situation in philosophy and had clarified the sort of pantheism that he wished to defend, he went on to attack his major spiritualistic rivals, Bradley and Royce. Both these thinkers claimed that their "absolute" was no hypothesis but a "presupposition in all thinking, . . . a logical necessity" (*PU*, 29). They assumed that the world was coherent, rational, or self-consistent and assumed that the world had to be so in order for people to think the truth. According to their doctrine, James asserted, the world appeared incoherent, but this was the fault of perception, which presented discontinuous bits and pieces of the world. By displacing percepts with concepts, people ordered chaotic life. But conceptualization had a side effect, the only cure for which was the assumption of the absolute continuity of thought. When concepts displaced percepts, the logic of identity was introduced as governing the behavior of thought and, hence, of things as conceptually ordered. This government fixed the distinctions between things: everything was construed as independent of everything else—unless one assumed prior and complete continuity between each and every thought.

According to both Bradley and Royce, admitting any discontinuity among things required the conclusion that the world was incoherent. Admitting some continuity, to the contrary, required the admission of complete continuity. To be sure, Bradley and Royce differed over particulars. Bradley agreed with James that people must encounter reality, if they encounter it anywhere, as much-at-once in the "bewildering mass of phenomenal diversity."[2] He also agreed with James that conception, governed by the logic of identity, was far more analytic than unifying. He claimed that in the long run, the logical regimentation of observations made things less and less comprehensible.

Bradley and James divided on the issue of "relations." Bradley asserted that entities were necessarily altered by the relations into which they entered. His strategy was to argue *ex vi terminorum* (1) that "everywhere there must be a whole embracing what is related, or there would be no differences and no relation!" (2) that whatever is related is altered by the relation entered into; and (3) that "there is no identity or likeness possible except in a whole, and every such whole must qualify and be qualified by its terms. And where the whole is different, the terms that qualify it and contribute to it must so far be different, and so far therefore by becoming elements in a fresh unity the terms must be altered" (180, 513–19). Thus, according to Bradley, the tradition of empiricism exemplified by Hume was wrong to construe things as externally related: things were always and necessarily related as parts of wholes.

James did not pit a doctrine of "external relations" against Bradley's doctrine of internal relations in 1908. To the contrary, he countered Bradley's doctrine by undercutting the philosophical premises that made the distinction between internal and external relations important. Arguing against mechanism, James claimed that things may be interrelated as parts of wholes; against idealism, however, he argued that they were not necessarily related this way. In any case, according to James, interrelated things could be observed as such, a position which countered both mechanism and idealism. The first part of James's position on "relations" made his

theological ultimate possible. The second part made absolute pantheism improbable. The third part undercut any need to depart
from the world of observation in order to think out his soteriology.

As James saw things, "to have the alternative forced upon us of
admitting either finite things each cut off from all relation with its
environment, or else of accepting the integral absolute with no
environment and all relations packed within itself, would be too
delicious a simplification" (PU, 35). Royce argued from this "forced
alternative" in much the same way that Bradley did, even if he was
more Humean in his analysis of immediate experience. For instance, he assumed that from a commonsense viewpoint, thoughts
and things appeared independent of each other. Their becoming
related through awareness made them no less independent because
any connection between thoughts and things was itself distinguished from both the thought and the thing and, as such, stood in
need of further connections, ad infinitum:

> The realist's many beings, as defined, are defined as wholly
> disconnected; and they must remain so. They cannot first say
> of them, for instance, that they are logically independent, and
> then truly add that nevertheless they are really and causally
> linked. No two of them are in the same space; for space would
> be a link. And just so; no two of them are in the same time;
> no two are in any physical connection; no two are parts of any
> really same whole. The mutual independence, if once real, and
> real as defined, cannot later be changed to any form of mutual
> dependence.[3]

The next step that Royce took was to deny the "original" realistic
hypothesis that the "many beings" were disconnected. If, to the
contrary, one assumed that they were "co-involved," it was impossible to escape the conclusion that they were interrelated parts of a
world that presented itself as one fact: there must be a higher mind
which "owns them" as objects. This higher mind must be the mind
that knows everything else, on pain of introducing the paradoxes
of the original realistic hypothesis.

James thought that if Royce was granted his premises, Royce's
position was sound. He also thought that Royce's position recapitulated Hegel's. James reflected that

> Hegel . . . considers that the immediate finite data of experi-
> ence are 'untrue' because they are not their own others. They
> are negated by what is external to them. The absolute is true

> because it and it only has no external environment, and has
> attained to being its own other. . . . Granting his premise that
> to be true a thing must in some sort be its own other, every-
> thing hinges on whether he is right on holding that the several
> pieces of finite experience themselves cannot be in any wise
> *their* own others. When conceptualistically or intellectual-
> istically treated, they of course cannot be their own others.
> Every abstract concept as such excludes what it doesn't in-
> clude; and if such concepts are adequate substitutes for reali-
> ty's concrete pulses, the latter must square themselves with
> intellectualistic logic, and no one of them in any sense can
> claim to be its own other. [PU, 53]

James himself had employed "intellectualistic logic" on the issue of the one and the many until his essays in radical empiricism. Then, motivated in part by the inapplicability of intellectual logic to the data of religious self-transformation, but more fundamentally by recognition of the historicity of things, he abandoned it. He accepted Hegel's claim about the connection between 'truth' and synthesis, but made this claim against his old opponent: "If, how-ever, the conceptual treatment of the flow of reality should prove for any good reason to be inadequate and to have a practical rather than a speculative or theoretical value, then an independent em-pirical look into the constitution of reality's pulses might possibly show that some of them are their own others in the self-same sense in which the absolute is maintained to be so by Hegel" (PU, 53).

Saints, for instance, were their own others in Hegel's precise sense: they had divested the objective world of its strangeness; they had done this when they encountered and were encompassed by their own other. James had discovered this by taking an inde-pendent empirical look into the rebirth of persons who had achieved well-being.

In light of this, James denied the adequacies of the logic of iden-tity for speculative purposes and accepted the coherence of Hegel-ian monism as a vision of some universe which might be true some time and some place. But he claimed that only *some* experiences that people investigated were their own others in Hegel's sense. Hence, "the real way of rescue from the abstract consequences of one name is not to fly to an opposite name, equally abstract, but rather to correct the first name by qualifying adjectives that restore some concreteness to the case. . . . Only when we know what the process of interaction literally and concretely *consists* in can we tell whether beings independent *in definite respects*, distinct, for example, in origin, separate in place, different in kind, etc., can or cannot interact" (*PU*, 32). Following this strategy, the formal problem of the one and the many collapsed. There was no need to fly from the abstract consequences of the name "One" to those of the name "Many."

James associated his criticism of logic with Bergson. But far from succumbing to the mysticism exemplified by Bergson's inversion of Hegel's position, James suggested that if people were able to look at conjoined experiences, if they were able to look at much-at-once, there was no philosophical motivation either to depart from perception or to invoke any absolute thought (or mystical intuition) for the sake of metaphysical speculation. His point was that investigators had observed "original" situations that both undercut the authority of the logic of identity and underwrote the continuability or composability, indeed, the reparability, of things-in-general. *Varieties* exemplified such observations.

James also thought that Fechner's work was exemplary in this regard. He recognized just how fanciful much of Fechner's metaphysics was, especially when it came to speculations on the inner life and consciousness of plants. Nevertheless, he was impressed with Fechner's attempt to argue from observations and analogies that superhuman consciousnesses existed and that people were intimately connected with them. He declared that he wanted to argue as Fechner had, but for a vision of superhuman beings that Fechner did not share: the vision of superhuman beings supported by the observation-reports of divine encounter that he had cataloged in *Varieties*. The shape of Fechner's argument was important because it presented "a vast analogical series, in which the basis of the analogy consists of facts directly observable in ourselves" (*PU*, 73).

Fechner was fascinating to James because he did not conclude with a skeletal statement of what might be analogously the case. He went on to characterize concrete hypotheses that were open and subject to investigation. His vision was thick, sometimes to the point of fiction. He said that the earth was an organism, and he speculated, for instance, on earth-things that might play the "same" role for the earth that brain fibers played for individual sentient beings. Fechner took questions like this and tried to give full answers. In general, he tried to picture how the ways of the world permitted "compounding of consciousness," in contrast to other pantheists whose visions ran "thin" by assuming a sort of inclusive consciousness without making any attempt to show it.

Without endorsing the particulars of Fechner's vision, James went on to present his own view on "the compounding of consciousness." First, he showed that people did observe both continuity and discontinuity. Then he commended philosophers to take another look at events, especially full-blooded personal activities. When they looked at life going on, he predicted, they would find that "the immediate experience of life solves the problems which so baffle our conceptual intelligence" (PU, 116). No mystical or rationalist strategy had to be deployed in order to realize that some things were their own others:

> How can what is manifold be one? how can things get out of
> themselves? how be their own others? how be both distinct
> and connected? how can they act on one another? how be for
> others and yet for themselves? how be absent and present at
> once? The intellect asks these questions much as we might ask
> how anything can both separate and unite things, or how
> sounds can grow more alike by continuing to grow different.
> If you already know space sensibly, you can answer the for-
> mer question by pointing to any interval in it, long or short; if
> you know the musical scale, you can answer the latter by
> sounding an octave; but then you must first have the sensible
> knowledge of these things. [PU, 116]

On these grounds, the philosophers' problem of the one and the many was an example of language gone on holiday, an instance of diseased thought. The philosophers had talked about their language as though it were reality. They had committed the sin of confusing words and objects. Read as a series of solutions to the problem of the one and the many, the entire Western philosophical tradition rested on a vicious intellectualism! This line of reasoning led James to proclaim that

> Socrates and Plato taught that what a thing really is is told
> us by its *definition*. Ever since Socrates we have been taught
> that reality consists of essences, not of appearances, and that
> the essences of things are known whenever we know their defi-
> nitions. So far we identify the thing with a concept, and then
> we identify the concept with a definition, and only then, in-
> asmuch as the thing is whatever the definition expresses, are
> we sure of apprehending the real essence of it or the full truth
> about it. [PU, 99]

The sort of "one" that monists insisted upon was precisely that definitive identity or essence of a thing demanded by conceptualization. James argued that if monists simply took conceptualization for the practical thing that it was, no problem would occur; but they failed to do this. They dropped into confusion, as did their opponents, when they began to employ concepts privatively as well as positively. The confusion took the same form as one in which a person denied that a human baby with a tail was human because humans were not defined as having tails. James noted: "It is but the old story, of a useful practice first becoming a method, then a habit, and finally a tyranny that defeats the end it was used for. Concepts, first employed to make things intelligible, are clung to even when they make them unintelligible" (PU, 99).

James's reflection on the course of philosophy since Socrates led to a remarkable confession. He said that he saw "that philosophy had been on a false scent ever since the days of Socrates and Plato, that an intellectual answer to the intellectualist's difficulties will never come, and that the real way out of them, far from consisting in the discovery of such an answer, consists in simply closing one's ears to the question" (PU, 131).

If 'rationality' meant 'logicality' and 'logicality' meant 'the logic of numerical identity', then James's choice was to "face the fact that life is logically irrational" (PU, 95). If, to the contrary, rationality was not equivalent to 'the logic of numerical identity' but an ability to respond to novel situations in effective ways, then his choice was to reflect on the behaviors which made discrete and intransigent parts of the human situation more integrated and compromising.

James took up the latter position. With Bergson, he said abruptly, "I say no more: I must leave life to teach the lesson." With Bergson, he argued that concepts governed by the logic of numerical identity had great practical applications, but no theoretical or speculative import, no application to the question how things got made. With Bergson, he suggested that answering the speculative question about how things got made involved taking the pose of the metaphysical realist, "a kind of passive and receptive listening quite contrary to the effort to react noisily and verbally on everything," an effort which "our idealistic contemporaries prescribe." Finally, with Bergson, James argued that if you "put yourself *in the making* by a stroke of intuitive sympathy with the thing," you would realize that "reality *falls* in passing into conceptual analysis; it mounts in living its own undivided life—it buds and bourgeons, changes and creates" (PU, 132, 113, 117–18).

But James parted company from Bergson on as many points as

he agreed on. Bergson viewed the universe monistically, as starting "with an original, harmonious unity, developed by way of a diversifying evolution toward a continually greater dispersion."[4] James countered this vision with his own "tychism," a picture of the world as tending toward an ultimate equilibrium as a matter of fact, not a matter of deduction. For Bergson, "life" transcended "experience." He thought "reality" was just as indescribable as Spencer had claimed. His understanding of "sympathetic intuition" was Cartesian: a sort of unverbalizable acquaintance. For James, experience transcended conceptualization; hence, reality was describable, but not as "thought," only as "biography" and "history."[5] His understanding of sympathetic intuition was molded by his radical empiricism: a reporting of events from the point of view of the agents in question.

For Bergson, activity, freedom, novelty and causation were all practically equivalent and finally identified with a predominant ontological substance: real duration, spirit, life. For James, there was no "metaphysical principle of activity," and everything living was active but not necessarily novel or free (cf. *ERE*, 79–95). From James's vantage point, Bergson's *élan vital*, and the continuity of things that it stood for, was an example of vicious intellectualism, naming a substance to back up what Bergson thought was actually going on: the self-diremption of the world-soul.

The continuity of consciousness that James argued for was simply "concatenous." The "compounding of consciousness" actually occurred in every experience of community, whether ordinary (for instance, family, polity, or institution) or extraordinary (for instance, religious encounter). His old objection to the self-compounding of states of consciousness—breaking the principle of self-identity—was "unfounded" in principle because every smallest state of consciousness was historical and "overflows its own definition." The historiographic description of things bore this out. History and biography were the locus for discovering situations in which "no part goes exactly so far and no farther, . . . no part absolutely excludes another, but . . . they compenetrate and are cohesive; . . . if you tear out one, its roots bring out more with them; . . . whatever is real is telescoped and diffused into other reals; . . . in short, every minutest thing is its hegelian 'own other,' in the fullest sense of the term" (*PU*, 129, 121). Indeed, if each and every experience came as a grouping of interactive things, then things in general were like a federal republic; particularly if every grouping had its own environment and had something with which to contend as unsystematizable.

James's Pluralistic Pantheism and "Critical Monism"

Once James thought he had secured the credibility of his vision of the world as a federal republic, the logical grounds obstructing his commitment to pantheism disappeared. If things were not self-identical but historiographically identifiable (maintaining coherence despite change), then "intellectualism's edge [was] broken." In particular, the logic of numerical identity was "inapplicable to our inner life, which spurns at its vetoes and mocks at its impossibilities." On the grounds of the logic of identity, something was either a self or not a self; something could not be a self and not a self. But history and biography showed that "every bit of us at every moment is part and parcel of a wider self" which "may be 'subconscious' to us, yet if in its 'collective capacity' it also exerts an active function, it may be conscious in a wider way, conscious, as it were, over our heads" (*PU*, 131).

James's moral objections to pantheism were overruled when he demonstrated that instances of compounded consciousness that he had observed, especially in *Varieties*, were more adequately construed as concatenated or strung along rather than consubstantial, as open-textured and environmentally located rather than self-enclosed and all-inclusive. So long as a pan-god had an environment, was in time, and was "working out a history just like ourselves, he escapes from the foreignness from all that is human, of the static timeless perfect absolute." On these grounds, good might be concatenous with more good, harmony with greater harmony, warranted assertions with better warrants, because divinity was "the ideal element in things solely, and is our champion and our helper and we his helpers, against the bad parts of the universe" (*PU*, 144, 133).

James's theism was a pantheism because it pictured whatever was conscious as continuable in a concatenated way, not because it pictured everything participating in one collective consciousness. Simultaneous characters participating in the same communities overlapped each other in their being—in their activities and their lives. If this was actually so, James thought, then why not admit what the varieties of religious experience suggested: that "we ourselves form the margin of some more really central self in things which is co-conscious with the whole of us" (*PU*, 131).

In the conclusions to his Hibbert Lectures, then, James made his inevitable return to the importance of religious experience. He asserted point-blank that "there *are* religious experiences" or divine encounters that "point with reasonable probability to the continuity of our consciousness with a wider spiritual environment from which the ordinary prudential man (who is the only man that scientific psychology, so-called, takes cognizance of) is shut off" (*PU*, 135).

When the facts of divine encounter were added to those of divided or split personality, the hypothesis of cosmic or wider-than-recognized consciousness found enough corroboration for James to hold it as presumptively true. He said that a "decidedly *formidable* probability in favor" of it emerged on the basis of analogies "with ordinary psychology, with certain facts of pathology, with those of psychical research, so-called, and with those of religious experience" (*PU*, 140).

James had warned in his Gifford Lectures that cosmic consciousness could not stand on the grounds provided by the varieties of religious experience without further support. His warning stemmed from the principle of inquiry that enjoined investigators from issuing ad hoc solutions. But James became convinced that the hypothesis of cosmic consciousness was no longer ad hoc when he found substantial roles for it in the explanation of exceptional mental states and in metaphysical, moral, religious, and aesthetic discourse.

In "A Suggestion about Mysticism," written and published in 1910, James postulated a "transmarginal" or cosmic consciousness of indefinite extent to account for "typically" mystical states. He had no suggestions to make about the "causes" of "mystical intuition." His hypothesis was that mystical states "may be only very sudden and great extensions of the ordinary 'field of consciousness'" (*EP*, 157). Employing Fechner's "wave scheme" of consciousness as he had in *Human Immortality* thirteen years before, he demonstrated what was going on when a person had exceptional experiences that he himself named mystical.

James noted that diagrammatically speaking, the 'width' of fields of consciousness was variable and that the 'bounds' of fields of consciousness rose and fell as narrower consciousnesses became wider and then narrower again. He noted also that when "by any accident" the threshold of consciousness was lowered in persons with narrower fields, their fields widened and things that were usually subliminal presented themselves in ways that were both exhilarating and convincing. "It is a refreshing experience; and—such is now my hypothesis—we have only to suppose it to occur in an exceptionally extensive form, to give us a mystical paroxysm, if such a term be allowed" (*EP*, 158).

According to James, the form of the field was a much-at-once in which an interactive group of "sensations, memories, concepts, impulses, etc.," were constantly equilibrating. When the threshold fell, from whatever cause, a mass of subconscious memories, conceptions, affections, and associations or "perceptions of relation" came into view all at once. "Sensations" were not included in the extension of consciousness, because they required physical stimulation. To the contrary, in mystical experience, sensation was supplemented in exceptional ways by things that would come to be classified as thoughts, and "if this enlargement of the nimbus that surrounds the sensational present is vast enough, while no one of the items it contains attracts our attention singly, we shall have the conditions fulfilled for a kind of consciousness in all essential respects like that termed mystical" (*EP*, 159).

According to this line of thought, mystical states occurred when the much-at-once of ordinary consciousness was vastly extended *without any analytic breakdown*—that is, without any conceptualization of any of the many things constituting it. James thought this explanation accounted for mysticism as he had characterized it in *Varieties*. It accounted for its transiency because any change of threshold was transient. It accounted for its noetic quality because any lowering of threshold uncovered more and novel perceptions. It accounted for its passivity, because what was discrete and central in the ordinary field of consciousness was overpowered by "a tremendous muchness" in which no vantage point was felt. Finally, it accounted for its ineffability by pointing out that without any vantage point or center of consciousness, there was no point from which to initiate description.

This explanation of mysticism emerged from reflections on exceptional experiences that James himself had during the period 1905–10. In three of these, he was reminded of a past experience somehow related to his own present but in ways that he could not determine. In these, "there was a strong exciting sense that my knowledge of past (or present?) reality was enlarging pulse by pulse, but so rapidly that my intellectual processes could not keep up the pace" (*EP*, 160). These experiences brought James a conviction of "fact-revealed," together with an informing sense of "muchness" which eluded articulation.

In a fourth experience, "the most intensely peculiar experience of my whole life," James suddenly found himself remembering a pair of dreams that he could not remember dreaming. The next night, he found himself dreaming three dreams at once, one that presented itself as "his" and two others that were invasive: "I seemed thus to belong to three different dream-systems at once, no one of which would connect itself either with the others or with my waking life" (*EP*, 160, 161). This convinced him that his consciousness extended indefinitely beyond its ordinary margins, whether he was getting into the dreams of other persons, having telepathic experiences, experiencing treble personality, having a thrombus in a cortical artery, or breaking down mentally.

James did not learn anything about the chance of salvation in his investigations of these exceptional states. But his account of them persuaded him that the notion of wider consciousness played a determining role in psychological theory. This made the hypothesis of cosmic consciousness much less ad hoc. Apparently, "the subconscious" comprised both hither and farther parts. Religious experiences made it clear to him that some exceptional experiences of wider consciousness were divine. The explanations of exceptional mental states and of religious experience leaned on each other and, in the doing, supported James's transformation from theism to pantheism.

Investigating psychical states, James discovered that ordinary self-consciousness was actually related indefinitely to other consciousnesses. Investigating religious experience, he discovered that when ordinary self-consciousness was engaged in "well-doing" but "let go," extraordinary consciousness brought well-being. Along with his argument that the logic of historical identifiability, not the logic of numerical identity, governed speculative discourse, these discoveries led James to the conclusion that "the absolute is not the impossible being I once thought it" (*PU*, 132). Mental facts did function both singly and together. Singular minds did function together in ways that constituted intelligent behavior more powerful than any activity of single minds or even single minds added together. The logic of inquiry, which depended on the assumptions of corrigibility and fallibility, only denied that the position of absolutism was intellectually coercive.

Indeed, the dissolution of the traditional problem of the one and the many that James executed in *A Pluralistic Universe* made his pluralism more a matter of practical emphasis than anything else. Concatenous continuity promised ultimate harmony or equilibrium if everything that could cooperate did so. After the publication of *A Pluralistic Universe*, one had no more reason to be either a pluralist or a monist in any strong sense (that is, ontologically or epistemologically) than one had reason to be a polygenist or a monogenist after Darwin's *Origin of Species*. Just as species or populations overlapped in some ways and maintained recognizable breaks in other ways, so did the experiences that constituted the world.

James's world was becoming repaired "through us," even if "we" did the repairing sometimes as divinely energized. His world got "its disconnections remedied in part by our behavior" (*PU*, 148). But people were more likely to turn to the tasks of peace and persuasion by committing themselves to the notion that "however much may be collected, however much may report itself as present at any effective center of consciousness or action, something else is self-governed and absent and unreduced to unity." Federal republican harmony depended on the assumption of "the more," on the sacredness of individuality, which practically meant residual interests.

Thus James's pluralism differed only slightly from the critical monism presented by his Danish contemporary Harald Höffding in his *Problems of Philosophy*. According to Höffding's doctrine of critical monism, which James taught in courses at Harvard and Stanford, "although you cannot exhaustively account for any item of fact by referring to the whole of which it is a member, yet so much of *what we call* a fact consists of its relations to other facts, that we are equally unable to see any fact wholly independent" (*EP*, 142). This reading of critical monism recapitulated James's radical empiricism without qualification. Both views committed adherents to a conservation of "the best things," even if critical monism emphasized the promise of triumph while James's pluralistic universalism underscored the inevitability of struggle. Each assumed what the other made salient.[6]

Surely, James argued, as he climbed down his faith ladder one more time, the logic of historical entities makes the notion of cosmic consciousness *conceivable*: it might be true somewhere, for it is not self-contradictory. Both ordinary human organizations of intelligence and extraordinary religious experiences suggest that it is actually becoming true and may be true even here and now. Understood concatenously and as environmentally situated, it is fit to be true because it dissolves the "mystery of universal determinism." Well-being would displace well-doing if it were true. Moreover, the "ethical republic," which construes the pursuit of happiness as regulative, warrants it morally. It *would be well if it were true, and it ought to be true*. It is one of those "certain special cases" in which "your acting thus may . . . be a means of making it securely true in the end" because "you" are one of the many without which the "one out of many" will never be constituted (*PU*, 140, 148).

If absolute idealism was just as conceivable as this federal republican pantheism, James argued, the latter was more practical because it was historical. It was more dramatic because it required people to do as well as they could to achieve the happiness they sought and to accept the surprising help they received along the way, while monism suggested that people were "really" well despite all the appearance of disease. James's pantheism was morally more appealing than monism, which construed the thought of evil as part and parcel of the thought of good, because it called for "extrication" from intolerable discontinuities and divisions.

From a federal republican point of view, then, the world was more rationally construed as a federal republic than as an empire or a kingdom. The way that James pictured the world lent an "aura of factuality" to the premises of the republic that regulated his quest for salvation, while his vision required his quest.[7] If this was circular reasoning which, according to James, it was, it was all the more propitious: "Thus do philosophy and reality, theory and action, work in the same circle indefinitely" (*PU*, 149).

The Difference That Religious Thought Makes

The last piece of his own work that James saw published was a panegyric on the pluralistic mysticism of Benjamin Paul Blood. For James, Blood was a long-time correspondent, informant, and fellow-traveler in psychedelic experimentation. "A Pluralistic Mystic" (1910) recalled the style of James's introduction to his father's *Literary Remains* (1884). In it, James located Blood as a "character" and seemed to let him articulate his own vision while actually regimenting it for other concerns. But where James had let the *incoherencies* of his father's vision set the issues that motivated his religious investigations, he let Blood's mystical vision of incoherence lend the kind of support for his own view of the world "which mystical corroboration may confer" (*EP*, 173).

James relished the fact that "monism can no longer claim to be the only beneficiary of whatever right mysticism may possess to lend *prestige*." Just as James had claimed that the theology of Henry James, Sr., sounded monistic enough to charm post-Kantian idealists, so he claimed that Blood's synopsis charmed "the monist in me unreservedly" (*EP*, 173, 178). Blood's world view pictured things pushing and pulling toward a state of affairs in which they ultimately lived and let live. He construed the process in words that echoed Emerson's notion of universal compensation.

But James claimed that Blood was pluralistic enough to insist that being and thought varied independently and that from all he could tell, the two never quite overcame the tension that existed between them. This pluralism echoed the one that James had discovered in his father's thought, where divinity was constantly having to triumph over brutal materials.[8]

Blood wrote that "contingency forbids any inevitable history, and conclusions are absurd. Nothing in Hegel has kept the planet from being blown to pieces." From James's vantage point, the important thing was that the universe was "game flavored as a hawk's wing"; reason and wonder always "blushed face to face." James agreed with Blood that the Western legend that pictured divinity hovering over primordial chaos creating a universe "sinks to burlesque if in that great argument which antedates man and his mutterings, Lucifer had not a fighting chance" (EP, 188, 189). James had argued all these things himself, but for those who found more authority in the confessions of mystics than in the professions of university men, Blood was an ally.

"A Pluralistic Mystic" outstripped even A Pluralistic Universe as a tour de force. Both works were written rather unsparingly by a James so certain of the overthrow of absolute idealism that his characteristic tentativeness lay wrecked. James's tone at the end of his last published piece was simply magisterial, calling attention, perhaps for the first time, to the teacher, not the teaching, and to his office, not his task. James said: "Let my last word, then, speaking in the name of intellectual philosophy, be his word:—'There is no conclusion. What has concluded, that we might conclude in regard to it? There are no fortunes to be told, and there is no advice to be given. Farewell!'" (EP, 190).

The drama of the message almost hid its function, which was to indicate that thought played a particular role in James's view, one that led not from premises to conclusions but from the presentation of problems and difficulties to the enactment of solutions and the application of salves. James's religious thought was harnessed in a way that forced the thinker to exit from thought, to undercut the orientation of the gnostic by passing thoughtfully from "words, that reproduce but ancient elements, to life itself, that gives the integrally new" (EP, 190).

James saw his pluralistic pantheism making this difference. For a price, it provided a public religious vision not only for the republic but for republicans around the world, a vision which guarded the dignity and distinctiveness of many faiths. The price was simply stated even if it took all of James's professional expertise to make it seem fair: The cost of discipleship was the elimination of coercive discourse and action on the one hand and the assumption that salvation and social responsibility were inseparable on the other. James construed his universe as a federal republic in order to deny the imperium of each "centre of action" over any other and to demand that each accommodate itself to the others enough to help achieve a common social goal, a goal his father had called the pacific gospel truth.

The arguments in *A Pluralistic Universe* and the pronouncements in "A Pluralistic Mystic" brought James very close to his father's religious Romanticism. To be sure, there were important differences. His father had tried to fuse both the Christianity and the democracy that he had inherited by showing others how Christ presented himself in the death of human personality and the new birth of individuals as social beings, dignified, indeed, divinized, by their impartial participation in universal friendship. But Christ did not present himself at all to William James, even if he was saturated with "protestant protestant" Christian attitudes. James had been disabused of his father's "democracy," not so much by the Civil War, which was still easily interpreted in terms of the doctrine of the vox populi, but by the ascendance of militarism and materialism in America. His observations made it impossible for him to view a world of unregulated friendship as a grounded possibility. He commended people to fight for a regulated world, a federated world, governed as much by the ideals of détente and disengagement among faiths as by those of mutual support and constructive transaction.

If James was not Christian, because Christ was no concern of his, he surely was not un-Christian either. He was linked to his father through Christian themes: for both, evil, not only without but within the human heart, motivated reflection—there was something wrong about people as they naturally stood; for both, redemption from evil was the goal; for both, salvation required regeneration whenever evil was present; and for both, the perfection of things was not complete until the golden rule had become natural in the common life of men.

These were all decidedly Christian inheritances, even if for the father they were once removed from "orthodox theism" and fully thrice removed for the son. Henry, Sr., kept Christian themes loosely knit in a supernatural frame of reference consisting of three terms: Creator, Creature, and Creation. He differed from more prominent Romantic writers by insisting that it made no sense to displace this vision with a "natural" one built on mind and nature alone and sided with them in their effort to know and glorify the divine "the only way they could," by knowing and glorifying the perfected life of man in the world. But he failed to see how Romantics knew what to look for without expressing what divinity was to be incarnated.

Henry, Sr., saw three lively religious options: one could be Stoic, or pluralistic, and accept tragedy; one could be a pantheist and accept comedy; or one could accept Christ as he appeared in humanity along with a responsible role in the history of salvation. Stoicism left the disconsolate without hope; pantheism left the destiny of man mysterious by focusing on the inherence of the psychical in the physical instead of centering on the incarnation of God in the human. That left something akin to progressive orthodoxy: a theology Scottish enough to make man's sin inevitable and God's grace indispensable but Romantic enough to pin hopes on a new earth and to see those hopes realized historically as the divine was incarnated in a regenerated humanity.

William James was once removed from orthodox Christianity by the Romanticism of his father's generation, twice by the idealism of his own, and yet another time by the natural history point of view that triumphed with Darwin. With the third saltation, he glorified neither a Christian Creator, nor a Christian Creation, nor a Christian Creature. He wove his themes of wrongness, regeneration, and salvation into a frame of reference consisting of an indefinite number of terms, and he wove them in ways that made the notions of creator, creation, and creature so overlap that it was no longer useful to construe them as basic categories of interpretation.

Still, the son was more the father's disciple at the end than at the beginning of his religious investigations. With his father he accepted a vision of perfection that called for the many to become one in ways that reverberated with the premises of his republic. He asked people to accept themselves as they appeared as social beings and, hence, to accept their responsible role in the history of salvation. If he did not view evil as inevitable or grace as indispensable in all cases, he reported actual instances of both. He, too, was Romantic enough to pin his hopes on new worlds to come and to commend their realization. He became a pluralistic pantheist, but not by melding the two options that his father had denied. Instead he worked his father's understanding of divinity as social harmony into a view of the world that if still bifurcated in brutal ways, promised all the intimacy that "orthodox" pantheism ever did, and much more.

Henry, Sr., was born too early, of course, to take Darwin's undoing of historical ascent seriously. He clung to a view of providential and progressive change that made one end inevitably triumphant. Like other New England theologians, he found a way to square "natural selection" with design and could easily have said with John Fiske that evolution was simply God's way of doing things. Hence, he still engaged in a two-worlds discourse which envisioned a fallen world dying and another, spiritual world rising from its grave. William James's pluralistic universe, to the contrary, was articulated in a one-world context. His was a metaphysics for a world without end.

Indeed, one of the last challenges that James tackled was the problem how a continuous world could be ordered "ordinally," or without end. His response to this challenge appeared as his chapters on "novelty" in *Some Problems of Philosophy*, edited and published after his death. There, he characterized his vision this way: "The world, it thinks, may be saved, *on condition that its parts shall do their best*. But shipwreck in detail, or even on the whole, is among the open possibilities" (*SPP*, 73). He suggested that "real novelty" divided this vision from absolute idealism. Monistic idealists assumed that either all the elements that conditioned the perfection of things were present from the very beginning or life was simply unintelligible, because the principle of continuity was broken.

But James argued that monistic idealists analyzed "continuity" in a way that could be challenged and that his competitive analysis both allowed for real novelty and fit historical and biographical observation. Pragmatically, "that genuine novelties can occur means that from the point of view of what is already given, what comes may have to be treated as a matter of chance." These contingencies might or might not make things more continuous. So the crucial question to ask was this: "In what manner does new being come?" (*SPP*, 75).

As early as 1867, James had challenged his father's ability to answer this question in any a priori way—that is, by working out a theory of creation (*LWJ*, 1:97). But perceptually, or taken as a matter of fact, not logic, James claimed that the question had to be answered by first noting novelties that people encountered from time to time. He argued that "new men and women, books, accidents, events, inventions, enterprises, burst unceasingly upon the world. It is vain to resolve these into ancient elements, or to say that they belong to ancient kinds." He thought it was vain to do this because these people and things were doing original work, ancient elements per se were not. Viewed historiographically, in other words, Darwin was right: things come "into being by discrete increments of novelty however small" (*SPP*, 78, 79). Darwin showed how novelty or chance played an indispensable role in evolution, in making events continuous. In the doing he undercut the whole enterprise of building conceptual theories of creation by demonstrating that—so long as one stuck to analyses of particular cases of change—the issue of creation-in-general never arose. Variants interacting with selective factors made novel things.

But Darwin's demonstration that change occurred incrementally caused conceptual problems for some philosophers. If each historical thing depended on other things emerging in a special way, evolution seemed to involve "infinitely" shaded gradations. The continuity of evolution seemed to be infinitely divisible, a characteristic which made it the subject of Zenonean paradoxes and Kantian antinomies. If each historical entity depended on other historical entities, which in turn depended on others, and if any historical entity was composite, or made up of an indefinite number of variant and selective factors, it was unclear how any change ever got accomplished. The problem was summed up by James this way: "The difficulty . . . is that of touching a goal when an interval needing to be traversed first keeps permanently reproducing itself and getting in your way" (SPP, 92).

But James argued that this conceptual problem applied to mathematics, not history. Georg Cantor may have solved the antinomies by introducing the concept of transfinite numbers, but the concept had no application to history where "each point must be occupied in its due order of succession; and if the points are necessarily infinite, their end cannot be reached, for the 'remainder,' in this kind of process, is just what one cannot neglect." On Darwinian grounds, historical changes came wholly when they did come, or they did not come at all. The steps that made them were not necessarily infinite. They were, to the contrary, both finite and perceptible. In retrospect, historical entities might be decomposed ad infinitum, but this sort of analysis did not reproduce "the operation by which they were originally brought into existence" (SPP, 92, 94). History proceeded by addition; analysis of history by division. So conceptual transformation of perceptual experience turned the infinite into a problem; perceptual experience did not.

James died before he could give a positive perceptual account of historical continuity, but it is unlikely that he would have departed in any serious way from the Darwinian analysis of change that he had espoused in one investigation after the other for thirty years. His allegiance to both "tychism," or the doctrine of chance, and to "synechism," or the doctrine of continuity, placed him with Peirce as thinkers steeped in Darwinism. Darwin had opened his eyes to the realizations that chance happenings sometimes produced fit results; that evolution depended on novelty as well as conservation; that 'things' were both one and many as a matter of fact; and that from a historical point of view, the world was without end—not because there were no ends but because there were an indefinite number of them. All these revelations confirmed James's belief that "work is still doing in the world-process, and that in that work we are called to bear our share. The character of the world's results may in part depend upon our acts. Our acts may depend upon our religion,—on our not-resisting our faith tendencies, or on our sustaining them in spite of 'evidence' being incomplete" (*SPP*, 112).

EPILOGUE

James as Epochal Thinker

James's cultural canonization was both immediate and enduring. Shortly after he died, Dewey wrote in one of his appreciative notes that James was one of the few philosophers whose death marked a public event. Newspapers, quarterlies, and academic journals in philosophy, psychology, theology, and psychical research, not only in America but also in Britain, France, Germany, and as far away as Japan, announced his death and lauded his life, assessed his contributions and reconstructed him as an American character without peer in his time.

Some memorials were utterly hagiographic. John Jay Chapman's, for instance, made James into a living angel by noting that "the world watched James as he pursued through life his search for religious truth; the world watched him, and often gently laughed at him, asking, 'When will James arise and fly? When will he "take the wings of the morning, and dwell in the uppermost parts of the sea"?' And in the meantime, James was already there. Those were the very places that he was living in."[1]

Three days after James's death, *le Temps* called him the most famous American philosopher since Emerson, a claim that the London *Times* endorsed. This view was echoed and amplified at home and abroad and shaped nearly every interpretation of James for generations to come. Influential spokesmen from Bergson in France to Russell in Britain to Troeltsch in Germany portrayed a James who not only represented the epoch when American philosophy came of age but almost single-handedly made it known and respectable in the rest of the Western world. A host of interpreters in the United States followed the same track, led especially by Royce, Santayana, and Perry. These three thinkers, so intimate with both James and the community of philosophers who survived him, were largely responsible for canonizing his work. The James that came to life after his death emerged from the pens of three thinkers who loved him, respected his positions, and bent over backwards to be fair to him. Perhaps inevitably, they also mirrored their own concerns in their appreciations of his work.

Royce, for instance, was already turning toward critical monism by the time that James died, but he was still an idealist. He read James's last work as a sort of idealism and characterized his thought on the whole in post-Kantian terms. Santayana wrote his first portrayal of James when he was on the verge of abandoning not only the Harvard philosophy department but also the United States. His more complete picture came nine years later in his lectures to British audiences on character and opinion in the United States. In both, Santayana measured James's worth against a tradition that he himself despised, at least outwardly. For all his keen and balanced perceptions of James, Perry was eager to construct his own neo-realism out of James's radical empiricism. Perhaps even more important, he wanted to domesticate James's public and religious philosophy for a philosophical community that was quickly turning from public concerns to professional ones, and from religious interests to irreligious ones.

Royce's James

Royce characterized James in epochal terms in his Phi Beta Kappa oration at Harvard in June 1911. He predicted that fifty years hence, educated Americans would recognize that James's thought played an indispensable role in the phenomenology of the American spirit, and even the world spirit. Like Edwards, who presented and transformed colonial Calvinism, and like Emerson, who emerged as the quintessential spokesman for the National Period, James was representative of a stage in American civilization yet he managed to retain an independent voice, critical of the period.

If James was wary of such talk about the stages of spirit, Royce argued, "fortune" proved him wrong. Death clarified James's significance for "the world's thought in his time." Considering the world's spiritual development, James was important on two counts: he transformed the evolutionary movement by actually applying evolutionary ideas and methods to the study of human life, and he accomplished the first great work in psychology understood as a natural science. These projects, Royce asserted, made James a world-historical figure and framed his essentially religious and ethical contributions to American spiritual development.[2]

In the American context, James was important because he did more to resolve the great social tensions of his day than anyone else.

Royce set James against the backdrop of an America trying simultaneously to retain its moral character after the Civil War and to become a world power. Because America's traditional moral character was, on many counts, antithetical to prospects of world power, demands arose for "new embodiments of the religious consciousness, for creeds that shall not be in conflict with the modern man's view of life" (20).

According to Royce, James met these demands. He brought the right genius to the right offices at the right time. His pragmatism was "a form of Americanism in philosophy" which provided religious and moral guidance for a transformed and restless people by emphasizing energy, practicality, and courage. These virtues, Royce said, belonged to "a people that is indeed earnestly trying to find itself, but that so far has not found itself." James interpreted these virtues, reminding energetic men to unblind themselves to the needs of the pathetic, recalling worldly men to the powers of unworldliness, demonstrating to courageous men how things were sufficiently evil to make some people's teeth chatter. Royce said that in these ways, James expressed "the better spirit of our people. He understood, he shared, and he also transcended the American spirit" (35, 30, 36). He pushed America beyond one of its self-images so that it knew itself better.

Within this distinctively Hegelian framework, Royce reviewed his criticisms of James's religious thought. His *Varieties* was a novel expression of American religious unrest. His Gifford Lectures offered no new ways of salvation, but "portrayed the meaning that the old ways of salvation had possessed, or still do possess, in the inner and personal experience of those individuals whom he has called the religious geniuses" (20). His crass supernaturalism was an attempt to account for the "meaning" of the religious process.

Royce noted that scores of people responded to James's *Varieties* as a "new gospel, the glad tidings of the subconscious." But the book was far more influential than true. Worst of all, James left "religion in the comparatively trivial position of a play with whimsical powers." At best, James's work signaled the "hopeful unrest" of an American Israel still wandering through the desert and evoked "the spirit of the frontiersman, of the gold seeker, or the home builder" and marked healthy American contempt for "social appearances." But his religious vision was inadequate, because it was "chaotic" and, as such, had to be taken up into the "larger view" provided by spirit triumphant (surely a claim that would have rankled James) (21, 22, 24, 25).

Indeed, Royce suggested, James was on his way toward accepting the indispensability of that "larger view" in his last works. James, he asserted, was actually an idealist of a Fichtean stripe. Having sown the seeds for this position in his *Will to Believe and Other Essays*, a book Royce called his "philosophy of life in its best form," he reaped the harvest in *A Pluralistic Universe*, where he exposed himself as "an ethical idealist to the core." Whatever James claimed about his own philosophy, Royce suggested that it was part and parcel of the ascent of reason that Hegel had discovered; Royce's James was a "prophet of the nation that is to be" who, in spite of his polemics against absolute idealism, "uttered some of the great words of the universal reason" (36, 43, 44, 45).

Canonization has its price, and the cost is usually some blend of exegesis and eisegesis. Royce, to be certain, was as intimate in his perceptions of James as anyone. Besides drawing attention to James's genius, he gave us a well-rounded picture of his sometime teacher, sometime student, and lifetime critic. But this early essay on James also helped to set enduring patterns of scholarship. Following Royce, criticisms of James have tended to look upon *The Will to Believe and Other Essays* as the heart of James's religious vision, if not his philosophy *sans phrase*; to locate James's place in the phenomenology of the American spirit as a way of evaluating his work; and, with special regard to his religious investigations, to emphasize his temper, outlook, and spirit at the expense of his methods, arguments, and conclusions.

Royce's James was a lovable genius whose influence was world-wide but whose philosophy was as restless and irresponsible as the wandering American spirit that was bound, ultimately, to come home. That made for a different James from the one presented in this book. My picture of James has not been couched in a story about world-historical ascent. I have shown that the methods, arguments, and conclusions in his religious investigations were as prominent as his spirit and that his *Will to Believe* was an important historical segment in a religious vision that changed as he first abandoned tenacity for philosophy, then actually searched for religious facts, and finally began to reconstruct his religious thought on the basis of his findings.[3]

Santayana's James

Santayana delivered "The Genteel Tradition in American Philosophy" the same summer that Royce immortalized James's "philosophy of life." Santayana cast James in mythic proportions as well, but without any overt Hegelian machinery. Moreover, he did not reflect so much on James's place in the historical ascent of spirit as on his descent from Calvinism and transcendentalism. In this early response to James, Santayana extolled his genius for escaping the confines of his American intellectual inheritance, a tribute that forecast Santayana's own expatriate experience.

Santayana argued that contemporary American thought descended from two contrary movements: Calvinism's agonized conscience and transcendental idealism's embrace with nature. He pictured American thought resting—and mostly stagnating—in the midst of the tension between Calvinism's "fierce pleasure in the existence of misery" and transcendentalism's evaporation of any sense of sin.[4] Three thinkers had made dynamic strides to overcome America's divided mind: Mark Twain, Walt Whitman, and William James.

But Twain only half escaped "the genteel tradition" because without it, he had no baseline for his jokes. Whitman made bohemian forays against the tradition, but he had too unfinished an intellect to bring about the reconstruction of American mentality. James completed a task that the other two had only started. He combined an understanding of the tradition with his own personal Romanticism to construct "a new theology, or romantic cosmology" that broke the spell of the old tension and "enticed faith in a new direction" (210).

Nine years later, Santayana developed and modified this picture of James in his lectures to British audiences that were later published as *Character and Opinion in the United States*. There, Santayana highlighted James's philosophical tentativeness in telling ways, but fell into caricature by claiming that James's fundamental doctrine was agnosticism. This James was not so much a religious investigator as a champion of others with religious predilections. "He did not really believe; he merely believed in the right of believing that you might be right if you believed."[5] He served as a sort of counsel for "the intellectual cripples and the moral hunchbacks" whose messages dotted the pages of *Varieties*. Santayana suggested that James's "vivisection" of religious experience was both technically successful and "an operation that eventually kills." Just as a man could die cured, "a description of religion that showed it to be madness might first show how real and how warm it was, so that if it perished, at least it would perish understood" (75, 81).

Santayana's agnostic James got depressed at the thought of a settled issue, viewed philosophy as having "a Polish constitution," and had no notion how to answer the question What is a good life? Moreover, he was just as restless and as philosophically irresponsible as Royce's James. He was a prophet who could, on occasion, express "thoughts of simple wisdom and wistful piety, the most unfeigned and manly that anybody ever had." But his philosophical intuitions outran his patience; he was "too impulsive for exact sympathy; too subjective, too romantic, to be just" (96, 94).

His James differs as much from mine as Royce's did, primarily because my picture is not tinted with the agnosticism that Santayana colors his with. James believed in certain principles of salvation. He not only championed other religious thinkers and saints but participated in religious investigations aimed at making practical recommendations and at drawing conclusions (presumptive, to be sure). Furthermore, he construed his operation on religious experiences as restorative not killing. Far from reveling in indecision, he developed new methods of adjudication to overcome philosophical impasse as well as new methods of appreciation to overcome Romantic subjectivism. Perhaps above all, he insisted that philosophers guide impulses by the judicious norm of inclusive integration in order to help attain the good life.

Perry's James

Ralph Barton Perry wrote his first appreciation of James in 1910. "The Philosophy of William James" first appeared in the *Harvard Graduates' Magazine*, a year later in the *Philosophical Review*, and ultimately in Perry's *Present Philosophical Tendencies* in 1921. In this piece, Perry wrote that James's "influence widened to the bounds of European civilization; while his versatility, his liberal sympathies, the coincidence of his ruling passions with the deeper interests of mankind at large, and above all the profound goodness of his heart, so diversified and humanized this influence that there were few indeed too orthodox or too odd to respond to it."[6] Hagiography like this makes the line between historical narrative and mythic construction somewhat hard to judge.

Perry's early James was a philosopher whose work was "so complete and so significant" that it touched every traditional philosophical problem and expressed "through the medium of personal genius the characteristic tendencies of an epoch." He suggested that James was so massive that the only suitable service a colleague could do *in memoriam* was give "a brief and proportionate exposition" of his work. Moreover, this was no mean feat because James's

275

thought was too original to suit "the hackneyed classifications of the schools." James's investigations amounted to "the study of man as he works out his salvation," an inquiry that could not bear division without remainder (349, 376).

But having said this, Perry went on to classify James's work in the manner of the new "professional" philosophers. Dividing James's thought into a philosophy of mind, a theory of knowledge, and a philosophy of religion, he accurately presented James's view of human intelligence as selective and interested, neither ontologically creative nor epistemologically detached. He was also careful to distinguish James's empirical view of knowledge from the concerns of *erkenntnistheorie* and insisted that James's contribution to the study of religion was as considerable and important as his psychology and philosophy. But Perry's division of James's work recast James in ways that would have bothered his teacher and, as regards James's understanding of the problem of salvation, gerrymandered his thinking to argue that James's philosophy of life was dominated by a "healthy-minded moralism" (374).

Perry's *Thought and Character of William James* appeared in 1935 and is still the best introduction to second-order reflections on James's life and work. In it, Perry carefully narrated stories of James's intellectual and cultural backgrounds, let James himself present his struggles with the problems of vocation, and then developed a picture of James's career as a psychologist and philosopher from correspondence, publications, reading materials, and diaries.

But *Thought and Character* often left elements of James's religious investigations submerged and sometimes detached them from the philosophical and psychological work crucial to their development. First, Perry suggested a simple narrative line for understanding the development of James's career. He said that James emphasized general psychology in the 1880s, ethics and religion in the 1890s, and systematic philosophy from 1900 to 1910. This downplayed the importance of James's introduction to his father's *Literary Remains* as an integral part of his own religious thought; left the impression that James's religious inquiries culminated in the theism of *The Will to Believe and Other Essays*; somehow made *Varieties* a part of "systematic philosophy"; and obscured the religious quality of *A Pluralistic Universe*.

Second, Perry divided James's ethical, social, and political sentiments from his religious thought, distinguishing ethics and politics as public enterprises from religion as a strictly personal undertaking. This made it next to impossible to realize that James's work in and on religion stemmed not only from concerns for personal self-esteem but also from James's diagnosis of the cultural confusions brought on by moral materialism at home and military imperialism abroad.

Third, Perry continued to distinguish James's "moral philosophy" of pluralistic meliorism from his "theistic" religious thought. He noted James's distinction between moralistic, "hardened" pluralism and practical religious pluralism, but made little of it; and he virtually ignored James's claim that optimism, pessimism, meliorism, and indifference were temperaments that emerged in the wake of a "religious demand" for salvation. For Perry, James's gospel was "moralistic," when James was "at his best." In support of this claim, he argued that since James used "the term 'healthy' for pluralism and 'sick' for monism, it is impossible to avoid the inference that a proper spiritual hygiene would bring man to that better state in which pluralism is palatable—that the stronger man eager for battle and enjoying the risk is the more ideal type" (*TC*, 2:354). James never firmly stood behind these diagnoses of pluralism and monism, much less drew the inference. Indeed, his examination of saintliness led him to conclude that in many ideal characters, the line between health and sickness blurred, and a sense of quiet assurance complemented the strenuous life.

So Perry's James differs from mine as well. Perry's historical narrative obscures both continuities and discontinuities in James's religious thought, which moves from tenacity in the 1870s, to philosophy in the 1880s, to the science of religions by the end of the 1890s, and to theological and psychological speculations during his last years. Far from divorcing the religious from the political, James gave up his free-market metaphors concerning religious faith and turned toward an interventionist science of religions in the wake of the "Philippine Tangle" and his abandonment of the doctrine of vox populi. Moreover, he continually defended his practical religious pluralism against both moralistic pluralism and religious monism from the early 1880s until he died.

Troeltsch's James

Royce, Santayana, and Perry differed in their characterizations of James's work, but each was received more or less officially. After all, each was closely associated with James. The first works that focused particularly on James's religious thought were not written by intimates. German authors wrote them. Karl August Busch published his *William James als Religionsphilosoph* in 1911. He portrayed *Varieties* as a psychological religious philosophy; drew connections between pragmatism and religion; characterized James as a melioristic theologian; and criticized James's work from a post-Kantian point of view.

Ernst Troeltsch wrote a far more acute analysis of James's religious investigations in 1912. He was able to see the radical implications of James's work that every early American interpreter missed. His "Empiricism and Platonism in the Philosophy of Religion: To the Memory of William James" asserted that James's work was the first thoroughgoing contribution from America to the philosophy of religion and countered American portrayals in telling ways.[7]

Troeltsch undercut Royce's Hegelizings, Santayana's view that James's basic doctrine was agnoticism, and Perry's false dichotomy between James's moral and religious thought. He claimed that James joined other Western philosophers of religion by abandoning sectarian norms of truth for inclusive integration based upon investigation of "the whole wide field of religious phenomena" (402). But Troeltsch then asserted that James's philosophy of religion challenged the entire Western tradition by systematically attacking every form of Platonism and Neoplatonism.

My William James coincides with Troeltsch's in a basic respect —by abandoning not only the quest for rational necessity but also the skepticisms, subjectivisms, and relativisms that motivated it. Troeltsch argued that European philosophy of religion from Plato through the Church Fathers to the modern idealists was constructed from five leading ideas. First, religion is a necessary fact of consciousness, either ethical or metaphysical or both. Second, this a priori spiritual law is the essence of every religious phenomenon. Third, this essence of religion realizes itself through an evolution necessarily resulting from the relationship between noumenal spirit and phenomenal experience. Fourth, this evolution makes the ultimate realization of spiritual law a problem, especially for sectarian Christians concerned with identifying Christianity as absolute. Fifth, all these investigations set out from the assumption that consciousness is a compound of the necessary and the contingent and that the nature of the compound is the paramount problem to resolve.

Both according to Troeltsch and as presented in this book, James's position was exactly opposite on every count. James pit his Darwinian methods against both the relativism and skepticism of the Sophists and the apriorism of the Platonists in order to establish normative and valid knowledge. Like European philosophers of religion, he also started from the full facts of consciousness, but his 'consciousness' was a bundle of continuous, contingent experiences, structured by a perception-thought-action loop; 'consciousness' was not an a priori unity; and individual consciousness was not internally related to consciousness in general. Second, James abandoned the search for an essence of religion and examined religion in empirical ways for the sake of resolving the problems of men. Third, in lieu of an "idea" of religion requiring pure realization, James focused on the descent of actual types of religious temperament from original divine encounters. Fourth, James paid no attention to the problem of identifying some particular religion as absolute, because the absolute and the necessary played no role in his investigations. Standards of appreciation emerged in historic movements of thought and adjustments among those movements. Finally, without allegiance to the "Platonic" view of consciousness, James displaced concern for the problem of the finite and the infinite with inquiries about the indefiniteness of any consciousness and the conjoining of particular consciousnesses. Hence, he was able to introduce theory about the role of the subconscious in religious experience and to consider both polytheism and pluralistic pantheism attractive options.

Given this view, Royce was wrong to call James an idealist, much less a closet Hegelian. The whole point of metaphysical idealism was to locate *rational necessity* in mind. But James did not locate it anywhere. Santayana was wrong to call James's basic doctrine agnosticism. Agnosticism (a term coined by Huxley in a positivist mood) depended quite precisely on the phenomenal/essential bifurcation that James's radical empiricism upended. Finally, Perry's contention that James was a moralist apologizing for religion to its cultured despisers was revealed as Perry's way of apologizing for James to Perry's increasingly irreligious profession. As James portrayed religion, it needed no apology; rather, it required reconstruction away from absolutism.

Troeltsch proclaimed both his initial attraction to James's positions and his ultimate rejection of them. The task, he said, was somehow to "incorporate the element of correctness in James's philosophy of religion into the structure of the transcendental, *a priori* philosophy of Kant and Schleiermacher." But he also admitted his inability to discover ways to accomplish the requisite sublimation, because James's position stood "sharply opposed at every point to transcendentalism." So he finally and simply warned his readers that transcendental method was an indispensable element in philosophy of religion. In the end, then, James was helpful for his insistence that philosophers give "serious heed to realities" but otherwise was expendable (420, 422). My James also saw the great role that transcendental methods played in philosophy of religion. However, he told his audience that philosophy of religion was expendable; that philosophy of religion should transform itself into a science of religions; and that religion would become more vital as a result.

Bixler's James

Troeltsch's rendition of James was presentist. His essay mounted toward the question What next in the philosophy of religion? In 1926, Julius Seelye Bixler became the first American to write a full-length study on James and religion, *Religion in the Philosophy of William James*. His essay was presentist as well. To his credit, Bixler disputed the notion that traditional religion battled modern science in James's work. He pursued James's antiabsolutism and fruitfully compared James's pluralism with other pluralisms; discussed James's view of will as free, believing, and purposive; and surveyed the development of James's thoughts on deity, immortality, mysticism, and the shape of religion.

As Bixler saw it, the crucial puzzle in James's religious thought was how to square two contending views of salvation, one that emphasized human autonomy and another that construed human well-being as ultimately secured by deity. The view of James that I present coincides with that of Bixler in that both concentrate on the relations between well-doing and well-being. Bixler saw this tension recapitulated in a three-stage development of James's conception of deity. *The Will of Believe and Other Essays* marked the first stage by presenting a purely functional view of deity. There, "God"— whatever it was—stimulated strenuous life or human well-doing. *Varieties* marked the second by distinguishing the "power" that let loose saintliness from normal human consciousness and by emphasizing the sense of peace and security as much as the strenuosity that ensued in the wake of religious experience. *A Pluralistic Universe* marked the third stage, combining conceptions of God as power and as inciter of human powers in a cooperative meliorism. Bixler shied away from James's own description of his last position as pluralistic pantheism, but nevertheless emphasized James's commitment to speculation about spiritual powers outside but continuous with human ones.

On the whole, Bixler was effective in demonstrating that interpreters were unjust when they divorced James's religious investigations as "tender" from the rest of his work as "tough"; that moral and religious sentiments were complementary in his work; and that Jamesian pragmatism contended with agnostic positivism. If Bixler failed to notice that James's radical empiricism competed with every *ontologie*, including both idealism and realism (Bixler read him as a realist), his presentist program may have caused the blindness. His study of James culminated in an assessment of James's contribution to the "contemporary" religious situation.[8]

For Bixler, "the main currents of the religious thought of our day have met in James to emerge in clarified form." Bixler still lived in a world where "we all have enough of what James called the 'mystical germ' in us to feel the glow that comes in moments when life takes on a larger significance, to understand what Schleiermacher meant by his beautiful phrase, 'sense and taste for the Infinite,' and to respond when the larger relationships of living seem in a measure to be revealed, all ineffable though the experience must be." So Bixler could end his book on a note of celebration: James's religious philosophy would surely appeal "to the members of the generation just coming to maturity." Because they were experimentalist, James's empiricism was attractive. Because they had witnessed the "colossal insanity" of total war, his pluralism made sense. Because theirs was "an age of vision," James's pragmatic, creative faith was fitting. Bixler's James spoke on behalf of Bixler's God, who "will summon the coming generation to belief and to action with the message which James loved to repeat: 'Son of Man *stand upon thy feet,* and I will speak to thee'" (208, 217, 218).

Bixler's "age of vision," of course, first became an age of worldwide economic depression, and then an age of happy warriors. Long before his "coming generation" began to die out, some Westerners had begun to believe that Jews, Gypsies, and Negroes were more like pigs than people or that Germans were blond beasts. Nuclear devastation had become an ever-present possibility. Perhaps more to the point, the urgency of debates about theistic religion and culture, debates to which both James and Bixler were parties, had begun to wane. As Alasdair MacIntyre has put it, "The role of theism in Victorian life was conflict-creating; that role is lost now." Bixler's book on James was written as part of the conflict, even if Victorian assumptions had largely disintegrated by the time it was published.[9]

Henry May demonstrated in *The End of American Innocence*

that Victorian America fell apart about 1912, "not because it was attacked but because attack, combined with the challenge of events, brought to light its old inadequacies."[10] He noted three things about James in this regard. First, James was part of the old culture that survived into the first decade of this century by virtue of his being "moral to the core, with deep idealist tendencies, devoted to standard culture though impatient of its stuffier tendencies." Second, James helped to bring about the passing of this older age by questioning and ultimately rejecting "with alternate moods of fearful doubt and gay defiance, all the familiar ways of looking at the universe." Third, while James was often "consigned to the special hell of gentility" along with his whole generation, he was more often sanctified by "young intellectuals" like Gertrude Stein and Floyd Dell, "liberators" like H. G. Wells, "radicals" like Walter Lippmann and Randolph Bourne, and "poets" like Wallace Stevens. May finally claimed that these three characteristics made James the central figure in early twentieth-century American intellectual life because "this was the man who came nearest bringing together the old and the new; this was the man who best embodied all that men of good will expected from the twentieth century" (146, 144, 142, 143).

My story of James's religious investigations, told without presentist aspirations, stops short of May's last claim, unless it is taken strictly as a report about the cultural insurgents, invaders, and rebels who undid the "standard culture" of nineteenth-century America. Then it becomes interesting to speculate about why none of the great undoers whom James influenced were academic philosophers or religious thinkers (unless Dewey is included, but Dewey can be more comfortably placed in the old culture than James).

A large part of the answer emerges in the story of the professionalization of American philosophy. That story coincides with another one about the appropriation of religious investigation by Christian divinity schools. Another part of the story emerges in a history of the passing of saintliness as an important sort of American character. Finally, of course, each of these histories is a strand emerging from a complex of data still too fresh to account for very well.

In any case, the study of James's work and the study of the life of his work since he died are two different things. James lived in situations unfamiliar to us. Unlike the James portrayed by Royce, my view was not built from contemporary notions of universal reason. Unlike Santayana's, it did not emerge from a thoughtful

polemic against some American tradition. Unlike Perry's, it does not mirror post-war professional disciplinary organization. Unlike Troeltsch's James, mine must not be overcome in a new development of the Western tradition in philosophy of religion. Unlike Bixler's, mine is not built from current religious concerns.

My James contributes no direct answers to presentist questions. I have tried to show James in his own world, pursuing his own interests as they spill over all sorts of categories that we make but that he did not. As such, James is a historical precedent that can provoke us to self-criticism but that does not assure any new identity. He gives us leverage to examine our own self-images and views, but only so long and insofar as we take care to see him as different and as distanced from us.

NOTES

Chapter 1

1. See Sidney E. Mead, *The Lively Experiment: The Shaping of Christianity in America* (New York: Harper and Row, 1963), especially pp. 90–102. I owe a general debt of gratitude to Mead's notion of "desectarianized" Christianity in American history.

2. For broad historical surveys of the Second Awakening, see Sydney E. Ahlstrom, *A Religious History of the American People* (New Haven: Yale University Press, 1972), and Winthrop S. Hudson, *Religion in America*, rev. ed. (New York: Scribner's, 1973). For a detailed interpretation of the Second Awakening which complements my characterization, see William G. McLoughlin, *Revivals, Awakenings, and Reform* (Chicago: University of Chicago Press, 1978), especially pp. 98–179.

3. This phrase is commonly attributed to James Freeman Clarke (1810–1888). See Daniel W. Howe, *The Unitarian Conscience* (Cambridge: Harvard University Press, 1970).

4. For discussion of the intensity with which "the premises of the republic" saturated both conservative and liberal rhetoric before the Civil War, see Sidney E. Mead, *The Old Religion in the Brave New World* (Berkeley: University of California Press, 1977).

5. See William A. Clebsch, *Christian Interpretations of the Civil War* (Philadelphia: Fortress Press, 1969).

6. Ibid., p. 14.

7. See Arthur M. Schlesinger, Sr., "A Critical Period in American Religion, 1875–1900," *Massachusetts Historical Society Proceedings* 64 (1930–32): 523–46.

8. McLoughlin, *Revivals, Awakenings, and Reform.*

9. *Nation*, Mar. 9, 1876.

10. Quoted in Hudson, *Religion in America*, p. 322.

11. See Horatio W. Dresser's classic *History of the New Thought Movement* (New York: Thomas Y. Crowell, 1919).

12. Ray Stannard Baker, *The Spiritual Unrest* (New York: Frederick A. Stokes Co., 1910), pp. 190–91.

13. Stephen Gottschalk, *The Emergence of Christian Science in American Religious Life* (Berkeley: University of California Press, 1973), p. 123.

14. See Theodore Dwight Bozeman, *Protestants in an Age of Science* (Chapel Hill: University of North Carolina Press, 1977); and H. S.

285

Levinson, "Religious Testimony and Empirical Restraint," *Reviews in American History* 6 (Dec. 1978): 518–23.

15. Bozeman, *Protestants in an Age of Science.*
16. *Nation,* Dec. 31, 1874, p. 437.
17. Ahlstrom, *A Religious History,* pp. 36–42.
18. M. H. Abrams, *Natural Supernaturalism* (New York: W. W. Norton, 1971), pp. 185–86.

Chapter 2

1. Matthew Arnold, *God and the Bible* (London: Smith, Elder and Co., 1906), p. viii.
2. Robert C. Solomon, *The Passions* (Garden City: Doubleday, 1977), p. 35.
3. This counters the view of James made popular by Ralph Barton Perry, according to which religious thinkers are inevitably tender minded insofar as they are religious.
4. See, for instance, "The Unseen Universe," in the *Nation,* May 7, 1875, pp. 366–67.
5. See below, p. 35–40.
6. "Quelques Considérations sur la méthode subjective" has been reprinted in *The Works of William James: Essays in Philosophy* (Cambridge: Harvard University Press, 1978), pp. 23–31. An English translation of the article is appended, pp. 331–38.
7. This article was largely incorporated into "The Sentiment of Rationality," which appeared in *The Will to Believe and Other Essays* (Cambridge: Harvard University Press, 1979), pp. 57–89.
8. See also "Quelques Considérations . . ." in *Essays in Philosophy,* pp. 27–28; "The Sentiment of Rationality" in *The Will to Believe,* p. 87.
9. This claim was developed further in "Great Men and Their Environment," *The Will to Believe,* pp. 163–89.
10. This claim was developed further in "The Dilemma of Determinism," *The Will to Believe,* pp. 114–40.
11. This claim was developed further in "The Moral Philosopher and the Moral Life," *The Will to Believe,* pp. 141–62.
12. "What is an Emotion?" originally appeared in *Mind* 9 (Apr. 1884): 188–205. It was subsequently reprinted, together with Carl Georg Lange's "The Emotions" and James's own "The Emotions," in Knight Dunlap, ed., *The Emotions* (Baltimore: Williams and Wilkins Co., 1922). Quotations will be cited from Dunlap's edition.
13. See "The Psychology of Belief," *Mind* 14(1889): 321–52; reprinted almost verbatim but with additions in *PP,* 2:283–324 as "The Perception of Reality."
14. Originally published in the *International Journal of Ethics* 1 (Apr. 1891): 330–54. Quotations are cited from *The Will to Believe,* pp. 141–62.
15. Quoted from William Kingdon Clifford, *Lectures and Essays,* ed. Leslie Stephen and Frederick Pollack, 2 vols. (London: Macmillan and Co., 1879), 2:183.

16. An invitation had been sent and accepted, but an actual date had not yet been set.
17. *Boston Evening Transcript*, Mar. 1, 1899.
18. Ibid.
19. Ibid.
20. Ibid.
21. Ibid.
22. Ibid.
23. James gave another set of lectures relevant to his religious investigations during this period. In 1897 he delivered his Ingersoll Lectures on Human Immortality, significant because they signaled James's break away from a theistic to a pantheistic idiom. I delay consideration of these lectures until my discussion of James's pluralistic pantheism in part 3. They foreshadow a theology James did not pursue seriously until after his Gifford Lectures.

Chapter 3

1. See Henry James, ed., *The Letters of William James* (Boston: Atlantic Monthly Press, 1920), 1:142–43.
2. *Primitive Culture*, 2 vols. (London: John Murray, 1871), 1:16.
3. Herbert Spencer, *The Study of Sociology* (Ann Arbor: University of Michigan Press, 1961).
4. William Kingdon Clifford, *Lectures and Essays*, ed. Leslie Stephen and Frederick Pollack, 2 vols. (London: Macmillan and Co., 1879), 1:82.
5. See Michael T. Ghiselin, *The Triumph of the Darwinian Method* (Berkeley: University of California Press, 1969), especially pp. 131–59.
6. See Edwin D. Starbuck, *The Psychology of Religion* (London: W. Scott, 1899).
7. Henry Maudsley, *Natural Causes and Supernatural Seemings* (London: Kegan Paul, Trench and Co., 1886), p. 257.
8. Ibid., p. 256.
9. James Leuba, "The Contents of Religious Consciousness," *Monist*, Jan. 1901.

Chapter 4

1. Henry Wood, *Ideal Suggestion through Mental Photography* (Boston: Lee and Shepherd Co., 1899), p. 54.
2. Ralph Waldo Trine, *In Tune with the Infinite or Fullness of Peace, Power, and Plenty* (New York and Boston: Thomas Y. Crowell and Co., 1897).
3. Edward Caird, *The Evolution of Religion* (New York: Macmillan Co., 1893).
4. H. H. Goddard, "The Effects of Mind on Body as Evidence of Faith Cures," *American Journal of Psychology* 10 (Apr. 1899): 430–502.

5. In "Song of Myself," *Leaves of Grass*, ed. Malcolm Cowley (New York: Viking Compass, 1959).
6. See Frank Miller Turner, *Between Science and Religion: The Reaction To Scientific Naturalism in Late Victorian England* (New Haven: Yale University Press, 1974), especially pp. 104–33.
7. James borrowed "these Crumps and Stigginses" from Emerson, but I have not found the reference.

Chapter 5

1. See Charles Wegener, *Liberal Education and the Modern University* (Chicago: University of Chicago Press, 1978), p. 109.
2. George Santayana, *Character and Opinion in the United States* (New York: W. W. Norton, 1967), p. 77.
3. See James Luther Adams, "A Letter From Friedrich von Hügel to William James," *Journal of the American Academy of Religion* 45 (1977): 497.
4. See M. H. Abrams, *Natural Supernaturalism* (New York: W. W. Norton, 1971), pp. 385–90.
5. Compare C. S. Peirce, *Collected Works*, ed. Paul Weiss and Charles Hartshorne, 6 vols. (Cambridge: Harvard University Press, 1931–36), 5:358–87.

Chapter 7

1. See *Sewanee Review* 10 (Oct. 1902): 493–97; *International Journal of Ethics* 13 (Jan. 1903): 236–46; and especially James H. Leuba, "Professor William James's Interpretation of Religious Experience," *International Journal of Ethics* 14 (Apr. 1904): 322–39.
2. See Henri Bergson, "On the Pragmatism of William James," in *The Creative Mind*, trans. Mabelle Andison (New York: Citadel Press, 1946), p. 211.
3. Walter B. Pitkin, "A Problem of Evidence in Radical Empiricism," *Journal of Philosophy* 3 (Nov. 22, 1906), 645–50.

Chapter 8

1. Josiah Royce, "Mind and Reality," *Mind* 7 (1882): 30–54.
2. Josiah Royce, "The Eternal and the Practical," *Philosophical Review* 13 (1904): 142. For the remainder of our discussion of this work, references to page numbers will appear in parentheses.
3. William James, "Reason and Faith," *Journal of Philosophy* 24 (1927): 199.
4. John McTaggart, *Some Dogmas of Religion*, 2nd ed. (London: Macmillan and Co., 1906), p. 66.
5. Bertrand Russell, "James's Conception of Truth," in *Philosophical Essays* (London: George Allen, and Unwin, 1966), p. 118. For the

remainder of our discussion of this work, references to page numbers will appear in parentheses.

6. Josiah Royce, "The Problem of Truth in Light of Recent Discussion," in *William James and Other Essays* (New York: Macmillan Co., 1911), p. 196. For the remainder of our discussion of this work, references to page numbers will appear in parentheses.

Chapter 9

1. See Charlene Haddock Seigfried, *Chaos and Context: A Study in William James* (Athens, Ohio: Ohio University Press, 1978).
2. See F. H. Bradley, *Appearance and Reality*, 2d ed. (London: Oxford University Press, 1897), pp. 119–42. For the remainder of our discussion of this work, references to page numbers will appear in parentheses.
3. Josiah Royce, *The World and the Individual*, 2 vols. (New York: Dover, 1959), 1:129.
4. Theodore Flournoy, *The Philosophy of William James*, trans. E. B. Holt and William James, Jr. (New York: Henry Holt and Co., 1917), p. 205.
5. See Horace M. Kallen, *William James and Henri Bergson: A Study in Contrasting Theories of Life* (Chicago: University of Chicago Press, 1914), chapters 2 and 3.
6. Perhaps more significantly, Josiah Royce's *Problem of Christianity*, 2 vols. (New York: Macmillan Co., 1913), marked his allegiance to a brand of critical monism as well. But James never saw this work, which was published three years after he died.
7. I borrow the phrase "aura of factuality" from Clifford Geertz, "Religion as a Cultural System," in *The Interpretation of Cultures* (New York: Basic Books, 1973), pp. 87–125.
8. James had clamored to Blood's call of "Ever not quite!" since 1897, when he reissued it on behalf of his own views as collected in *The Will to Believe and Other Essays* (Cambridge: Harvard University Press, 1979). Cf. p. 6.

Epilogue

1. Quoted in Gay Wilson Allen, *William James* (New York: Viking Press, 1967), p. 494.
2. Josiah Royce, "William James and the Philosophy of Life," in *William James and Other Essays* (New York: Macmillan Co., 1911), pp. 10–11. For the remainder of our discussion of this work, references to page numbers will appear in parentheses.
3. Royce made many telling criticisms of James's religious thought in other works, but these have been explored only quite recently. See, for instance, Bruce Kuklick, *Josiah Royce: An Intellectual Biography* (Indianapolis and New York: Bobbs-Merrill, 1972).
4. George Santayana, "The Genteel Tradition in American Philosophy,"

in *Winds of Doctrine: Studies in Contemporary Opinion* (New York: Scribner's, 1913), p. 189. For the remainder of our discussion of this work, references to page numbers will appear in parentheses.

5. George Santayana, *Character and Opinion in the United States* (New York: W. W. Norton, 1967), p. 77. For the remainder of our discussion of this work, references to page numbers will appear in parentheses.

6. Ralph Barton Perry, "The Philosophy of William James," in *Present Philosophical Tendencies* (New York: Longmans, Green and Co., 1921), p. 378. For the remainder of our discussion of this work, references to page numbers will appear in parentheses.

7. Ernst Troeltsch, "Empiricism and Platonism in the Philosophy of Religion," *Harvard Theological Review* 5, no. 4 (1912): 401–22. For the remainder of our discussion of Troeltsch's work, references to page numbers will appear in parentheses.

8. Julius Seelye Bixler, *Religion in the Philosophy of William James* (Boston: Marshall Jones Co., 1926), culminates in a last chapter, "James and the Religious Thought of Today," pp. 199–218. For the remainder of our discussion of this work, references to page numbers will appear in parentheses.

9. Alasdair MacIntyre, "The Debate about God," in *The Religious Significance of Atheism*, ed., Alasdair MacIntyre and Paul Ricoeur (New York: Columbia University Press, 1969), p. 19.

10. Henry F. May, *The End of American Innocence: The First Years of Our Own Time, 1912–1917* (New York: Knopf, 1959), p. 397. For the remainder of our discussion of this work, references to page numbers appear in parentheses.

BIBLIOGRAPHICAL ESSAY

Part I: The Problem of Religion in James's America

The most complete bibliography of American religion is Nelson R. Burr, *A Critical Bibliography of Religion in America*, 2 vols. (Princeton: Princeton University Press, 1961). The most useful books that include studies of religion during James's lifetime are Sydney E. Ahlstrom's panoramic *Religious History of the American People* (New Haven: Yale University Press, 1972); Winthrop S. Hudson's *Religion in America*, rev. ed. (New York: Scribner's, 1973); Martin E. Marty, *Righteous Empire: The Protestant Experience in America* (New York: Dial Press, 1970); Robert T. Handy, *A History of the Churches in the United States and Canada* (New York: Oxford University Press, 1976). I am more heavily indebted to Sidney E. Mead, *The Lively Experiment: The Shaping of Christianity in America* (New York: Harper and Row, 1963) and *Old Religion in the Brave New World: Reflections on the Relation Between Christendom and the Republic* (Berkeley: University of California Press, 1977) than to other listed works that interpret the religious history of Americans.

The best short piece on the impact of science and scholarship, Darwinism, biblical criticism, and recognition of alien religions during the period 1875–1900 is Arthur M. Schlesinger, Sr., "A Critical Period in American Religion, 1875–1900," first published in the *Massachusetts Historical Society Proceedings* 64 (1930–32): 523–46, but reprinted many times, most recently in *Religion in American History: Interpretive Essays*, edited by John M. Mulder and John F. Wilson (Englewood Cliffs, N.J.: Prentice-Hall, 1978). A longer and stunning essay on the period 1890–1920 has been written by William G. McLoughlin in his *Revivals, Awakenings, and Reform* (Chicago: University of Chicago Press, 1978).

For explorations of Scottish Realism and its American Calvinist assimilation, see Elizabeth Flower and Murray G. Murphey, *A History of Philosophy in America*, 2 vols. (New York: Putnam's, 1977), especially volume 1; Bruce Kuklick's chapter "Scottish Realism and the Evolutionary Controversy" in his *Rise of American Philosophy: Cambridge, Massachusetts, 1860–1930* (New Haven: Yale University Press, 1977); Theodore Dwight Bozeman, *Protestants in an Age of Science* (Chapel Hill: University of North Carolina Press, 1977); Morton White, *Science and Sentiment in America: Philosophical Thought from Jonathan Edwards to John Dewey* (New York: Oxford University Press, 1972); and

Herbert W. Schneider, *A History of American Philosophy*, 2d ed. (New York: Columbia University Press, 1963).

There are two fine studies of the thought of Henry James, Sr. Giles Gunn's introduction to his edition of *Henry James, Sr.: A Selection of His Writings* (Chicago: American Library Assoc., 1974) and James G. Moseley, *A Complex Inheritance* (Missoula: Scholars Press, 1975). See also Ralph Barton Perry, *The Thought and Character of William James*, 2 vols. (Boston: Little, Brown, and Co., 1935), especially volume 1, part 1; and F. O. Matthiessen, *The James Family: A Group Biography* (New York: Knopf, 1961).

The best work on New Thought is Charles S. Braden, *Spirits in Rebellion: The Rise and Development of New Thought* (Dallas: Southern Methodist University Press, 1963). But consult Horatio W. Dresser's classic *History of the New Thought Movement* (New York: Thomas Y. Crowell, 1919). His insights are limited by his allegiance to the movement. See also Stephen Gottschalk, *The Emergence of Christian Science in American Religious Life* (Berkeley: University of California Press, 1973), for comparisons between various sorts of mental healing sects and Mary Baker Eddy's Christian Science.

For studies of the Romantic mood in nineteenth-century America, see F. O. Matthiessen, *The American Renaissance* (New York: Oxford University Press, 1941), and Sydney E. Ahlstrom, *A Religious History of the American People*. I am especially indebted to M. H. Abrams's incisive work on tradition and revolution in Romantic literature, *Natural Supernaturalism* (New York: Norton Press, 1971). For connections between the principles of democracy, the Romantic norm of inclusive integration, and the emergence of university education in America, see Charles Wegener, *Liberal Education and the Modern University* (Chicago: University of Chicago Press, 1978).

Frank Miller Turner, *Between Science and Religion: The Reaction to Scientific Naturalism in Late Victorian England* (New Haven: Yale University Press, 1974), contains sound characterizations of sectarian science. But see also John Passmore's chapter "Materialism, Naturalism, and Agnosticism" in *A Hundred Years of Philosophy* (London: Duckworth, 1957).

For an excellent study of James's own religious melancholia and recovery, read William A. Clebsch, *American Religious Thought* (Chicago: University of Chicago Press, 1973), pp. 125–70. See also Gay Wilson Allen, *William James* (New York: Viking Press, 1967). The best work with which to initiate serious study of William James as a person and thinker is Ralph Barton Perry, *The Thought and Character of William James*. But Perry constantly transforms James's religiousness into moralism. For a brief but excellent characterization, see the introduction and preface to John J. McDermott, *The Writings of William James: A Comprehensive Edition* (Chicago: University of Chicago Press, 1977). John E. Smith's works, *The Spirit of American Philosophy* (New York: Oxford University Press, 1963), *Themes in American Philosophy* (New York: Oxford University Press, 1970), and *Purpose and Thought: The Meaning of Pragmatism* (New Haven: Yale University Press, 1978), all contain sensitive treatments of James's religious thought. J. S. Bixler, *Religion in the Philosophy of William James* (Boston: Marshall Jones

Co., 1926), might be considered an earlier attempt at the sort of study I am developing, but Bixler construes 'religion' as part of some overall Jamesian philosophy, not as a determinable field of interest analyzed in terms of problems that need to be solved or difficulties managed for the sake of satisfaction.

Two excellent studies of James focus on the relationship between human emotion, belief, and will, but both are marred by presentisms. Both John Wild, *The Radical Empiricism of William James* (Garden City: Doubleday and Co., 1969), and Hans Linschoten, *On the Way Toward a Phenomenological Psychology: The Psychology of William James* (Pittsburgh: Duquesne University Press, 1968), attempt to accommodate James's thought to the demands and requirements of existential phenomenology. Bruce Wilshire, *William James and Phenomenology* (Bloomington: University of Indiana Press, 1968), and Richard Stevens, *James and Husserl: The Foundations of Meaning* (The Hague: Martinus Nijhoff, 1974) are presentist as well, accommodating James's psychology to the exigencies of transcendental phenomenology. Of course, as Kuklick points out, to the extent that James lives in a post-Kantian philosophical world, there are bound to be similarities between James's work and Husserl's investigations. See Henry S. Levinson, *Science, Metaphysics, and the Chance of Salvation: An Interpretation of the Thought of William James* (Missoula: Scholars Press, 1978) for my own presentist criticism of phenomenological interpretation.

The doctrine of the Will to Believe has been the subject of continuous analysis since it first appeared. Ralph Barton Perry's chapter "The Right to Believe" in his *In the Spirit of William James* (Bloomington: University of Indiana Press, 1938) is the classic positive analysis of the piece. There are a host of well-known attempts to dismiss the doctrine, from Ettie Stettheimer, *The Will to Believe as a Basis for the Defense of Religious Faith* (New York: Science Press, 1907), to A. J. Ayer, *The Origins of Pragmatism* (San Francisco: Freeman, Cooper, and Co., 1968). Several recent explications of the doctrine well worth the reading are Stephen T. Davis, "Wishful Thinking and 'The Will to Believe,'" *C. S. Peirce Society Transactions* 8 (1972): 231–45; Peter Kauber and Peter H. Hare, "The Right and Duty to Will to Believe," *The Canadian Journal of Philosophy* 4 (1974): 327–43; and James L. Muyskens, *The Sufficiency of Hope: The Conceptual Foundations of Religion* (Philadelphia: Temple University Press, 1979), pp. 94–102. See also Henry S. Levinson, *Science, Metaphysics, and the Chance of Salvation*, pp. 218–41, for criticism of these and other discussions of the doctrine of the Will to Believe.

I do not know of any suitable literature on James's turn to a "science of religions," on his Lowell Lectures on abnormal mental states, or, shockingly, on his doctrine of human blindness. But see Ralph Barton Perry, *The Thought and Character of William James*, 2: 280–335. John J. McDermott, *The Writings of William James*, has urged James scholars to pay more attention to the connections between James's social, (technically) philosophical, and religious thought. My discussion of James's religious responses to public crises begins to address this concern.

The best historical introduction to the pragmatic movement in American philosophy and, indeed, of William James's role in it is H. S. Thayer,

Meaning and Action: A Critical History of Pragmatism (Indianapolis: Bobbs-Merrill, 1968). See also the works of Ralph Barton Perry and John E. Smith cited above, as well as Edward Madden, *Chauncey Wright and the Foundations of Pragmatism* (Seattle: University of Washington Press, 1963); Arthur O. Lovejoy, *The Thirteen Pragmatisms and Other Essays* (Baltimore: Johns Hopkins University Press, 1963); Charles Morris, *The Pragmatic Movement in American Philosophy* (New York: George Braziller, 1970); Jean Wahl, *Les Philosophies pluralistes d'Angleterre et d'Amérique* (Paris: Librarie Felix Alcan, 1920); and Philip Wiener, *Evolution and the Founders of Pragmatism* (Philadelphia: University of Pennsylvania Press, 1972).

Part II: The Gifford Lectures, 1901–1902

I know of no other book which presents a sustained analysis of each and every Gifford Lecture that James delivered. William Clebsch's discussion in *American Religious Thought* is valuable but extremely compact. Wild's discussion in *The Radical Empiricism of William James* nearly reduces the work from investigation to speculation, never mentions Darwin's impact on James, and emphasizes James's understanding of the tensions between science and religion in a way that obfuscates James's contributions to "the science of religions." James E. Dittes, "Beyond William James," in *Beyond the Classics: Essays in the Scientific Study of Religion*, edited by Charles Y. Glock and Phillip E. Hammond (New York: Harper and Row, 1973), presents a major thesis opposed to claims in this book: to wit, that James's Gifford Lectures "were not intended, the book was not written for the purpose of contributing to a common enterprise of accumulating scientific generalization. They were offered to express a personal outlook, an attitude, a philosophy, a spirit." James M. Edie has given an overview of the lectures from a contemporary, phenomenological viewpoint in "William James and the Phenomenology of Religious Experience," collected in *American Philosophy and the Future*, edited by Michael Novak (New York: Scribner's, 1968). Many standard works introducing the psychology of religion give brief overviews of James's Gifford Lectures. The best is Robert Thouless, *An Introduction to the Psychology of Religion* (London: Cambridge University Press, 1971). Consideration of James's work within the context of the development of the discipline of religious studies is meager. But Eric J. Sharpe, *Comparative Religion: A History* (New York: Scribner's, 1975), is a fine work which places James and other Americans like Starbuck, Leuba, and Coe alongside Britishers like Max Müller, Tyler, Frazer, Lang, and Jevons at the creation of religious studies.

The only previous work which analyzes James's use of Darwinian methods and models of analysis in his Gifford Lectures is Henry S. Levinson, *Science, Metaphysics, and the Chance of Salvation*. The phenomenologists never mention Darwin in connection with James, but see Wiener, *Evolution and the Founders of Pragmatism*, Thayer, *Meaning and Action*, Kuklick, *The Rise of American Philosophy*, Flower and Murphey, *A History of Philosophy in America*, and Cynthia Russett,

Darwin in America (San Francisco: W. H. Freeman and Co., 1976), for the general impact of Darwin's work on Cambridge philosophy and academic investigation at the turn of the century. Nicholas Rescher, *Methodological Pragmatism* (New York: New York University Press, 1977), recognizes the evolutionary character of James's criteriology, but develops a distinction between thesis Darwinism (James and others) and methodological Darwinism (himself) that is simply too neat to account for James's Darwinism. For recognition of the historiographic nature of James's Darwinian methods, consult D. T. Campbell, "Evolutionary Epistemology," in *The Philosophy of Karl R. Popper*, edited by P. A. Schilpp (Glencoe: Northwestern University Press, 1977). For general discussions of "survival theories" of religion see Sharpe, *Comparative Religion*, and E. E. Evans-Pritchard, *Theories of Primitive Religion* (Oxford: Oxford University Press, 1965).

See Clebsch, *American Religious Thought*, for an analysis of the "religious facts" presented in *Varieties*; also Cushing Strout, "William James and the Twice-Born Sick Soul," *Daedalus* 97 (1968): 1062–82. Royce claimed that James's commitment to "full personal facts" in *Varieties* and after made James a metaphysical idealist. See "William James and the Philosophy of Life," in *William James and Other Essays on the Philosophy of Life* (New York: Macmillan Co., 1911). Kuklick argues for this Roycean interpretation of James in *The Rise of American Philosophy*. I disagree, largely on the grounds that James developed his radical empiricism during the period 1900–1907 and never explicitly rejected it, even in *A Pluralistic Universe*. Idealism as a metaphysics is a sort of ontology, but James's radical empiricism was presented as a metaphysics without ontology. James was an idealist, but his idealism was conceptual, not metaphysical. See Nicholas Rescher, *Conceptual Idealism* (Oxford: Basil Blackwell, 1975), for the distinction.

Cordell Strug's dissertation, "William James and the Gods: A Peek at the Conceptual Underbelly of the 'Varieties of Religious Experience' " (Purdue, 1973), analyzes James's view of the subconscious, but in a far too dualistic way. Milec Capec's earlier work, "The Reappearance of the Self in the Last Philosophy of William James," *Philosophical Review* 62 (1953): 526–44, does not commit the sin of dualistic interpretation, but also does not demonstrate the reappearance of the self in *Varieties* either. See Linschoten, *On the Way Toward a Phenomenological Psychology*, for a general discussion of "subliminal activity" as it appears in James's philosophical psychology; also Gardiner Murphy's introduction to *William James on Psychical Research*, edited by Gardiner Murphy and Robert O. Ballou (New York: Viking Press, 1960).

For an instructive comparison, read Charles Peirce, "The Fixation of Belief," in *Collected Papers*, edited by Charles Hartshorne and Paul Weiss, six volumes (Cambridge: Harvard University Press, 1931–36), alongside James's discussions of "the value of saintliness," "mysticism," and "philosophy." There are close parallels between Peirce's scientific method of fixation and James's evaluation of saintliness, between Peirce's "personal tenacity" and James's "mysticism," and between Peirce's "a priorism" and James's "philosophy." There is no literature which subjects James's appreciation of religions to sensitive criticism.

John E. Smith, *Purpose and Thought*, identifies the basic terms of James's theory of religion the way I do. The more common opinion among interpreters of James is that he had no theory of religion.

Part III: Religion in a World of Pure Experience, 1902–1911

Of the many books and articles on James's radical empiricism, few are incisive, and fewer still make any effort to relate his essays on radical empiricism to his religious investigations. Excellent works include Wild, *The Radical Empiricism of William James*, Thayer, *Meaning and Action*, John E. Smith, "Radical Empiricism" in *Themes in American Philosophy*, McDermott, *Writings of William James*, as well as his introductions to James's *Essays in Radical Empiricism* (Cambridge: Harvard University Press, 1976) and *Essays in Philosophy* (Cambridge: Harvard University Press, 1978). Also consult T. R. Martland, Jr., *The Metaphysics of William James and John Dewey* (New York: Philosophical Library, 1963) and D. C. Mathur's *Naturalistic Philosophies of Experience* (St. Louis: Warren H. Green, 1971). For careful and sustained analysis of James's doctrine of relations, read Charlene Haddock Seigfried, *Chaos and Context: A Study in William James* (Athens, Ohio: Ohio University Press, 1978). Paul M. van Buren, "William James and Metaphysical Risk," in Novak, ed., *American Philosophy and the Future*, analyzes the religious elements of James's radical empiricism. The only work to recognize fully James's turn to pantheism is Kuklick, *The Rise of American Philosophy*.

My position on James's pragmatism and the problem of religious truth comes close to one that Thayer articulates in his introduction to James's *The Meaning of Truth* (Cambridge: Harvard University Press, 1975). Thayer claims that James's work contains an implicit distinction between cognitive truth and pragmatic truth: cognitive truth is a necessary but not sufficient condition of pragmatic truth. I think this is a sound *reconstruction* of James's theory, but one that James himself failed to make. For other important interpretations, read "William James, the Tough-Minded: An Appraisal," in Flower and Murphey, *A History of American Philosophy*; A. J. Ayer, *The Origins of Pragmatism*; Arthur O. Lovejoy, *The Thirteen Pragmatisms*; Robert A. Oakes, "Pragmatism, God, and Professor Matson: Some Confusions," *Philosophy and Phenomenological Research* 32 (1972): 397–402; Israel Sheffler, *Four Pragmatists* (New York: Humanities Press, 1974); and William James Earle, "William James," in *The Encyclopedia of Philosophy*, edited by Paul Edwards et al., 8 vols. (New York: Macmillan Co., 1967).

Kuklick's discussion of James's battle with Royce's Absolute is superb in *The Rise of American Philosophy*, even if his James turns out far too Roycean. Richard Bernstein's introduction to James's *Pluralistic Universe* (Cambridge: Harvard University Press, 1977) is a good corrective, demonstrating James's *dissolution* of the problem of the one and the many, a problem idealists of any ilk were required to *solve*. Horace Kallen, *William James and Henri Bergson: A Study in Contrasting Theories of Life* (Chicago: University of Chicago Press, 1914), is still the best work contrasting the two. For analysis of James's relations with Fechner, Bradley, and Höffding, consult Perry, *Thought and Character*.

Following Murray Murphey's seminal "Kant's Children: The Cambridge Pragmatists," *C. S. Peirce Society Transactions* 4 (1968): 3–33, a current tendency, best developed by Kuklick's *The Rise of American Philosophy*, is to read James as part of a Kantian philosophical movement and to downplay James's self-conscious Americanness. It is no coincidence that interpreters who take this position systematically fail to discuss the deep and perduring connections between the desectarianized, republican Christianity of Henry James, Sr., and William James's own rendition of "American Religion."

Epilogue

The most complete bibliography of publications about James is Ignas K. Skrupskelis, *William James: A Reference Guide* (Boston: G. K. Hall and Co., 1977). Perry, *Thought and Character*, Matthiessen, *The James Family*, and Allen, *William James*, each gives an account of reactions to James's work and life upon his death. But no in-depth study of the cultural canonization of James has been written. I am not pretending to give one here.

Royce, "William James and the Philosophy of Life," was first published in *William James and Other Essays* (New York: Macmillan Co., 1911). It is now available in *The Basic Writings of Josiah Royce*, edited by John J. McDermott, 2 vols. (Chicago: University of Chicago Press, 1969). The best studies of Royce are Bruce Kuklick, *Josiah Royce: An Intellectual Biography* (Indianapolis and New York: Bobbs-Merrill, 1972) and John E. Smith, *Royce's Social Infinite* (New York: Liberal Arts Press, 1950).

Santayana, "The Genteel Tradition in American Philosophy," was first published in *The University of California Chronicle* in 1911. It also appeared in his *Winds of Doctrine: Studies in Contemporary Opinion* (New York: Scribner's, 1913). This edition serves as the source for my quotations. It is now available in *Selected Critical Writings of George Santayana*, edited by Norman Henfrey, 2 vols. (Cambridge: Cambridge University Press, 1968). Santayana, *Character and Opinion in the United States*, is still in print. Criticism of Santayana's work, including his interest in religion, is sorely needed. For a good study of some of his philosophical arguments, read Timothy L. S. Sprigge, *Santayana: An Examination of His Philosophy* (London: Routledge and Kegan Paul, 1974).

Perry, "The Philosophy of William James," first appeared in the *Harvard Graduates' Magazine* 19 (1910). He reprinted it in the *Philosophical Review* 20 (1911). Ultimately, he appended it to *Present Philosophical Tendencies: A Critical Survey of Naturalism, Idealism, Pragmatism, and Realism Together with a Synopsis of the Philosophy of William James* (New York: Longmans, Green and Co., 1921). See Kuklick, *The Rise of American Philosophy*, for a study of Perry's work and philosophical aspirations.

Julius Seeyle Bixler, *Religion in the Philosophy of William James*, is the only book-length study of James's religious thought written in English that precedes this one. There are no readily available works on Bixler's life and thought.

Troeltsch, "Empiricism and Platonism in the Philosophy of Religion: To the Memory of William James," was published in the *Harvard Theological Review* 5, no. 4 (1912): 401–22. A good place to start studying both Troeltsch's historicism and his commitment to transcendentalism is his *Die Absolutheit des Christentums und die Religionsgeschichte*, translated by David Reid and introduced by James Luther Adams as *The Absoluteness of Christianity and the History of Religions* (Richmond: John Knox Press, 1971).

My understanding of turn-of-the-century developments in American culture relies heavily on Henry F. May, *The End of American Innocence: The First Years of Our Own Time, 1912–1917* (New York: Knopf, 1959). Kuklick pursues the professionalization of philosophy, especially at Harvard, in *The Rise of American Philosophy*. Joseph M. Kitagawa's "The History of Religions in America," in *The History of Religions: Essays in Methodology* edited by Mircea Eliade and Joseph M. Kitagawa (Chicago: University of Chicago Press, 1959), begins to expose, perhaps unintentionally, the domination of religious studies by divinity-school interests. Alasdair MacIntyre, "The Debate about God: Victorian Relevance and Contemporary Irrelevance," in *The Religious Significance of Atheism*, edited by Alasdair MacIntyre and Paul Ricoeur (New York: Columbia University Press, 1969), emphasizes how distant Victorian theological debate is from current intellectual enterprises. See Sacvan Bercovitch, *The Puritan Origins of the American Self* (New Haven: Yale University Press, 1975) and his *The American Jeremiad* (Madison: University of Wisconsin Press, 1978), Philip Greven, *The Protestant Temperament: Patterns of Child-Rearing, Religious Experience, and the Self in Early America* (New York: Knopf, 1977), and David E. Stannard, *The Puritan Way of Death: A Study in Religion, Culture and Social Change* (New York: Oxford University Press, 1977), for current and often fruitfully competitive insights into the development, not so much of early American character, as of early characters in America. No study of equal significance has been written to account for transformations of American characters in James's time.

My own view of historical criticism, idiosyncratic as it is, has developed in a decade of conversations with William A. Clebsch, whose "The Liberating Function of History," prepublished for presentation and discussion at the 1968 summer session of the Wenner-Gren Foundation for Anthropological Research, turned my head toward this sort of scholarship. Murray G. Murphey, "Toward an Historicist History of American Philosophy," *Transactions of the C. S. Peirce Society* 15, no. 1 (1979), articulates the position that I am most comfortable defending, though I think the meanings of "historicism" have run their course. In any case, as I view the study of history, presentism is by far the greatest sin.

I have also had occasion to refer to Daniel W. Howe, *The Unitarian Conscience* (Cambridge: Harvard University Press, 1970); William A. Clebsch, *Christian Interpretations of the Civil War* (Philadelphia: Fortress Press, 1969); Ray Stannard Baker, *The Spiritual Unrest* (New York: Frederick A. Stokes Co., 1910); Matthew Arnold, *God and the Bible* (London: Smith, Elder and Co., 1906); Robert C. Solomon, *The Pas-*

sions (Garden City: Doubleday, 1977); E. B. Tylor, *Primitive Culture*, 2 vols. (London: John Murray, 1871); William Kingdon Clifford, *Lectures and Essays*, edited by Leslie Stephen and Frederick Pollack, 2 vols. (London: Macmillan and Co., 1879); Herbert Spencer, *The Study of Sociology* (Ann Arbor: University of Michigan Press, 1961); Michael T. Ghiselin, *The Triumph of the Darwinian Method* (Berkeley: University of California Press, 1969); Edwin D. Starbuck, *The Psychology of Religion* (New York: Scribner's Sons, 1899); Henry Maudsley, *Natural Causes and Supernatural Seemings* (London: Kegan Paul, Trench and Co., 1886); James H. Leuba, "The Contents of the Religious Consciousness," *Monist* 11 (Jan. 1901): 138–53; Henry Wood, *Ideal Suggestion Through Mental Photography* (Boston: Lee and Shepard Co., 1899); Ralph Waldo Trine, *In Tune with the Infinite or Fullness of Peace, Power, and Plenty* (New York: Thomas Y. Crowell and Co., 1897); H. H. Goddard, "The Effects of Mind on Body as Evidence of Faith Cures," *American Journal of Psychology* 10 (Apr. 1899): 430–503; Walt Whitman, *Leaves of Grass*, edited by Malcolm Cowley (New York: Viking Press, 1959); James Luther Adams, "A Letter from Friedrich von Hügel to William James," *Journal of the American Academy of Religion* 45 (1977): 497; James H. Leuba, "Professor William James's Interpretation of Religious Experience," *International Journal of Ethics* 14 (Apr. 1904): 322–39; Henri Bergson, *The Creative Mind* (New York: Citadel Press, 1946); Walter B. Pitkin, "A Problem of Evidence in Radical Empiricism," *Journal of Philosophy* 3 (Nov. 22, 1906): 645–50; Josiah Royce, "Mind and Reality," *Mind* 7 (1882): 30–45; Josiah Royce, "The Eternal and the Practical," *Philosophical Review* 13 (Mar. 1904): 113–42; William James, "Reason and Faith," *Journal of Philosophy* 24 (Apr. 1927): 197–201; John McTaggart, *Some Dogmas of Religion* (London: Macmillan and Co., 1906); Bertrand Russell, "James's Conception of Truth," in *Philosophical Essays* (London: George Allen, and Unwin, 1966); F. H. Bradley, *Appearance and Reality*, 2d ed. (London: Oxford University Press, 1897); Josiah Royce, *The World and the Individual*, 2 vols. (New York: Dover, 1959); Theodore Flournoy, *The Philosophy of William James*, translated by E. B. Holt and William James, Jr. (New York: Henry Holt and Co., 1917); Josiah Royce, *The Problem of Christianity*, 2 vols. (New York: Macmillan Co., 1913); Clifford Geertz, *The Interpretation of Cultures* (New York: Basic Books, 1973).

INDEX

Abbott, Lyman, 7, 22
Abrams, M. H., 19, 286 (n. 18),
    288 (chap. 5, n. 4), 292
Absolutism, 53–54, 88, 95, 279
Action. *See* Activity
Activity, 36, 39, 41, 54–55, 58, 87,
    98, 107, 125–30, 151–52, 154–
    55, 160–61, 163, 198–202, 257
Adams, James Luther, 288 (chap.
    5, n. 3), 298, 299
Adler, Felix, 8
Aestheticism, 25
Affectional facts, 172–74, 183,
    185–89, 214–15. *See also* Feel-
    ings
Agnosticism, 40, 43, 50, 275, 279,
    292
Ahlstrom, Sydney, 19, 285 (n. 2),
    286 (n. 17), 291, 292
Allen, Gay Wilson, 289 (n. 1),
    292, 297
Americanism, 101, 272
American spirit, 12, 22, 271–73
Andison, Mabelle, 288 (chap. 7, n.
    2)
Anhedonia, 25–26, 42, 44–45, 47,
    110
Animism, 156
Anthropology, 74–76, 216, 218;
    doctrine of survivals in, 75–76,
    108, 156–57, 199, 213, 295
Appreciation: defined, 81–82, 122;
    mystical, 123, 139–46; philo-
    sophical, 146–52; of religious
    life, 81–82, 98, 122–52 passim,
    279–95
Apriorism, 148–52, 278, 279, 295
Argument, dogmatic structure of,
    85
Arnold, Matthew, 25, 40, 286 (n.
    1), 298

Asceticism, 65, 119–20, 129, 133,
    135–36
Augustine, Saint, 112
Automatisms, 116–17
Ayer, A. J., 293, 296

Baconianism, 15–17
Bain, Alexander, 47
Baker, Ray Stannard, 9, 285 (n.
    12), 298
Ballou, Robert O., 295
Beecher, Henry Ward, 7, 18, 22
Belief, 46–51, 65, 104, 112–15,
    126–28, 134, 138–44, 146, 148,
    155, 179, 214, 224, 229, 236–37;
    fixation of, 33, 122, 142, 150–
    52, 221, 273, 295; religious,
    157–59, 209, 218–19
Beliefs: competing, 51–56, 86–87;
    and will, 48–51, 293. *See also*
    Will
Bercovitch, Sacvan, 298
Bergson, Henri, 179, 189, 250,
    254, 256–57, 270, 288 (chap. 7,
    n. 2), 289 (n. 5), 299; *élan
    vital*, 257
Berkeley, George, 196
Bernstein, Richard, 296
Besant, Annie, 106
Biography, 190–91
Bixler, Julius Seelye, 290 (n. 8),
    292–93, 297; on James, 280–81
Blavatsky, Helena P., 8
Blood, Benjamin Paul, 263–65,
    289 (n. 8)
Bourne, Randolph, 282
Bozeman, Theodore Dwight, 285
    (n. 14), 286 (chap. 1, n. 15),
    291
Braden, Charles S., 292
Bradley, F. H., 106, 200, 235, 250–

52, 289 (chap. 9, n. 2), 297, 299
Brentano, Franz, 47
Brinton, Daniel, 73
Brooks, Phillips, 22
Brown, Thomas, 15
Büchner, Ludwig, 26, 29, 37, 40
Bunyun, John, 110
Burnouf, Emile, 72
Burr, Nelson R., 291
Busch, Karl August, 277
Bushnell, Horace, 5

Caird, Edward, 106, 287 (chap. 4, n. 3)
Calvinism, 8, 92, 98, 106, 111, 127–28, 266, 271, 274, 291; and Henry James, Sr., 13–14; Old School, 7, 15–18; and republicanism, 11. See also Republicanism
Campbell, D. T., 295
Cantor, Georg, 268
Capec, Milec, 295
Carlyle, Thomas, 18–19, 29–30, 33
Carnegie, Andrew, 6–7
Carus, Paul, 8
Causes: of maintenance, 78–82, 87; of production, 78–82, 87
Certainty, 126, 128, 148, 178, 224
Chance, 27, 43, 138, 233, 268–69
Change, 76–81, 86, 113, 127, 128–29, 176–77, 188, 190–91, 268; conceptual, 228; and permanence, 191
Chaos, 11, 137, 141, 175, 189–98, 205–7, 247
Chapman, John Jay, 270
Charcot, Jean, 116
Christianity, 3–24 passim, 25, 38, 59–60, 73–74, 92–93, 105–11, 117–18, 245, 265–66
Clarke, James Freeman, 285 (n. 3)
Clebsch, William A., 285 (n. 5), 292, 294, 295, 298
Clifford, William Kingdon, 22, 30, 38, 53, 54, 286 (n. 15), 287 (chap. 3, n. 4), 299; on society, 80
Close-mindedness, 59–60, 75, 133–34, 136, 143, 157, 158, 159

Coe, George A., 118, 294
Coherence: epistemological, 222, 225
Coleridge, Samuel, 18–19
"College bred," 20, 241
Common sense, 14, 45, 57, 122, 124–26, 137, 173–74, 179, 182, 211, 212, 217, 228–29, 245, 246
Common-Sense Realism (Scottish), 15–18, 35, 291
"Compounding of consciousness," 254–55, 257, 258
Comte, Auguste, 73, 75
Conception, 19, 36, 47, 48, 52, 65–66, 86, 100–101, 151, 172, 182–83, 186, 194, 250–51, 256, 260, 268
Conduct. See Activity
Confession, 144–45, 153–54
Consciousness, 96–98, 278–79, 280; continuity of, 161–66, 172, 190–92, 219–20, 224, 245–47, 257, 258–59, 261; discontinuity of, 163, 190–91, 246; field of, 115–16; margin of, 116–17; religious, 95–98, 135; structure of, 179, 181–85, 196–97
"Consequences of action," 160–61, 164, 226
Continuity: principle of, 267–68; and coherence, 86
Conventionalism, 217
Conversion, 5, 84, 98, 111–18, 161, 165; volitional, 113–14
Correspondence: epistemological, 195–98, 222, 225, 230
"Cosmic consciousness," 141, 245–47, 259–63
Cowley, Malcolm, 288 (chap. 4, n. 5), 299
Creation: experience of, 201; theory of, 267–68
Curtis, Thomas F., 17

Darwin, Charles, 6, 7–8, 15, 27, 35, 36, 46, 73, 75, 76–81, 126–29, 211, 217, 226, 261, 266–69, 294
Darwinism, 5–6, 7, 27, 35–39, 43, 74–82, 177, 211, 222, 291, 295; natural selection, 35, 37, 78–81, 126–29; social, 6; spontaneous

variation, 35, 78–82, 129
Davidson, Thomas, 250
Davis, Stephen T., 293
Dell, Floyd, 282
Democracy, 11–14, 19, 32, 64,
  133–34, 178, 241, 245, 248–49,
  265, 292
de Saint Pierre, Abbé, 109
Determinism, 43, 180. See also
  Fatalism
Dewey, John, 176–77, 179, 189,
  206, 210, 250, 270, 282
Dialectical thought, 150
Diderot, Denis, 109
Dittes, James, 294
Divine encounter, 59, 67, 76, 90–
  91, 93–94, 98–103, 112, 121,
  153, 155, 185, 187, 214–15, 232,
  259, 261, 279
Divinity, 67, 90–91. See also
  James, William, on divinity
Doctrine of Human Blindness, 59–
  64, 97, 120, 122, 293
Doctrine of the More, 63, 160–64
Doctrine of the Will to Believe,
  51–56, 67–68, 93, 293
Doctrine of Reflex Action: and
  theism, 36–43
Dogmatism, 88
Doubt: and inquiry, 46–47, 140–
  45, 148–49, 213, 215, 233
Draper, J. W., 8
Dresser, Horatio, 9, 23, 106, 285
  (n. 11), 292
Dresser, Julius, 9, 23, 64, 106
Dualism, 173–75, 182–88, 197,
  202, 219
Duhem, Pierre, 221

Earle, William James, 296
Ecclesiasticism, 154
Eddy, Mary Baker, 10, 23, 292
Edie, James M., 294
Edwards, Jonathan, 13, 18, 121,
  127, 271
Effort, 56–59, 93, 138, 199, 226,
  238, 242
Eliade, Mircea, 298
Elliott, Stephen, 5
Emerson, Mary Moody, 92
Emerson, Ralph Waldo, 3, 12, 18–
  19, 263, 270, 271, 288 (n. 7)

Emotion: absence of, 44–45; and
  belief, 105–6, 293
Emotions, 43–46, 104–5; theory
  of, 57; James-Lange Theory, 44–
  46
Empiricism, 15–18, 36, 37, 54,
  181, 189, 206, 247, 248–49;
  Humean (or ordinary), 189–91,
  195, 222–23, 251–52; and reli-
  gious testimony, 18, 103; undi-
  vided from theism, 18. See also
  Radical empiricism
Epicureanism, 25–26, 38, 90–91.
  See also Aestheticism
Epistemology, 40, 95, 103, 124–25,
  148, 173–74, 182, 194–98, 201,
  209–10, 218, 222–25, 236–38,
  261. See also Erkenntnistheorie
E pluribus unum, 11, 242, 247
Erkenntnistheorie, 40, 209–10,
  218, 230, 237, 276. See also
  Epistemology
Essence, 86–90, 255–56, 278–79
Essentialism, 86–88, 255, 278–80
Evans, Warren Felt, 9. See also
  New Thought
Evans-Pritchard, E. E., 295
Evidence, 17–18, 38, 53, 55–56,
  58, 90, 142, 145, 151, 153, 155,
  161–62, 214–15, 269
Evil, 10, 19, 27–29, 31–32, 57–58,
  60, 92, 96, 98, 105–8, 111, 135,
  154, 207, 263, 265–66
Evolutionism, 27, 36, 178, 211,
  212, 249, 271; empirical, 176,
  194; as a religious doctrine, 105
Experience, 67–68, 155, 182, 191–
  95, 197, 200, 207, 256–57; co-
  conscious, 198, 214–15, 219–20,
  248, 358–59; the long run of,
  54, 213, 217–18, 227–28, 233,
  236–38; mystical, 139–46, 187–
  88; religious, 44–45, 71–167
  passim, 183–85, 187–89, 194,
  196, 198, 202, 207, 214–20, 232,
  234, 239, 244–45, 258, 261, 274,
  280

Faith, 28–29, 31–32, 36–43, 45,
  51, 55, 269; and science, 17. See
  also Subjective method
"Faith-state," 118–20, 164

Fallibilism, 213–14
Fatalism, 27, 42, 43, 80, 218
Fechner, Gustav, 189, 198, 244, 254–55, 259, 296–97
Feelings, 44–46, 172, 185–86, 194, 200. *See also* Affectional facts
Fiske, John, 6, 7, 267
Fletcher, Horace, 64
Flournoy, Theodore, 100, 116, 289 (chap. 9, n. 4), 299
Flower, Elizabeth, 291, 294, 296
Fourier, François, 13
Fox, Emmet, 9
Fox sisters (Margaret, Leah, Catharine), 72
Francis of Assisi, Saint, 84, 109
Frazer, James G., 90, 156, 294
Freedom, 257
Freud, Sigmund, 116
"Full personal facts," 98, 104, 118, 121, 138–39, 158–59, 166, 172–75, 176, 198, 279, 295
Function, 244

Geertz, Clifford, 289 (n. 7), 299
Ghiselin, Michael T., 287 (n. 5), 299
Gifford Lectures, 9, 59, 63, 71–167 passim, 171, 172, 174, 175, 192, 202, 204, 209, 217, 221, 222, 227, 231, 239, 243, 259, 272, 294–96
Glock, Charles, 294
Gnosticism, 37, 41–43, 264. *See also* Pantheism, gnostic
Goddard, H. H., 107, 287 (chap. 4, n. 4), 299
Godkin, E. L., 3
Gottschalk, Stephen, 285 (n. 13), 292
Greven, Philip, 298
Gunn, Giles, 13, 292
Gurney, Edmund, 72, 100

Hall, G. Stanley, 33–34
Hammond, Phillip E., 294
Handy, Robert T., 291
Harris, William Torrey, 35
Hartmann, Eduard von, 34, 232
Hartshorne, Charles, 288 (chap. 5, n. 5), 295

Healthy-mindedness, 58, 92–94, 98, 104–9, 206. *See also* Optimism
Hegel, G. W. F., 42, 204, 249, 252–53, 264
Hegelianism, 34, 35, 43, 106, 150–51, 176, 253–54, 272–73
Henfrey, Norman, 297
Higher education, 19–21, 33–34, 123, 241, 292; and religion, 19, 64
Historicism, 124, 298
Historicity, 86, 122, 179, 229, 246–47, 253, 257, 258, 268
History, personal, 190–91
Hodge, Charles, 7, 16, 22
Hodgson, Shadworth, 34, 179
Höffding, Harald, 189 ,262, 297
Holism, 72, 77, 79–80
Holmes, Oliver Wendell, 32
Holt, E. B., 289 (chap. 9, n. 4), 299
Hopkins, Samuel, 3
Howe, Daniel W., 285 (n. 3), 298
Howison, George, 206, 250
Hudson, Winthrop, 285 (nn. 2, 10), 291
Hügel, Friederich von, 132
Human Blindness. *See* Doctrine of Human Blindness
Humanism, 57, 64, 77, 139, 149, 189. *See also* James, William, humanism
Humanities, 20, 64, 71
Human sciences. *See* Humanities
Hume, David, 52, 190, 251–52
Husserl, Edmund, 293
Huxley, Thomas Henry, 18, 22, 27, 30, 38, 40, 279
Hypnotism, 72, 116

Idealism, 10, 31, 32, 166, 174, 179, 197, 218, 244–46, 251, 266, 271, 278, 281, 296; absolute (*or* transcendental), 176, 180, 189, 203, 205, 206, 207, 210, 222, 232, 243, 246, 250, 262, 264, 267, 273, 274; Berkeleyan, 189, 196; Bradleyan, 222; communitarian, 19; conceptual, 99–100, 295; ethical, 273; Fichtean, 273; metaphysical, 176, 279, 295;

monistic, 43; moral, 130–31; personal, 176–78, 189; post-Kantian, 146–47, 150–52, 271; religious, 9–10; Roycean, 222. *See also* Religion, and idealism

Identity, logic of, 150, 163–65, 171–72, 190–91, 202, 218, 242, 243, 246–47, 251, 253–54, 256, 258, 261; relative, 190

Ideology, 123

Illumination, 98, 141–44

Immortality, human, 243–45, 287 (n. 23)

Imperialism, 7; and sectarianism, 22, 60–63, 135–39

Inclusive integration, 19–20, 22, 57, 123–24, 135, 156, 159, 191–92, 243, 275, 278, 292

Individualism: methodological, 79–81

Industrialism, 7, 22

Infinite, problem of the, 166, 171, 180, 268–69, 279

Ingersoll, Robert, 7

Inquiry, 46, 50, 51, 54, 74, 78, 81, 88–89, 139–40, 144, 193–96, 198, 213, 226–28, 237, 239, 249, 261; and mysticism, 140–41

Instinct, tribal, 95, 132–33, 159

Instruments: concepts as, 82, 230; theories as, 229

Intellectualism, 30, 147, 156–57, 237, 253, 258; vicious, 255–56, 257

Interest, 35–37, 155, 187

Interpretation, 230

Intimacy, 165, 191, 203, 248–50

Intuition, 85–87, 102–3, 142, 144, 146, 257

Intuitions: dumb, 103, 109

Investigation. *See* Inquiry

James, Henry, Sr. (father), 10–14, 15, 19, 243, 250, 265–67, 292, 297; Calvinism, 13; on God, 10–14, 57, 263–66; on human perfection, 95–96, 265–66; republicanism, 10–14, 265–66; on salvation, 11–13, 92, 265–66; and Swedenborg, 17

James, Henry (brother), 61

James, Henry (son), 287 (chap. 3, n. 1)

James, William: acedia, 25–27; on appreciation, 213–20; on common sense, 124–26, 228–30, 245, 246, 247; concern for destiny, 3, 19, 276–77; concern for self-esteem, 19, 26, 49, 276–77; cultural canonization of, 270–83; Darwinism, 27, 35–39, 43, 75–87, 122–31, 139, 159, 191, 226, 266, 268–69, 294; on the definition of religion, 87–91; divine encounter, 17, 101–2; on divinity, 50, 59, 67, 90–91, 93, 99–105, 117–18, 127, 156, 157, 163–64, 165, 173, 175, 202–3, 205, 207, 213, 219, 243, 246, 247, 249–50; doctrine of interaction, 79–81, 257; doctrine of reflex action, 36; on emotion, 104–5; on essences, 88–89; "faith-ladder," 231–34, 235, 262; on fit survival, 39, 76–82, 86–87, 95, 124–31, 158–59, 209, 217, 242, 269; on God, 40–43, 50, 180, 202–3, 227, 232, 234, 242, 243, 249–50, 258, 265–66, 280; and Henry James, Sr., 14; on higher education, 20–21; on human consciousness, 96–98; humanism, 20, 59–64, 171, 174, 175–81, 202, 205, 225–26, 242–43; on human perfection, 96, 131; on knowledge, 193–98, 278–79; meliorism, 91, 99, 206–8, 232–34, 248–49, 277, 280; metaphysics, 30, 59, 155–56, 157, 166, 172–208, 227, 248; on philosophy, 20–21, 33, 201, 241, 248, 255–56; pluralistic pantheism, 171, 198–208, 227, 240–69; on prayer, 26; on reasoning, 88–89, 248; religious disease, 25–32, 292; religious tenacity, 32–33, 34, 71, 273, 277; republicanism, 19, 60–64, 127–28, 134–37, 192, 216, 241–43, 250, 257–58, 262–65, 266; Romanticism, 18–21, 95, 123–24, 156;

on salvation, 22, 51, 92, 103, 123–24, 163–64, 206–8; science of religion, 58–59, 71–94, 95, 114, 143, 152, 156–59, 165, 213, 216, 277, 280, 293, 294; on society, 76–81, 204–5, 276–77, 293; theory of religion, 153–56, 296; youth, 4, 25–27. *See also* Pessimism; Religious investigations; Religious hypothesis
James, William, Jr. (son), 289 (chap. 9, n. 4), 299
James-Lange Theory, 43–46, 63, 186. *See also* Emotions
Janet, Pierre, 116
Jefferies, Richard, 62
Jevons, F. B., 73, 90, 294
Judgments: existential, 82–83, 84; spiritual, 82–83, 84
Jung, Carl, 116

Kallen, Horace, 289 (n. 5), 296
Kant, Immanuel, 34, 147, 181, 209, 279, 297
Kauber, Peter, 293
Kitagawa, Joseph M., 298
Knowledge, 41, 192–98, 249; historical, 211, 214; incorrigible, 222–23; intuitive, 142–44; religious, 142; shared, 197–98, 211
Kuklick, Bruce, 289 (epilogue, n. 3), 291, 293, 294, 295, 296, 297, 298

Lamarck, Jean Baptiste, 78, 81
Lang, Andrew, 73, 294
Lange, Carl Georg, 286 (n. 12)
Lawrence, William (bishop), 23
Leuba, James H., 87, 118, 172–73, 174, 184, 208, 287 (n. 9), 288 (chap. 7, n. 1), 294, 299
Levinson, Henry S., 286 (chap. 1, n. 14), 293, 294
Lincoln, Abraham, 5
Linschoten, Hans, 293, 295
Lippmann, Walter, 282
Locke, John, 16, 34
Lotze, Rudolf, 178
Lovejoy, Arthur O., 200, 294, 296
Lowell, James Russell, 101
Luther, Martin, 109

MacAuley, Jerry, 7, 119
McCosh, James, 7, 15–16
McDermott, John J., 292, 293, 296, 297
Mach, Ernst, 221
MacIntyre, Alasdair, 281, 290 (n. 9), 298
McKinley, William, 7, 104
McLoughlin, William, 8, 285 (nn. 2, 8), 291
McTaggart, John, 234–35, 288 (chap. 8, n. 4), 299
Madden, Edward, 294
Martland, T. R., Jr., 296
Marty, Martin E., 291
Materialism, 18, 22, 37–38, 40, 63, 99, 135–39, 165, 179, 243, 244–45, 248–49, 265, 292; medical, 84–85, 200, 218; moral, 63, 130–31, 136–38; popular, 27; and theism, 64–67, 71
Mathur, D. C., 296
Matthiessen, F. O., 292
Maudsley, Henry, 22, 86, 287 (chap. 3, n. 7), 299
Maxima and minima, problem of, 221–22
May, Henry F., 281–82, 290
Mead, Sidney E., 285 (nn. 1, 4), 291
Meaning, 65–66, 150–51
Mechanism, 251
Melancholy, 25–32, 43–45, 50, 56, 83; philosophical, 26–28; religious, 109–11, 114–15, 135
Meliorism, 91, 99, 206–8, 216. *See also* James, William, meliorism
Mental states, 84; abnormal, 59–60, 71
Mesmer, Franz, 9, 72
Militarism, 22, 136, 138, 265
Mill, John Stuart, 124, 178
Miller, Dickinson, 220
Mind-cure, 9–10, 23, 63–64, 105–9
Monism, 29, 36, 43, 80, 166, 180, 205, 238–39, 245, 253, 255–56, 257, 261, 263, 267, 277; critical, 258–63
Moody, Dwight L., 6–7, 21, 109
Moore, G. E., 182, 220, 235

"Moral equivalent of war," 136, 240
Moralism, 13, 14, 19, 25–26, 57–58, 91–93, 96, 99, 138, 276–77. *See also* Stoicism
Morality, 17, 43, 45–46, 50, 55, 86–87, 91–94, 112, 119, 243, 262–63, 272
Morbid mind. *See* Sick soul
Morris, Charles, 294
Morse, Frances R., 67
Moseley, James G., 292
Mulder, John M., 291
Mulford, Prentice, 64
Müller, F. Max, 72, 73, 74, 294
Munsterberg, Hugo, 200
Murphey, Murray G., 291, 294, 296, 298
Murphy, Gardiner, 295
Muyskens, James L., 293
Myers, Frederic, 46, 72, 116
Mystical methods of criticism, 102, 123, 139, 188
Mysticism, 42, 62, 84, 102, 146–48, 152, 163, 172, 188, 218, 222, 254, 255, 259–63, 295; pluralistic, 263–65

Narrow-mindedness. *See* Close-mindedness
National destiny, 3–7, 12, 19, 22, 27, 60–62, 240–42
Natorp, Paul, 182
Naturalism, 8, 16, 99, 109–10, 153, 176, 177, 206, 292
Necessity, rational, 278, 279
Neoplatonism, 278–79
New Thought, 9–10, 23–24, 63–64, 92, 93, 105–9, 110, 292
Nietzsche, Friedrich, 130
Nisbet, J. F., 85
Nordau, Max, 85
Novak, Michael, 294, 296
Novelty, 37, 77, 171–72, 267–69

Objectivity, 100–101, 150, 166–67, 172–75, 182–88, 202, 215
Occam's razor, 41
One and the many, problem of the, 43, 57–59, 166, 171–72, 192, 203–4, 243–47, 253–56, 261, 296

Ontology (*ontologie*), 40, 95, 177–78, 179, 183, 201, 209, 219, 261, 281, 295
Open-mindedness, 20, 63, 75, 129, 133, 137, 159
Optimism, 9, 19, 23, 27, 33, 58, 91, 99, 104–9, 135, 145, 206, 216, 232, 248–49, 277
Order, 49, 67, 91, 96, 99, 137–39, 141, 175, 177, 189–98, 204–5, 242–43
Ostwald, Wilhelm, 221
Over-belief, 163–64, 231–34, 239, 242

Pacifism, 7, 171, 240
Panpsychism, 177–78, 179
Pantheism, 41–42, 162–63, 165, 222, 243–47, 249, 266, 296; gnostic, 41–43; pluralistic, 198–208, 279, 280
Paracelsus, Philippus Aureolus, 9
Parmenides, 204
Passmore, John, 292
Paul, Saint, 84
Paulsen, Fredrich, 189
Payson, Annie, 63
Peirce, Charles, 32, 65–66, 142, 150, 179, 204, 268, 288 (chap. 5, n. 5), 295
Perception, 18–19, 36, 40, 43, 45, 47, 86, 96–97, 100, 154, 172, 182, 186, 190, 194–97, 200, 250–51, 254, 260, 267–68, 279
Perry, Ralph Barton, 270–71, 275–77, 279, 286 (n. 3), 290 (n. 6), 292, 293, 294, 297
Personality, 9, 71, 75, 108, 115, 157–59, 174–75
Pessimism, 8, 25–32, 37–38, 42, 44–45, 50, 51, 55, 59, 91, 98, 99, 109–11, 135, 216, 232, 277. *See also* Religious disease; Sick soul
Phenomenology: existential, 293; transcendental, 293
"Philippine Tangle," 22, 60–62, 277. *See also* Imperialism
Philosophy, 20–21, 62, 67, 71, 74, 82, 93, 123, 133–34, 139, 146, 155, 241, 273–74, 295; limitations of, 56–59, 74; motives for,

33–43, 48; professional, 275–
76, 279, 282–83, 298. *See also*
James, William, on philosophy
Pitkin, Walter B., 201, 288 (chap.
7, n. 3), 299
Plato, 255, 256, 278
Platonism, 278–79
Plausibility, 161–62, 173, 175, 214
Pluralism, 166, 261, 266, 280, 281;
philosophic, 57–59, 91–92, 277;
religious, 57–59, 91–94, 138,
180, 238–39, 277
Poincaré, Jules Henri, 221
Pollock, Frederick, 286 (chap. 2, n.
15), 299
Polytheism, 166, 279
Positivism, 8, 32, 40–41, 43, 57,
73–74, 99, 199, 212–13, 279
Possibility, 206, 219
Post-Kantianism, 181–82, 229,
263, 293, 297
Pragmatism: absolute, 210; as cosmology, 205–8; and metaphysics, 227, 238–39; and philosophical disputes, 151–52, 164–
65, 172, 201, 203–5, 281; philosophical movement, 64–68, 152,
171–72, 293; theory of meaning,
40, 65–66, 159–60; theory of
truth, 36, 171, 209–39, 296
Prayer, 26, 44, 67, 153, 154, 164
Presentism, 280–83, 293, 298
Probability, 233
Propositions, 236
Psychology, 9, 16, 44, 47, 51, 60,
73, 76, 81–82, 100, 112–17, 161,
173–74, 259, 271; associational,
200; and religion, 114–18; and
religious investigations, 44
Pure experience, 175, 181–86,
199–202, 247; and knowledge,
191–98

Quimby, Phineas Parkhurst, 9

Radical empiricism, 166, 167, 171,
172, 174, 176–208, 242–43,
246–47, 262, 279, 295, 296–97
Radical skepticism, 50, 148, 223–
24
Ramsey, William, 221
Rationalism, 65–66, 103, 147, 149,
150–52, 163, 181, 189–91, 195,
206, 222–23, 247, 248, 255
Rationality, 127–29, 147, 156,
188–89, 256; practical, 37, 41,
43, 86–87; and progress, 127–
33; sentiment of, 36–37, 42;
theoretical, 36, 42, 88
Realism, 15, 252, 256, 281; natural, 189, 197
Reality, 46–47, 99–100, 110, 118,
158, 177, 180, 195, 204–5, 217,
224, 230, 234–38, 250, 253,
255–57; the perception of, 46–
48; symbols of, 158; unseen,
98–103, 119–20, 201–2, 213
Reasoning, 45, 88–89, 126–27,
218–19, 231–34, 248; circular,
225–30, 233
Redemption. *See* Salvation
Reference, objective, 184, 188,
195–98
Reid, Thomas, 15
Relations: conjunctive, 172, 175,
180, 181, 189–98, 246–47; disjunctive, 189–98; external, 183,
193, 209–10, 247, 251–52; internal, 251
Relativism, 218, 233, 278
Religion: American, 3–9, 11, 22,
23–24, 61, 65, 92, 109, 132, 291,
297; definition of, 87–91; experimental, 17; and health, 9–10,
23–24, 32, 63–64; and idealism,
9–10; institutional, 3–4, 6–7, 14,
21, 23, 74, 89–90, 107–8, 131–
33, 153–54; and morality, 91–
94; natural, 29–30; and neurology, 81–87; once-born, 109; personal, 89–90, 131–32; and science, 8, 9, 15–18, 137, 219, 222;
of science, 22, 30–31, 40; twice-
born, 109–111, 135. *See also*
Idealism; Morality
Religious attitudes, 98–99, 103,
137
Religious demand. *See* Salvation;
Well-being
Religious disease, 25–32, 46, 50,
56, 64; cures for, 28–29, 32–33,
34, 42–43, 46, 50–51, 56, 59.
See also Faith; Fatalism; Melancholy; Pessimism

Religious experience, 44–45, 67–68, 71–167
Religious facts, 55–61, 71, 95–121, 216, 231–32
Religious geniuses, 81–83, 90–91, 98, 99, 111, 154, 160–62, 214–15
Religious hypothesis, 51, 55–56; evidence for, 54–56, 219. See also Religious facts
Religious investigations, 18, 32, 34–35, 44, 50, 59–62, 198–99, 221–22, 226, 231–33, 273, 275, 282, 287 (n. 23), 294–96. See also James, William, science of religions
Religious originals. See Religious geniuses
Religious truth, 139, 142, 209–39; in Gifford Lectures, 212–20
Renouvier, Charles Bernard, 30, 31, 45
Republicanism, 4, 6, 127–28; and Calvinism, 11; Henry James, Sr., on, 10–14; of William James, 19–22. See also Calvinism
Rescher, Nicholas, 295
Research, psychical, 32, 71–72, 108, 172, 259, 270
Revivalism, 6, 21, 93, 109, 117, 140
Ricoeur, Paul, 290 (n. 9), 298
Rockefeller, John D., 23
Romanticism, 18–21, 22, 29, 42, 57, 61, 77, 95–96, 123, 140–41, 156, 165, 189, 203, 265–66, 274–75, 292; and optimism, 19
Rousseau, Jean-Jacques, 27, 109
Royce, Josiah, 150, 203, 204, 206, 226, 232, 235, 243, 250–52, 270, 277, 278, 279, 282, 288 (chap. 8, nn. 1, 2), 289 (chap 8, n. 6; epilogue, nn. 2, 3), 295, 296, 297, 299; on James, 271–73; on pragmatism, 209–14, 217, 218, 220, 236–38; on realism, 252
Ruskin, John, 28, 29
Russell, Bertrand, 220, 235–36, 270, 288 (chap. 8, n. 5), 299; on pragmatism, 235–36
Russell, John E., 220

Russett, Cynthia, 294

Sacrifice, 13, 94, 153–54
St. John Green, Nicholas, 32
Saintliness, 59, 61, 93–96, 117, 118–21, 135, 206, 214–16, 230, 232, 253, 277, 280, 282; "error by excess," 133–35; value of, 122, 295
Salter, William, 31
Salvation, 5, 22, 30, 82, 103, 114–15, 117–18, 120–21, 128–29, 160, 164, 165, 175, 177, 180, 215, 220, 227, 230, 232, 234, 235, 239, 242–43, 248, 263, 264–69, 272, 276, 277, 280; Henry James, Sr., on, 10–14, 58; William James on, 22, 51, 58; principles of, 137–39
Sankey, Ira, 21
Santayana, George, 123, 277, 278, 279, 282, 288 (chap. 5, n. 2), 289 (epilogue, n. 4), 290 (n. 5), 297; on James, 123, 270–71, 273–75
Schaff, Philip, 5
Schiller, F. C. S., 189, 210, 245, 250
Schleiermacher, Friedrich, 279, 281
Schlesinger, Arthur M., Sr., 285 (n. 7), 291
Schneider, Herbert, 292
Schopenhauer, Arthur, 34, 37, 232
Science: and faith, 17–18; and religion, 8, 15–18, 137, 157–59, 291, 294; as religion, 22, 30–31, 41; of religion, 58–60, 71–76, 95, 114–18, 152, 161, 213, 216, 217, 279–80; theistic, 18. See also James, William, science of religion
Sciences: evolutionary, 5, 74–81, 223; human, 20, 64, 71; natural, 73, 91, 114–18
Scottish Realism. See Common-Sense Realism
Sectarianism, 20–22, 30, 34, 41, 95, 104, 123, 124, 136, 245; Christian, 3–4, 8, 13, 15, 21, 41, 278; and imperialism, 22, 104; and science, 21–22, 292

Seigfried, Charlene Haddock, 289 (chap. 9, n. 1), 296
Selection: natural, 35, 37, 228, 267–68; rational, 127–31, 213–14, 228
Self, 48–51; divided, 111–13, 160; sense of, 48–51
Self-avowal, 112–18
Self-surrender, 9, 42, 93–94, 106–8, 113–14, 119, 140, 153, 157, 207
Self-transformation, 111–18, 121, 157, 160–61, 165, 218, 253. See also Conversion
Sharpe, Eric J., 294, 295
Sheffler, Israel, 296
Sick soul, 44–45, 93, 95, 98, 105. See also Melancholy; Pessimism
Sigwart, Christoph, 178, 221
Skepticism, 50, 60, 148, 156, 212–13, 278. See also Radical skepticism
Skrupskelis, Ignas K., 297
Smith, John E., 292, 294, 296, 297
Social impulse, 146, 152
Sociality of coercion, 3, 6, 11–12, 16, 59, 95, 132–33, 136, 138, 145, 264
Sociality of persuasion, 3, 4, 6, 11–12, 16, 20, 33, 61, 132, 136–40, 145, 240, 262
Society: Henry James, Sr., on, 11–12, 14, 17; William James on, 19–20, 55–56, 61–62, 76–81, 129–31; and religion, 5, 6
Society for Psychical Research, 71–72, 100
Sociology, 216
Socrates, 255, 256
Solipsism, 193, 211, 213, 217
Solomon, Robert, 25, 286 (n. 2), 298–99
Sophism, 278
Spencer, Herbert, 6, 27, 29, 34–36, 39, 44, 73, 74–75, 76–81, 257, 287 (chap. 3, n. 3), 299
Spinoza, Benedict, 109
Spiritualism, 8–9, 23, 32, 72, 106, 243, 248–49; empirical, 249
Sprigge, Timothy L. S., 297
Stannard, David E., 298
Starbuck, E. D., 84, 111–14, 118,

287 (n. 6), 294, 299
Statesmanship: intellectual, 21; the language of, 156
Stein, Gertrude, 282
Stephen, Leslie, 286 (chap. 2, n. 15), 299
Stettheimer, Ettie, 293
Stevens, Richard, 293
Stevens, Wallace, 282
Stevenson, Robert Louis, 62
Stewart, Dugald, 15
Stoicism, 25–26, 37–38, 90–93, 266. See also Moralism
Stout, G. F., 200
Strauss, D. F., 17, 72
Strong, Augustus, 22
Strong, Josiah, 6–7
Strout, Cushing, 295
Strug, Cordell, 295
Subconscious, doctrine of the, 46, 60, 113–18, 161–63, 258, 272, 279, 295
Subjective method, 38–39, 45, 51
Subjectivism, 181, 213, 215–16, 275, 278
Subjectivity, 100–101, 166–67, 172–75, 182–88, 201–2, 216
Subliminal self, 72, 113–18, 219. See also Subconscious
Substitution, conceptual, 194–96
Success, bitch goddess of, 63, 136, 220
Suggestive method, 107–8
Supernaturalism, 95, 145, 227; crass, 121, 153, 159–66, 180, 219, 234, 272; natural, 29–30, 71, 141, 165. See also Religion, natural
Swedenborg, Emanuel, 9, 11, 17
Synechism, 268

Taylor, A. E., 235
Taylor, Nathaniel, 3
Tenacity, personal, 32–33, 71, 129, 139, 142–43, 150, 152, 221, 295. See also James, William, religious tenacity
Teresa, Saint, 84
Testimony, religious, 18, 112, 139–40, 149, 151, 153, 160–62, 166, 175, 214–15

Thayer, H. S., 293, 294, 296
Theism, 222, 234, 242; and empiricism, 18; of Henry James, Sr., 11; of William James, 40–43, 159–64, 243; and materialism, 64–67, 71; orthodox, 13, 15–18, 43, 71, 109, 124, 163, 165, 243, 249, 265
Theology, 66–67, 86, 90, 106, 120, 125–26, 146, 148–50, 154–56, 161–64, 167, 206, 207, 234, 242; aesthetic value of, 149, 155–56, 239, 248; philosophical, 73, 95, 103, 146–51, 218, 221–22, 239; scientific, 18
Thouless, Robert, 294
Tiele, C. P., 73
Tolerance, 22, 63–64, 159, 216, 234
Tolstoy, Leo, 23, 110
Transcendentalism, 3, 4, 9, 11, 15, 16, 17–18, 105, 274; methodological, 279–80, 298
Trine, Ralph Waldo, 9, 23, 64, 106, 287 (chap. 4, n. 2), 299
Troeltsch, Ernst, 290 (n. 7), 298; on James, 277–80
Truth, 8, 16–18, 35–36, 39–40, 43–56, 65, 77, 84–87, 125, 127, 128, 139, 140, 143–46, 148, 150–52, 162–63, 166–67, 174, 194–96, 205, 208, 251, 253; absolute, 224, 226, 242; definition of, 225; and emotional satisfaction, 236; and facts, 236–37; historicity of, 229; and justification, 220–30, 236–39; and knowledge, 223–25; mystics on, 139–40; presumptive, 226, 229–30; and utility, 236–37
Turner, Frank Miller, 288 (n. 6), 292
Twain, Mark, 274
Tychism, 257, 268
Tylor, E. B., 73, 74–75, 156, 294; on doctrine of survivals, 75–76, 299

Tyndall, John, 16, 18, 22, 27

Vacherot, Etienne, 72
Van Buren, Paul M., 296
Variation, 35, 37, 82, 89, 268
Varieties of Religious Experience, 10, 44, 59
Victorian ways of thinking, 28–30, 73, 136, 281–82, 298
Vindication, 221, 230, 232–33
Vitalism, 179
Voluntarism, 212, 214, 215, 233
Vox populi, 5, 40, 61, 241, 265, 277
Vivekananda, Swami, 8

Wahl, Jean, 294
Wegner, Charles, 288 (chap. 5, n. 1), 292
Weiss, Paul, 288 (chap. 5, n. 5), 295
Well-being, 58, 91–94, 103–4, 128–29, 138, 157, 163, 192, 215, 226–27, 233, 234, 240, 242, 253, 261, 262, 280
Well-doing, 56–57, 91–93, 240, 261, 262, 280. *See also* Effort
Wells, H. G., 23, 282
Wesley, John, 90
White, Andrew D., 8
White, Morton, 291
Whitefield, George, 121
Whitman, Walt, 27, 62, 108, 274, 299
Wiener, Philip, 294
Wild, John, 293, 294, 296
Will, 48–51, 199–200
Wilmer, Richard, 5
Wilshire, Bruce, 293
Wilson, John F., 291
Winchell, Alexander, 8
Witherspoon, John, 16
Wood, Henry, 9, 106, 287 (chap. 4, n. 1), 299
Wordsworth, William, 141
Wright, Chauncey, 16, 32–33
Wrongness. *See* Evil